A COMPENDIUM

OF THE

HISTORY OF THE UNITED STATES

FROM THE

EARLIEST SETTLEMENTS TO 1872

DESIGNED TO

ANSWER THE PURPOSE OF A TEXT BOOK IN SCHOOLS
AND COLLEGES AS WELL AS TO MEET THE WANTS OF
GENERAL READERS

BY

ALEXANDER H. STEPHENS

AUTHOR OF THE "CONSTITUTIONAL VIEW OF THE LATE WAR BETWEEN
THE STATES," AND PROFESSOR ELECT OF HISTORY AND POLITICAL
SCIENCE IN THE UNIVERSITY OF GEORGIA

———·:≻:·———

American Foundation Publications
Post Office Box 355
Bridgewater, VA 22812
www.afpub.com
1999

AMERICAN FOUNDATION PUBLICATIONS
Post Office Box 355
Bridgewater, VA 22812
www.afpub.com

First published 1872 by E. J. Hale & Son, Publishers
Murray Street, New York.
Columbia, S. C., W. J. Duffie.

Entered according to Act of Congress, in the year
1872, by ALEXANDER H. STEPHENS
In the Office of the Librarian of Congress,
at Washington.

This reprint by
American Foundation Publications 1999

ISBN 1-928596-00-2

FOREWORD

Never in the history of the world has there been a generation which knows less about more than the one in which we live. The "dumbing down" process that has taken place in this country, thanks to efforts of our "educational" institutions, has truly been a stunning spectacle. As a result, we have become the most miseducated people the world has ever known.

No little credit for this remarkable state of affairs must be given to our government-controlled schools and the textbooks they use. Modern textbooks are filled with mistakes and errors, as well as outright lies and slanders. They specialize in the trivialization of history and have come to look like nothing so much as hardcover editions of *People* magazine. They carefully record the shouting and pouting of disaffected revolutionaries, but give little attention the noble and wise leaders God has graciously given our country throughout its history. Thus, high school graduates know more about Marilyn Monroe and Elvis than they do about George Washington and Patrick Henry.

The results constitute a tragedy of Titanic proportions. Indoctrination has taken the place of education. Style and technique now substitute for wisdom. Principle has been discarded for pragmatism. We now have a generation which is not only unable to distinguish between truth and error but, what is worse, does not care about such things.

Men aspire to political office not out of a desire to preserve and promote our traditions but merely to enjoy the publicity and perks that now come with power and privilege. There is, by and large, no understanding of (or concern for) the nature of our union, the legitimate powers of the Federal Government, the rights of the individual States, or the constitutional protections of citizens. If you ask about these grand principles you receive a blank stare in response ("legitimate powers"?). We have become a land of unholy forgetfulness.

Americans are as ignorant of the Constitution as they are of the Egyptian Book of the Dead, yet think they understand it perfectly well. Everyone now knows that the Constitution was formulated by "the People" and established this nation as a "democracy." It is now a commonplace that the Constitution secures the supremacy of the Federal government over the States. We are a nation indivisible and no longer a union. The States are nothing more than subsidiaries of "U.S.A., Inc." whose job it is to carry out the dictates flowing from the imperial throne in Washington D.C. These are the unquestioned beliefs of the majority.

Thus, at the end of the twentieth century, we find ourselves under the dual tyranny of an unrestrained central government and the public opinion polls (the new "voice of the People"). It is the worst of all possible situations. God Democracy reigns supreme and no one dares to suggest that he is a lawless usurper.

In our present dilemma, books that reject the modern revision of our past and dare to set forth truth in-

FOREWORD

stead of propaganda are worth the proverbial King's ransom. This is why the reappearance of this volume is so important.

Alexander Hamilton Stephens was one of the most gifted Constitutional scholars this country has ever produced. He was a genius who became a political power in the mid-nineteenth century. A Georgian, child of a poor farmer, he was elected to the state legislature and afterwards to the Federal Congress where he served until 1859.

Mr. Stephens was a mere wisp of a man, often in ill health, and never weighing more than 100 pounds. His size, as one might imagine, was a constant source of jibes from his friends as well as his enemies. Once a political opponent offered to "grease his ears and swallow him whole." Unruffled, Mr. Stephens replied that such an action would be most unfortunate, since the gentleman would then "have more brains in his stomach than he did in his head!"

Stephens opposed the secession of the Southern states after the election of Lincoln in 1860. He did so not because he believed secession was unconstitutional, but because he believed it was not best for the South or for the country. After losing the debate over the issue in his native state, he submitted to the judgment of his peers and was later chosen to become the Vice President of the Confederacy. This position Mr. Stephens filled for the duration of the war. After the war he was arrested and imprisoned for five months before being released to return home to Crawfordsville, Georgia.

Mr. Stephens would spend his declining years speaking and writing. He published his monumental *Constitutional History of the Late War Between the States* in 1870. This still remains one of the greatest expositions of the nature of our republic. This present volume was finished two years later in 1872—a decade before his death on March 4, 1883. He commenced this history of the country because he had noticed that most history books confined their accounts to the Presidential elections and the admission of new States and omitted any explanation of the history of the political philosophy of the country. He determined to write a history that would train young minds in the basic principles of our governmental system. His concern was to emphasize the objects of the provisions of the Constitution, the powers delegated to the Federal government, the true character of the States and their relation to the Federal government, the crises through which our union had passed and their results.

Stephens' biographers note, "Mr. Stephens rightly conceived that in a country where every man is expected to exercise the primary functions of government, and any man may be called on to administer its trusts, a knowledge of these facts was of the first importance; and he therefore gave in his History, a condensed, but clear and impartial account of the formation of the Government and the principles of its organization, of the great questions on which public opinion was divided, the parties which arose upon these questions, and the contests between them."

FOREWORD

(*Life of Alexander H. Stephens,* Richard Malcolm Johnson and William Hand Browne. J. B. Lippincott & Co: Philadelphia, 1884.)

The strength of Mr. Stephens' *History* lies in his grasp of the principles which were foundational in the formation of our country. His survey of the founding of each of the original thirteen colonies and the States which were later carved from the territories is most enlightening. His treatment of the leading men and movements which have had a formative influence on our nation's development is invaluable. And, as one would expect, his analysis of the War Between the States is unsurpassed.

There are, however, at least in this writer's opinion, a couple of places in Stephens' analysis which do not meet the high standards of the work as a whole and thus, should be noted by the reader. He is, without question, far too generous in his judgment of the radical Roger Williams. Stephens' approval of Williams' political opinions betrays a lack of theological discernment. He certainly would not have approved of the practical outworkings of Williams' philosophy of "complete religious liberty" as it affects constitutional integrity. The Puritans of New England had their faults and made many mistakes, but, contrary to Mr. Stephens, the way in which they dealt with Roger Williams was not one of them.

The second place that one must call for caution is the treatment given of the Salem witch trials. This section is not from Stephens' pen but is an extended quotation from McCabe's *Pictorial History of the*

United States. McCabe's treatment of this sad event leaves a great deal to be desired and the reader is encouraged to check out other sources (including Cotton Mather's own *Magnalia Christi Americana*) for a more balanced account.

But these minor reservations should not lessen our enthusiasm for this volume. This book is a valuable addition to the growing body of material which gives a more thorough and truthful view of our country's past. Readers will learn here things of which the vast majority of Americans have never heard but which are essential to understanding our past and the rationale for our political structures. Those who study this volume will gain an appreciation for the development of the Christian social order that occurred in this country and which is vital to its future restoration.

It is greatly to be hoped that the resurrection of such books as this portends better things for us in the next century. That alone makes the reprinting of A. H. Stephens' *A Compendium of the History of the United States* a cause for celebration and thanksgiving.

Columbus Day, 1998
Steve Wilkins

HISTORY OF THE UNITED STATES

ALEXANDER H. STEPHENS

INTRODUCTION.

1. It is the purpose of the author of this work to give to the Youth of the country, as well as general readers, a condensed History of the United States of America; embracing all important facts connected with the discovery and early occupation of the country, within their limits, by immigrants from other lands; together with the facts attending the formation of their Governments, and the establishment of those free institutions which have so marked, as well as distinguished them, among the nations of the earth.

2. In the prosecution of this design, the first object will be, after a brief presentation of the facts attending the discovery of the continent of America, to trace, during their Colonial condition, the History of each one of the separate political Communities known as British Colonies thereon, which afterwards became united under the style of the United States of America, and then to trace the History of these States, so united under their existing Union, down to the present time.

3. The first part of the work will be the History of the Colonies; the second part will be the History of the States. With this view, for proper system, the work will be divided into two Books.

---

1. What is stated to be the purpose of the Author in preparing this History?
2. In the prosecution of the design, what will be the first object? What the second?
3. What will be the First Part of the work? What the Second? How many Parts will the work be divided into, and what will they be called? What will Book I. treat of? What will Book II. treat of?

Book I. will treat of the discovery, the early settlement, and colonization of the country by the ancestors of the present inhabitants, and the events which led to the assumption of sovereign or absolute self-governing powers by the respective Colonies.

Book II. will treat of the achievement and establishment of their independence as States, and their subsequent career under their present Federal Union.

HISTORY OF THE UNITED STATES.

BOOK FIRST.

CHAPTER I.

THE DISCOVERY OF AMERICA.

1. AMERICA, including what is styled South and North America, and which is sometimes called the Western Continent, was not generally known to the people of Europe until the year of our Lord 1492, when it was discovered by Christopher Columbus, a native of Genoa, one of the cities of Italy. Some Norwegians and Icelanders, at an earlier period, had discovered Greenland and the northern portions of North America, as far south, it is supposed by some, as Massachusetts Bay, to which region they gave the name of Vinland.

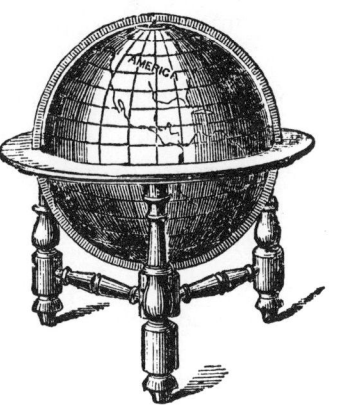

2. But their discoveries had been forgotten, and the knowledge of this Hemisphere had been lost to men of

---

1. What does the general name of America include? What is it sometimes called? In what year was it discovered? By whom? What is said of the Norwegians and Icelanders?
2. To whom does the glory of the discovery properly belong?

letters on the Eastern Continent long prior to the discovery by Columbus; to him, therefore, justly belongs the glory of having discovered the Western World.

3. Columbus was a navigator, and supposed that India, which was known to be in the East, could be reached by sailing due west, without doubling the Cape of Good Hope, at the southern extremity of Africa. From observations of the earth's shadow on the moon during eclipses, as well as from other considerations, he, with others, had come to the conclusion that the earth was round; and hence he reasoned that by sailing due west he must ultimately reach some land beyond the western sea. Other facts of a different character also excited him to undertake a western exploration. Driftwood floating from the west was sometimes thrown upon the coasts of the Madeiras, and the dead bodies of two men of an unknown race had also been found upon the coast.

4. The East Indies, from the earliest ages, had been a mine of wealth to the more western nations, but the overland journey was long and toilsome, and attended with many difficulties and dangers, and at this period it had become a favorite project of Europeans to discover a direct passage by sea. It was more with a view of opening up this new route to India that Columbus set out on his voyage of exploration, than with any idea of discovering a new continent.

5. For aid in the prosecution of his enterprise, he first made application to the government of Genoa, his native place; failing in this, he applied to John II., king of Portugal. King John seems to have amused him and detained him at his court for some time, while he privately fitted out an enterprise, which was intended to forestall his undertaking, and deprive him of the glory of the

---

3. What made Columbus think the earth was round? The earth being round, what did his reason teach him?
4. What is said of the East Indies? What was the object of Columbus?
5. Of what city and country was Columbus a native? To whom did he first apply for assistance? To whom next? How was he treated by King John?

achievement. On the discovery of this fact Columbus left Portugal in disgust.

6. About this period he sent his brother, Bartholomew Columbus, to the court of Henry VII., king of England, but so many delays occurred that the discovery of the West Indies had actually been made before the king gave a favorable answer to his application.

7. In 1486 he applied for aid to Isabella, queen of Arragon. The war that the united kingdoms of Castile and Arragon, under the dominion of Ferdinand and Isabella, had long waged against the Moors of Granada, was drawing to a close. Soon after its close, he was invited by the queen to her presence. He was received with distinguished favor, and a favorable answer was given to his application.

8. His demands "that he should be appointed admiral of all the seas which he might explore, and governor of all the continents and islands which he might visit; that these offices should be hereditary in his family; and that the tenth of everything bought, bartered, found, or got within the bounds of his admiralship, abating only the charge of the conquest, should be settled upon him, and should descend to his heirs in case of his death," were agreed to; and a fleet of three vessels, properly manned and equipped, was placed under his command. These vessels were victualled for twelve months, and had on board ninety mariners, besides several adventurers and servants, amounting in all to one hundred and twenty persons. The whole cost of the expedition was about twenty thousand dollars.

9. The names of the three vessels were the *Maria*, the *Pinta*, and the *Nina*. Of these the *Maria* was the largest; and in this vessel Columbus himself sailed. The *Pinta* was commanded by Martin Alonzo Pinzon, and the

---

6. What is said of his application to the King of England?
7. To whom did he apply in 1486? How was he received?
8. What were his demands? Were they agreed to? How many vessels were furnished him? What was the cost of the expedition?
9. What were the names of the vessels? From what port did they sail? On what day?

Nina by his brother, Vincent Yanez Pinzon. They sailed from Palos, a port in Spain, on the morning of Friday, the 3d of August, 1492. In three days they came in sight of the Canaries. Here they were detained several weeks on account of injuries received by the *Pinta.* Columbus endeavored to procure another vessel in place of the *Pinta*, but was unable to do so. The repairs were completed at length, and on the 6th of September, from Gomera, one of the Canaries, these three small vessels boldly sailed westward over a trackless and unknown sea.

10. On the 13th of September, when far from land, as they supposed, the sailors were much alarmed by discovering the variation of the needle of the compass, a phenomenon which had not been observed before. Though Columbus himself did not understand the cause of the variation, yet he invented some plausible reason for it, and succeeded in calming their fears and in reconciling them to the continuance of their course westward. But their fears of never again seeing land soon overmastered them and caused great discontent, which broke out in loud murmurs and mutinous threats of forcing the admiral to return. It was with great difficulty that he could retain his ascendancy over them; and at length he yielded so far to their importunities as to promise that, if there were no signs of land within three days, he would return to the East.

11. Before the three days expired many signs of land began to appear; flocks of strange birds were observed; the sea became more shallow, and pieces of floating timber were seen. On the night of the 11th of October, Columbus himself saw a light, moving as if borne in the hand of some person, which he considered as evidence, not only of the nearness of land, but also that the land was inhabited. At two o'clock on the morning of the 12th a gun was fired by

---

10. What alarmed the sailors on the 13th of September? Had this variation ever been observed before? How did Columbus account for it? What threats did the sailors make? What did Columbus do then?

11. What occurred before the three days expired? When was land first discovered? What land was it? How did Columbus name it?

CHAP. I.] THE DISCOVERY OF AMERICA. 9

the *Pinta*, as a token that land was in sight. The land proved to be one of the Bahama Islands, called by the natives Gu-an-a-han'-i, or Cat Island, named by Columbus San Salvador, which, in English, means the Holy Saviour.

LANDING OF COLUMBUS.

12. The landing, which took place on the morning of the 12th of October, 1492, was accompanied with every demonstration of gratitude and joy. Columbus, richly dressed in a scarlet uniform, and bearing the royal standard of Spain, was the first to land and press his foot upon the new earth, of which he took possession for and in the name of Ferdinand and Isabella, sovereigns of Castile and Arragon. Then kneeling, he kissed the earth, and gave thanks to

---

12. When did the landing take place? In whose name did he take possession? What is said of the Indians?

God for His goodness. Meantime the natives stood around filled with wonder and astonishment at the formidable appearance of these strange and wonderful men, whom they supposed to have descended from the sun; little thinking that these new-comers would soon be their destroyers.

13. Columbus afterwards discovered and touched at several other islands, amongst them Hispaniola and Cuba, all of which he claimed for his sovereigns, and all of which he supposed to be parts of India. Hence, to these islands has been given the name of West Indies, and the Aborigines, or those then inhabiting both the islands and the continent, have received the general name of Indians.

14. Of the origin of these tribes or peoples nothing is known with certainty. The manner in which they crossed the Atlantic or the Pacific, and the period at which they arrived on the shores of America, are equally buried in obscurity. But it is evident that for many years, it may be for many ages, prior to the advent of Columbus, America had been occupied by these heretofore-unknown races. Some nations in the southern part of North America, and some also in South America, had built large cities and had attained to a considerable degree of civilization. But their civilization differed greatly in many respects from that of the East.

15. Many curious remains of ancient structures erected by the aborigines of America still exist. In deep forests, in places far remote from the habitations and cultivated fields of white men, the traveller will sometimes suddenly find himself in the presence of massive ruins, whose appearance indicates that they were first erected many centuries ago. Large forest-trees, several hundred years old, are sometimes found growing amongst and on these ruins.

---

13. Did Columbus make further discoveries? What name did he give the Islands? What were the natives called?
14. What is known of the origin of those tribes? Had they been long in America? What is said of their civilization?
15. What is said of ancient buildings found in forests?

16. Perhaps the most highly-civilized and enlightened of all the aboriginal Americans were the Aztecs, in Mexico, the inhabitants of Central America, and the people inhabiting the regions of Peru and Chili in South America. In all these regions the Spaniards, who visited them after Columbus' discovery was known, found large cities, well and strongly fortified, with many thousand inhabitants, with large and spacious palaces, and with markets regularly supplied with all the necessaries of life, and with fine and elegant goods in great variety. Cortez, the celebrated warrior who penetrated and conquered Mexico, sometime afterwards, in a letter to the Emperor Charles V., says, writing of the city of Cholula: " The inhabitants are better clothed than any we have hitherto seen. People in easy circumstances wear cloaks above their dress; these cloaks differ from those of Africa, for they have pockets, though the cut, cloth, and fringes are the same. The environs of the city are very fertile and well cultivated. Almost *all the fields may be watered; and the city is much more beautiful than all those in Spain;* for it is well fortified and built on level ground. I can assure your highness, that from the top of a mosque I reckoned more than four hundred towers, all of mosques. The number of inhabitants is so great that there is not an inch of ground uncultivated."

17. The city of Mexico, which was the capital, exceeded Cholula in size, in population, and in the beauty and magnificence of its buildings. " The palace of Montezuma (the king) was so large a pile that it opened with thirty gates into as many different streets." The Aztecs, by which name the inhabitants of Mexico have been known in history, had made considerable progress in the arts of civilization. Their buildings, their paintings, and sculpture, were very remarkable in many respects.

---

16. Which nations were most highly civilized? What is said of their markets? What does Cortez say of them?
17. What is said of the city of Mexico? Describe the Palace of Montezuma. What is said of the paintings and sculptures?

18. But the civilization of the inhabitants of Peru in South America was of a higher and more refined character than that of Mexico. The people were milder and gentler in their manners, and their religion did not possess the savage feature of offering human sacrifices to idols, as that of the Aztecs did. They had a tradition that about four hundred years before the arrival of the Spaniards in the country, Manco Capac, their first Inca, by which name their kings were called, a white man of wonderful knowledge, clothed in flowing garments, came amongst them from some unknown region, and taught them agriculture and many useful arts; " to construct reservoirs and aqueducts; to make ploughs, harrows, and shoes for their own feet. His wife taught the women to spin, to weave, and to make their own garments."

19. His descendants and successors pursued the same gentle policy, and over whatever territories their sway became extended, whether by conquest or otherwise, they taught the inhabitants " to plough, and manure, and cultivate the soil." They constructed numerous aqueducts, many miles in length, by which almost the whole country of Peru was watered, some relics and monuments of which remain unto this day.

20. The tribes of Indians in that portion of North America now known as the United States were possessed of but little knowledge; their arts were very few; their buildings were rude huts called wigwams, and agriculture was practised to a very limited extent. War and the chase were the favorite occupations of the men. Whatever labor was done was done by the women. They were ignorant of letters; literature they had none, and their traditions were few and uncertain. But even these people dwelt not in unrelieved darkness. They were simple in their manners,

---

18. Describe the Peruvians. What tradition did they have? What did Manco Capac and his wife teach the people?
19. What policy was pursued by the descendants of Capac? What did they construct?
20. What is said of the Indians in the country now known as the United States?

faithful to their word, grateful for kindness, and believed that, when they were taken away by death, they would go to happy hunting-grounds prepared by the Great Spirit.

21. Columbus, on his return to Spain, was received with distinguished honor by Ferdinand and Isabella. He afterwards made several voyages to the New World, planted colonies, and built cities and forts. On his third voyage he visited the continent of South America, and landed at several places on the coast of Cumana. The mainland of North America he never saw. But after all his great services to Spain; after having added a New World to the dominions of that country, it was his misfortune to meet with ill-treatment and injustice. He was superseded in his command, and, under a charge of high treason, was sent home in chains. The charges against him were not sustained, and he was set at liberty, but the remainder of his life seems to have been inactive and uneventful. He died in obscurity and poverty at Val-la-do-lid', in Spain, on the 20th of May, 1506, in the 71st year of his age.

22. America was so called from Americus Vespucius, another navigator, who, after the report of Columbus' wonderful discovery had excited so much interest among the scientific men in Europe, set out on a new exploration, and made much more extensive discoveries than Columbus had. In 1499 he published a map of the coast and a description of the lands he had visited. His delineations of the coast were so accurate, and his descriptions of the countries were so vivid and so delightfully written, that, by the common consent of his contemporaries, the New World was called America.

---

21. How was Columbus received in Spain ? Did he make other voyages ? What treatment did he receive after this ? What was he charged with ? Where did he die ? At what age ?
22. From whom was America named ? And why ?

CHAPTER II.

SETTLEMENT OF VIRGINIA.
1607—1609.

The first permanent British Settlement in America, at Jamestown.

1. It does not come within the scope and purpose of this work to set forth the progress of the Spaniards and Portuguese in their conquest and occupation of the Southern portion of the continent. The history of that progress has very little to do with the history of the British colonies, or of the United States. What connection there may be will be noticed at the proper time. It will suffice at present to state that the Spaniards extended their conquests over Mexico, East and West Florida, Central America, nearly the whole of South America, except the Empire of Brazil, which was taken possession of by the Portuguese. It may interest the youthful reader to be told that Brazil is the only independent country or state on the Continent of America which is now governed by descendants of any of the royal families of Europe.

VIRGINIA COAT OF ARMS.

2. The French, at an early day after the discovery of America, made voyages to the New World, and planted many colonies and settlements. Nova Scotia, and all that region north of the River St. Lawrence now known as British America, were first occupied by them. They also planted the colony of Louisiana, and built the city of New Orleans, near the mouth of the Mississippi. From the

---

Chapter II.—**1.** What nations took possession of South America ? What is said of Brazil ?
2. In what region did the French plant colonies ? What was the consequence of the conflicting claims of the French and English ? Upon what were the claims of Great Britain founded ?

conflicting claims of Great Britain and France to vast tracts of country, the colonists of both countries frequently suffered greatly, not only from wars between those two countries, but also from wars with the neighboring Indian tribes.

3. The claim of Great Britain to plant colonies in North America to the exclusion of others, was founded upon the right of priority of discovery, which, by the general consent of nations, is regarded as good and valid. In the year 1497 John Cabot, a Venetian, in the service of Henry VII., King of England, discovered the mainland of North America, fourteen months before Columbus landed upon the mainland of South America. In the year 1498 the Cabots, father and son, John and Sebastian, explored the coast-line from Labrador as far south as the Chesapeake Bay. And in 1517 Sebastian Cabot sailed up Hudson's Straits and Bay until he reached the sixty-seventh degree of North latitude; it being an object of the British Government, even at that early day, to find a northwest passage to India.

4. The first attempts of the English to plant colonies in North America failed. About the year 1578 an expedition, to which Queen Elizabeth contributed, was fitted out for Labrador, the object of which was to work the mines of gold which were supposed to abound in that region. The colony consisted of about one hundred settlers, but they were afraid to be left in that dreary region, and so returned without even an effort to accomplish anything. But the hopes of colonizing the country at some point were not abandoned. In 1578 a charter was granted by Queen Elizabeth to Sir Humphrey Gilbert, empowering him to take possession of extensive regions of country. Gilbert sailed for North America, but was compelled to return without accomplishing his purpose.

---

3. What discoveries were made by the Cabots? What was the object of the British Government?
4. What is said of the first attempts of the English to found colonies?

5. A new expedition was fitted out in 1583 by Gilbert and his brother-in-law, Sir Walter Raleigh, under the same charter. This time they went through the ceremony of taking possession, in the Queen's name, of the island of Newfoundland. On their return, Sir Humphrey Gilbert was drowned. Sir Walter Raleigh, not discouraged by the unfortunate termination of the former expeditions and the sad fate of Gilbert, determined on planting a colony further south. He obtained a grant or charter for colonizing all the country between the parallels of 33° and 45° north latitude, on the coast of North America. In honor of Elizabeth, the virgin Queen, in whose reign the charter was granted, and on account of the great beauty of the lands embraced in it, the name of Virginia was given to the whole country covered by this patent. Some settlements were made by Raleigh, under this extensive grant, on the Roanoke in North Carolina in 1585–1587, but they were subsequently abandoned.

6. Though these first efforts at colonization failed, yet the spirit of adventure was kept alive, and the claim of the English, founded upon the discovery of Cabot, was not abandoned. It was, however, one hundred and fifteen years after the discovery of America by Columbus that the English succeeded in making their first permanent settlement on the continent. This was effected under the following circumstances and auspices. In 1606 James I., King of England, who had succeeded Elizabeth on the throne, divided the country embraced in the Gilbert and Raleigh charter into two districts. The northern district he granted by a new charter to a company organized in England, known as the Plymouth Company. The country embraced in this district was called North Virginia. The southern district was granted to another company organized in Eng-

---

5. What was accomplished by Sir Humphrey Gilbert and Sir Walter Raleigh ? What was the extent of Sir Walter Raleigh's grant ? What was the country called, and why ?
6. How long after the discovery of America before the first permanent settle-

CHAP. II.]   THE COLONY OF VIRGINIA.   17

land, known as the London Company. This district was called South Virginia. South Virginia extended from Cape Fear to the Potomac; North Virginia from the mouth of the Hudson River to Newfoundland. The region between the Potomac and the Hudson Rivers was to be neutral ground, on which the companies were at liberty to form settlements within fifty miles of their respective boundaries.

7. By the London Company, so organized, the first English colony was firmly planted on the continent in the year 1607, at Jamestown, on the River James, in the present

SETTLEMENT AT JAMESTOWN.

State of Virginia. The river was so called in honor of the King, James I. of England.

---
ment was made by the English ? How was it effected ? What were the names of the two new companies ? How was the Raleigh grant divided ? What name was given to each part ?

7. Where was the first colony planted ? What name did it take, and why ? Of

The colony took the general name of Virginia. The number of settlers consisted at first of one hundred and five persons. But few of them were laborers, and all were single, that is, unmarried men. The plan of government was set forth in the charter. The officers consisted of seven members of Council, viz., Bartholomew Gosnold (the navigator, who, in the year 1603, had visited and explored the shores of Massachusetts), John Smith, Edward Wingfield, Christopher Newport, John Ratcliff, John Martin, and George Kendall. Mr. Wingfield was chosen president or governor.

8. The season after their arrival proved very sickly, and nearly half their number died before the cool weather set in. Among those that died was Bartholomew Gosnold, one of the ablest men of the Council. The native people, the savages, called Indians, as before stated, were numerous in the neighborhood, and were sometimes hostile. Captain Newport, who had command of the squadron in which the settlers had come over, after a short stay sailed for England, leaving the colony in a very feeble condition. Provisions were scarce, the water was bad, and many of the men were sick. To add to their misfortunes, they quarrelled among themselves. They excluded Captain Smith from the Council; deposed Mr. Wingfield, the president, and put Mr. Ratcliff in his place. Their condition rapidly grew worse, until they gave the management of their affairs to Captain Smith, whose great skill, capacity, and courage, soon restored harmony, brought order out of chaos, and laid the foundations of a permanent prosperity.

9. The government of the settlers, with the right to pass all laws, was vested in the members of the Council, who were appointed by the stockholders of the Company; the

---

what number did the first settlers consist? What are the names of the first Council appointed? Who was first president?
  8. What is said of the condition of the colony? Who died? What is said of the Indians? How long did Captain Newport remain? How did the colonists act? How was harmony restored?
  9. What was the government of the colony at first? What was the estab-

governor, or president, was also, according to the charter, appointed by the stockholders. Changes in these particulars soon followed, as we shall see. The religion of the Church of England was established as the religion of the colony, and the right of trial by jury was secured to all persons charged with murder, or other crimes which were punishable with death. There was no restriction on trade, lands descended according to the common law, and permission to coin money was granted to the colony.

CHAPTER III.

THE COLONY OF VIRGINIA—CONTINUED.

1609—1621.

Captain John Smith—Jamestown—Pocahontas—Arrival of Lord Delaware, etc.

1. CAPTAIN JOHN SMITH was born in Lincolnshire, in England, in the year of our Lord 1579. He was apprenticed to a merchant, but not liking the business, he ran away from his master and went to Holland, where he enlisted as a soldier. After some time he went to Austria, which country was then at war with the Turks. He joined the Austrian army, and soon became distinguished for his great personal bravery and skill in single combat. He was rewarded for his services by a patent of nobility conferred upon him by the Duke of Transylvania.

2. After many singular adventures he was taken prisoner by the Turks and sold as a slave. He secured the favor of his mistress, and she, intending to do him a kindness, sent him to her brother, an officer in the Crimea, which was

---

lished religion? What civil rights were secured by the charter? What is said of trade and other matters?

CHAPTER III.—**1.** Where was Captain Smith born? What army did he join? **2.** How was he treated after being taken prisoner? How did he make his escape?

then a part of the Turkish Empire. Contrary to her expectations, her brother treated Smith with great cruelty. But his spirit was not broken, and he determined to make his escape whenever a favorable opportunity presented itself. He was employed in threshing grain about three miles from the dwelling of his master, and one day, when the bashaw came as usual to oversee him at his labor, he killed him with the flail used in threshing, hid the dead body, and made his escape on his master's horse.

3. On his way back to England he passed through Russia, Poland, Germany, France, and Spain. He reached England just in time to join the companies which were then forming for settlement in America. He became attached to the expedition under the command of Newport, and was made one of the Council.

4. Soon after the affairs of the colony were committed into his hands, as mentioned in the last chapter, he made treaties with the Indians, kept them quiet for a time, and calmed the fears of the settlers. Following the instructions of the London Company, as soon as the colony became tranquil, he determined to set out upon a voyage of discovery. With a party of men he went up the Chickahominy River, a branch of the James. They were attacked by Indians about thirty miles above the junction of the two rivers. His companions were slain, and he was made prisoner.

5. He had the great good fortune to persuade his captors that he was a magician, by showing them his pocket-compass, and by writing to his friends in Jamestown. His life was spared, but he was kept a close prisoner, and carried bound to Powhatan, the king. After consultation with the principal chiefs, and due deliberation, it was determined by Powhatan that the prisoner should die. His head was laid

---

3. What countries did he pass through on his return to England?
4. What river did he explore? What happened to him and his men?
5. What did he persuade his captors, and how? What happened then? What was Powhatan's conclusion?

CHAP. III.]   THE COLONY OF VIRGINIA.   21

upon a log of wood, and a huge club was raised by the strong arms of Powhatan himself, to strike the fatal blow.

6. But the blow was not struck, and the prisoner's life was saved. Pocahontas, the daughter of Powhatan, a beautiful girl of about twelve years, had been, all this time, a silent spectator of the scene. When she saw the upraised club about to descend upon the victim's head, she

POCAHONTAS RESCUING CAPTAIN SMITH.

sprang forward, threw herself upon his breast, and with eyes streaming with tears, begged his life of her father. Moved with pity, he hesitated, then glancing around, he saw in the faces of the chiefs present that they also were deeply moved. The club fell from his hands. He took his weeping daughter in his arms, and gave the prisoner his life.

6. Was he killed ? How was his life saved ? Can you describe the scene ?

7. The next day Captain Smith was conducted to Jamestown in safety, after having been a prisoner about seven weeks. Before his return to Jamestown he made a treaty with Powhatan, the Indian king agreeing to be at peace with the English, and always to regard Captain Smith as his son. But soon afterwards he again became angry with the whites, and made a plot by which he hoped to be able to destroy them all at one blow. The colony was saved by Pocahontas. The night before the time set for the execution of the plot was dark and stormy; notwithstanding the storm and darkness, this devoted girl proceeded to Jamestown, revealed the plot to Captain Smith, and returned to her own home the same night. The colony was saved, and through the influence of Smith peace was once more made.

8. In the year 1609, a great misfortune befel the colony. Captain Smith was seriously wounded, accidentally, and was compelled to return to England for the benefit of his health. He never revisited Jamestown; but in the year 1614 he sailed from England for the coasts north of Virginia. He made a prosperous voyage; explored the coast, and made a map of it, from the Penobscot River to Cape Cod. This map he presented to the king's son, Charles (who became Charles I.), and who gave to the country the name of *New England,* though it lay within the limits of the Plymouth grant, designated as North Virginia. It has been called New England ever since. Captain Smith died in the year 1631, in London, at the age of fifty-two.

9. Towards the close of the year 1608, two hundred immigrants came over, which increased the population, or settlement, to about five hundred in all, at the time of Smith's departure. But in less than six months after he

---

7. What was done next day? What happened afterwards? How was the colony saved?
8. What misfortune befel the colony in 1809? What voyages and explorations did Captain Smith make afterwards? In what year did he die? At what age?
9. How many settlers were in the colony when Captain Smith left? How

CHAP. III.]　　THE COLONY OF VIRGINIA.　　23

left they were reduced by death and otherwise to about sixty in number. The Indians, no longer restrained by the presence of Smith, became hostile. They attacked the outlying settlements and compelled the inhabitants to flee to Jamestown. Provisions now became scarce, and great suffering ensued. Many, it is said, died for want of food. In their extremity it was determined to abandon the settlement. At this juncture a vessel with crew and passengers, who had wintered in the West Indies, arrived at Jamestown. Their whole number now amounted to about two hundred.

10. The intention to abandon the settlement was not given up, and the colonists had actually set sail, when the opportune arrival of Lord Delaware with a supply of provisions and immigrants changed the aspect of affairs. The colonists returned to Jamestown, and were induced by Lord Delaware to remain. Affairs grew brighter at once under Lord Delaware's wise administration. The Indians ceased to be troublesome; disorder was repressed; industry was encouraged, and the health of the colony improved. But Lord Delaware's own health failed in a short time, and he was compelled to return to England. He was succeeded as governor by Sir Thomas Dale.

11. In September, 1611, Sir Thomas Gates, who had been appointed governor, to succeed Sir Thomas Dale, arrived with six ships and three hundred immigrants, and a large amount of provisions. The population now amounted to about seven hundred, and the colony was enabled to send detachments up the river, where Henrico and other new settlements were made. Sir Thomas Gates also brought over a number of cows, goats, and swine, now for the first time introduced into the New World.

---

many were there six months afterwards? What was the conduct of the Indians? What did the colonists intend to do?
10. How were they induced to remain? Who succeeded Lord Delaware as governor?
11. When did Sir Thomas Gates arrive? How many immigrants? What domestic animals?

12. In the year 1613 Pocahontas, although she had been so good a friend to the colony, was stolen by a party of white men, led by Captain Argall, and a large sum was demanded for her ransom. Powhatan refused to pay the sum demanded, and war was about to ensue, when a young Englishman, named Rolfe, fell in love with Pocahontas and proposed to marry her. Her father consented. She embraced the Christian religion, was baptized, and was soon afterwards married. In the year 1616, in company with her husband, she went to England, where she attracted a great deal of attention. She died in that country at the age of twenty-two, a short while before the time of her intended return to America. She left one son, an infant, named Thomas. From this union descended some of the most illustrious names in the annals of Virginia.

13. Tobacco, an Indian name of a plant which was unknown to Europeans until Columbus met with its use amongst the natives of Cuba, was first planted by the colonists in Virginia in the year 1614. Its use was violently opposed by King James, who wrote and published a book against it; but notwithstanding the royal opposition, it soon became, and still continues, a regular article of commerce throughout the world. The name of this plant, according to the best authority, was given to it from the name of the island Tobago, one of the West Indies, where it was cultivated.

14. In 1614 Sir Thomas Gates was succeeded as governor by Sir Thomas Dale, who continued in office until 1616, when he returned to England, and was succeeded by Mr. George Yeardley. Mr. Yeardley's term of office continued but about one year. His successor was Captain Argall, a cruel, avaricious, and tyrannical man. His rule, which lasted for three years, was exceedingly arbitrary and op-

---

12. What happened in 1613? What was the consequence of the seizure of Pocahontas? When and where did she die? What is said of her descendants?
13. When was tobacco first planted in Virginia?
14. Who succeeded Sir Thomas Gates? When did Captain Argall become governor? What is said of his administration? Who succeeded him?

pressive. He proclaimed martial law in time of peace, and enforced his laws and edicts at the point of the bayonet. The rigor of his administration excited much discontent, and at length the complaints of the Virginians making their way to the Company, Mr. George Yeardley was appointed captain-general, with instructions to examine into the wrongs of the colonists and to redress them.

15. Mr. Yeardley arrived at Jamestown in April, 1619, and immediately abolished the oppressive laws of Argall, and removed the burdens imposed by him. By order of the Company the power of the governor was limited by a council, and the people were admitted by the governor to a share in the administration of public affairs, by the institution of a colonial Assembly. This Assembly met for the first time at Jamestown, on the 19th of June, 1619, convened by order of the governor, Sir George Yeardley, without the express sanction of the Company, but which was afterwards given. This was the first legislative body ever assembled in this country in which the people by deputies enacted laws for their own government, and the time of its meeting may be considered as the birthday of American free institutions.

16. In the year 1620 ninety females were sent over to the colony, and in the following year sixty more, and these, being women of irreproachable character, were immediately married by the farmers; and their domestic and home ties thus becoming fixed in the New World, the thought of returning home to England gradually passed from their minds. The permanence and the prosperity of the colony were thus insured. One hundred convicts were also sent as laborers to the colony, in accordance with the policy about this time adopted by the English Government of sending criminals to the colonies as a punishment. Many

---

15. What course did Mr. Yeardley pursue ? When did the first Legislative Assembly meet in Virginia ?
16. What took place in 1620 ?

of these convicts, removed from their usual haunts of vice and dissipation, became useful citizens.

17. Some time anterior to this period the Spaniards and Portuguese had bought from the chiefs on the coast of Africa, negro captives, and had carried them to other parts of the world, especially to South America and the West Indies, and had sold them as slaves. This traffic they had continued without intermission, and in this year (1620) a Dutch vessel brought to Jamestown twenty of these unfortunate beings, and sold them to the colonists of Virginia. This was the introduction of negro-slavery in the British American colonies, which has been the source of so much trouble, as we shall see.

By the close of the year 1620 the population of the colony amounted to nearly two thousand.

CHAPTER IV.

SETTLEMENT OF NEW YORK BY THE DUTCH. HOW IT BECAME A BRITISH COLONY.

1609—1664.

1. THE Island of Manhattan, now called New York, was first discovered by Henry Hudson in the year 1609. He was an Englishman by birth, but was at that time in the service of the Dutch East India Company, by whom he was employed to search for a northwest passage to India. He discovered and sailed a considerable distance up the river which now bears his name. In consequence of these discoveries of Hudson, the Dutch laid claim

NEW YORK COAT OF ARMS.

---

17. What is said of the African slave-trade ? In what year were Africans first brought to Virginia ? What was the number of the population by the close of the year 1620 ?
CHAPTER IV.—**1.** By whom was New York first settled ? What was New York then called ? What name did the Dutch give the country ?

CHAP. IV.] THE SETTLEMENT OF NEW YORK. 27

to the country, and, in the year 1610, they erected a fort near the place where the city of Albany now stands. They also built a few log-huts on the Island of Manhattan, and to this settlement they afterwards gave the name of New Amsterdam. To the country they gave, in 1621, the general name of New Netherlands.

2. But the English also claimed that region as part of North Virginia, and also upon the general ground of the discovery of the continent by Cabot, and also upon the ground that Hudson himself was an Englishman; and, in 1613, they sent Captain Argall from Virginia to dispossess all intruders on the coast. Captain Argall, in this expedition, not only subdued New Amsterdam, whose governor promised to pay tribute, but he also took possession of all the French settlements in Acadia, as Nova Scotia was then called. But his possession of this latter place was merely temporary, and soon after he left the coast the French colonists returned to their homes. In 1614 the Dutch governor of New Amsterdam, or New York, as it is now called, refused to pay tribute and threw off the English yoke, and for fifty years the colony remained undisturbed by the English.

3. In the interval the progress of the Dutch was not rapid, but their settlements were gradually extended across the country from the Connecticut to the Delaware. On the Connecticut they had frequent disputes with their English neighbors, and also frequently received assistance from them in their contests with the Indians, for which species of warfare they appeared to be peculiarly unfitted. On the Delaware they had to contend against the claims of both the Swedes and the English. The Swedes were subdued, in 1651, by Peter Stuyvesant, the Dutch governor, and the Swedish population were absorbed by the Dutch. The foundations of the city of Albany were laid in 1623.

---

2. What other people claimed it? On what grounds?
3. What is said of the progress of the Dutch? With whom did they have to contend?

4. In 1664 New Amsterdam was seized upon by Colonel Nicholas for the Duke of York, the inhabitants making no resistance, and the whole of the Dutch possessions of the New Netherlands passed quietly into the hands of the English, under the name of New York, from the Duke of York, brother of the King of England.

CHAPTER V.

THE COLONY OF MASSACHUSETTS.

1620—1631.

Settlements at Plymouth, Salem, Dorchester, Lynn, Charlestown, Watertown, Roxbury, and Boston.

1. The first attempt at settlement in the region of country or district granted to the Plymouth Company in England, styled in the grant North Virginia, but afterwards known as New England, was made, in the year 1607, at or near the mouth of the Kennebec River, on the coast of Maine. This settlement was attempted about the same time the colony at Jamestown was planted by the London Company. Forty-five persons constituted the colony on the Kennebec. They were sent out by the Plymouth Company under the presidency or governorship of George Popham. The colonists suffered great hardships during the winter of 1607–1608. Governor Popham himself died during that winter. In the Spring, when no ships came with supplies, Raleigh Gilbert, who now succeeded to the presidency, learning that he had become heir to a consid-

MASSACHUSETTS COAT OF ARMS.

---

4. When did the country pass into the hands of the English ?
Chapter V.—1. In what year was the first attempted settlement made in what was called North Virginia ? What was its fate ?

erable property by the death of his brother, abandoned the enterprise, and the whole company returned to England.

2. Other attempts at colonization were made by the Plymouth Company, after the publication of Captain John Smith's map in 1614, as before stated, but these need not be particularly noticed, as all of them failed, from some cause or other.

3. But a colony was firmly planted in Massachusetts, the first in New England, rather by the permission than the favoring auspices of this Company, as we shall see. This was in 1620, by a religious sect known as Puritans.

4. "The name Puritan was given to them on account of their austerity of manner and the rigid observance of the forms of their religion. In religion they were Calvinistic, and were dissenters from the Church of England." Their manner of teaching, preaching, and acting brought them in contact with the public authorities in England at a time when there was no such thing as toleration in matters of religion; they were persecuted for obstinate refusal to conform to the requirements of the existing ecclesiastical establishment.

5. During the reign of Henry VIII. many of them had taken refuge in Switzerland and Germany. They had been hospitably received by their brethren in the faith there, and had sat at the feet of the great doctors of Strasburg, Zurich, and Geneva, and had been, during some years, accustomed to a more simple worship, and to a more democratical form of church government, than England had yet seen.

6. Some of these returned to their country after the accession of Elizabeth to the throne. But in vain did they look to her for any toleration to their peculiar views in matters of faith and worship. Persecution again awaited

---

2. Were other attempts to make settlements made? What became of them? In what year was the first permanent settlement made?
3. What people made the first settlement, and how did it come about?
4, 5, 6, 7, etc. What does Macaulay say of the Puritans and their origin?

them, and, in the language of Macaulay, "Persecution produced its natural effect on them. It found them a sect, it made them a faction. To their hatred of the church was now added hatred of the crown. The two sentiments were intermingled, and each embittered the other.

7. "In 1603 Queen Elizabeth died, and was succeeded by James of Scotland. A change, to some extent, had taken place in the principles and practices of the Puritans. The persecutions which they had undergone had been severe enough to irritate, but had not been severe enough to destroy. They had not been tamed into submission, but baited into savageness and stubbornness. After the fashion of oppressed sects, they mistook their own vindictive feelings for emotions of piety; encouraged in themselves, by reading and meditation, a disposition to brood over their wrongs; and, when they had worked themselves up into hating their enemies, imagined that they were only hating the enemies of heaven. In the New Testament there was little, indeed, which, even when perverted by the most disingenuous exposition, could seem to countenance the indulgence of malevolent passions.

8. "But the Old Testament contained the history of a race selected by God to be witnesses of His unity and ministers of His vengeance, and specially commanded by Him to do many things which, if done without His special command, would have been atrocious crimes. In such a history it was not difficult for fierce and gloomy spirits to find much that might be distorted to suit their wishes. The extreme Puritans, therefore, began to feel for the Old Testament a preference, which, perhaps, they did not distinctly avow even to themselves, but which showed itself in all their sentiments and habits. They paid to the Hebrew language a respect which they refused to that tongue in which the discourses of Jesus and the epistles of Paul have come down to us. They baptized their children by

the names, not of Christian saints, but of Hebrew patriarchs and warriors.

9. " In defiance of the express and reiterated declarations of Luther and Calvin, they turned the weekly festival by which the Church had, from the primitive times, commemorated the resurrection of her Lord, into a Jewish Sabbath. . . . . It was a sin to hang garlands on a Maypole, to drink a friend's health, to fly a hawk, to hunt a stag, to play at chess, to wear lovelocks, to put starch into a ruff, to touch the virginals, to read the Fairy Queen. Rules such as these, rules which would have appeared insupportable to the free and joyous spirit of Luther, and contemptible to the serene and philosophical intellect of Zwingle, threw over all life a more than monastic gloom. The extreme Puritan was at once known from other men by his gait, his garb, his lank hair, the sour solemnity of his face, the upturned white of his eyes, the nasal twang with which he spoke, and, above all, by his peculiar dialect. He employed, on every occasion, the imagery and style of Scripture. Hebraisms violently introduced into the English language, and metaphors borrowed from the boldest lyric poetry of a remote age and country, and applied to the common concerns of English life, were the most striking peculiarities of this cant, which moved, not without cause, the derision both of prelatists and libertines."

10. This portraiture of the character of the Puritans, like most of the word-painting of Macaulay, is perhaps overwrought and too highly colored. It exhibits the darker side only of this wonderful people, and shows nothing of the many fine and tender traits, as well as high heroic virtues, for which they were equally distinguished.

11. A sect of these Puritans known as Brownists, from the name of their founder, had taken refuge at Leyden, in Holland, from the annoyances to which they were liable in

---

10. Is Macaulay's estimate just ?
11. What induced the Puritans to leave Holland ?

England. They resided in that city for some years, under the pastoral charge of Mr. John Robinson; but not finding their situation altogether congenial, they came to the determination to remove to America. As they desired to settle within the limits of the territory then known as Virginia, they sent two of their number, Robert Cushing and John Carver, to England, for the purpose of obtaining the consent of the London Company.

12. Their application was favorably received, and, through the influence of Sir Edwin Sandys, secretary of the company, a patent under the company's seal was obtained, and a tract of land was assigned them. They wished, also, that their enterprise should receive the approbation of the king; but James hated the Puritans, and the greatest favor they could obtain from him was his promise to let them alone. Money was obtained from a company of London merchants on terms that constituted the merchants partners in the adventure. Ten pounds in money advanced by the merchant was made equal to seven years of labor of the emigrant. The profits were to be reserved to the end of that time, when a distribution was to be made. This association of Puritans was, from their migrations, also called Pilgrims.

13. They procured two vessels, the *Speedwell*, of sixty tons, and the *Mayflower*, of one hundred and eighty tons burthen. They set sail on the 22d of July, 1620, but the *Speedwell* was soon found to be unseaworthy, and they were compelled to put back for repairs. They sailed again from Southampton on the 5th of August, but were compelled to put back the second time. They returned to Portsmouth, at which place they abandoned the *Speedwell*, with some of the party whose courage failed them. The *May-*

---

12. How was their application to the London Company received? Why did not the king favor their enterprise? What were the terms of their contract with the merchants? Why were the Puritans who settled at Plymouth called Pilgrims?
13. What were the names of the vessels in which the Pilgrims sailed? When did the *Mayflower* finally set sail?

flower finally set sail on the 6th of September, with one hundred and one persons on board.

14. Their destination was the mouth of the Hudson River, but they were conducted by their captain, whether ignorantly or of set purpose, to a much more bleak and inhospitable region, north of that river. After a voyage of sixty-three days they came in sight of Cape Cod, and on

LANDING AT PLYMOUTH.

the 10th of November they cast anchor in that harbor. Having no charter from the king, they, as yet, had no form of government. One, purely democratic, was adopted before landing, drawn up in writing, and signed by the men, forty-one in number. Mr. John Carver was unanimously chosen governor for one year.

---

14. What was the place of their destination? What was the length of their

15. Several days were spent in searching for a suitable place to land. At last the desired harbor was found, and on the 22d of December, 1620, the Pilgrims landed. The place they named Plymouth, after or in honor of the place in England from which they had sailed. No time was spent in idleness; trees must be felled, and houses built. Lots were assigned to families, and on the third day they began to build. The winter was very severe, and the sufferings of the colonists were great. By the first of April, 1621, all but forty-six of those who had landed were dead. Among the dead were Governor Carver, his wife, and son. At one time there were but seven well persons in the whole settlement. With the return of spring came health and renewed vigor.

16. In March, a short time before the death of Governor Carver, a treaty of amity was made with Massasoit, the great chief of the Wampanoags, with Samoset, a chief of the same tribe, and eight smaller chiefs. This treaty was of great service to the colony, as, in its weak and suffering condition, it could easily have been destroyed by savage enemies. It was kept inviolate by both parties for fifty years. As spring advanced the health of the colonists improved. But their supply of provisions was barely sufficient to last them until harvest. Massasoit taught them the cultivation and use of maize or Indian corn, the first of which was planted in the month of May, 1621. In November, a ship arrived with thirty-five immigrants, wholly without provisions. The following winter their sufferings were much increased; sometimes for months they had no grain at all.

17. William Bradford, who was chosen governor after the death of Carver, was so much beloved that he was con-

---

voyage? When did they first come in sight of land? What was the form of government adopted before landing?
15. What was the day of their landing? Why did they call the place Plymouth? What is said of their sufferings and condition during the winter? What eminent man died?
16. What treaty was made? What was their condition in the winter of 1621?
17. Who succeeded Carver as governor? What is said of him? What is mentioned as one of the causes of scarcity?

tinued in office the greater part of the time until his death, nearly forty years in all. The harvest of 1622 was scanty, and the settlers would have suffered greatly had it not been for the friendship of the Indians. One of the causes of scarcity was the deep religious feeling of the leading Puritans, who had desired, in imitation of Apostolic times, to have a community of property. But even amongst the Puritans there were some who would not work, as long as they were permitted to eat the fruit of the labor of others. And so the system was changed, and, in the spring of 1623, each family had allotted a parcel of ground to cultivate for itself. All had now to work for themselves, or to do without the necessaries of life. After the harvest of that year there was never any general want of food.

18. In 1623, the Pilgrims, as they were called, as before stated, were involved in an Indian war, through the conduct of another small English colony, which had in the meantime been established at Weymouth, near Boston harbor. Thomas Weston, one of the London merchants who had advanced money to settlers, moved by the hope of gain, had obtained a patent from the Plymouth Company in England for a small district in Massachusetts Bay, on Boston harbor. To this place he sent a company of about sixty men, who were dissolute in their habits, and by their aggressions gave so much offence to the Indians that a plot was laid to entirely exterminate the English. Massasoit, the friendly chief, grateful to the colony at Plymouth for kindness received from them, revealed the plot to the governor, who immediately sent Captain Standish to the new settlement for its defence. Captain Standish took with him but eight men. Hastening to the scene of action, he was in time, not only to prevent the attack, but also to surprise the Indians. He attacked them unexpectedly, slew the principal instigators of the plot, and drove

---

18. How were the Pilgrims involved in war in 1623 ? What is said of Weston and his settlement ? Who revealed the plot of the Indians ? What is said of Captain Standish ?

the rest into a swamp, where many of them miserably perished. Weymouth was soon after abandoned, and the settlers returned to England.

19. In the year 1624, other immigrants arrived at Plymouth. They brought with them cattle, swine, poultry, clothing, and provisions. The progress of Plymouth colony was slow. Four years after the landing of the Pilgrims there were thirty-two houses in the settlement and one hundred and eighty inhabitants; at the end of ten years there were only three hundred.

20. The connection of the colony with the London merchants from whom they had received money, embarrassed them greatly. The merchants complained that they received no return for the money advanced, and interfered in various ways with the affairs of the colony, causing the immigrants great inconvenience. At last the colonists were able to buy out the rights of the London adventurers, and by this means were relieved of debt and an unpleasant connection.

21. In November, 1620, a short time before the landing of the colonists at Plymouth, a new charter was granted by James I. of England, in lieu of the one before granted to what was known as the Plymouth Company. This was to a new company in England, at the head of which stood the Duke of Lenox. This new company was styled the "Grand Council of Plymouth." This charter granted to the new company all the territory between the "*fortieth* and *forty-eighth* degrees of north latitude, and extending throughout the main land from sea to sea."

In this new grant or charter the name of "North Virginia," previously applied to this district of country, was dropped, and that of "New England" substituted for it.

---

19. What is said of the progress of Plymouth ? How many inhabitants were there in the colony ten years after the landing of the Pilgrims ?
20. What was the colony's embarrassment ? How relieved ?
21. When was the charter for North Virginia changed ? What was the new

22. In 1628 a number of persons in England, wishing to emigrate to North America, purchased from the "Grand Council of Plymouth" "that part of New England which lies between three miles to the south of the Merrimack River, and three miles to the south of Charles River, and extending from the Atlantic to the South Sea." Under this purchase John Endicot, a man of note, with about one hundred colonists, made a settlement at Salem.

23. In 1629 the proprietors of this purchase of public domain, who were residents of England, obtained from Charles I., King of England, who had succeeded his father James I., a charter, granting them powers of government over colonists who might settle within its limits. The title of the corporation created by the royal grant was "The Governor and Company of Massachusetts Bay in New England." About three hundred persons soon after embarked for the new colony of Massachusetts.

In 1630, for the purpose of stimulating emigration to the new colony, the proprietors agreed "to form a council of those who should emigrate, and who might hold their sessions thereafter in the new settlement" or colony. Under this arrangement *John Winthrop* was chosen the first governor of the colony of Massachusetts, so planted—and during the year 1630 about fifteen hundred new settlers came over from the mother country and made their home in Massachusetts. New settlements were made at Charlestown, Dorchester, Watertown, Lynn, Roxbury, and Boston.

24. In October, 1631, a general meeting of all the freemen in the colony was held in Boston, when John Winthrop was re-elected governor, and Thomas Dudley was

---

company called ? What was that part of the country included in the new charter called ?
22. When was the settlement at Salem made ? Under what purchase of land was it made ?
23. When was the charter for the colony of Massachusetts Bay granted ? By whom was it granted ? What year was the first settlement made under it ?
24. Who was the first governor ? About how many colonists came over the year Winthrop was made governor ? What was the first government of the colony of Massachusetts ?

chosen deputy governor. The colony of Massachusetts was thus established.

At first the government, under the rights and privileges granted by the charter, was a pure democracy. All the freemen assembled and gave their votes for their magistrates and other officers, as well as upon all matters of government. This was afterwards changed. In different localities the freemen held meetings, and chose deputies or delegates to meet in a common council, which was called "The General Court," and which was empowered to pass all proper laws. This "General Court" was to meet four times a year. The pure democratic form of government in this way gave place to what is called the representative system: that is, where the people make laws and govern themselves by chosen deputies, or select delegates to act for them.

25. For several years after the settlement at Plymouth, that colony had no direct political connection with the other settlements in Massachusetts. It was under a government exclusively its own, and in the regulation of all local affairs recognized no authority but its own. Its government was purely democratic.

CHAPTER VI.

Progress of Virginia.
1621—1660.

We turn now again to Virginia.

1. On the 24th of July, 1621, the Colonial Assembly, of which mention has already been made, received the express sanction of the London Company by an ordinance. This ordinance may be considered as the written Consti-

---

25. What was the government of the settlement at Plymouth for many years? Chapter VI.—1. What took place July 24, 1621? What is said of this ordinance?

tution of the colony. Its provisions were liberal, giving to the people the election of two burgesses from each borough, who formed what was called the House of Burgesses, and who, with the Council appointed by the company, constituted the General Assembly. They had power to make laws, subject to the approval of the governor (who was appointed by the company), and the approval of the company in London, and "no orders of the court in London were to be binding on the colony unless ratified by the Assembly."

2. Beside the right of trial by jury, all other civil rights of Englishmen were secured, to be determined according to their own regulations, with the restriction just stated. In the charter of Virginia, as now amended, was recognized for the first time by the mother country the principle of the great and inestimable right of local self-government, by the people of the British colonies respectively on this continent.

3. Sir Francis Wyatt succeeded Yeardley as governor in 1621. At this period the colony was in a very flourishing condition. There were about eighty settlements, and the population amounted to not less than three thousand. The inhabitants enjoyed civil rights; the land was fertile; trade was free, and peace continued with the Indians. In the midst of their prosperity and seeming security, a terrible calamity suddenly befell them. They had no suspicion that the Indians had become unfriendly, but such was the fact. O-pe-chan-can-ough, the brother of Powhatan, had succeeded him as king, in 1618. He had no love for the strangers, but concealed his hatred until he could mature his plans, by which he hoped to be able to destroy them all. At noon on a certain day, the Indians were to fall upon every settlement, and murder the whites.

---

2. What civil rights were secured ?
3. Who succeeded Yeardley ? What was the population at this time ? What terrible misfortune befell the colony at this time ?

4. The plot was so well kept secret that even on the morning of the day of the massacre, the Indians mingled freely with the whites, and sat at their tables at their morning meals. Nothing in the manner of the savages gave the slightest intimation of their evil designs. The plot might have been entirely successful and the massacre complete, had it not been for the warning of a converted Indian named Chanco, who, on the morning of the attack,

INDIAN MASSACRE.

brought the news of the plot to Jamestown. Only the night before had he learned it. Messengers were immediately dispatched in every direction to warn the inhabitants, but it was too late to warn all. At twelve o'clock, on the first of April, the attack was made, and over three

---

4. Who revealed the plot? How many persons were killed? How many plantations destroyed?

hundred men, women, and children, were slain in a single hour. Of eighty plantations, all but seven or eight were laid waste, the survivors fleeing to Jamestown.

5. A general war of extermination against the Indians followed. The whites lost all confidence in the red men; hunted them like wild beasts, and used all the wily arts of cunning and treachery for their destruction. At length the Indians were driven back from the river a considerable distance into the wilderness; their strength was broken, and the colony was again safe. This was a dreadful blow to Virginia, from which it took some years to recover. Many settlers returned to England, and two years after the massacre there were not two thousand inhabitants in the colony.

6. Meantime the London Company was hastening to its dissolution. The stockholders, who were very numerous, had become divided into two political parties, and the subject of the king's prerogative was freely discussed at their meetings, much to the king's annoyance. He charged the disasters of the colony to the mismanagement of the company, and commissioners were appointed by the privy council to examine into its affairs. They seized the charter, and all the books and papers of the company, and, after examination, made an unfavorable report. The king then demanded of them a surrender of their charter, which being refused, the case was then carried into the court of King's Bench, and decided against them. The company was then declared dissolved, and the government of the colony devolved on the crown, under the charter.

7. While the controversy between the king and company was going on, the colonists were left to take care of themselves. In February, 1624, the General Assembly declared "that the governor should not impose any taxes on the

---

5. What was the result of the war?
6. What is said of the condition of the London Company? What was the result of the investigation by the commissioners? and the suit?
7. In February, 1624, what did the Assembly declare? What did they refuse to do?

colony, otherwise than by authority of the General Assembly; and that he should not withdraw the inhabitants from their private labor to any service of his own." They also refused to give a declaration of unlimited submission to the king, when urged by the royal commissioners, but they sent a petition to the king praying for a confirmation of their civil rights under their charter.

8. The king refused to recognize the Assembly, and issued a special commission, appointing a governor and twelve councillors, to whom the entire control of the affairs of the colony was committed. King James died in 1625, before any action was finally taken by the commissioners. He was succeeded by his son, Charles I. Charles was disposed to favor the colonists, and desired to ingratiate himself with them, in order that he might obtain a monopoly of their tobacco trade. He did not interfere in any way with their franchises, seeming to know but little and to care but little about the political condition of the Virginians. Sir George Yeardley succeeded Wyatt as governor in 1626. The House of Burgesses continued its meetings; the king did not interfere in any way; emigrants arrived in great numbers; and agriculture and commerce were flourishing.

9. In November, 1627, the governor, Sir George Yeardley, died, and the council elected Francis West governor in his place, until another should be appointed by the king. During his administration, the king requested the House of Burgesses to pass a law by which he alone could purchase the tobacco of the colony. The House refused to comply with the request, as it would be injurious to their trade. The king appointed Sir John Harvey governor in the place of Yeardley. He was no stranger in the colony, had been a member of the council, and was very unpopular.

---

8. What did the king do then ? In what year did King James die ? What was the principal object of King Charles ? Who succeeded Wyatt in 1626 ?
9. What request did the king make of the House of Burgesses ? Did they agree to it ? Who was appointed governor by the king ? What occurred then ?

A strong party was formed against him, and the opposition became at last so strong that he was impeached by the House of Burgesses and removed from office. The Assembly appointed two commissioners to prosecute the charges against him in England. The king would not hear the complaints against Harvey, but re-appointed him governor, in which office he continued until 1642, when he was succeeded by Sir William Berkeley.

10. About this time the colony was left for awhile to take care of itself, as the attention of the king was entirely taken up with the struggle between himself and his Parliament. The majority of the people of Virginia were staunch friends of the cause of the king in that contest, and the parliamentary party in the mother country, who were contending against him, met with no favor from them. That party was condemned as composed chiefly of Puritans, and as the religious creed of the Puritans was in great disfavor in Virginia, they were looked upon with suspicion, and those of their number who refused to conform to the ceremonies of the Church of England, which the House of Burgesses had declared to be the established religion of the colony, were banished. Puritan missionaries from New England were silenced, and ordered to leave the colony.

11. Never, since the great massacre of 1622, had there been any real peace with the Indians; and in 1644 they made a sudden attack upon the frontiers, and killed about three hundred of the inhabitants before they were repulsed. When resisted, a panic seemed to seize them, and they fled to the wilderness. The war continued for about two years, and the power of the Indians was completely broken. Their aged chief, Opechancanough, was taken prisoner, and soon

---

10. What took place about this time in England ? What is said of the majority of the people of Virginia ? How were Puritan missionaries treated by the House of Burgesses?
11. What took place in 1644 ? How many were slain ? How long did the war last ? With what result ?

after died in captivity. In 1646, a treaty was made with Necontowanee, the successor of Opechancanough, by which the Indians relinquished the lands of their fathers and retired further into the wilderness.

12. At this time the colony was in a very flourishing condition; commerce was largely increased; more than thirty ships were engaged in the carrying trade. The population, in 1648, amounted to twenty thousand. After the triumph of the parliamentary party in England, and the execution of the king, Charles I., many royalists fled from that country to Virginia, where they were warmly welcomed. Virginia was the last of the colonies to acknowledge the authority of the commonwealth under Cromwell. In 1651, a fleet was sent over to reduce the colony to submission; and when it was found that the Parliament offered to secure to the colonists all the rights of Englishmen, on condition that they would adhere to the Commonwealth, they yielded.

13. Richard Bennett, one of the parliamentary commissioners, was elected governor, and Sir William Berkeley retired to private life. In 1655 and 1658, the House of Burgesses exercised the right of electing and removing the governor, and on receiving intelligence of the death of Cromwell, they re-asserted the right, and required Matthews, the governor, to acknowledge it. On the death of Matthews, Cromwell being dead, and the government of England in an unsettled state, the House of Burgesses elected Sir William Berkeley governor. He refused to serve under the usurped authority of Parliament, when Charles II., who was then in exile, was proclaimed their lawful sovereign, and invited to come over and be king of Virginia. From this incident in her history Virginia received the name of "The Old Dominion."

12. What was now the condition of the colony? What took place after the triumph of the parliamentary party in England?
13. In 1655 and 1658 what right did the House of Burgesses exercise? Who was elected governor after Cromwell's death? How did Virginia receive the name of the Old Dominion?

14. Charles was, not long afterwards, restored to the throne of England. Of all his subjects, the Virginians were the last to renounce and the first to return to their allegiance to the House of Stuart.

CHAPTER VII.

SETTLEMENT OF NEW HAMPSHIRE.
1623—1680.

1. THE accounts given, even by the best authorities, of the early English settlements in the colony of New Hampshire, conflict very much with each other. Some maintain that they were made in 1623 under a grant by the Plymouth Company, in 1622, to Sir Fernando Gorges and Captain John Mason, to a district of country designated as Laconia. Others maintain that there were no permanent settlements made within the present limits of New Hampshire until after the grant of the 7th November, 1629, to Captain John Mason.

NEW HAMPSHIRE COAT OF ARMS.

2. Much of this confusion arises from the great number of grants made at different times, to different parties, by the Plymouth Company in England, to the same district of country, and out of which sprung most of the troubles and evils that so greatly retarded the growth of this colony. After a very thorough investigation of the subject, the following statement may be received as a correct narrative of all the essential facts.

3. On the 10th of August, 1622, a conveyance or grant

CHAPTER VII.—1. What is said of the accounts given of the early settlements in New Hampshire?
2. What does the confusion on the subject arise from?
3. When was the first grant made to Sir Fernando Gorges and Captain John

was made by the Plymouth Company in England (at the head of which stood the Duke of Lenox), to Sir Fernando Gorges and Captain John Mason, of all the rights and jurisdiction vested in that corporation by their Royal Charter of the 3d of November, 1620, for colonizing in New England, over a district of country including part, at least, of New Hampshire; but this district, over which their rights and powers of colonization were so conveyed, was not designated in the grant as Laconia.

The Laconia grant was made to the same parties on the 17th of November, 1629. But under the grant to Gorges and Mason, of the 10th of August, 1622, as stated, two settlements, which proved to be permanent, were made within the present territorial limits of New Hampshire.

4. These were on the Piscataway river, one of them near the mouth of this river and near the present site of Portsmouth. This one was, for a long time, called Strawberry Bank, or Mason Hall, in honor of the principal house in the place, erected by Captain Mason, under whose auspices the settlement was made. The other was higher up on the same river, and received the name of Dover, which it still bears. Both of these settlements were made in 1623, under the grant of the 10th of August, 1622, to Gorges and Mason. The settlement near the mouth of the Piscataway was under the special management of David Thompson, chief overseer of Captain Mason at this place; and the one at Dover under the like supervisorship of William Hilton.

After these settlements were so made, to wit, on the 7th of November, 1629, and before the Laconia grant, Captain John Mason obtained a grant to himself alone, from the

---

Mason? By whom was this grant made? By what authority was it made? Did it include any part of New Hampshire? When was the Laconia grant made, and to whom? Under what grant were the two settlements made?

4. Where were these settlements made? What was the first one of them named? What was the name of the other? In what year were these two settlements made? To whom was the grant of the 7th of November, 1629, made? Did it include these settlements? What name was given to the country embraced in this grant?

same Plymouth Company, for a district of country which included within its specified boundaries the settlements already made by him; and to the whole of the district of country embraced in this grant to him was given the name of New Hampshire.

It was in this grant, by the Plymouth corporation to John Mason individually, made on the 7th of November, 1629, the colony of New Hampshire received its name.

5. After this grant, accessions were made to the two settlements previously established, but no new settlement was attempted for several years.

In the winter of 1635-6 Captain John Mason, the founder of New Hampshire, died, and as no one for many years succeeded to his proprietary rights, the colony was neglected and made little progress.

In 1638 a new settlement was made at Exeter by John Wheelright and some followers, who were compelled to leave Massachusetts on account of some peculiarities in their religious faith.

In like manner the settlement at Hampton was made in 1640, by Stephen Bacheler and some adherents.

6. But after the death of Captain John Mason each of the settlements in New Hampshire was left without any government, except that which each constituted for itself.

Dover, Exeter, Hampton, and Portsmouth (as Strawberry Bank, or Mason Hall, was afterwards called), were each severally governed by its own laws, and they severally recognized no other authority than their own, in the administration of justice and the regulation of all local affairs. In 1641, however, or about that time, Massachusetts claimed to exercise some sort of jurisdiction over these communities, by virtue of certain grants by the Plymouth Company to that colony. The dispute between the government of

---

5. Were any settlements made for some time afterwards? Who was the founder of New Hampshire, and when did he die? How did his death affect the colony? When were other settlements made, where, and how?
6. After the death of Mason, how were these settlements governed? What took place in 1641, or about that time?

Massachusetts Bay, and the rightful Proprietary, under the Mason grant of the 7th of November, 1629, was not ended until 1680, when it was very justly determined, by the proper authorities in England, against the claim of Massachusetts.

7. But during all this time, the colony of New Hampshire remained almost stationary. It increased very little either in population or wealth. In 1653 the entire population did not exceed one thousand. The people, however, during the whole period, were greatly distinguished for their virtues and love of liberty. These were as pure as the air from the tops of their own White Mountains, the highest in New England!

CHAPTER VIII.

SETTLEMENT OF CONNECTICUT.

1633—1639.

1. THE first settlement in Connecticut was made in 1633, at or near the place where Hartford now stands, by the

CONNECTICUT COAT OF ARMS.

Dutch, under the name of Good Hope. They were moved to this enterprise to keep out the English, who, they learned, were about to occupy the territory, under a grant given by the Plymouth Company to Lord Warwick, transferred by him to Lords Say and Brooke. The Dutch, unable to hold the country, yielded their claim in 1634, and the dividing line was drawn, nearly the same as

---

7. How did the colony remain from 1641 to 1660? What is said of the population in 1653? What is said of the people during this time? What is said of the White Mountains in New Hampshire?

CHAPTER VIII.—**1.** When was Hartford first settled? By whom? What was it called? When was the government of Connecticut organized?

now exists between New York and Connecticut. In 1635 John Winthrop, the agent of the Proprietaries, erected a fort at the mouth of the Connecticut, which he called Saybrooke. In the next year the government of Connecticut was organized under a commission from Massachusetts.

2. In the spring or summer of 1636, a party of about one hundred emigrants, weary with the continued turmoil and religious dissensions of Massachusetts, set out under the leadership of Rev. Thomas Hooker and John Haynes, a former governor, across the wilderness, for the fertile valley of the Connecticut. They arrived in July. Of these emigrants, some remained at Hartford; some went up the river and founded Springfield, and some went down to Wethersfield.

3. In 1637 the colony was threatened with destruction by an Indian war, of which we shall say more hereafter.

4. In 1637 John Davenport, a clergyman of London, and his friend, Theophilus Eaton, a rich merchant, with some associates, arrived in Boston. They were cordially welcomed and pressed to remain, but the religious controversies of that community were so incessant and harassing that they preferred to go into the wilderness, where they could dwell in peace. Eaton, with a few men, during the winter explored the coast, and found a desirable place, which they purchased from the natives. In the spring of 1638 the company sailed from Boston, and landing on the shores of the beautiful bay, at the spot selected by Eaton, they founded the city of New Haven. Eaton was elected governor. During the remainder of his life, for more than twenty years, he was annually elected to the same office.

5. At this time there were three separate political communities in that territory now known as Connecticut:

---

2. What took place in the spring and summer of 1636 ? What places did these men settle ?
3. What great calamity threatened the colony in 1637 ?
4. Who arrived in Boston in 1637 ? Why did they not remain in Massachusetts ? What city did they found ?
5. How many sections in Connecticut in 1638 ?

Saybrook under the Proprietaries; the Connecticut colony organized by Massachusetts; and the New Haven colony under Eaton.

6. In 1639 the settlements on the Connecticut River held a convention at Hartford, and adopted a Constitution and form of government. The Constitution was liberal, and admitted every one to the rights of citizenship who took the oath of allegiance to the commonwealth. No jurisdiction was allowed to the king. The governor and other officers were to be elected annually, and the representation in the Assembly was apportioned among the townships according to population.

7. The settlement or colony at New Haven remained separate, under a code of laws of their own making, which, from their very rigid character, have been styled the " Blue Laws."

CHAPTER IX.
THE SETTLEMENT OF RHODE ISLAND.
1636—1688.

Roger Williams—His Flight—Providence—Charter of Rhode Island—Sir Edmund Andros.

RHODE ISLAND COAT OF ARMS.

1. THE colony of Rhode Island was founded in 1636, by Roger Williams. This celebrated divine, and apostle of civil as well as religious liberty, deserves special notice, in connection with the events attending the early settlement of the famous Plantations established under his auspices. He was a native of Wales, and born in 1599. Having been reared and educated in the Episcopal faith, and being of ardent temperament, and

---

6. What was done by the people in 1639? What is said of the Constitution, laws, etc.?
7. How did the colony of New Haven remain?
CHAPTER IX.—1. When was the colony of Rhode Island founded, and by whom? What is said of Roger Williams?

thoroughly imbued with a spirit of piety, he entered the ministry at an early age, taking orders in the church of his fathers. Not long afterwards, upon a fuller investigation of doctrines, he became a Dissenter, and connected himself with the denomination known as Baptists.

ROGER WILLIAMS.

2. He came to America in 1631, and settled in Salem, Massachusetts. He preached there regularly, and occasionally at Plymouth, enforcing his peculiar views with great zeal and eloquence. His teachings, however, were deemed not only heretical but seditious by the Puritan Fathers at both these places. He was tried and condemned on charges of this character, and made flight from Salem in the Winter of 1635–36. It was about the middle of January, 1636, according to the best accounts, and under cover of night, he sought safety in exile.

3. His heresy, according to Bancroft, consisted in maintaining "that the civil magistrate ought to restrain crime, but never control opinion: should punish guilt, but never violate the freedom of the soul." He denounced the law that compelled all persons to attend worship, as an infringement of the rights of conscience.

4. Soon after his arrival in Massachusetts he considered it as part of his spiritual mission to become acquainted with the language, customs, and manners of the neighboring Indian tribes, that he might impart to them a knowledge of the Gospel of Christ. He was on friendly terms, therefore, with the Sachems Massasoit, Ousamequin, and

---

2. When did he come to America ? Where did he settle ? Where did he preach ? What was he tried for ? What was the result ?
3. What was Williams's heresy according to Bancroft ?
4. What is further said of Williams ? How long did he wander in search of a place suitable for such a new settlement as he wished to make ? How did he travel ? Where were his wife and children ?

Canonicus. In the huts of these and other barbarian chiefs, he sought and obtained, for a while, that shelter and protection which were denied him by his Christian brethren.

He wandered " for fourteen weeks," according to his own statement, most of the time " in the bitter winter season," in quest of a place where he could found a settlement for himself and family, and such other persons as might be disposed to join him. In these wanderings he was alone and on foot. His wife and children had been left at Salem.

5. At length, on the Pawtucket (now the Seekonk) River, and on the east side of that river, he found a place which he thought would suit his purpose. He went to see Ousamequin, the Sachem of Pokanoket, within whose territory the place lay, and obtained from him permission to occupy the lands selected for the purpose stated by him. These lands are said to be within the limits of the present town of Seekonk, in Massachusetts. Here Williams with his own hands reared a habitation; and here he began to plant, in the Spring of 1636. Here, also, a few friends joined him, but his and their troubles and wanderings were not ended.

6. Governor Winslow, of the Plymouth settlement in Massachusetts, soon notified him that Seekonk was within the boundaries of his jurisdiction, and as he was " loath to displease " the authorities at Salem, he mildly admonished him to leave. This admonition Williams and five other friends, who were then with him, immediately heeded. He set out with them again in search of a resting place. This they found near the mouth of the Moshassuck River. The site chosen was near an excellent spring of pure water, which was noted for many years afterwards. Here they renewed their work of building and planting, and here the settlement of the colony of Rhode Island was commenced.

---

5. Where did he at length find a place ? What Indian Chief gave him permission to settle there ? What did he do towards making a settlement at this place ?
6. Why did not Williams and his followers remain at Seekonk ? Where did they, at last, find them a resting place ? What name did Williams give to the place, and why?

"To the town there founded, Williams, with his habitual piety, and in grateful remembrance of God's merciful providence to him in his distress, gave the name of PROVIDENCE."

7. This place was within the jurisdiction of Canonicus, the Chief or Sachem of the Narraganset Indians. Canonicus was Williams's friend, and made him the grant of land for his settlement in consideration of kindness and good will alone. Of Ousamequin and Canonicus Williams himself said: "When I came I was welcome to Ousamequin, and to the old prince Canonicus, who was most shy to all English to his last breath;" and in speaking further of Canonicus, he said that "it was not thousands, or tens of thousands, of money could have bought of him an English entrance into this bay."

Of his grant he said, "By God's merciful assistance I was the procurer of the purchase, not by moneys, nor payments, the natives being so shy and jealous, that moneys could not do it, but by that language, acquaintance, and favor with the natives, and other advantages, which it pleased God to give me."

8. The foregoing is an outline sketch of this most remarkable man, who, fleeing from persecution, penetrated the wilderness with a view of establishing a colony where there should be perfect freedom of conscience in the worship of God. According to the most probable accounts, the wife of Williams, with her two children, came from Salem to Providence, in the Summer of 1636, in company with several persons who wished to join their exiled pastor.

The population of this settlement soon increased considerably by immigrants from Massachusetts and from England. It was a refuge and asylum for those in all countries

---

7. Within the jurisdiction of what Indian Chief or Sachem was this place? Upon what consideration did he permit Williams and his followers to settle? What did Williams say of the Sachems Ousamequin and Canonicus?
8. According to most probable accounts, when did Williams's wife and children join him? Who accompanied them? Did the settlement increase, and how? What was the design of Williams in planting his colony? Give the substance of the covenant or Constitution by which the settlement was governed.

who were persecuted and suffered " for conscience' sake." The design of Williams was " that his colony should be open to all persons who might choose to reside there, without regard to their religious opinions." This inducement brought many. He was careful, however, to provide for the maintenance of law and order. In his Constitution, every one forming a constituent member of the Society was required to subscribe the following covenant: " We whose names are here under-written, being desirous to inhabit in the town of Providence, do promise to subscribe ourselves, in active or passive obedience, to all such orders or agreements as shall be made for the public good of the body, in an orderly way, by the major consent of the present inhabitants, masters of families, incorporated together into a township, and such others whom they shall admit unto the same, *only in civil things!*"

9. This written Constitution, drawn up by Williams himself, and subscribed by every member of his Society, as above set forth, formed the entire basis of the first government of the settlement at Providence. It embodied the principles of a pure democracy, with the exercise of unrestricted religious liberty. It was the germ of those free institutions under which the colony flourished so long a time afterwards.

10. On the 30th of August, 1636, a Synod was held at New Town (Cambridge), Massachusetts, to settle certain religious doctrines then in dispute between several Puritan ministers in that colony. The result was the condemnation of the tenets of quite a large class of prominent and influential men. These, for what was considered their seditious principles, were banished by the General Court of

---

9. Who subscribed it? What was the character of the government established by this Constitution? What was it the germ of?
10. What was the object of the Synod at New Town in 1636? What was the result? Where did those who were banished seek refuge? How did Williams receive them? What was the Indian name of the island now called Rhode Island? Why was it called Rhode Island? Who settled this island in 1638? What was the character of the government instituted? When was the first Baptist church, as claimed by some, organized in America, and by whom?

the colony of Massachusetts Bay, and went in quest of a new settlement. They came to Providence, where they were kindly received by Williams, through whose generous assistance a gift to the Island of Rhode Island, then called Aquidnick, was obtained from the Indian Chiefs. The name of Rhode Island was substituted for that of Aquidnick, because of its supposed resemblance to the Isle of Rhodes in Greece.

Upon this island, in 1638, at Newport, the new comers formed a new settlement. William Coddington, their preacher and leader, who was a native of England, and who had come to Massachusetts in 1630, was chosen their chief magistrate. The government instituted by them here was purely democratic, as was that at Providence.

At Providence, in 1639, Williams organized a Baptist church. This was, perhaps, as some assert, the first regularly organized Baptist church in America.

11. In the year 1643 Williams went to England as agent for both settlements, and, through the aid of friends, obtained from the Earl of Warwick and his Council (who had charge of British-American affairs at that time) a free and absolute charter of civil incorporation, by the name of the "Incorporation of Providence Plantations in Narraganset Bay." This charter set forth the boundaries of Rhode Island, as they in the main still exist; and embraced all the settlements upon the lands procured from the Indian Sachems through the influence of Williams. These settlements, and all afterwards made within these limits under this charter, continued to be governed until after the restoration of Charles II., King of England; and

---

11. What did Williams do in 1643 ? How long was the colony of Rhode Island under the government of the charter he obtained from the Earl of Warwick ? What was the title of the new charter obtained by Williams from Charles II. in 1663 ? How long did the charter of Charles II. remain as a foundation of the government of the people of Rhode Island ? What occurred for a year or two during the reign of James II. of England ? Who was the despot who for a period during this reign deposed the rightful officers and held in a state of repression the rightful government of the colony under the charter of Charles II. ? What did the people of Rhode Island do as soon as this despot was removed from power ?

until 1663, when Williams succeeded in obtaining from this monarch another charter for the government of the same country, under the title of "The English Colony of Rhode Island and Providence Plantations in New England." This charter, without any essential change, remained the foundation of the government of the people of Rhode Island for nearly two centuries, as we shall see.

For one or two years during the reign of James II. of England, which lasted from 1685 to 1688, this charter was subverted by the usurpation and tyranny of Sir Edmond Andros, as were all the other New England charters. The rightful officers and magistrates in Rhode Island under the charter of Charles II. were deposed, and the rightful government of the colony under it was held in a state of repression during the arbitrary rule of this infamous despot; but as soon as he was removed from power the people of Rhode Island reinstated their former officers and magistrates, under their old charter, and re-instituted their rightful government, which had for a period been in a state of repression by the exercise of unjust and tyrannical powers.

CHAPTER X.

THE NEW ENGLAND CONFEDERATION.

1643—1675.

The Pequod War—Captives made slaves of—First negro slaves in New England—New Connecticut Charter.

1. The colonies of Plymouth, Massachusetts Bay, New Hampshire, and Connecticut, as well as Rhode Island, having been firmly established, as we have seen, all of them, except New Hampshire, increased and grew rapidly for several years after their organizations.

---

1. Which one of the New England Colonies did not prosper? In which ones of them were new settlements made? Where did the settlers come from, and to what sect did they belong? What war broke out?

New settlements and new towns were erected in Massachusetts and Connecticut. Large numbers of emigrants every year came over from England, mostly of the sect known as Puritans. But the Pequod war, which broke out, for a time threatened the existence of all these colonies.

2. This war was projected by Cassacus, the leading Sachem of the tribe known as Pequods, and which was the most formidable of all the tribes of the aborigines in New England. This daring chief conceived the idea, and determined upon the design, of exterminating all the English settlements, by a union against them of all the Indian tribes. For this purpose he visited the chiefs of the Mohegans and Narragansetts, and endeavored to get them to join him in his designs. In this he most probably would have been successful, but for the urgent appeal and controlling influence of Roger Williams, as we have seen, who had won the confidence of these chiefs.

3. Ill-blood, however, was engendered by the murder of several of the colonists by the Pequods, committed, as was supposed, by his instigation. In 1634, Captain Stone and Captain Norton, commanding trading vessels on the Connecticut River, were thus killed in a most savage manner.

In 1636, Captain Oldman, commanding another trading vessel on the same river, at Block Island, was in like manner butchered by Pequods, who took possession of the ship with its cargo. This aroused the indignation of the colonists generally to such a pitch, that war was determined upon by the colonies of Massachusetts and Connecticut. Before entering upon it, however, they, through the influence of Roger Williams, secured the alliance of the Mohegan and Narragansett chiefs.

---

2. Who projected this war? What was his object? Through whose influence was this object probably defeated?
3. What occurred in 1634? Who was killed in 1636 by the Indians? Was war declared? What was done by Massachusetts and Connecticut before war was declared?

4. Massachusetts raised four companies, under the command of Captain Stoughton of Dorchester, Captain Patrick of Watertown, Captain Trask of Salem, and Rev. John Wilson, pastor of the church at Boston. They took the field against the Pequods early in 1637. Captain Patrick, who went in advance, sailed to Saybrook, and there joined Captain Underhill of Massachusetts, who had been sent out the winter before with a few men, to aid the colonists of Connecticut, by strengthening the garrison at that post. After being joined by Captain Mason, in command of the Connecticut forces, under the guide of friendly Indians, they approached the forces of Pequods, who were collected in their strongest fort, on the Mystic river. Here a battle was fought on the 20th of May, 1637, under the general direction of Captain Mason, in command of the Connecticut forces. The Pequods were utterly routed, their fort was destroyed, and their wigwams burnt. It was Captain Mason who gave the order, "Burn them." This seemed to be the only successful way of assault upon the enemy in his stronghold. Seven hundred Indians were estimated to have fallen in this engagement, by sword or fire; many of them were burned to death. About two hundred captives were taken. These were women and children. The loss on the side of the colonists was very small; some say two only.

5. Cassacus made his escape, and fled to the Mohawks; by them or some of his own men he was afterwards assassinated.

The women and children taken as captives were divided between the conquerors, the two colonies of Connecticut and Massachusetts Bay, and their allied Indian tribes, by

---

4. How many companies did Massachusetts raise? When did they take the field? Who commanded the Connecticut forces? Where and when was the battle fought? Who gave the order to burn them? How many Indians were supposed to have fallen in this battle, by sword or fire? How many colonists fell?

5. What became of Cassacus? What became of the women and children taken as captives? What was the general result of this war?

CHAP. X.] THE NEW ENGLAND CONFEDERATION. 59

whom they were reduced to slavery. Many of them were sent, by the Puritan Fathers of Connecticut and Massachusetts, to the West Indies, and there sold as slaves for life. In this war, the great tribe of the Pequods was extinguished.

6. In 1636 was built at Marblehead, in Massachusetts, the first American slave-ship; it was called the *Desire*, and was intended for the African slave-trade, in which several of the European nations were then engaged. The first cargo of negro slaves brought into Massachusetts was by the *Desire*, on the 20th of May, 1638. Many of the most prominent men of the colony purchased slaves out of this cargo; so that Massachusetts was only a few years behind Virginia in the introduction, within the English settlements on this continent, of this unfortunate race as slaves.

7. In 1637, Hugh Peters and Sir Henry Vane, distinguished Puritan leaders in England, came to Massachusetts. Sir Henry Vane, from his talents and acquirements, was very popular. He was elected Governor of the colony. This remarkable man was the eldest son of the Baronet of that name, and was born at Hadlow in 1612. Few men of his age in England had fairer prospects for rising to distinction in that country than he had when he came to America.

Mrs. Anne Hutchinson, a most remarkable woman, teacher, and preacher, came over about the same time. Her doctrines put the people of Massachusetts into quite a ferment. She maintained that what was styled " the covenant of works," was of more importance than " the covenant of grace." These religious questions controlled popular elec-

---

6. Where was the first slave-ship built in the colonies? and what was it called? What was it intended for? When was the first cargo of negro slaves introduced into Massachusetts?
7. What two distinguished Englishmen came to Massachusetts in 1637? What is said of Sir Henry Vane? What is said of Mrs. Ann Hutchinson? What became of Sir Henry Vane? What became of Mrs. Hutchinson?

tions at the time. Sir Henry Vane sided with Mrs. Hutchinson in her peculiar views. By a majority of the voters these views were deemed altogether heretical and seditious. The result was the defeat of Vane for the Governorship at the next election. He returned to England, where he acted a very conspicuous part in the war which soon broke out between King Charles I. and the Parliament. Mrs. Hutchinson and her sect were banished from Massachusetts. She sought refuge in the colony of Roger Williams. Here she was kindly received, though her doctrines were as little acceptable to him as they were to her persecutors. He tolerated all religious opinions. The fate of this remarkable woman was a sad one. She, with a few adherents, left Rhode Island, and settled at "Ann Hook," now Pelham, then under the jurisdiction of the Dutch. Here they were all massacred some years afterwards by the Indians, except a grand-daughter, who was carried off as a prisoner.

8. In 1638 a college at Cambridge, Massachusetts, was founded by Rev. John Harvard. It is now known as Harvard University. The first printing press in the colony was also established this year, by Rev. Jesse Glover, and put under the management of Stephen Day. The first thing issued from this press was the Freeman's Oath, in January, 1639; the second, an almanac; the third, the Psalms in metre.

9. But, notwithstanding the general prosperity of these colonies, it was thought best, especially after the Pequod war, for the mutual security and protection of each in the enjoyment of their rights of local self-government, to form a confederated union between themselves. This was con-

---

8. When was Harvard University founded? When was the first printing press established in New England, and by whom? What were the first things published?
9. After the Pequod war, what did the colonies of Massachusetts Bay, Plymouth, Connecticut, and New Haven, do for their better protection? When was this confederation formed? What was the title of it? What was the object of it? How many commissioners did each colony send? What qualification was required of the commissioners? Why was Rhode Island excluded? Was the action of the commissioners binding on the colonies without their subsequent sanction? What was the agreement as to slaves or fugitives from service?

summated in 1643. The parties to it were the colonies of Massachusetts Bay, Plymouth, Connecticut, and New Haven. Massachusetts, as we have seen, had taken civil jurisdiction over the colony of New Hampshire. The colony of Rhode Island was excluded on account of its religion.

The title assumed for the union thus formed by these four distinct colonies was, "The United Colonies of New England." The declared object of the Confederation was, a protection of the lives, liberties, and property of the whole, against foreign or domestic enemies. Each colony was to be perfectly free in the management of its own internal affairs, while external matters that pertained to the general welfare of all were entrusted to the management of eight commissioners, two of whom were to be selected by each colony. The only qualification required of the commissioners was church membership. The measures adopted by these commissioners were not to be binding upon the several colonies, without their subsequent express sanction and ratification. Fugitives from service, or slaves, were to be delivered up on demand. This was the first confederation between any of the British colonies in America, and continued with general harmony until the attempted annulment of all the charters of the colonies so confederated, in 1685, as we shall see.

10. One of the principal powers entrusted to the commissioners, under the articles of confederation, was the regulation of Indian affairs; and very soon after their organization, a very important duty in this respect devolved upon them. Uncas, the chief of the Mohegans, attacked one of the subordinate chiefs of Miantonomah, then Sachem of the Narragansetts. This Sachem, as has been stated, was the nephew of old Canonicus. He appealed to the commissioners of the confederation for permission to make war

---

10. What was the first important duty that devolved upon the commissioners? What is said of Uncas and Miantonomah? What was the decision of the commissioners as to Miantonomah after Uncas had him as a prisoner? What became of him?

against Uncas and his tribe, for the outrage he had committed, without being interfered with by the colonists. The permission was given, and he invaded the Mohegan territory; but was defeated, betrayed, and taken prisoner. Uncas carried him to Hartford, Connecticut, where his fate depended upon the decision of the commissioners. They held their session at Boston. This was in September, 1643. A decision of the commissioners was, that Uncas could do with his prisoner as he pleased, provided, that if he chose to put him to death, the execution should be without torture, and not in the jurisdiction of any one of the colonies; and if he should not put him to death, then Miantonomah was to be sent prisoner to Boston. Uncas instantly resolved upon the execution; and just as soon as he had his victim beyond the border, he struck a hatchet into his head, and before life was entirely extinguished, cut a piece of flesh from the shoulder of his "fallen foe," which he eagerly devoured, "declaring that it made his heart strong, and was the sweetest morsel he ever ate."

11. In 1653, the English Council of State having declared war against Holland, the people of New Haven and Connecticut were anxious for the United Colonies to declare war against New Netherlands. To consider the subject, a special session of the commissioners was held at Boston in May. Six out of eight of these were in favor of the measure. This was a constitutional majority, according to the articles of confederation; but Massachusetts insisted that, according to the articles of union, the commissioners had no power to declare an "offensive war," and this, therefore, could only be done by the unanimous consent of all the colonies; and as Massachusetts would not give her consent, the war was not declared.

12. The first American edition of the Bible was Eliot's

---

11. What important question came before the Confederation in 1653, and how was it decided?
12. When was the first American edition of the Bible published, and what was the character of this edition?

translation of it, in the Indian language, printed at Cambridge, Massachusetts, in 1661.

13. On the restoration of Charles II. of England, in 1660, Whaley, Goffe, and Dixwell, three of the regicide judges, who had pronounced sentence of death against Charles I., made their escape, and came to New England. A royal order for their arrest soon followed them. The commissioners for the United Colonies of New England issued their proclamation against these fugitives; but they, through the aid of faithful friends, remained undiscovered, and were never taken. "Dixwell lived openly at New Haven, under a feigned name; the other two remained in concealment, sometimes in Connecticut, and sometimes in Massachusetts."

14. In 1661, Governor Winthrop, of Connecticut, went to England, to see after the charter of his colony under the restoration of Charles II. Through the influence of the aged Lord Say, he succeeded, in 1662, in getting a confirmation of a charter for his colony, with exceedingly liberal provisions, in securing the rights of self-government to the people of Connecticut, and with boundaries including the whole of the New Haven colony. The people of New Haven were very much opposed to this invasion of their independence on the part of Connecticut. They appealed to the commissioners for the United Colonies of New England for redress; but none was obtained.

New Haven being thus absorbed in Connecticut under this new charter, the two colonies henceforth sent but two representatives to the meetings of the commissioners for the United Colonies of New England, instead of four, as before. Connecticut was now divided into four counties, New Haven, Hartford, Middlesex, and New London.

---

13. What are the names of the three regicide judges who fled to New England on the restoration of Charles II. of England, in 1660? Where did Dixwell live, and how? How did the other two escape arrest?
14. What did Governor Winthrop of Connecticut do in 1661? Through whose influence did he succeed? In what year was his new charter obtained? What effect had it upon the colony at New Haven?

Under this new charter, the colony of Connecticut enjoyed great liberty for a number of years. The entire population of the confederation was at this time something over one hundred thousand.

15. Some important facts connected with the history of the colonies composing this confederation, of another but not less interesting character, will now be mentioned.

On the 1st of June, 1638, there was a great earthquake, which extended throughout all these colonies. Its centre seemed to be in Connecticut. It shook the ships which rode in the harbors, and the islands around about. It lasted but a few moments, but the earth was unquiet at times for twenty days afterwards. There were two great tempests also this year. The one on the 3d of August raised the tide on the Narragansett shore fourteen feet above the common Spring tides, and the one on the 25th of September caused the highest swell of the sea ever before observed on that coast.

16. The winter of 1641–42 was the severest ever experienced by the colonists. The bay of Boston was frozen so hard that teams, with loaded wagons, passed from the town to the neighboring islands.

17. In 1658 another notable earthquake occurred; but in 1662 there was still another, of which the accounts are much fuller. This was followed up by a succession of shocks, which occurred at intervals for more than six months, extending into 1663. During these shocks, it is said that in Canada small rivers and springs were dried up, and that a large ridge of mountains subsided to a plain.

18. In 1668 a great comet appeared, with an immense coma or train, which greatly alarmed the superstitious,

---

15. What remarkable event happened throughout New England on the 1st of June, 1638? What is said of the two great tempests also the same year?
16. What is said of the winter of 1641–42?
17. What is said of the winter of 1662–63? What is said of the great earthquakes that occurred?
18. What is said of the great comet?

especially as an unusually hot summer and a very malignant disease, which occurred at the same time, were attributed to its baneful influence.

CHAPTER XI.

SETTLEMENT OF MARYLAND.

1621—1660.

Lord Baltimore—His charter—Religious liberty first established—The Clayborne insurrection—Prosperity and peace of the colony.

1. CAPTAIN SMITH, of Virginia, as we have before said, was the first to explore the Chesapeake Bay. In 1621 the country now known as Maryland was explored by Virginia settlers, and trading posts were established. William Clayborne, the agent of a company formed in England, endeavored to monopolize this trade, and for this purpose obtained a license, under which he claimed rights for years after, as we shall see.

MARYLAND COAT OF ARMS.

2. In 1628 Sir George Calvert, Lord Baltimore, visited Virginia with some intention of founding a colony within its limits, but the government of Virginia was at that time intolerant towards the religion of the Roman Catholic Church, of which he was a member; he therefore turned his attention to some region beyond the jurisdiction of that colony. In 1629 he explored the country lying on the Chesapeake Bay; with which being much pleased, he returned to Eng-

---

CHAPTER XI.—1. In what year were trading posts established in Maryland?
2. Who visited Virginia in 1628? For what purpose? Why did he not settle in that country? What were the boundaries prescribed by his charter?

land and made application for a charter, which was easily obtained. His death prevented the execution of his purpose in obtaining it; this devolved upon his son and heir. The boundaries prescribed by the charter were the Atlantic Ocean, the fortieth parallel of north latitude, the meridian of the western fountain of the Potomac, the river itself from its mouth to its source, and a line drawn due east from Watkins Point to the Atlantic Ocean.

LORD BALTIMORE.

3. This charter was the most liberal in its provisions of all the original grants by the Crown to founders of settlements in America. It gave to the colonists full power of legislation, and all the essential rights of self-government, without any interference from the mother country. It clearly defined and secured the freedom of the settlers, with proper limitations upon the rights and privileges of the Proprietaries. It contained a guaranty against taxation by England, and established full toleration to men of all religions. Indeed, it was one of the leading objects of Lord Baltimore, in planting the colony, to furnish an asylum to the persecuted of all Christian churches. In this design Lord Baltimore was only a few years in advance of Roger Williams. The colony was called Maryland, in honor of Henrietta Maria, wife of Charles I. of England.

4. Mr. Bancroft, writing of the colonization of Maryland, says: "Calvert deserves to be ranked among the most wise and benevolent lawgivers of all ages. He was the first, in the history of the Christian world, to seek for

---

3. What is said of this charter? What was one of the principal objects of Lord Baltimore?
4. What does Mr. Bancroft say of Calvert and his object?

religious security and peace by the practice of justice, and not by the exercise of power; to plan the establishment of popular institutions with the enjoyment of liberty of conscience; to advance the career of civilization by recognizing the rightful equality of all Christian sects. The asylum of Papists was the spot where, in a remote corner of the world, on the banks of rivers which, as yet, had hardly been explored, the mild forbearance of a Proprietary adopted religious freedom as the basis of the State."

5. Sir George Calvert was succeeded by his son, Cecil Calvert, second Lord Baltimore, who became Proprietary of Maryland. In November, 1633, his brother, Leonard Calvert, sailed from England in two vessels, the Ark and the Dove, with about two hundred emigrants, mostly Roman Catholic gentlemen, with their servants. On their arrival in February following, at Point Comfort, in Virginia, they were received with courtesy by Governor Harvey. Passing up the Potomac, Calvert chose a site for a settlement at an Indian village called Yoacomoco, which he purchased from the natives, who quietly yielded possession. To the town he gave the name of St. Mary's. He pursued a kind and liberal course towards the natives, supplying them with hoes, axes, clothes, and knives. A permanent treaty was made with the Indians. Their women taught the wives of the settlers how to make corn-bread, and their warriors instructed the men in forest sports.

6. In 1635 the freemen of the colony held their first Legislative Assembly, one object of which was to protect their rights against the encroachments of Clayborne. His license to trade with the Indians having been made void by Lord Baltimore's charter, he endeavored to excite a rebellion. He made an attack on the colonists near the Isle of Kent, but was defeated; his men were taken prisoners,

---

5. Who succeeded Sir George Calvert? What was the character of the emigrants? Where did they settle? What did the Indian women teach the wives of the settlers?
6. In what year did the first legislative Assembly meet? For what purpose? What is said of Clayborne?

but he made his escape into Virginia. The Maryland Assembly declared him a traitor, and his estates were confiscated. Governor Calvert demanded him of the Governor of Virginia, but he sent him to England. Clayborne endeavored to obtain redress in England, but without success; and the right of Lord Baltimore to the jurisdiction of Maryland was fully confirmed.

7. For several years after this defeat of Clayborne, the colonists enjoyed undisturbed peace and were eminently prosperous. The rights of the people were clearly defined and protected by law; the rights of the Proprietary were respected; civil liberty and freedom of religious worship were enjoyed by all; the lands were fertile; commerce began to prosper, and tobacco became a profitable article of culture. Efforts were made, and not in vain, to convert some of the neighboring Indians to Christianity. The honest and upright conduct of the governor and the authorities of Maryland, in all their dealings with the natives, prepared the way for the acceptance of the religion of the strangers.

8. Four stations were established among them. Tozoc, a chief, and his wife were baptized, taking the names of Charles and Mary. Not long after one hundred and thirty other converts received baptism. But these efforts of good men were rendered nugatory by the machinations of the bad. Clayborne, the evil genius of Maryland, returned to the country, and, in 1642, instigated the Indians to hostilities. This trouble, however, was soon suppressed; but in the next year (1643) he raised a rebellion, which kept the colony in a state of turmoil for three years. The governor himself was driven from the colony and took refuge in Virginia. The public records were lost or destroyed.

---

7. After Clayborne's defeat, what was the condition of the colonists? What is said of the efforts to convert the Indians?
8. How many converts received baptism? What put a stop to these efforts?

9. At length, after two or three years of misrule, the legitimate government of Maryland triumphed, and peace was once more restored. This government, ever actuated by the magnanimous spirit of Christian forbearance, passed a general Act of Amnesty, and all offenders were pardoned.

10. During the civil wars in England, the internal tranquillity of Maryland was much disturbed. When the fleet, with commissioners, was sent over to reduce the Virginians to submission to the authority of Parliament, Clayborne again seized the opportunity to create disturbance in the colony by endeavoring to establish his own authority. Leonard Calvert, the governor, died in 1647, and Stone, his successor, was more than once deprived of his office. The religious parties in the colony became political; and while the Protestants were in the ascendant they persecuted the Catholics for their religious opinions, forgetful of the liberty that had been allowed to them when the Catholics were in power. For six years, from 1652 to 1658, civil discord reigned. The authority of the Proprietary was, however, finally restored, and in 1660 all parties acknowledged Philip Calvert governor. On the restoration of Lord Baltimore to his Proprietary rights, he proclaimed a general pardon for all past political offences, and for many years thereafter the colony enjoyed undisturbed repose.

---

9. What was the result of the contest with Clayborne?
10. What effect did the civil wars in England have on the colony of Maryland? On the restoration of Lord Baltimore, what was done by him?

CHAPTER XII.

SETTLEMENT OF NEW JERSEY.

1622—1738.

The Danes—The Duke of York—College at Princeton.

1. In 1622 the Danes effected settlements on the Delaware River and at Bergen. In 1623 the Dutch built a fort on the east side of the Delaware, to which they gave the name of Nassau. An attempt at colonization was made by the English in 1640, but they were opposed by both the Swedes and the Dutch, and their settlement was broken up.

NEW JERSEY COAT OF ARMS.

2. In 1664, Charles II., King of England, made a grant of the Dutch colony of New Netherlands, after his acquisition of it, to his brother, the Duke of York. This charter conveyed the whole territory lying between the Connecticut River and the Delaware. The Duke conveyed to Lord Berkeley and Sir George Carteret the territory which now constitutes the State of New Jersey. In compliment to Sir George Carteret, who had been governor of, and who had defended, the Island of Jersey during the civil war in England, it was called New Jersey.

3. Liberal inducements were held out by the Proprietaries to settlers to come into the colony. No rent was to be collected for five years; no taxes were to be paid except

---

CHAPTER XII.—**1.** What people first settled in New Jersey? In what year did the English make their first attempt?
2. What was done by King Charles in 1664? Why was the country called New Jersey?
3. What inducements were held out to settlers? What was the occasion of disputes? What took place in 1670?

those imposed by the General Assembly or Legislature of the colony, and liberty of conscience in religious matters was to be allowed. A settlement had been made at Elizabethtown, and one or two other places, under licenses from Colonel Nichols, Governor of New York, who was ignorant of the transfer to Lord Berkeley and Sir George Carteret, which was the occasion of disputes between the settlers and Proprietaries for many years, the former claiming priority of title. The disputes ran so high after 1670, when the earliest rents fell due, that an insurrection broke out, and the governor, Sir Philip Carteret, after a struggle of two years, abandoned the government and returned to England.

4. Sir Philip Carteret, the first governor, who had arrived in 1665 with thirty emigrant settlers, and fixed his residence at Elizabethtown, which remained the capital for several years, was a prudent and judicious ruler. His disputes with the settlers did not grow out of any mismanagement of his. After his return to England, the government was conferred on a son of Sir George Carteret, who had favored the popular party.

5. In 1673, the Dutch recovered New York and New Jersey, but they were soon afterwards restored to the English. The Duke of York then obtained a new charter for both provinces in one, and appointed Sir Edmund Andros, the tyrant, governor. He vested all legislative power in the governor and council, thus making the government entirely arbitrary, and destroying the rights of the people. In 1674, Lord Berkeley, disgusted with the conduct of the Duke of York, sold his share of New Jersey to Edward Byllinge, an English Quaker, who shortly afterwards transferred his claim to William Penn, and New Jersey was divided between Penn and Sir

---

4. What was the character of Sir Philip Carteret? Who succeeded him as governor?
5. What took place in 1673? In 1674?

George Carteret, Penn taking West Jersey, and Sir George Carteret East Jersey. The dividing line was drawn from the ocean at Little Egg Harbor, to the northwestern corner of the province.

6. In 1675, Sir Philip Carteret became Governor, and returned to the colony. He was a man of education and refinement, and distinguished for many of the highest traits of a British nobleman. He was devoted in his attachment to the principles of *Magna Charta*, and to the rights of the colonists, under it, British subjects. The inhabitants gave him a joyful welcome, for they were very weary of the tyranny of Andros. He postponed the payment of rents, and granted further concessions to the colonists, and by his kind and liberal course, once more restored peace and order to the colony. But Andros still remained their bane and pest; he destroyed their commerce, exacted tribute, and even arrested the Governor and conveyed him to New York. He released him only by command of the Duke of York.

7. In 1677, Burlington, in West Jersey, was settled by about four hundred Quakers, who arrived from England in that year. This province (West Jersey) rapidly filled with inhabitants, mostly Quakers. Many of them were men of considerable means; and being careful, prudent, and industrious, the country throve in their hands. The claims of the Duke of York over New Jersey were urged until 1680, when a legal decision was given, in the English courts, in favor of the Proprietaries, and the colony at length became independent of him.

8. The first Legislative Assembly of West Jersey met in 1681. In 1682, William Penn, and eleven others of the Society of Friends, purchased the province of East

---

6. How was Sir Philip Carteret received on his return ? What was done by Andros ?
7. In what year was Burlington settled ? By whom ?
8. In what year did the first Legislative Assembly meet ? In what year did Penn purchase East Jersey ? Who was the first governor ?

CHAP. XII.] SETTLEMENT OF NEW JERSEY. 73

Jersey from Sir George Carteret. Twelve other persons united with them, and to these twenty-four Proprietors the Duke of York executed another grant or charter, when they proceeded to organize a Proprietary Government. Robert Barclay, the first governor, was appointed for life. He died in 1690.

9. In 1685, the Duke of York became James II., King of England; when, having no regard to his engagements as the Duke of York, he attempted to usurp the government of New Jersey; but he himself was dethroned by the revolution in England, of 1688. During the reign of William and Mary, who succeeded James II., New York again claimed jurisdiction over New Jersey. The disputes about jurisdiction and title continued until the next reign, when the Proprietaries of New Jersey resigned their claim to the crown, and the government of New Jersey devolved upon the King of England, under the various charters which had been granted to the Proprietaries. This was in 1702. Queen Anne united it under one government with New York, and appointed Lord Cornbury governor, each colony, however, retaining its own Assembly.

10. The two colonies continued to be governed in this manner until the year 1738, when a separate governor was appointed for New Jersey. Lewis Morris was the first governor under this arrangement. The college at Princeton was founded in 1746, under the auspices of the General Assembly of the Presbyterian Church.

---

9. What is said of the Duke of York as king? In what year did the Proprietaries resign their claims?
10. In what year was Princeton College founded?

CHAPTER XIII.

SETTLEMENT OF DELAWARE.

1632—1690.

The Dutch—The Swedes—Gustavus Adolphus.

1. This Colony took its name from the river and bay which form its eastern boundary.

2. The first attempt by Europeans to settle this section of country was made by the Dutch. Not long after the settlement of New Netherlands, as we have seen, an expedition was sent out from Texel, an island in the Zuyder Zee, under the auspices of Van Rensselaer, Godyn, Bloemart, and De Laet, men of character and distinction in Holland. Godyn had previously purchased of the Indians, about thirty miles of territory, from Cape Henlopen to the mouth of the Delaware River. The expedition was committed to the charge of De Vries, a celebrated navigator. The colonists, consisting of about thirty emigrants, with stores of seeds and agricultural implements, **embarked in December, 1631, and landed in May, 1632.** The place selected for their future abode was near where Lewistown is now situated.

DELAWARE COAT OF ARMS.

On the return of De Vries to Holland, the affairs of the settlement were left in the hands of one Osset as governor. A misunderstanding arose between him and the Indians.

CHAPTER XIII.—1. What did Delaware take its name from?
2. By whom was the first European attempt made to settle Delaware? What navigator conducted the expedition? What year was the settlement made? At what place? To whom was the management of affairs left on the return of De Vries? What was the fate of this settlement?

One of the chiefs was killed in the hot blood that ensued. A general spirit of revenge was aroused among the savages, who, seeking an opportunity, fell upon the little colony unawares, and utterly exterminated it. This was within twelve months after it was planted.

3. In 1637, Oxenstiern, who had been Prime Minister of Gustavus Adolphus, King of Sweden, determined to carry out the wish and design of that great Protestant chieftain to found a colony in America. This design had been formed by him as early as 1626, but the German war in which he became engaged, and in which he lost his life, at the battle of Lützen, 16th of October, 1632, prevented its execution.

Oxenstiern, in carrying out this design, professed "to be but the executor of the wish of Gustavus Adolphus." Under his direction and auspices an expedition, consisting of two vessels, the *Key of Calmar* and the *Griffin*, was fitted out in 1637. As many emigrants, consisting of Swedes and Finns, as these vessels could bring, reached the Delaware Bay early in the year 1638.

4. The general management and supervision of the colony had been entrusted by Oxenstiern to Peter Minuits, the Hollander, who had been first governor of New Amsterdam. Under his direction the first settlement (and which was the first permanent European settlement made in Delaware) was near the mouth of a creek, which he named Christiana, in honor of the infant Queen of Sweden. Here a fort was soon built, to which he gave the same name. It was near the site of the present city of Wilmington. The colony itself was called New Sweden.

5. Other emigrants soon followed, and the colony in-

---

3. Who planned another settlement? What is said of Gustavus Adolphus? When did new settlers arrive? Of what nation were they?
4. To whom was the management of the colony entrusted? Where was the first settlement made? What was the name given to the creek and fort, and in honor of whom? What name was given to the colony?
5. Did other emigrants come? Did the colonists of New Netherlands and New Sweden get along harmoniously together?

creased rapidly in numbers. More than a hundred families came over in one expedition, not long afterwards. Jealousies soon sprung up between the colonies of New Netherlands and New Sweden.

6. In 1651, the Dutch built Fort Casimir, on the site of New Castle, within five miles of Christiana. This was deemed a menacing encroachment by the Swedes. In 1654, Rising, the governor at that time of New Sweden, determined to seize Fort Casimir and drive the Dutch away. This by skill and stratagem he succeeded in doing; but his success proved the destruction of his own colony. Peter Stuyvesant, the governor of New Netherlands at this time, treated the aggression of Rising on Fort Casimir as an act of war. He raised more than six hundred men, and invaded the colony of New Sweden. Resistance to this force was unavailing. The entire population of all the settlements of Delaware was not much over one thousand persons. Rising therefore was compelled to accept such terms of peace as were offered. These were, the quiet possession of all their estates by the Swedish colonists, upon their acknowledgment of the authority and jurisdiction of the Dutch government of New Netherlands. This was in 1655.

"Such," says Bancroft, "was the end of New Sweden, the colony that connects our country with Gustavus Adolphus, and the nations that dwell on the Gulf of Bothnia. It maintained its distinct existence for a little more than seventeen years, and succeeded in establishing permanent plantations on the Delaware."

7. In 1664, when the Duke of York took possession of the colony of New Netherlands, as we have seen, the settlements on the Delaware passed with it.

---

6. What did the Dutch do in 1651? Who was governor of New Sweden in 1654? What did he do? Who was the Dutch governor of New Netherlands at the same time? What did he do? What was the result of the war?

7. Under what jurisdiction did the settlements on the Delaware pass in 1664? To whom did the Duke of York transfer the same section of country? How long did it remain a part of Penn's colony? When did it become separate, and how?

Afterwards, as we shall see, the Duke of York, in 1682, transferred to William Penn his rights and jurisdiction over this section of country, to which was given the name of "the lower counties of Delaware." These Swedish settlements thus remained a portion of the colony of Pennsylvania until the year 1690, when the deputies to the Legislative Assembly of Pennsylvania from these " lower counties" raised the question that, as Penn had only the Duke of York's conveyance to his rights of jurisdiction over their territory, which did not extend to the powers of government, and had no Royal Charter granting him power of government over them, the lower counties were not rightful parts of the colony of Pennsylvania, and they therefore withdrew and formed a Legislature to themselves for the three lower counties. In this way they became a distinct colony to themselves, so far as concerned their local affairs, with the name of Delaware, which name they have ever since retained.

Penn himself approved the separation, but claimed Proprietary rights under the Duke of York's conveyance to him, which claim was acceded to.

CHAPTER XIV.

SETTLEMENT OF PENNSYLVANIA.

1638—1724.

William Penn—The Quakers.

1. The first European settlements made in that section of country to which the name of Pennsylvania was afterwards given, were made by the Swedes soon after their arrival on the Delaware, in 1638. These settlements were under the government of New Sweden until 1655, when

---

Chapter XIV.—1. By whom was Pennsylvania first settled? When did the Swedes arrive on the Delaware? When did they become subjected to New Netherlands?

that colony was subjected to the Dutch Government of New Netherlands, as we have seen.

2. In 1664, when the English Duke of York took possession of the Dutch colony of New Netherlands, these Swedish settlements, lying on the upper Delaware, passed with this conquest, as well as the "lower counties," and they so remained for seventeen years.

COAT OF ARMS OF PENNSYLVANIA.

3. In 1681, Charles II., King of England, granted to William Penn a Royal Charter for all that section of country since known in honor of the grantee as Pennsylvania. Penn proposed the name of Sylvania, but the king prefixed his name to the one proposed.

William Penn, who thus became so famous as the founder of this colony, belonged to that sect of Christians who style themselves Friends, but who are by the world styled Quakers.

4. The Quakers in England were subject to numerous disabilities and annoyances, and Penn, weary of the persecutions to which they were subject, became fixed in the determination to seek in the New World an asylum for himself and his suffering brethren. His father bequeathed him a claim of sixteen thousand pounds sterling against the government, for which he was willing to receive land. The king, Charles II., always in want of money, was very glad to pay this debt in that way, and gave him a grant of twenty-six millions of acres, covering a territory nearly corresponding with the present bounds of the State of Pennsylvania.

---

2. When did they pass to the Duke of York ?
3. When was the Royal Charter granted to the colony of Pennsylvania ? By what king was it granted, and to whom was it granted ? What is said of William Penn ?
4. What is said of the Quakers ?

5. The charter constituted Penn and his heirs absolute Proprietaries, reserving to the crown their allegiance and the sovereignty. They had power to make laws and to erect courts of justice. The rights of the colonists were guarded, and the freemen were to assist in framing the laws by which they were to be governed. The great principle of the right of local self-government by the people was in this charter fully recognized. To encourage emigration, the lands were offered for sale in lots of one thousand acres, at one penny per acre, and many Quakers became purchasers.

WILLIAM PENN.

In May, 1681, two ship-loads of emigrants came over under the direction of Markham, a relative of Penn, and began a settlement near the mouth of Schuylkill river. They were instructed to lay the foundations of a new city, with broad streets, and so planted with gardens as to form a "greene country towne." He also wrote to the Indians in a kind and friendly spirit, assuring them of his peaceful intentions, and entreating them, as children of the same Great Spirit, to have the same feelings towards the emigrants.

6. Before Penn left England, in 1682, he purchased from the Duke of York his Proprietary rights over the three lower counties of Delaware. In August of that year, accompanied by one hundred emigrants, he sailed for America, and landed at New Castle on the 24th of October. The Swedes, Dutch, and English all gave him a hearty welcome. Other emigrants soon came, so that in a

---

5. What is said of Penn's charter? Was the principle of the right of local self-government recognized in it? What did Penn write to the Indians?
6. How many emigrants did he bring in 1682?

short time the Quaker population amounted to about two thousand. Penn's plan of government consisted of a Governor, a Council of Three, and a House of Delegates, to be chosen by the freemen. All were freemen who believed in Christ, and sustained a good moral character.

7. A short time after his arrival, Penn met the chiefs of the various tribes of Indians in the neighborhood, and formed with them treaties of amity and good will. He promised to treat them justly; a promise which was never broken, and it is said that no Quaker was ever killed by an Indian. From the Swedish settlers he purchased a tract of land lying between the Schuylkill and Delaware, which he laid off for the building of his "greene country towne," to which he gave the name of Philadelphia. The city grew rapidly; in three years it had more than six hundred houses, and the colony had a population of eight or nine thousand.

8. During the same year, 1682, a party from Germany settled in and near Germantown. They soon formed plantations of corn and wheat; and being peaceable, industrious, and energetic, they became prosperous in a high degree. On the 4th of December, 1682, the first Legislative Assembly was held. The second Assembly was held at Philadelphia in March, 1683. At this session the form of government was somewhat modified. Laws were made to restrain vice. Labor on the Sabbath was forbidden, and to prevent lawsuits, three "peace-makers" were appointed for each county.

9. Penn's presence having become necessary in England, in 1684 he returned to that country. After the accession of the Duke of York to the throne, under the title of James II., Penn used his influence with him in favor of the op-

---

7. What is said of treatment of the Indians? Did this city flourish?
8. When was Germantown settled? By whom? At what time was the first Legislative Assembly held in Pennsylvania?
9. What revolution took place in 1688? How was Pennsylvania governed in the meantime? What was done to William Penn? Who was appointed governor?

pressed Quakers and other dissenters. In pursuance of his solicitations and entreaties, great numbers of Quakers were liberated who had been in prison for many years. Penn's charter was the only one of the colonial charters that were not attempted to be revoked about this time. In 1688, the great revolution drove James II. from the throne; but for two years the government of Pennsylvania continued to be administered in his name. This gave quite an offence to the reigning monarchs, William and Mary, and Penn was imprisoned and his government taken from him. Benjamin Fletcher was appointed governor. Some of the magistrates refused to acknowledge his authority, and some resigned.

10. When the Assembly met they refused to legislate under any other charter than that given by Charles, declaring that to be as good as the one given by King William. They never noticed the governor, and entirely ignored his presence. At length King William became satisfied that Penn's attachment to the Stuarts was not treasonable, and his government was restored to him. He sent Markham as his deputy; an Assembly was called, and the people framed for themselves a liberal constitution, and refused to levy taxes until this was granted. When Penn returned he approved what the people had done.

In 1690 Delaware was permitted to have a separate Legislature, as we have seen.

11. Penn had determined to remain in the colony; but hearing that the charters of all the colonies were about to be taken away, he thought his presence in England necessary. The charter was rendered permanent, and the Proprietorship remained in his family until the great American Revolution, when the colony became the State of Pennsyl-

---

10. When the Assembly met, what did they do ? In what year did Delaware obtain a separate government ?
11. What caused Penn's return to England ? Did he accomplish his purpose? What took place at the breaking out of the American Revolution ? When did Benjamin Franklin come to Philadelphia ?

vania, as we shall see. After the breaking out of that war the Proprietary claim was purchased by the Commonwealth for five hundred and seventy thousand dollars. Penn died in 1718, leaving three sons, minors. Six years after his death, Benjamin Franklin came to Philadelphia as a journeyman printer. He soon became eminent as an experimental philosopher and for his great practical common sense.

CHAPTER XV.

SETTLEMENT OF NORTH CAROLINA.
1563—1729.

Early Explorations—Final Permanent Settlements—Indian Wars.

COAT OF ARMS OF NORTH CAROLINA.

1. The coast of the Carolinas was first explored by the French in 1563, and so called by them in honor of Charles IX. (Carolus), King of France. No permanent settlements were made by them. A small colony of twenty-six persons, Protestants, was left at Port Royal, South Carolina, in 1563, by John Ribault, but no reinforcements being sent to them they abandoned the place. In 1564, Admiral de Coligny, the great Protestant leader of France, was able to send out a new expedition under Laudonniere, but these settled on the coast of Florida, on the river May, now called St. Johns.

2. Sir Walter Raleigh, in 1585, twenty-two years before the building of Jamestown, in Virginia, attempted, as we

---

CHAPTER XV.—1. Who first explored the coast of the Carolinas? From what is the name derived? What is said of the early settlements of the French? 2. In what year did Sir Walter Raleigh attempt his settlement? What was its fate?

have before stated, the first settlement ever made within the present limits of the United States by the English, near the mouth of the Roanoke River, in North Carolina, with one hundred and seven persons. The settlers were left under the care of Ralph Lane as governor. By their injudicious conduct the settlers gave great offence to the natives, whom they despised, and a conspiracy was formed for their destruction. Fortunately, when their situation had become exceedingly critical, Sir Francis Drake arrived with a fleet of twenty-three vessels and removed them to England. They had remained at the settlement about one year.

SIR WALTER RALEIGH.

3. No other attempt was made to colonize this region for many years. In 1630, Sir Robert Heath obtained a patent for an extensive region of country lying south of the 36th degree of north latitude. But as he made no settlements, his patent was declared void after a few years. Between the years 1640 and 1663, numbers of persons from Virginia and other colonies, as well as from other countries, settled that portion of North Carolina lying nearest to Virginia. These settlements, several of them on the Chowan River, were made without grants from any quarter. But Governor Berkeley, of Virginia, claimed jurisdiction, visited the colony, to which the name of Albemarle was given in honor of the Duke of Albemarle, and appointed William Drummond governor.

4. In 1663 the whole country from the 30th to the 36th degree of north latitude was conveyed by Charles II., King

---

3. What took place between 1640 and 1663? What was done by Governor Berkeley?
4. What grant was made in 1663? What is said of the constitution of John Locke? What name was given to this colony?

of England, to eight noblemen, who were joint Proprietors, with full power to settle and govern. The constitution for the government of the colonists under this grant was drawn up by the celebrated philosopher John Locke, and exhibits great wisdom and forecast in many of its features. Religious freedom was specially provided for in it. The general provisions of the charter were liberal to settlers. Under this charter, in the year 1665, a colony was planted near the mouth of Cape Fear River, and Sir James Yeamans was made governor. To this colony was given the name of Clarendon, in honor of Lord Clarendon, one of the Proprietaries. There thus became established within the limits of North Carolina two separate colonies, Albemarle and Clarendon, each having its own governor. But this arrangement did not long continue, though during its continuance it was the occasion of considerable trouble.

5. The Proprietaries of Carolina, by virtue of their charter from Charles II., claimed all the lands it covered, and jurisdiction over all the inhabitants within its limits. The inhabitants of Albemarle were not satisfied. They desired to hold their lands upon the same tenure as lands were held in Virginia, and broke out in open revolt; but they became quiet when assured that their wishes in this respect should be complied with. Under Stephens, who succeeded Drummond as governor, the first laws of the colony were enacted by an Assembly, composed of the governor, council, and twelve delegates; the latter chosen by the people, and the former by the Proprietaries. These laws were liberal, carefully guarding the rights of the settlers, and granting religious liberty to all. This was in 1669.

6. In 1670 the colonies of Clarendon and Albemarle were united under the name of North Carolina. But the

---

5. What was the cause of disputes in North Carolina ? In what year were the first laws of the colony enacted ?
6. In what year did the union of Clarendon and Albemarle take place ? What was the cause of the slow progress of the colony ? What is said of the insurrection of Culpepper ?

progress of the colony was slow, in consequence of the general bad administration of public affairs, and the turbulent and insurrectionary character of the colonists. In 1674 the population was only about four thousand, and the annual product of tobacco eight hundred thousand pounds. In 1677 the colonists, headed by Culpepper, broke out into open insurrection against the authorities. They imprisoned the Proprietary officers and seized the public revenue. The revolt continued successful for two years, when the people, becoming uneasy, sent Culpepper and Holden to England to offer submission to the Proprietaries, on condition that their proceedings were ratified.

7. Culpepper was seized and tried for high treason, but was saved through the influence of Lord Shaftesbury. The Proprietaries sent the notorious Seth Sothel as governor, to restore order to the colony. Corrupt and tyrannical, under his administration the disorders became greater than ever. For six years the colonists bore with his oppressions and exactions. He was then seized, to be sent to England for trial, but he begged that he might be tried by the Assembly. This was done, and he was banished from the colony. He was succeeded by Philip Ludwell. In 1695, John Archdale, a Quaker, was appointed. His jurisdiction extended also over South Carolina. He succeeded in restoring comparative quiet. The wisdom and prudence of his administration were generally acknowledged; considerable settlements were made, and the export of tar and rice was commenced. Churches were erected, and provision was made for the support of public worship.

8. In 1705, Thomas Carey was appointed governor, but was soon removed to give place to Edward Hyde, whereupon he incited a rebellion; and, at the head of an armed force, attacked Edenton, was repulsed, and finally by the aid

---

7. What is said of the administration of Seth Sothel? Of John Archdale?
8. Who became governor in 1705? When removed, what did he do? Describe the Tuscarora War of 1712.

of troops from Virginia the rebellion was suppressed in 1711. In 1712, the Tuscarora and Coree Indians formed a conspiracy to destroy the white settlers. Twelve hundred warriors entered into the plot. They carried on their design with great cunning and secrecy. From their principal town they sent out small parties, who entered the settlements, as friends, by different roads. The massacre was to begin the same night. On that night they entered the planters' houses and demanded provisions. They pretended displeasure with the provisions, and then the slaughter began. Men, women, and children, were slain without distinction or mercy.

9. The savages ran from house to house and slaughtered the scattered families wherever they went. About Roanoke one hundred and thirty-seven settlers fell a sacrifice to savage fury in one fatal night. These were German Palatines, led by Baron de Graffenreid, a Swiss, and had but lately come into the country. They were nearly all slain, but some few escaped, and by alarming their neighbors prevented the total destruction of that colony. The militia of the country collected as rapidly as possible, and held the savages in check until assistance was sent from another quarter, as we shall see.

10. The progress of the colony had been so slow that in 1717 the number of taxable inhabitants did not exceed two thousand, having gained no more than six hundred in forty-one years. The interior of the country had not been explored, and the great fertility of that region was altogether unknown. At length the beauty of the country and richness of the soil became known, and emigrants to that colony rapidly poured in. At the commencement of the war of the Revolution the population amounted to one hundred and eighty-one thousand.

---

9. How many were killed about Roanoke? Who were these? How was the colony saved?
10. What is said of the slow progress of the colony? How many inhabitants were there at the commencement of the Revolution?

11. In 1729 the Proprietaries sold their rights to the King, and henceforth the government of the colony devolved upon the crown under the charter. The last Proprietary governor was Sir Richard Everhard; the first royal governor, George Barrington.

CHAPTER XVI.

SETTLEMENT OF SOUTH CAROLINA.

1670-1707.

Port Royal—Charleston—Seth Sothel—Indian War.

1. "THAT germ of civilization," says Dr. Ramsay in his

COAT OF ARMS OF SOUTH CAROLINA.

History of South Carolina, "which took root, flourished, and spread in South Carolina, was first planted at or near Port Royal, in 1670, by a few emigrants from England, under the direction of William Sayle, the first governor of the province," under the royal charter of Charles II. They removed the next year to the western bank of the Ashley river, and there laid the foundation of old Charleston. The site was not well chosen, for it could not be approached by vessels of large burden, and was therefore abandoned. A second removal took place to Oyster Point, formed by the junction of Ashley and Cooper rivers, and there, in the year 1680, the foundations of the present city of Charleston were laid. In one year thirty houses were built. The names of only two of these original settlers of Charleston have been handed down to posterity, viz.: William Sayle and Joseph West.

---

11. What took place in 1729? Who was the last Proprietary governor? Who the first royal governor?
CHAPTER XVI.—1. When was the first settlement made by the English in

2. William Sayle was the first governor, but he died soon after his arrival, and was succeeded by Joseph West, who, for upwards of twenty years, bore the chief sway in the colony. The colonists brought with them the same constitution of government which had been drawn up for North Carolina by John Locke.

3. It was found impossible to carry out in all particulars the provisions of this constitution, but the colonists resolved to come as nigh it as possible, and accordingly elected a council and representatives. Of the first laws passed nothing is known. The first law which has been found on record in the office of the secretary of the province, is dated May 26, 1682.

4. By appointment of the council, Joseph West succeeded William Sayle as governor until the pleasure of the Proprietors could be known. Sir John Yeamans as Landgrave claimed the office, and the Proprietors judged it expedient that the government should be committed to him. He brought with him from the Barbadoes about fifty families, and nearly two hundred slaves. This was the beginning of negro slavery in South Carolina (1671). During the administration of Yeamans the Spaniards caused considerable trouble, by sending emissaries to Charleston to excite the inhabitants to revolt; to encourage servants to run away from their masters; and to instigate the savages to exterminate the whites.

5. In 1673 the colony was strengthened by the arrival of numbers of Dutch from the New Netherlands, which had passed into the hands of the English. Many of the inhabitants of that colony sought new homes.

6. Disputes having arisen between the Proprietors and

South Carolina? At what place? In what year were the foundations of Charleston laid?
2. Who was the first governor? Who succeeded him?
3. What is said of the laws?
4. When was negro slavery introduced into South Carolina? By whom?
5. How was the colony strengthened in 1673?
6. Who succeeded Yeamans? How many governors were there in the space of five years? What was the cause of this rapid succession?

Sir John Yeamans concerning the heavy expenses of the colony and the deficient returns therefrom, he retired to Barbadoes, where he soon after died. He was succeeded by Joseph West in 1674. West's administration continued for eight years. After this, in the short space of four years, to wit: from 1682 to 1686, there were no less than five governors: Joseph Morton, Joseph West, Richard Kyrle, Robert Quarry, and James Colleton. This rapid succession of governors was caused by the close and bitter contests between the two parties existing in the colony. From the very first there were seeds of strife and discord, which soon sprang up and grew strong and rank.

7. Of the two parties, one was composed of cavaliers, to whom large grants of land had been made, who were attached to the Church of England, and who favored the prerogative and authority of the Proprietors; the other was composed of dissenters from the Church of England, and democrats in principle; these looked with a jealous eye upon any class which claimed prescriptive rights and privileges either in church or state. The former contended that the laws received from England ought to be implicitly obeyed; the latter looked at local circumstances, and contended that the laws brought from England should be observed only so far as they were consistent with the interest of the colony. In this situation no governor could long support his power. Whenever he endeavored to exert his authority, his person was insulted and his administration complained of until he was removed from office.

8. During Morton's second administration, in 1686, the Spaniards laid waste the settlements of Port Royal. Morton then prepared to attack St. Augustine, but was prevented by the interference of the Proprietors. During the same year large accessions were made to the strength of the

---

7. What was the character of the two opposing parties ? How was the governor treated by his opponents ?
8. What took place in 1686 ? How was the colony strengthened this year ?

colony by numbers of Protestant refugees, known as Huguenots, from France, who were compelled to flee from that country by the revocation of the edict of Nantes.

9. Soon after the accession of Colleton, in 1686, he determined to exert his authority and compel the people to pay up their arrears of quit-rents. The quit-rents were trifling in amount per acre, but there were so many thousand acres out of which no profit was drawn, that the rents were really burdensome. The governor, being determined to exert his authority in collecting the rents, wrote to the Proprietors to appoint deputies to assist him in the execution of his office. But he soon found that the more rigorous he was the more turbulent the people became. The colony was a scene of confusion.

10. Mortified at his loss of power and his utter inability to enforce the collection of rents, Governor Colleton came to the conclusion, by the advice of his council, to declare martial law. Accordingly he called out the militia, as if some danger threatened the country, and at their head martial law was publicly proclaimed. But this proceeding served only to exasperate; the Assembly met and resolved that it was an assumption of power and an unwarrantable encroachment on their liberties. It was in vain that the governor endeavored to carry out his measures. In 1690 a bill was passed by the Assembly, disabling Landgrave James Colleton from holding any office or exercising any authority within the province; and they gave him notice that within a certain time he must leave the colony.

11. In the midst of these disturbances, the notorious Seth Sothel, who had been banished from North Carolina, made his appearance, and pretending to be one of the Proprietors, usurped the government. At first the people acknowledged his authority, but soon finding him destitute

---

9. What did Colleton undertake ? With what success ?
10. What course did Colleton pursue ? In 1690 what act was passed by the Assembly ?
11. What is said of Seth Sothel ? His conduct ?

of honor and principle, they abandoned him. He trampled upon every principle of common justice and equity. The fair traders from Bermuda and Barbadoes were seized as pirates and imprisoned until such ransom as he chose to exact was paid; bribes from felons and traitors were accepted; plantations were forcibly taken into possession; planters were compelled to pay large sums of money for permission to retain possession of their property; indeed, every species of exaction that a rapacious and avaricious tyrant could think of to exact money, was resorted to by him.

12. At length the people became so weary of his extortions, that they determined to take him by force and send him to England. Then he begged permission to remain in the country, promising to submit his conduct to the judgment of the Assembly. At the meeting of the Assembly thirteen different charges were preferred against him; he was found guilty, deprived of the government, and banished from the country. An account of his conduct was sent to the Proprietors, which filled them with astonishment, and they ordered him to England for trial. Philip Ludwell was appointed governor in his place, 1692.

13. During Ludwell's administration the struggle between the people and the Proprietors continued. The French refugees were a source of controversy, and in this the people were clearly wrong. The refugees were orderly, industrious, and religious; they fled from the lovely valleys of their own land because they were persecuted Protestants, and sought a home where they could worship God in peace; but because they were Frenchmen the English settlers were their enemies, and thought that they were not entitled to the privileges and advantages of natural born subjects. But the Proprietors favored them, and instructed Governor Lud-

---

12. What did the people resolve on doing? What was done? Who succeeded him?
13. What took place during Ludwell's administration? Why was Ludwell removed?

well to allow them the same liberties as other citizens. Ludwell was removed in 1693, for encroachments on the prerogatives of the Proprietors, in proposing to the Assembly to consider a new form of deed for holding lands.

14. Thomas Smith was appointed to succeed him. Complaints soon poured in upon him from all quarters. The French refugees were uneasy in regard to the titles to their property, and for this had good reason. There was no provincial law to secure their estates to the heirs of their body, or their next of kin; and they feared that on the death of the present owners their lands would escheat and their children become beggars. The English colonists also perplexed the Governor with ceaseless complaints. At length he wrote to the Proprietors that he despaired of ever uniting the people in interest and affection; that he and many more had resolved to leave the province, and he recommended that one of the Proprietors be sent with full powers to redress grievances, and settle differences in the colony.

15. Following the suggestions of Governor Smith, the Proprietors appointed John Archdale, a Quaker, a man of judgment and experience, and a Proprietor. His arrival caused great joy in the colony, and his very presence seemed to have the power to banish animosity and discord. His wise and judicious course gave satisfaction to all parties, Proprietors and colonists, except the French refugees. For these he found it impossible to do anything, on account of the strong feeling of dislike still existing in the minds of the English settlers. Rents were remitted; roads were constructed; canals were cut; the Indians were protected from insult, and a fair and friendly trade and intercourse were established with them; and though no positive enactments were made in favor of the French settlers, yet through his

---

14. Who succeeded him ? What gave the French settlers uneasiness ? What did the governor write to the Proprietors ?
15. What was done by the Proprietors ? What was accomplished by Archdale ? What took place in 1696 ?

influence the antipathies against them were greatly softened, and in the next administration, in 1696, they were admitted to the same rights as the English settlers.

16. Joseph Blake succeeded Archdale. From 1696 to 1710, there were four Governors: Joseph Blake, James Moore, Sir Nathaniel Johnson, and Edward Tynte. In 1702, towards the close of Governor Moore's administration, war broke out between England and Spain, and as the Spaniards of Florida were near neighbors to the Carolinians, they became involved in war. In 1702, Moore fitted out an expedition against Florida, and endeavored to take St. Augustine. He sailed from Charleston with a force of twelve hundred colonists and friendly Indians. The expedition was not a success. Moore was unable to take the fort at St. Augustine, and was compelled to raise the siege. By this unfortunate expedition the colony became involved in a heavy debt, and paper promises to pay were given to creditors in the place of money.

17. Soon afterwards an expedition was made against the Appalachees Indians, who had become quite troublesome, Governor Moore invaded their country; burned their towns and villages; killed several hundred of them, and obliged the others to submit to the English government. The Governor received the thanks of the Proprietors, and by his success in this expedition wiped off the ignominy of that against St. Augustine. He also procured a number of Indian slaves, whom he employed or sold for his own advantage.

18. During the administration of Sir Nathaniel Johnson, from 1702 to 1709, party spirit ran high and civil commotions continued. He was succeeded by Governor Tynte, and after his death, in 1710, the quarrels in regard to the succession came very near involving the colony in all the

---

16. Who succeeded Archdale ? What war broke out in 1702 ? What expedition was undertaken by Governor Moore ? What was accomplished ?
17. What is said of the expedition against the Appalachees Indians ?
18. What is said of the administration of Sir Wm. Johnson ? Describe the contest between Gibbes and Broughton.

horrors of a civil war. The rival candidates for Governor were Robert Gibbes and Colonel Broughton, and each one insisted that he was entitled to the office by the votes of the deputies of the Proprietors. The difficulty was occasioned by one of the deputies voting in the morning for one of the candidates, and in the afternoon declaring for the other. Soon afterwards he died suddenly, and after his death it was ascertained that his second vote had been obtained by bribery.

19. The strife ran very high between the candidates, and it was finally agreed that Gibbes should administer the government until the pleasure of the Proprietors could be known. They appointed Charles Craven, who then held the position of Secretary to the Governor. During his administration the colony was involved in two wars with the Indians: one with the Tuscaroras in North Carolina, and the other with the Yamassees. We have seen that North Carolina was involved in war with the Tuscaroras. South Carolina became a party to this war.

20. Four thousand pounds were voted by the Assembly for the expenses of the war with the Tuscaroras, and Governor Craven lost no time in sending assistance to North Carolina. A body of militia consisting of six hundred men, commanded by Colonel Barnwell, marched against the savages. Two hundred and eighteen Cherokees, seventy-nine Creeks, forty-one Catawbas, and twenty-eight Yamassees joined the Carolinians in this expedition. A dreadful wilderness, two hundred miles across, had to be traversed before the seat of war could be reached. In spite of every difficulty Barnwell advanced, employing his Indian allies to hunt for provisions by the way. At length he came up with the savages, and attacked them with great execution. In the first battle he killed three hundred Indians and took about one hundred prisoners. The Tuscaroras retreated to

---

19. Who was appointed governor by the Proprietors?
20. Describe the expedition against the Tuscaroras. Who commanded it?

their breastwork; they were there surrounded; many of them were killed, and the rest sued for peace. Their request was readily granted, as Barnwell's men were much fatigued, and suffering from hunger and wounds.

21. It is computed that the loss of the Tuscaroras was near one thousand killed and wounded in this war. Of Barnwell's party five white men were killed and several wounded. Thirty-six friendly Indians were killed, and between sixty and seventy wounded. Hostilities were soon afterwards renewed, and again the Tuscaroras were terribly defeated by Col. James Moore. After this defeat the survivors abandoned their country and joined the Five Nations in the North.

CHAPTER XVII.

VIRGINIA, RESUMED.
1660–1754.

The Bacon Rebellion—College of William and Mary.

1. THE intelligence of the Restoration of Charles II. to the throne of England was received with great enthusiasm in Virginia. The last to acknowledge the Parliament, the first after the death of Cromwell to proclaim the King, the most loyal of all English subjects, it was natural that they should rejoice at the turn affairs had taken, and entertain hopes of a brighter and better future. The terms in which the King addressed the colonists were well calculated to stir all loyal hearts, and keep alive and ardent the feelings of hope and expectation. But these hopes were doomed to disappointment. It became the policy of the government of England to make the commerce of the

---

21. What was the estimated loss of the Tuscaroras? Barnwell's loss? What became of the Tuscaroras finally?
CHAPTER XVII.—**1.** How was the intelligence of the Restoration received in Virginia? Were the hopes of the people realized? What became of the policy of the mother-country?

colonies entirely subservient to that of the mother-country. This policy was very injurious to the colonies, as it placed such restrictions on their commerce as, in a great measure, to destroy the profits arising from it.

2. The first act was to lay a duty of five per cent. on all merchandise exported from or imported into any of the colonies or dominions belonging to Great Britain. This was followed, in a short time, by the "Navigation Act," by which the plan of monopolizing to England the commerce of the colonies was perfected and reduced to a complete system. This act enjoined "that no commodities should be imported into any British settlement in Asia, Africa, or America, or exported from them, except in vessels built in England or in the plantations; of which vessels the masters and three-fourths of the mariners should be English subjects; and that no sugar, tobacco, *cotton*, wool, indigo, or woods used in dyeing, of the growth or manufacture of the colonies, should be shipped from them to any country except England; and that none but natural-born subjects, or such as had been naturalized, should exercise the occupation of merchant or factor in any English settlement, under the penalty of forfeiture of goods and chattels." This act was afterwards extended, in 1663, so as to prohibit the importation of any European commodity into the colonies, unless laden in England, in vessels navigated according to the tenor of the act.

3. The Parliament was not content with even these restrictions on the trade of the colonies, but went still further. They taxed the trade of the several colonies with each other, imposing a duty on the exportation of all commodities enumerated in the Navigation Act, from one colony to the other, the same as that levied on the consumption of those articles in England. This system, though it may have been advantageous to the interests of England, was

---

2. Give some of the provisions of the Navigation Act.
3. What other hardships did Parliament lay on the colonies ? What is said of this system in its bearings on England and the colonies ?

injurious to the colonies, and excited indignation and opposition, especially in Virginia, where the extensive commerce and pre-eminent loyalty of the people rendered the pressure of the burden more severe, and the infliction of it more exasperating.

4. There was, however, some compensation for these severe restrictions. The colonies were allowed the exclusive privilege of supplying England with tobacco, the cultivation of which was forbidden in England, Ireland, Guernsey, and Jersey. But the compensation did not equal the burden, and the discontent was general. Virginia remonstrated and petitioned for relief, but in vain. The King enforced the act with rigor.

5. The discontents in Virginia were augmented by the grants of land made by the King to his favorites, which were in violation of former grants, and were inconsistent with the rights of Virginians. A war breaking out with the Susquehanna Indians, who ravaged the frontiers, added to the distress, and increased the discontent of the people. Sir William Berkeley, who had been Governor for many years, had generally been popular with all classes; but at last the discontents of the people began to affect his standing, and he was accused of "wanting honesty to resist the aggression of the mother-country, and courage to repel the Indians." These charges were urged chiefly by Nathaniel Bacon, a young lawyer, ardent and ambitious.

6. Bacon was educated in London, had emigrated to Virginia in 1673, and was appointed a member of the Council shortly after his arrival. He was well qualified to be a leader of the people. A man of engaging address, young, bold, and ambitious, he harangued them upon their grievances, inflamed their passions against their rulers, and declaimed especially against the languid manner in which

---

4. What compensation was there for these hardships?
5. How were the discontents augmented in Virginia? What was the effect on the popularity of Sir William Berkeley?
6. When did Bacon arrive in Virginia? Describe him. What is said of his election? What did Governor Berkeley do?

the war against the Indians was then carried on. Without warrant or authority of law, an assembled multitude of men elected him General. Whereupon he immediately applied to the Governor for a commission, and for his official sanction of the popular election, offering to march at once against the Indians. Governor Berkeley refused, and issued a proclamation commanding, in the King's name, the multitude to disperse. The popular voice was loud in Bacon's favor. They demanded a bold leader. He was just such a one as they desired. The more their demand was insisted on the more firmly the Governor adhered to his proclamation. Bacon was threatened with outlawry as a traitor.

7. Bacon was not intimidated or disconcerted; but feeling that he had gone too far to recede, instead of causing his followers to disperse, he marched at the head of six hundred armed men directly to Jamestown, surrounded the house where the Governor and Council were assembled, and repeated his demand. Berkeley refused with firmness, and, boldly presenting himself before the angry multitude, defied their malice; but the Council, less courageous, hastily prepared a commission, and, by their entreaties, prevailed on the Governor to sign it. Bacon and his men then began their march against the Indians; but no sooner were the Council relieved of their fears than they annulled the commission, denounced Bacon as a rebel, and commanded his followers to deliver him up. The Governor readily approved this act of the Assembly, as he had signed the commission only at their earnest entreaty.

8. Enraged at this treatment, Bacon with all his forces returned to Jamestown. The aged Governor, unsupported and almost abandoned, fled to Accomac, on the eastern

---

7. What steps did Bacon take next ? By whose influence did he get his commission ? After his departure, what was done by the Council ?
8. What was then done by Bacon ? By Berkeley ? What was done by Bacon to give his authority a legal sanction ?

shore of the Chesapeake. Collecting those who were well affected towards his administration, he opposed the insurgents and several skirmishes were fought with various success. Some of his councillors accompanied him, some went home to their plantations, and the actual government of the colony was, for the time being, in the hands of Bacon. He sought to give it a legal form, and for this purpose caused a convention to assemble, and prevailed upon the members to pledge themselves to support his authority. The convention published a declaration charging the origin of the troubles upon Sir William Berkeley, and requiring the people to support Bacon against all forces, until the King could be informed of the true state of the case.

9. The colony was now in a state of civil war. A party of Bacon's men burned Jamestown, laid waste that part of the country whose inhabitants adhered to the old administration, and confiscated the property of the loyalists, their opponents. The Governor retaliated, seized the estates of many of the insurgents, and executed several of the leaders. When intelligence of the troubles reached England, the King issued a proclamation declaring Bacon a traitor, and granting pardon to all who would forsake him. He also dispatched a fleet with some troops to the assistance of Governor Berkeley.

10. But a new and unexpected turn was given to the course of events by the sudden death of Bacon. So, completely had he been the soul of the movement, that immediately after his death the hopes of his followers sunk, his party dissolved; and without any attempt at re-organization, without any choice of a new leader, they entered into negotiation with Sir William Berkeley, and laid down their arms, on obtaining a promise of general pardon. Such was the termination of a civil war which, at one time, seemed

---

9. Relate the proceedings of the different parties. What was done by the King of England ?
10. What event put a sudden stop to the affair and restored Berkeley to power ?

to threaten the destruction of the colony. Many valuable lives were lost, and much property was destroyed, by a civil war which seems to have effected no good, and to have accomplished none of the purposes for which it was begun. Whether the outbreak may properly be termed a rebellion or not, and Bacon a usurper, after his death his followers, being left without a head, gladly submitted to the authority of Sir William Berkeley, on condition of receiving a general pardon.

11. Berkeley returned to England about 1678, and was succeeded by Culpepper, who was appointed Governor for life; he was, however, removed in 1683 or 1684, and Effingham appointed his successor. In 1685 occurred in England the rebellion of James, Duke of Monmouth. When it was suppressed, many of those persons implicated in it were sent to Virginia and Maryland, to be sold to the colonists as slaves for ten years. The Virginia House of Burgesses declared them free. Meanwhile, the restrictions on the commerce of the colonies continued through the subsequent portion of the reign of Charles II., and through that of James II., until the revolution of 1688, which placed William and Mary on the throne—an event beneficial to Great Britain and her colonies.

12. During the reign of William and Mary a college was established in Virginia, to which the sovereigns gave their patronage and their names. The King gave to the college outstanding quit-rents to the value of two thousand pounds, and also other grants. From this period Virginia enjoyed almost uninterrupted peace, and continued to increase in wealth and population until the breaking out of the old French war in 1754, considerably over half a century. Its central situation, removed alike from the French in Canada and the Spaniards in Florida, saved it from their hostile

---

11. Who succeeded Berkeley in 1678? What event occurred in England in 1685? What revolution occurred in 1688?
12. What college was founded in Virginia in the reign of William and Mary? How did the central situation of Virginia affect its tranquillity?

incursions, and insured comparative repose. Religious intolerance disappeared; and though Episcopacy continued to be the established religion, and the laws against dissenters were unrepealed, yet they were a dead letter, and men of all names and sects could worship as they pleased, and the "Old Dominion" became the worthy Mother of States and Statesmen.

CHAPTER XVIII.

NEW YORK, RESUMED.
1664-1754.
Sir Edmund Andros—French and Indian Wars.

1. IMMEDIATELY after its subjugation, as we have seen, New Amsterdam and the whole of the conquered province received the name of New York. Considerable numbers of the Dutch inhabitants left the country, and sought new homes elsewhere. The Governor, Stuyvesant, himself acquiesced in the change, and passed the remainder of his days as a British subject. Nichols, the first governor after the conquest, retained many of the Dutch forms of government; but a change to English customs was gradually brought about; trial by jury was introduced, and on the 12th of June, 1665, New York was incorporated, under a Mayor, five Aldermen, and a Sheriff. In 1666, war with Holland having broken out, apprehensions were entertained that efforts might be made to recover the province; but no attack was made, and at the treaty of peace New York was regularly ceded to England in exchange for Surinam, by a general stipulation that each one of the belligerents should retain what its arms had acquired since the commencement of the war.

2. In 1667 Nichols resigned his appointment, and was

CHAPTER XVIII.—**1**. Who was first governor of New York after its conquest? **2**. Who succeeded Nichols? What took place towards the close of his administration? When was New York restored to the English?

succeeded by Colonel Lovelace, who was governor for six years. During his administration the colony was prosperous. Towards the close of his term, war having again broken out with the Dutch, a small squadron was fitted out by them to prey upon the commerce of the English colonies in America. This squadron suddenly made a descent upon the city of New York, and captured it during the absence of Colonel Lovelace. It was restored to the English at the treaty of Westminster, in 1674.

3. Sir Edmund Andros was Governor under the Duke of York, as successor of Colonel Lovelace, until the year 1682, when Colonel Thomas Dongan was appointed. It was during his administration that a representative Legislative government was first established in New York. So much discontent was excited under Andros' arbitrary system, that the Proprietary was induced to grant the same form of government that was enjoyed by the other colonies. The Assembly consisted of a Council of ten members, and a House of Representatives chosen by the people, composed of eighteen members; but its laws were to be ratified by the Proprietary before they could take effect. It was in this way the principle of the right of local self-government took root in this colony. The people for a time seemed content with the mere privilege of having representatives, though they had only two sessions of the Legislature in the next six years.

4. The administration of Dongan was distinguished by the attention which he gave to Indian affairs. The interior of New York was inhabited by several of the aboriginal tribes. These at first were known as the Five Nations. After they were joined by the Tuscaroras from the Carolinas, they were known as the Six Nations. Colonel Dongan, in 1684, seeing great danger from the encroachments of the

---

3. When was a representative government established in New York ? Of whom did the Assembly consist ?

4. In what way was the administration of Dongan distinguished ? What advantageous treaty was formed ?

French in Canada, in conjunction with Lord Effingham, Governor of Virginia, entered into a treaty with the Five Nations, embracing all the English settlements and all the Indian tribes in alliance with them. This treaty, which was long and faithfully adhered to, was of immense advantage to the English settlers, as it erected a firm barrier between them and the French on the north, and prevented their encroachments for many years.

5. In 1684, De la Barre, the Governor of Canada, invaded the territory of the Five Nations with an army of seventeen hundred men, with the intention of defeating and driving them from their country. But his troops suffered so much from famine, hardship, and sickness, that he was compelled to ask peace of those whom he had come to destroy. He invited the chiefs of the Five Nations to meet him at his camp; they accepted the invitation. In the conference which ensued, he accused the confederates of conducting the English to the trading grounds of the French, and threatened them with a war of extermination if they did not alter their behavior. The Indian chief Garangala, who well knew the weakness and helpless condition of the French army, treated his threats with contempt, and replied to him in a bold and independent speech.

6. De la Barre was mortified and enraged at his reply; but, submitting to necessity, he concluded a treaty of peace and returned to Montreal. His successor, De Nouville, led a larger army against the confederates, but with no better success. He fell into an ambuscade, and was defeated with heavy loss. These wars served to strengthen and perpetuate the enmity of the Indians against the French, and their attachment to the English.

7. After James II. ascended the throne, in 1685, and declared the abrogation of the old colony charters, New York

---

5. What took place in 1684 ?
6. What was the result of De la Barre's expedition ?
7. What took place after James II. became king ? What is said of the administration of Andros? What revolution occurred in 1688 ? Who seized the government in New York ?

and the Jerseys were added to the jurisdiction of the four colonies of New England, and Sir Edmund Andros was appointed captain-general and vice-admiral over the whole. His hard rule, however, was a brief one; but during his administration additional taxes were imposed, and a printing-press was strictly forbidden in the colony. In 1688 occurred the revolution in England which placed William and Mary on the throne. When intelligence of their accession was received in New York, and while the principal officers and magistrates were assembled to consult for the general safety, Jacob Leisler, a captain of militia, seized the fort and held it for the Prince of Orange, under the old charter. Nicholson, the deputy of Andros, fled to England. A few of his adherents, Courtlandt, the mayor of the city, Colonel Bayard, Major Schuyler, and other gentlemen, retiring to Albany, seized the fort there, declaring they held it for King William, but would have no connection with Leisler. Leisler sent his son-in-law, Milbourne, against them; they gave up the fort, and retired to the neighboring colonies. In revenge, Leisler confiscated their estates.

8. Meantime the province was ruled by a committee of safety, with Leisler at their head. In a few months a letter arrived from the ministry in England, directed to " such as for the time being take care of administering the laws of the province," as they existed under the charter, and conferring authority to perform all the duties of Lieutenant-Governor. This letter Leisler understood as addressed to himself, and accordingly assumed the authority conferred by it, and issued commissions and appointed his executive council. A convention was called, consisting of deputies from all the towns and districts, who enacted various regulations for the government of the colony.

9. War about this time was declared between France and

---

8. What is said of Leisler's position, and the condition of New York?
9. What war was declared? Who became governor of Canada? What is said of him? What treaty did he make? When was Schenectady burnt?

England. Count Frontenac, a veteran and skillful officer, succeeded De Nouville as Governor of Canada, and soon, by his energetic measures, aided by a large reinforcement, he raised the affairs of the French from the brink of ruin to a position that enabled them to act on the offensive. He held a great council with the Five Nations at Onondaga, and as he found them somewhat inclined to peace, he persuaded them to remain neutral in the war between the French and English; and to raise the drooping spirits of the Canadians, he determined to give them immediate employment against the English colonies. On the 19th of January, 1690, a party of about two hundred French and some Cahuuaga Indians set out for Schenectady; they arrived at eleven o'clock at night on the 8th of February, and the first intimation the inhabitants had of danger or of the presence of enemies was conveyed in the noise of their own bursting doors. Before they made the attack, the French and Indians, finding the inhabitants buried in profound repose, and no guards set, divided themselves into different parties; at the same time they set fire to the town in various places.

10. The village was burnt; sixty persons were massacred, and twenty-seven were carried into captivity; the rest escaped and made their way naked through the snow towards Albany, at which place some arrived in extreme distress, while many perished on the way. A party of young men and Mohawk Indians immediately set out from Albany in pursuit of the enemy, overtook them, and killed and captured twenty-five.

11. To avenge these barbarities, and others perpetrated in New England, preparations were immediately commenced for an invasion of Canada. An army was raised in New York and Connecticut. These forces, united under the

---

10. How many made their escape ? How many of the enemy were killed and captured ?
11. What was done to avenge these barbarities ? With what success ? Who commanded the expeditions against Canada ?

command of General Winthrop, were to march against Montreal. They proceeded as far as the head of Lake Champlain, but finding no boats prepared for their use they were obliged to return. The expedition against Quebec was equally unsuccessful. Sir William Phipps, with a fleet of more than thirty vessels, sailed from Boston into the St. Lawrence, landed a party, and made an attack, both by land and water, upon Quebec. But he was obliged to abandon the enterprise, in consequence of the army which was to co-operate with him having returned to New York, thus allowing the whole force of the enemy to repair to the assistance of the garrison.

12. When Leisler was informed of the retreat he caused Winthrop to be arrested; but this so aroused the indignation of all parties that he was compelled to release him. The failure of the expedition was in fact attributable to Milbourne, who, acting as commissary-general, had failed to furnish the necessary supplies.

13. Leisler was superseded by Colonel Slaughter, who arrived in the province in 1691. Leisler was shortly afterwards arrested, tried, and executed, on a charge of treason, for refusing to surrender his authority to the person legally appointed to receive it. Milbourne, his son-in-law, was tried and executed with him. Colonel Slaughter was unwilling to sign their death-warrant; but their enemies took advantage of his fondness for wine, gave him a dinner-party, and while intoxicated they induced him to sign the order for their execution, and the next morning, before the governor became sober and could recall the warrant, the unfortunate men were hurried to death. In a few months Slaughter himself died, just after the conclusion of a treaty, offensive and defensive, with the Five Nations.

14. In 1691, near the close of the year, Major Schuyler,

---

12. When informed of the retreat, what did Leisler do? Who was to blame for the failure?
13. Who succeeded Leisler? What was Leisler's fate?
14. What expedition was undertaken near the close of the year 1691? What is said of the war between the Indians and French?

who had acquired great influence over the Indians of the Five Nations, undertook an expedition against Montreal, at the head of a considerable body of colonial and Indian forces. He inflicted heavy losses upon the French, but was compelled to retreat. The war was waged with great fury between the Indians and French; prisoners were tortured and put to death, without the least regard to the rights of humanity or the laws of war. Both parties seemed inspired with a desire to excel each other in cruelty as in prowess in battle.

15. Colonel Fletcher, the next Governor of New York, arrived in 1692. He was a man of great energy of character, but violent and passionate in his disposition. His administration is remarkable for nothing except for the effort to obtain control of the Connecticut militia, by virtue of a commission from the King, in which he signally failed; the matter was submitted to the Attorney and Solicitor-General of England, who decided in favor of Connecticut. He also endeavored to induce the Assembly to declare Episcopacy the established religion of the colony. A bill was passed for settling ministers in the several parishes, but an amendment was added by the council that people might choose their own ministers, provided the Governor should exercise the Episcopal power of approving and collating the incumbents. This amendment the Assembly negatived, for which the Governor called them before him and rated them soundly. His abuse they bore with patience, but remained firm in their position.

16. In 1697 the peace of Ryswick was concluded, which gave security and repose to the colonies, but left the Five Nations exposed to the animosity of the French. Lord Bellamont, who succeeded Colonel Fletcher, protected the Five Nations from the fury of the French. He supplied

---

15. Who was next Governor of New York? What is said of him? What is his administration remarkable for?
16. When was peace made? How did Lord Bellamont act towards the French and Indians?

them with arms and ammunition, and notified Count Frontenac that if the French attacked them, he would send the whole disposable force of the colony to their aid. By his firmness and decision Count Frontenac was induced to forego his purpose of war, and shortly afterwards peace was made between the French and Indians.

17. During the administration of Fletcher, piracy had increased to an alarming extent, to which great evil Bellamont was particularly desirous of putting an end; but the government declining to furnish an adequate naval force, he engaged with others in a private undertaking against the acknowledged outlaws of all nations. Among the undertakers were Lord-Chancellor Summers and the Duke of Shrewsbury; the King himself, also, had a tenth share. Having procured a vessel, the command was given to Captain Kidd, and he was despatched on a cruise against the pirates. Kidd had been but a short time at sea when he made a new contract with his crew, and on the Atlantic and Indian Oceans he became himself one of the most daring, successful, and celebrated pirates that ever infested the seas. After a bloody career of three years he had the wonderful audacity to appear in public in Boston. He was there seized, sent to England, and tried and executed. The noblemen who had procured him his commission were charged with complicity with him, and this feeling became so powerful, that a motion was made in the House of Commons that all who were concerned in the adventure might be deprived of their employments. The motion was rejected by a large majority,

CAPTAIN KIDD.

---

17. What is said of piracy and the efforts of Lord Bellamont to put an end to it? Describe Captain Kidd's career.

and the unfortunate shareholders in the adventure were proven entirely innocent of any participation, either in the designs or profits of Captain Kidd.

18. Lord Bellamont's administration was wise and prudent, and promised to be highly beneficial, but was suddenly cut short by his death in 1701. He sought to allay the feuds and soften the asperities of party spirit. He was mainly instrumental in procuring a grant of one thousand pounds for the benefit of young Leisler when he made application for indemnification for the losses sustained by his family. Lord Cornbury was appointed his successor, a man eminent for his meanness and profligacy, dismissed by his friends to place him out of the reach of his creditors. His oppressive and extravagant rule, and the baseness of his private character, exposed him to universal odium. He was removed in 1709 by Queen Anne, who appointed Lord Lovelace his successor.

19. Lord Lovelace died soon after his arrival, and General Hunter was appointed to succeed him, in 1710. He brought with him nearly three thousand Germans, a part of whom settled in New York, the remainder in Philadelphia. An invasion of Canada by the united forces of New York, New Jersey, and Connecticut, took place in 1711. It was unsuccessful, and nothing was accomplished by it. To defray its expenses the Assembly passed several bills which the council persisted in amending. The Governor took sides with the council, and finally dissolved the Assembly. At the ensuing election most of the members elect were opposed to the Governor. This Assembly was dissolved by the death of the Queen. The next met the same fate from the Governor. The people at length became weary of contending, and elected representatives whose views were in unison with those of the Governor.

---

18. What was the character of Lord Bellamont's administration ? What grant was he instrumental in procuring ? Who succeeded him ? What is said of his successor ? Who was appointed by Queen Anne in 1709 ?
19. What emigrants did General Hunter bring over with him ? Relate the contests between the Governor and the Assembly.

20. General Hunter quitted the province in 1719, and his authority devolved on Peter Schuyler, the oldest member of the council. His successor was William Burnet, son of the celebrated Bishop Burnet, a man of good sense and kind feelings. His attention was directed chiefly to Indian affairs, and the danger to be apprehended from the vicinity of the French. Turning his views to the wilderness, he perceived that the French were employed in erecting a chain of forts from the St. Lawrence to the Mississippi. To defeat their design he built a trading-house and afterwards a fort at Oswego, on Lake Ontario. But the French had abundant resources, and were not easily foiled. They penetrated into the wilderness, and erected a fort at Niagara, commanding the entrance into the lake; they had previously erected Fort Frontenac, commanding the outlet.

21. Mr. Burnet held a conference with the chiefs of the Five Nations, at Albany; spoke to them of the wrongs the French had done to them, and of the kindness they had received from the English. He so moved upon them by his eloquent representations that they were persuaded to give a deed surrendering their country to the King of England, to be protected for their use, and confirming their grant of 1701, concerning which there was only an entry in the books of the secretary for Indian affairs.

22. But in the meantime the electors of the colony had become dissatisfied at the length of time which had elapsed since there had been an election for members of the Assembly. There had been such complete harmony between the Governor and the Assembly elected in 1716, that there had been no dissolution for eleven years, and the people became dissatisfied. Yielding to their clamors, he dissolved the Assembly in 1727, and a new election was held. As might have been expected, a majority in the next Assembly were

---

20. What is said of Governor Burnet and his administration? What steps did he take to defeat the designs of the French?
21. Give an account of his conference with the Five Nations, and its result.
22. What was the result of the election held in 1727?

opponents of the administration, and disputes immediately arose between them and the Governor.

23. The court of chancery, in which Mr. Burnet presided, had become exceedingly unpopular. It had been instituted without the concurrence of the Assembly, and some of its decisions had given great offence to influential individuals. The Assembly passed resolutions intimating that its decrees were void, and declaring the court a "manifest oppression and grievance." Mr. Burnet immediately dissolved the Assembly. In the spring, however, an ordinance was passed to remedy certain abuses and to reduce the fees of the court.

24. Mr. Burnet was shortly afterwards appointed Governor of Massachusetts, and was succeeded by Col. Montgomery in New York. His short administration was only distinguished by his love of ease, which so absorbed his attention that he had no time to devote to public affairs. He died in 1731, and the executive authority devolved upon Rip Van Dam, the senior member of the council. During his administration the French were permitted to erect a fort at Crown Point, within the limits of New York, which became a source of constant annoyance, being a rallying-point for hostile bands of Indians.

25. In August, 1732, Van Dam was superseded by William Crosby, who was at first popular, on account of having defended the colonies in the British Parliament; but he soon lost the affections of the people by his encroachments on the liberty of the press. He prosecuted Zenger, the printer of a newspaper, for publishing an article which he thought derogatory to the dignity of his Majesty's government. For printing the offensive article Zenger was thrown in prison, and not brought to trial until after the lapse of thirty-five weeks. He was ably defended by An-

---

23. What is said of the court of chancery ? What was the action of the Assembly in respect to it ?
24. Who succeeded Mr. Burnet ? How was his administration distinguished ? What took place during Rip Van Dam's administration ?
25. Who succeeded Van Dam ? What is said of his administration?

drew Hamilton, the eminent Quaker-lawyer of Philadelphia, and acquitted.

26. In 1736, Crosby was succeeded by George Clark. During his administration the contest between the Governor and the Assembly was revived. It was the Governor's wish to control the public revenue; the Assembly declared that the moneys raised should be applied to the extinguishment of certain specific debts, and refused to appropriate any sum for any length of time, or for any purpose, except as in their judgment they thought right. The Assembly was dissolved; but a new Assembly was no more tractable, and for a time the Governor yielded and promised his cordial co-operation in all measures calculated to promote the prosperity of the colony. Harmony did not long continue. At the next session the Assembly, persisting in its refusal to raise a revenue for a longer period than one year, was again dissolved.

27. In 1740 the Assembly again met, and still continued their opposition to their Governor's wishes. Their resolute adherence to their views of duty and right was construed by the Governor into a desire for independence, and in a speech delivered in 1741 he alludes to a "jealousy which for some years had obtained in England, that the plantations were not without thoughts of throwing off their dependence on the crown."

28. Clark was superseded in the government by George Clinton, in 1743. Like most of the governors, he was received with joy by the people. But, more fortunate than the greater number, he seems to have retained his popularity by timely concessions to the popular will. To manifest his confidence in the people, he gave his assent to a bill limiting the duration of the present and all succeeding Assemblies. The Assembly, actuated by a similar desire

---

26. What is said of the controversy between Governor Clark and the Assembly?
27. What charge does Governor Clark bring against them in 1741?
28. Who succeeded Clark? In what year? What can you tell about his administration?

to promote the public welfare, readily adopted the measures he recommended for the defence of the colony against the French, who were then at war with England. In 1745 the Indian allies of France made frequent incursions into New York, as well as the other English colonies. Their depredations continued, with little intermission, until the termination of the French dominion in Canada.

29. At the commencement of the French and Indian war of 1754, the population of the colony of New York did not exceed one hundred thousand.

CHAPTER XIX.
NEW ENGLAND CONFEDERATION, RESUMED.
1675—1754.

King Philip's War—Sir Edmund Andros—Charters Suppressed—Connecticut Charter Oak—End of the Confederacy—Old Charters Revived—Massachusetts and Plymouth United—Queen Anne's War—Witchcraft.

1. THE public manifestations of loyalty to Charles II. throughout New England, after the Restoration, were more in appearance than reality. There was a general apprehension pervading the minds of a large majority of the people, that their chartered rights would not be regarded by this monarch. It is true he had confirmed the charter of Massachusetts, yet he had done it in a way, and with qualifications, which increased this apprehension. In his act of confirmation he required a toleration of the Church of England, and dispensed with colonial church membership as a qualification to hold office.

2. These apprehensions were still more increased upon the arrival, not long after, of a board of Royal Commis-

---

29. What was the population of the colony of New York in 1754?
CHAPTER XIX.—1. What is said of the manifestations of loyalty to Charles II. in New England? In confirming the charter of Massachusetts, what changes did he make?
2. What is said of the board of commissioners? On what matters did disputes arise between this board and Massachusetts? What put a temporary quiet to these disputes?

sioners, who were sent over, on some pretext or other, to determine certain civil as well as military matters in each of the colonies of the confederation, and also to Rhode Island. They were to look after the peace and security of the whole country generally. These commissioners met with a very jealous reception in Massachusetts, much more so than in Plymouth, Connecticut, or Rhode Island. A very serious dispute soon arose between them and the General Court of Massachusetts, about her claim of jurisdiction over New Hampshire. The commissioners returned to England without any satisfactory adjustment of this dispute. Massachusetts was cited to appear by agents or attorneys, to answer in England certain complaints alleged against her by them. This she neglected to do, and matters were assuming quite a serious aspect in that quarter, when a new trouble arose, which diverted attention temporarily from a quarrel with the mother-country. It was a dangerous quarrel with the Indians at their doors. This was the breaking out of what is known as King Philip's War.

KING PHILIP.

3. King Philip was the second son of Massasoit, who had always been a warm friend of the English; but he

---

3. Who was King Philip? What is said of the cause of his hatred to the colonies?

CHAP. XIX.] NEW ENGLAND CONFEDERATION. 115

was far from sharing the feeling of his father. He concealed his hatred, and went silently to work maturing a plan by which he hoped to be able to exterminate all the colonists. The cause of his hatred was the wrongs which, as he complained, had been inflicted upon his brother and upon others of his tribe, who were put to death after being tried and found guilty of murder, by a jury composed of colonists and Indians. This was done under an Indian treaty with the Confederation, and he complained that it all came from the controlling influence of the whites.

4. For five years Philip labored diligently in inducing other tribes to join in a league for the destruction of the whites. At the end of that time he found that he could bring three thousand warriors into the field. The war began by an attack upon Swanzey, in Plymouth, in June, 1675. The Confederation stood together in the common defence. The war was waged with great fury and various success until August, 1676, when it was terminated by the death of Philip, the destruction of his tribe the Wampanoags, the destruction of the Nipmucks and the Narragansetts, and the captivity of Philip's wife and son, yet a lad. His son was taken to Boston, and there it was debated whether he should be put to death or sold into slavery. This youth, the last prince of the Wampanoags, the grandson of Massasoit the lifelong friend of the colonists, was adjudged by the authorities to be sold as a slave, and was ordered to be sent out and so disposed of in Bermuda.

5. The loss of the Confederation in this war was very great. Six hundred of the inhabitants, composing a large portion of its military strength, were either killed in battle or otherwise lost. Twelve or thirteen towns were destroyed, and

---

4. How long was he striving to stir up strife between the two races ? Where and when did the war begin ? When did it end ? What was its result ? What became of King Philip's son ?
5. What was the loss of the Confederation in the war ? What was the population of the Confederation at this time ?

about six hundred buildings, chiefly dwelling-houses, were burnt. A heavy debt was contracted, and their resources were greatly diminished. At the beginning of this war the entire population of New England was not above one hundred and twenty-five thousand.

6. After this war, the dispute between Massachusetts and the mother-country, in regard to New Hampshire as well as Maine, was renewed. The latter was ended, in 1677, by Massachusetts paying twelve hundred pounds sterling for the proprietary rights of Gorges to the territory of Maine.

The dispute as to New Hampshire was ended in 1679, by a judicial decision in England, against the claim by Massachusetts of jurisdiction over that colony. A new and very liberal charter was granted to New Hampshire on 18th September, 1679. John Cutts, of Portsmouth, was appointed chief magistrate, under the name and style of President. After this New Hampshire remained a separate colony.

The first General Assembly under the new organization met at Portsmouth, 16th of March, 1680, which passed many wholesome and liberal laws. One of their declarations was that no act, imposition, law, or ordinance should be imposed upon the inhabitants of the province, but such as should be made by the Assembly and approved by the President of the council. Under the code then adopted, New Hampshire soon began to flourish.

7. It was not long after this that King Charles II. entered upon the execution of a purpose to annul all the New England colonial charters. His acts, in the proceeding which ensued, were most arbitrary and tyrannical. In 1684 a judgment was obtained by him in the High Court of Chancery, abrogating the Massachusetts charter. All the other New

---

6. After the war was over, what is said of the disputes between Massachusetts and the mother-country ? Who was the first chief magistrate of New Hampshire under the new organization ? When did the first General Assembly meet ? What is said of its action ?

7. What is said of the conduct of Charles II. as to the New England charters ? When and how was that of Massachusetts abrogated ? What is said of the oth-

England charters, soon after, were also declared void by revocation or annulment. Very great excitement in all the colonies was the necessary consequence. The New England Confederation, which had existed since 1643, was now at an end. James II., who succeeded Charles II., his brother, to the throne of England in 1685, appointed Joseph Dudley to take charge of the government of Massachusetts, New Hampshire, Maine, Plymouth, Rhode Island, and Connecticut. He was superseded in 1686 by the infamous Sir Edmund Andros, who, with a council to be appointed by the King, was empowered, under the title of captain-general and vice-admiral, to make all laws and levy taxes at discretion over the whole of the same country. Upon his arrival in Massachusetts, his conduct bore every mark of a usurping despot. He removed all the civil authorities, and put a restraint not only on the freedom of the press, but upon the freedom of personal locomotion. All public meetings were prohibited, and no one was allowed to leave the country without his permission. He afterwards went to Rhode Island and broke the seal of the charter of that colony, and declared its government at an end. In 1687 he went to Hartford, and demanded the charter of Connecticut. The Assembly was in session, but the demand was evaded until night. When candles were lighted the charter was brought in and laid upon the table. As Andros was about to take it up the lights were suddenly put out; and when they were restored, the document was gone. It had been, according to previous arrangement, seized by one of the patriots, and carried away for safe keeping. It was hid for the time in the hollow of a venerable oak, which afterwards remained famous as the old Charter Oak for more than a century.

8. The charter of Connecticut was in this way saved from

ers? What effect had this upon the Confederation? Who succeeded Charles II. to the throne of England? In what year? Whom did James appoint governor of the New England colonies? Who superseded Dudley, and when? What is said of Andros? What did he do at Hartford?

8. What became of the Connecticut charter? What is said of Cotton Mather? What effect did his appeal to the King have?

destruction, but the government under it was repressed for the time being. Andros had complete control, under his commission from the King, and by his exactions and atro-

CHARTER OAK.

cities rendered himself and his administration extremely odious to all the people within the limits of his sway. Cotton Mather, an eminent divine of Massachusetts, was despatched as a common agent to England to seek redress. But the King remained firm in his purpose, and even enlarged the jurisdiction of Andros, so as to extend it over the colonies of New York and New Jersey.

9. Relief, however, came shortly afterwards, not from the King, but from his overthrow. James II., by his arbitrary measures, both in church and state, excited a general apprehension throughout the realm that the rights and liberties of the people of England were not safe in his hands. Parliament declared against his authority, and invited William, Prince of Orange, husband of Mary, his eldest daughter, to come over and take his place upon the throne. The invitation was accepted. James fled the kingdom. William and Mary were proclaimed by Parliament as the

---

9. How did relief come ? What became of James ? When did this change in the government of England take place ? What became of Andros ? What was the result in Massachusetts ? What in Rhode Island ? What in Connecticut ? What in Plymouth ?

legitimate sovereigns of the nation, under what was called the settlement of 1688. The inhabitants of New England received the news of the change with acclamations of joy. Andros and about fifty of his most active partisans were seized in Boston and sent to England for trial. The administration of civil affairs in Massachusetts was immediately restored to their former officers, who had been displaced by Andros. The same was done in Rhode Island, as we have seen, as also in Connecticut. There the old charter was brought from the hollow of the oak, in which it had been securely kept from the grasp of the tyrant, and the former officers resumed their functions under it. In the colony of Plymouth, when it was known that Andros had been arrested, Clark, his agent or deputy, was imprisoned, and Thomas Hinckly, former governor, was immediately restored to office.

10. In 1691 King William of England granted a new charter to the colonies of Massachusetts and Plymouth. By this charter these two colonies, which before that had been separate, were incorporated into one. It was accepted by both of them in 1692, and ever since then the original colony of Plymouth has been a part of Massachusetts, and under the same government. At the time of the union the population of Massachusetts was about forty thousand, and that of Plymouth about seven thousand. The district of Maine was also embraced in the same charter. In it the King reserved to himself the power of appointing the governor and other officers, but conceded to the people the right of self-government in all other respects, and insured to all classes the protection of person and property. Sir William Phipps was the first governor under this new organization.

11. Meantime France favored the cause of the exiled

---

10. When did the colonies of Plymouth and Massachusetts become united under the same government? At the time of the union, about what was the population of each? What is said of this new charter of William's? Who was the first governor under the new charter?

11. What is said of France, after the revolution and settlement in 1688? What is said of Schenectady? What is said of Salmon Falls, in New Hamp-

British King James II., and soon after the English revolution and settlement of 1688, war broke out between that country and England. The colonies of New England and New York were great sufferers, being exposed to continual incursions of the French and Indians from Canada. On the night of February 8th, 1690, Schenectady, in New York, was destroyed, and many of the inhabitants were slain. Salmon Falls, in New Hampshire, shared the same fate. Thirty of the inhabitants were killed and fifty-four were carried into captivity. The whole northern frontier became a scene of horrors from the same enemies.

The Confederation determined to carry the war into the enemy's country. A fleet of eight vessels was fitted out, and a force of eight hundred men, under command of Sir William Phipps, was sent against Port Royal, in Acadia, as Nova Scotia was then called. The expedition was successful; Port Royal was captured, and all Acadia was subjugated. But an expedition against Canada, the object of which was the capture of Quebec, failed, as we have seen. In 1696 Port Royal was recovered by France, and the possession of all Acadia followed. The peace of Ryswick, which was concluded in 1697, gave a brief repose to France and England, and also to the colonies.

12. In 1702, after a lapse of only five years, war again broke out between the two countries, and the colonial border warfare recommenced.

In 1707 an unsuccessful expedition was undertaken against Port Royal. Haverhill was burned by the Indians in 1708; more than one hundred persons lost their lives, and many were carried into captivity. The same year a force of three thousand men was sent against Canada, but returned without accomplishing anything. But the idea of taking Port Royal was not given up. Some regiments

---
shire ? What did the colonies determine to do ? What did Sir William Phipps do ? When did this war between England and France cease ? When and where was peace made ?

12. How long did peace last ? What is said of Haverhill ? What of Port Royal ? What was its name changed to, and why ?

were sent from England under Colonel Nicholson, with a fleet, to coöperate with the colonists in an attack on that place. Success crowned their efforts. Port Royal was taken, and the name was changed to Annapolis, in honor of Queen Anne, sister of Mary, who was now on the throne of England.

13. Encouraged by this success, a grand expedition against Quebec and Montreal was undertaken in 1711. Fifteen ships of war, forty transports, and six storeships sailed from Boston; but in proceeding up the St. Lawrence Bay the fleet was scattered by a storm, and one thousand men were lost. This terrible disaster caused the complete failure of the expedition; the force of four thousand men, which was proceeding overland, returned home, as they could accomplish nothing without the coöperation of the fleet. For ten years the colonies of New England suffered all the miseries of this harassing warfare. The danger was so urgent that they were compelled to keep one-half the whole body of the militia, amounting to six thousand men, on duty.

The peace of Utrecht, which was concluded in 1713, between France and England, gave the colonists rest from war, but left them heavily burdened with a public debt. To supply the want of money to pay the soldiers, bills of credit were issued. These bills very greatly depreciated in value a result which it was impossible to prevent—and great financial embarrassment and distress followed.

On the 24th of February, 1717, there was the greatest snow storm ever known in New England. Cotton Mather said that in some places the snow was sixteen feet deep, "covering many cottages over the tops of their chimneys." Many people as well as cattle perished in it.

On the 11th of December, 1719, the aurora borealis, or northern lights, as it is called, was observed for the first

---

13. What was done in 1711? What became of the fleet? What became of the land-force? What is said of the state of things for ten years? When was the peace of Utrecht made? What was done to supply the want of money? What was the result? What is said of the snow storm, northern lights, and earthquake?

time by the colonists after the settlement of the country. It caused great wonder and excited the apprehension of the superstitious.

On the 29th of October, 1727, there was a noted earthquake, which extended throughout New England, causing alarm, but doing no serious injury.

14. Heretofore no mention has been made of the trials and executions for witchcraft in New England, one of the darkest and most melancholy episodes in the history of that country. The first trials occurred in 1645, when four persons were put to death for that crime in Massachusetts. The following account of this sad delusion is given by a writer of New England:*

"For more than twenty years after the executions for witchcraft in 1645, we hear but little of similar prosecutions. But in the year 1688 a woman was executed for witchcraft in Boston, after an investigation conducted with a degree of solemnity that made a deep impression on the minds of the people. Suspicions having been thus violently roused, the charges of witchcraft began gradually to multiply, till at length there commenced at Salem that dreadful tragedy which rendered New England for many months a scene of bloodshed, terror, and madness, and at one time seemed to threaten the subversion of civil society.

15. "In the year 1692 the frenzy of the colonists reached the highest pitch of extravagance. Suspicions and accusations of witchcraft became general among them; and on this fanciful charge many persons were put to death. This pestilential visitation first showed itself in the town of Salem. A fanatic, who was a minister of a church there, had two daughters subject to convulsions. He fancied they were bewitched, and fixed his suspicions on an Indian

---

14. When were the first trials for witchcraft in Massachusetts ? When did the great excitement break out ?

15. What is said of the state of things in 1692 ? Where did the frenzy against it first show itself? Were children put to death for it ? What is said of the termination of the frenzy ?

---

* Greenville Miller.

girl who lived in the house as the accomplice and tool of Satan in the matter. By harsh treatment he made the poor savage acknowledge herself a witch. Among a people like the New Englanders, this was throwing a firebrand into a powder-magazine; and the explosion was dreadful.

"Every woman subject to hysterical affections instantly believed herself bewitched; and was seldom at a loss to discover the guilty cause of her malady. Persons accused of the imaginary crime of witchcraft were imprisoned, condemned, hanged, and their bodies left exposed to wild beasts and birds of prey. Counsellors who refused to plead against these devoted victims, and judges who were not forward in condemning them, were doomed to share their fate as accomplices in their guilt.

"Children of ten years of age were put to death; young women were stripped naked, and the marks of witchcraft sought for on their bodies with unblushing curiosity. Scorbutical or other spots on the bodies of old men were reckoned clear proofs of a heinous commerce with the infernal powers. Dreams, apparitions, prodigies of every kind, increased the general consternation and horror. The prisons were filled, the gibbets left standing, and the citizens were appalled. Under this frightful delirium the miserable colonists seemed doomed to destruction by each other's hands. The more prudent withdrew from a country polluted by the blood of its inhabitants, and the ruin of the colony seemed inevitable, when, ceasing to receive countenance from those in authority, this awful frenzy passed away almost as suddenly as it had arisen, leaving to future ages a fearful warning against such popular insanity."

16. From the peace of Utrecht, in 1713, until the breaking out of war between Great Britain and France, in 1744, during the reign of George II., the colonies of New England

---

16. What is said of the state of things in New England from the peace of Utrecht, 1713, to the breaking out of the war between Great Britain and France in 1744?

enjoyed almost uninterrupted peace. In Massachusetts, after the appointment of Mr. Burnet as Governor, in 1728, disputes were kept up, with little intermission, through his administration into the succeeding one, between the Governor and the Legislature, in regard to his salary and other financial matters. The Assembly ultimately triumphed.

In 1744 war again broke out between the allied powers of France and Holland, and Great Britain. Soon after the commencement of hostilities the French made a descent upon Nova Scotia, which had remained in possession of Great Britain ever since its capture, in 1710. The governor of Cape Breton took possession of Canseau, in Nova Scotia, made its garrison and inhabitants prisoners of war, and then made an attack upon Annapolis, but was defeated. These operations roused the New England colonies to make an effort to subjugate all the French possessions north of them. And finding that the strong fortress of Louisbourg, on the island of Cape Breton, was used as a hiding-place for privateers, by whose operations they were much annoyed, they determined to capture it.

17. Having obtained the sanction of the British government, and the promise of the coöperation of Commodore Warren with a large fleet, they began active preparations to carry out the design. Funds were raised by voluntary subscriptions and issuing bills of credit; troops were raised from the different New England colonies and equipped, and by the last of April, 1745, an army of more than four thousand men, commanded by Colonel Pepperell, was before Louisbourg. The French were surprised at the sudden appearance of the British fleet and the landing of the army, but they determined to defend the place.

The colonists had a supply of provisions for two months; and having easily captured all the approaches to the town, they regularly began the siege. Two weeks were occupied

---

17. What attempt was made to take Louisbourg? Was it successful? How long did the siege last? When did the surrender take place, and in what year? Who planned it, and who executed it? What honor did they receive?

in dragging their cannon from the landing-place, two miles through a deep morass, to their encampment, where the guns could be of use. Meantime, the fleet off the harbor captured a French man-of-war having on board a reinforcement of more than five hundred men. Discouraged by this loss, and despairing of receiving any assistance and supplies, the French commandant, after a siege of seven weeks, surrendered. The surrender took place on the 17th of June. Colonel Pepperell, who commanded the expedition, and Shirley, Governor of Massachusetts, who planned it, were both rewarded with the honor of knighthood for its success.

18. Mortified at their loss, the French made extraordinary efforts to retrieve it, and to inflict chastisement on New England. A fleet was equipped, consisting of forty vessels-of-war and fifty-six transports, having on board a force of near four thousand men, under the command of the Duke D'Anville. This fleet sailed from France in the spring of 1746. The news of its approach spread terror throughout New England, but a succession of disasters deprived it of power to harm. A violent storm scattered it, and only a few vessels arrived at Halifax. These were in no condition to make a descent on New England. They sailed, however, for the purpose of attacking Annapolis, but were again scattered by a storm, and made the best of their way back to France.

A treaty of peace between the three powers was signed at Aix la Chapelle, in October, 1748. By this treaty Cape Breton was restored to the French, a general restitution of places captured during the war being made by all the belligerent powers. But the question of boundary between

---

18. What did France do in consequence ? When did her great fleet sail ? What was its number ? What effect had it upon New England ? What became of the fleet ? When and where was peace made ? What became of Cape Breton by the treaty ? Was any definite plan settled in this treaty about the boundary between the jurisdiction of France and Great Britain in America ? What is said of the boundary between New England and Canada ? between Nova Scotia and the French possessions ? What about the great lakes and about New Orleans ?

the possessions of France and Great Britain in America was left unsettled, and it was rapidly becoming one of grave importance. In many cases the claims of the two countries were conflicting. There was no well-defined boundary-line between Canada and New England; none between Nova Scotia and the French possessions; and the extent of Louisiana, which France had also acquired, was altogether indefinite. About this time, also, the French began to entertain the grand scheme of building a chain of forts along the great lakes and down the Mississippi to their colony of New Orleans, which was now in a flourishing condition.

CHAPTER XX.

SOUTH CAROLINA, RESUMED.

1709—1754.

The Yamassee War.

1. On the southwestern border of South Carolina, next to the Savannah river, there was a strong and warlike tribe of Indians, known as the Yamassees. These were, perhaps, the most warlike of all the southern tribes. Becoming angry with the whites, and jealous of their increasing power, they determined, if it were possible, to destroy them entirely. To effect this object they united in a great league all the tribes of Indians from Cape Fear, in North Carolina, to Florida.

2. They began the war by an attack upon Pocotaligo about daybreak on the morning of the 15th of April, 1715. They here killed about ninety persons. The inhabitants of Port Royal were warned in time, and made their escape to Charleston by means of a vessel which was then lying in the harbor. A few families in the country, who had not

---

CHAPTER XX.—**1**. Describe the Yamassees—their situation. What did they determine ?
2. How did they begin the war ? Where else also did they wage it ? What orders were given by the Governor ?

time to embark, were either killed or carried into captivity. The war was also waged in the country towards North Carolina, and the danger became so great that serious fears were entertained for the safety of Charleston itself. The Governor ordered out every man under arms, except the slaves, and even some of the more trusty of them were armed.

3. At the head of two hundred and forty men, Craven marched directly against the enemy, and sent a courier to Colonel Mackey, with orders to raise, at once, what forces he could, and then to proceed by water to meet him at Yamassee town. The Governor rested at night on the Combahee River, within sixteen miles of the enemy, and was attacked early next morning by about five hundred Yamassees. After a considerable fight, he routed the Indians and drove them back with great loss, while he had but one man killed and several wounded. Being without guides, and seeing great numbers of the enemy on the opposite side of the river, he returned to Charleston.

4. Col. Mackey, in the execution of the duty assigned him, surprised and drove the Indians from their town, in which were stored large quantities of provisions and plunder. He here learned that two hundred of the enemy had posted themselves in another fort, and he sent one hundred and forty men to attack them. At this time a young man named Palmer, who, at the head of sixteen men, had been on a scout, came to Mackey's assistance, and at once scaled the walls, but was driven back. He returned to the charge, and was successful. He drove the enemy out, and as they fled they were shot down in numbers by Mackey's men.

5. But though the Indians were checked here, they gained some advantages on the northern border of the colony. A party entered the plantation of Mr. John Herne, near the Santee, and treacherously killed him after being kindly en-

---

3. With how many men did the Governor march against the Indians? What was the result of the fight?
4. What was done by Colonel Mackey? What is said of Palmer?
5. What advantage was gained by the Indians? What is said of Captain Barker? his fate?

tertained. Captain Thomas Barker immediately collected a body of ninety men and advanced to meet them. Trusting to an Indian guide, he was led into an ambuscade in a great thicket of bushes, where the enemy lay concealed on the ground. Capt. Barker and several of his men were instantly killed, and the rest fled in disorder.

6. The panic now became so great that nearly all the inhabitants of the parish were fleeing towards Charleston. On one plantation, however, seventy white men, with forty negroes, had thrown up a breastwork, resolving to defend themselves to the last extremity. For some time they were successful, but after a while they became discouraged, and, while listening to proposals of peace, they suffered themselves to be surprised. Very few escaped with their lives. The Indians were shortly afterwards met, defeated, and driven back by the Goose Creek militia, commanded by Captain Chicken, who proved himself a true gamecock on that occasion. The province was thus made secure on the north.

7. In the meantime the whole country became deserted to within twenty miles of Charleston. Many began to fear the destruction of the colony. The enemy numbered from eight to ten thousand warriors, while the Carolina muster-roll could show but about twelve hundred men fit to bear arms. Yet Craven determined to send forces into the wilderness to meet the enemy upon their own ground. In his summons of the Assembly he said: "Expedition is the life of action; bring the women and children into our town, and all provisions from all exposed plantations. Virginia and New England must be solicited for aid." Francis Holmes was sent as agent to New England to purchase arms. Lieutenant-General James Moore, and Colonels John

---

6. What is said of the panic ? What took place on Goose Creek ?
7. What was the number of Indian warriors ? the Carolina muster-roll ? What language did Craven use in his summons ? Who were appointed to command the troops ?

Barnwell and Alexander Mackey, were chosen to lead the troops.

8. The war was pushed so vigorously that the Yamassees were soon driven from the country to the region beyond the Savannah River. They took up their residence in Florida, from which place they continued for some time, in small parties, to infest the borders of Carolina. But the province was now well defended by a number of forts, garrisoned by six hundred Carolinians, one hundred Virginians, four hundred negroes, and a hundred friendly Indians. When a new Assembly met, in February, 1716, the war was almost entirely over, and the chief object of solicitude then was to secure a permanent peace with all the neighboring tribes.

9. After this signal failure to destroy the colony, the Indians became so well convinced of the invincibility of the Carolinians, that they never again combined against them or made any attempt to penetrate in hostile bands to the neighborhood of the capital. Governor Craven's family affairs requiring his presence in England, by permission of the Proprietors he left the colony on the 25th of April, 1716, leaving Colonel Robert Daniel deputy Governor. But he would not and did not leave the province until after the conclusion of the war, and all apprehension of danger had ceased.

10. In 1717 Robert Johnson, son of Sir Nathaniel Johnson, was appointed Governor. He was the last Governor under the authority of the Proprietors. With few intervals of calm the colony had been a scene of strife and bickering, between the people and Proprietors, from its first planting, until in 1719 the explosion took place which destroyed the Proprietary government. The members of the convention which overthrew the previous government proclaimed

---
8. What was the result of the war?
9. What is said of Governor Craven?
10. Who succeeded Craven as Governor? What took place in 1719? Who was proclaimed Governor by the convention? Who was appointed by the King? How was he received by the people?

James Moore, Governor; but early in the year 1721 General Francis Nicholson arrived at Charleston with a royal commission as Governor. He was received with every demonstration of joy by the people, and by his wise measures the peace of the colony was preserved; all parties seemed to unite in the desire to promote the general welfare and prosperity. In 1729 the Lords Proprietors under the Carolina charter sold their rights to Parliament, and for the next forty years the peace of the colony was preserved, not only at home, but also with the neighboring tribes of Indians.

CHAPTER XXI.

SETTLEMENT OF GEORGIA.

1732—1754.

Savannah—Darien—Frederica—Augusta—Ebenczer—Sazlburgers—Spanish War.

1. THE colony of Georgia was founded by James Edward Oglethorpe. A charter for this purpose was obtained by him on the 9th of June, 1732, from George II. of England. The country embraced in its limits was named Georgia, in honor of the King who granted the charter; and it extended from the Savannah River westward to the British boundary in that direction, which was the Mississippi River. The same country had been embraced in the Carolina charter, and in 1717 the Palatine and Lords Proprietors of South Carolina had granted to Sir Robert Montgomery that portion of it which lies between the rivers "Savannah and Altamaha," under the title of "Margravate of Azilia;" but as no settlements had been made under either of these grants, west of the Savannah River, the whole country embraced within the chartered

---

CHAPTER XXI.—**1.** Who was the founder of the colony of Georgia? In what year was the charter granted? What was the object of the colony?

SETTLEMENT OF GEORGIA.

limits of Georgia was now therefore granted to Oglethorpe. The object of Oglethorpe, who was a member of Parliament, and who was distinguished alike for benevolence, patriotism, and statesmanship, was not only to provide a home and means of subsistence for the poor inhabitants of Great Britain, but to furnish a refuge for the distressed Salzburgers and other Protestants on the continent of Europe. The entire management and government of the settlers was conferred for a period of twenty-one years upon Oglethorpe, and a board of trustees consisting of twenty-one noblemen and gentlemen of England, at the head of which stood Lord Percival.

COAT OF ARMS OF GEORGIA.

2. In November, 1732, one hundred and sixteen persons embarked at Gravesend under the direction of the founder of the new colony, who arrived early in the next year at Charleston, where they were cordially received by Governor Craven, of that State, and the inhabitants generally. From Charleston they proceeded to Beaufort, and while the colonists were landing at Beaufort, Oglethorpe ascended the boundary river of Georgia, and chose for the site of his city the bluff where Savannah now stands. At a distance of half a mile dwelt the Yamacraws, a branch of the Muskogees, who, with Tomo-chichi, their chief, immediately sought an alliance with him. The chief presented him a buffalo-robe, painted on the inside

OGLETHORPE.

---

2. Who was the founder of this colony? Where did he first settle? In what year? Describe the interview with Tomo-chichi.

with the head and feathers of an eagle, saying: "The feathers of the eagle are soft and signify love; the buffalo-skin is warm, and is the emblem of protection. Therefore love and protect our little families."

3. Oglethorpe's fame soon penetrated the wilderness, and in a short time treaties were made with the lower Muskogees, the Creeks, and even with the Cherokees of the mountains and the Choctaws on the borders of the Gulf of Mexico. The Muskogees begged him to have pity on the broken and feeble remnant of the Yamassees. The red-men all had great confidence in him, for he always acted in good faith, and had a most noble mien and sweet disposition.

4. The Salzburgers were *descended* from the Vallenses, a name derived from the Alpine valleys of Piedmont; but the Salzburgers themselves are so called from Salzburg, the broad valley of the Salza, which lies between the Norric and Rhetian Alps. All the inhabitants of this valley were denominated Salzburgers. Many of them were Protestants (Lutherans)—what proportion it is impossible to say; but it must have been considerable, if we may judge from the large numbers that were compelled to seek safety in other countries.

5. A persecution was begun under Leopold, Duke of Austria, in 1729, and continued with great violence until 1732. The victims experienced every species of outrage which fanaticism could suggest. They were whipped, imprisoned, murdered, banished, and their property was confiscated. All natural ties were disregarded. Children were torn from their parents. Husbands and wives were banished far from each other. Over thirty thousand of these suffering people were exiled and compelled to seek safety in other countries.

6. In December, 1732, the Trustees of Georgia, warranted

---

3. With what tribes did Oglethorpe make treaties?
4. From whom were the Salzburgers descended? Of what religion?
5. What caused the Salzburgers to leave their country?
6. How many families came over? When did they arrive at Savannah?

by a special fund raised for that purpose, invited fifty families of these Salzburgers to remove to the colony. We find that forty-two men, some with families, numbering in all seventy-eight persons, availed themselves of the offer. They arrived at Charleston, S. C., early in March, 1734. They left that city on the 9th, and on the 11th entered the Savannah River. On the 12th they arrived at Savannah, where they were very cordially received. Oglethorpe himself went down to the river, met them, and bade them welcome to their new homes.

7. Having all safely disembarked, the next object of interest was to select a location for settlement. Gen. Oglethorpe informed Baron Von Reck, who conducted the expedition, that his people might make their own selection. They desired to be removed some distance from the sea, amongst hills and dales, and where the country was supplied with springs of fresh water. Accordingly, Oglethorpe, in company with Paul Jenys, Esq., Speaker of the South Carolina House of Assembly; Baron Von Reck, Mr. Gronau, Dr. Twiffler, their physician, and one of the Lutheran elders, with some Indians made a tour of observation. They penetrated nearly thirty miles into the interior, and chose a place on "the banks of a river of clear water, the sides high; the country of the neighborhood hilly; the valleys of rich cane-land, intermixed with little brooks and springs of water."

8. The Salzburgers who were in the company were highly delighted with the situation and appearance of the country. And feeling deeply moved with pious gratitude to God for His great goodness in conducting them to such a lovely land of safety, after singing a psalm, they set up a stone which they found upon the spot, and named the place "Ebenezer," "the stone of help;" for they could say with truth, "Hitherto the Lord hath helped us." In this manner was laid the foundation of the settlement of the Salzburgers.

---

7. At what place did they fix their settlement? Can you describe the country?
8. What name did they give their settlement? Why?

9. This location was in a region of the country afterwards known as St. Matthew's Parish; subsequently erected into a county and called Effingham, in honor of Lord Effingham, who, in the British Parliament, some years afterwards, defended the resistance of the colonies to the mother-country, and resigned his commission in the army rather than fight for what he believed to be an unjust cause. The county is still called Effingham.

Oglethorpe was exceedingly judicious in the location of his settlements, with a view to the protection of the colonists from attack, either from the Indians or the Spaniards. In 1735 a company of Scotch Highlanders was settled at Darien, and in 1738 a company of immigrants was located at Frederica, on St. Simon's Island. A settlement was also made at Augusta.

10. The civil and military affairs of the entire colony of Georgia, including the settlements of Ebenezer, Savannah, Darien, Frederica, and Augusta, were under the control of the Trustees, with Oglethorpe the chief executive officer; but the immediate superintendence of the settlement at Ebenezer was assigned to the Rev. John Martin Bolzius and his colleague, Mr. Gronau, by whom the affairs of the settlement were most judiciously managed.

11. The Trustees, in their regulations for the government of Georgia, forbade the importation of rum and the introduction of negro-slaves. Georgia was the only colony which prohibited the introduction of negroes. All the others, from the time that Virginia received the first cargo, sooner or later had patronized the African slave-trade. The enforcement of the prohibition against rum was attended with serious difficulty in all parts of the colony except at Ebenezer. Strictly temperate themselves, they required not the stimulus

---

9. In what county is Ebenezer? Why was the county so called? In what year was Darien settled? By whom? In what year was Frederica settled?
10. How was Georgia governed?
11. What regulations of the Trustees caused difficulty?

of ardent spirits, and they saw that its habitual excessive use was injurious to piety and good morals.

12. On the 20th of October, 1735, the *Symond* and *London Merchant*, with two hundred and twenty-seven emigrants for the colony of Georgia, some from England, about eighty Salzburgers, and twenty-seven Moravians, sailed from Gravesend. Among the passengers were John and Charles Wesley, who were coming over to preach the gospel to the Indians, and to try to improve the moral and religious condition of the colony. To his intercourse with these Moravians and Salzburgers, and to his observation of their great calmness and resignation in a time of severe trial, John Wesley attributes his own conversion.

13. On his return to England, two years after his first visit to Georgia, Mr. Wesley writes thus in his journal: "It is now two years and nearly four months since I went to America to teach the Georgia Indians the nature of Christianity; but what have I learned of myself in the meantime? Why (what of all I least expected), that I, who went to America to convert others, was never myself converted to God,"—words that should be most deeply and solemnly pondered by all.

14. In a few years after the establishment of the settlement of Salzburgers, their produce of raw silk amounted to ten thousand pounds a year. Indigo also became a staple article of production. Orphan-schools were established immediately after their arrival. Indeed, in their fundamental rules and regulations they made it obligatory upon all members of the congregation to contribute to this end according to their ability.

15. In 1738, Rev. George Whitefield, the most eloquent

---

12. In what year did John and Charles Wesley visit Georgia? What does John Wesley attribute to this visit?
13. What did he write in his journal after his return to England?
14. What is said of the silk culture of the Salzburgers? orphan-schools? What did they make obligatory?
15. In what year did Mr. Whitefield visit Georgia? What is said of his views of African slavery?

preacher of his day, came to Georgia. He visited the settlement at Ebenezer, and was so deeply impressed, and was so much gratified with the good the orphan-school was doing in training and educating the homeless and destitute, that he determined to found a similar one By his fervent zeal he was able to obtain sufficient funds in England and America. His institution was established a few miles from Savannah. It flourished under his fostering care during his life, and, with some modifications in its organization, still exists as a monument to his memory. Mr. Whitefield at first was opposed to the introduction of negro-slaves, but afterwards changed his mind and spoke in its favor, for which he was sharply reproved by Mr. Bolzius. But he justified himself by saying that God had some wise ends to accomplish in reference to African slavery; and that he had no doubt it would terminate to the advantage of the Africans. The problem is not yet fully solved.

16. Spain claimed the territory of Georgia as her own, and looked upon its colonization by the English as an intrusion upon her rights. She therefore made a demand for its surrender, which being refused, she prepared to expel the intruders. But there were other sources of irritation. Trade was not free, and the Spanish laws regulating it were frequently violated by the English merchants on the coasts of Florida, and when caught and punished they were regarded by their countrymen as martyrs to free trade rather than as law-breakers. Runaway negro-slaves from South Carolina were also welcomed by the Spanish authorities in Florida, and lands were given to them in that province.

17. Seeing that war was inevitable, Oglethorpe went to England in 1737 to prepare for the contest. In that country he raised and disciplined a regiment of six hundred men, and in less than a year returned prepared for defence,

---

16. What nation claimed Georgia ? What other causes of dispute existed ?
17. What did General Oglethorpe do ? In what year was war declared ? What expedition was undertaken in 1740 ?

having been appointed commander-in-chief of all the militia forces in Georgia and South Carolina. From this time he was known as General Oglethorpe. War was at length declared by England against Spain in 1739, and Oglethorpe was ordered to invade Florida. He immediately hastened to Charleston; supplies were voted, and at as early a day as possible in 1740, at the head of two thousand men, some of them Carolinians and some friendly Indians, he set out on the expedition against St. Augustine. Up to this time about twenty-five hundred immigrants had settled in Georgia.

18. General Oglethorpe found St. Augustine much more strongly fortified, and the garrison much more numerous, than he had expected. After a few weeks' siege his Indian allies began to desert; his troops became enfeebled by sickness; and he was compelled to raise the siege and retire.

19. In 1742 this invasion was retaliated by a formidable land and naval force of about three thousand men. In this difficulty Oglethorpe, receiving no assistance from South Carolina, was obliged to rely upon his own resources. The Spanish commander, instead of sailing direct to Savannah, proceeded to the mouth of the Altamaha. Oglethorpe, having but seven or eight hundred men, was obliged to retreat from Cumberland Island to St. Simon's, on which was the town of Frederica, the object of attack. After the landing of the enemy, Oglethorpe intended, small as was his force, to attack them by surprise at night. For this purpose he had approached to within about two miles of their camp, when a French soldier of his party fired his musket and ran into the enemy's lines. His situation was now very critical, for he knew that the deserter would make known his weakness.

20. Returning to Frederica, he had recourse to the fol-

---

18. With what result?
19. What took place in 1742? After the Spaniards landed, what did Oglethorpe intend? What prevented?
20. What stratagem did he resort to? What was the result of the stratagem?

lowing expedient: he wrote to the deserter, desiring him to urge the Spaniards to an immediate attack, and to inform them of the defenceless state of Frederica. But if he could not bring on an attack, he urged him to persuade them to remain where they were three days longer, as within that time he expected six British ships of war with two thousand troops from Carolina. This letter he intrusted to a Spanish prisoner, under promise to deliver it to the deserter, but he gave it, as was intended, to the Spanish commander-in-chief, who put the deserter in irons. This letter perplexed the Spaniards very much, and while deliberating what course to pursue, three ships with troops on board, which the governor of South Carolina had sent to Oglethorpe's assistance, did actually appear in sight. Believing these to be the vessels mentioned in the letter, and firmly convinced that the letter was not a stratagem, the Spaniards, in a moment of consternation, burned their fort and fled, leaving their cannon and military stores.

21. By this stratagem a great victory was gained without bloodshed, and Oglethorpe acquired the reputation of a skillful general. Indeed, he was not without considerable military experience. He had served in a European campaign on the staff of Prince Eugene.

In 1743 he returned to England, and never revisited his colony again. Thirty-two years afterwards, Frost, in his History of the United States, says: "He was offered the command of the British army in America," and "that he professed his readiness to accept the appointment if the ministers would authorize him to assure the colonies that justice would be done them; but the command was given to Sir William Howe." He died in August, 1785, at the age of ninety-seven, the oldest general in the British army, and two years after he had witnessed the establishment of his colony as a sovereign and independent State, as we shall see.

---

21. In what year did Oglethorpe return to England? When did he die? At what age? What further is said of him?

22. From the first settlement of Georgia until the year 1741, the government was entirely and solely administered by General Oglethorpe; but in 1741, by order of the Trustees, the colony was divided into two counties, one called Savannah, the other Frederica, each having a president and four assistants. This arrangement continued only two years, when the Trustees ordered that both counties should be united under one executive, and that the president and assistants of the county of Savannah should have the government of the whole province. In 1750 they ordered a Colonial Assembly to be called, consisting of sixteen members, proportioned according to the population of the different districts. About this time also the Trustees yielded to the policy of the mother-country, as well as the wishes of the colonists, in allowing the introduction of negro-slaves.

In 1752, one year before the expiration of their charter, the Trustees surrendered their rights under it to the Crown; and after that, the government of the colony passed to the " Board of Trade and Plantations," composed of the Lords Commissioners appointed to the superintendence of colonial affairs, of which the Earl of Halifax was then at the head.

In the same year a settlement was made at Midway, which afterwards became greatly distinguished.

On the 6th of August, 1754, Captain John Reynolds, of the Royal Navy, was appointed Governor of Georgia, under letters patent from the Crown. By virtue of the authority therein contained, the government of the colony devolved upon a Legislature or General Assembly of the colonists, in conjunction with the Governor and his council, and another body known as councillors. These councillors, or upper house, were colonists appointed by the King, while the lower house, or commons of the Assembly, were colonists chosen by the people of the respective settlements.

---

22. How was the government administered for the first ten years ? What change then took place ? When did the Trustees surrender their rights ? How was the colony then governed ? Who was the first governor ?

CHAPTER XXII.

HISTORIC FACTS PRELIMINARY TO THE FRENCH AND INDIAN WAR OF 1754.

Spanish Discoveries and French Settlements on the Mississippi and the Lakes—De Soto—Joliet, Marquette, and La Salle.

1. FERDINAND DE SOTO, Governor of Cuba, was the first European who ever visited the valley of the Mississippi, and crossed that majestic current of waters. He sailed from Havana in May, 1539, and landed in Florida at the Bay of Spiritu Santo in June following. The first season's wanderings, from June to October, brought him to the country of the Appalachians, not far from the head of Appalachee Bay. The number of his followers is not definitely stated; Bancroft says, " they were a numerous body of horsemen, besides infantry, completely armed; a force exceeding in numbers and equipments the famous expeditions against the empires of Mexico and Peru."

FERDINAND DE SOTO.

Early in the spring of the following year this band of adventurers renewed their march, passing northward, lured by an Indian guide, towards the gold regions of North Carolina. They passed the waters of the Altamaha, through middle Georgia, and at length, in April, reached the head-waters of the Ogeechee; their course being still north, it seems, until they reached the head-waters of the

---

CHAPTER XXII.—**1**. What is said of De Soto? What of the course of his marches? What of the battle of Mobile?

Savannah and the Chattahoochee; thence southwest and afterwards southward through Alabama, until, October 18, they reached a town on the Alabama River called Mabilla, or Mobile. Here a battle was fought with the natives, in which the Indian village was destroyed, with many hundred killed. The Spaniards lost eighteen killed, and all their baggage, which was burned in the town.

Thence they passed northward and northwest, until, on the 25th of April, 1541, we find them at the Mississippi River, to which they were guided by the natives. They crossed in May, most probably at the lower Chickasaw Bluff, not far from the thirty-fifth degree of north latitude. About the middle or last of July they reached the northernmost point of their journeyings in the neighborhood of the Mississippi, at Pacaha, a place which cannot now be identified. From this point they journeyed north and northwest, more deeply still into the continent, until they reached the highlands of White River, more than two hundred miles from the Mississippi.

2. In all their wanderings they had found no gold, and the prospect of finding this, the great object of their expedition, seeming more remote than when they began their wanderings, they again turned south. In the region west of the Mississippi, on the Washita River, they found an agricultural people with fixed places of abode, who lived more upon the produce of the soil than of the chase. They were gentle and harmless in their natures, peaceable in their dispositions, and presented a higher type of civilization than their neighbors. The Spaniards treated them with great cruelty.

In March, 1542, the adventurers determined to descend the Washita to its mouth, in hopes of getting tidings of the sea. After innumerable difficulties they reached the Mississippi at the mouth of the Red River, about the 17th

---

2. What further is said of the marches of De Soto?

of April. At this place they were told by the natives that the lower banks of the Mississippi were an uninhabited waste. They would not believe the tale, and De Soto sent one of his officers with eight men down the river to explore the country. In eight days they were able to advance only thirty miles. De Soto's mind became filled with gloomy apprehensions. His men and horses were dying, and the natives were becoming dangerous.

3. Bancroft thus describes the closing scenes in De Soto's life, and his death: "He attempted to overawe a tribe of Indians near Natchez, by claiming a supernatural birth, and demanding obedience and tribute. 'You are a child of the sun,' replied the undaunted chief; 'dry up the river and I will believe you. Do you desire to see me? Visit the town where I dwell. If you come in peace I will receive you with special good-will; if in war, I will not shrink one foot back.'

"But De Soto was no longer able to abate the confidence or punish the temerity of the natives. His stubborn pride was changed by long disappointments into a wasting melancholy, and his health sunk rapidly and entirely under a conflict of emotions. A malignant fever ensued, during which he had little comfort, and was neither visited nor attended as the last hours of life demand. Believing his death near at hand, he held the last solemn interview with his faithful followers, and, yielding to the wishes of his companions, who obeyed him to the end, he named a successor.

"On the next day (May 21st, 1542) he died. Thus perished Ferdinand De Soto, the Governor of Cuba, the successful associate of Pizarro. His miserable end was the more observed from the greatness of his former prosperity. His soldiers pronounced his eulogy by grieving for his loss; the priests chanted over his body the first requiems that

---

3. What does Bancroft say of the closing scenes of De Soto's life?

were ever heard on the waters of the Mississippi. To conceal his death his body was wrapped in a mantle, and in the stillness of midnight was sunk in the middle of the stream. The discoverer of the Mississippi slept beneath its waters. He had crossed a large part of the continent in search of gold, and found nothing so remarkable as his burial-place."

4. In the year 1670 two Catholic priests, Joliet and James Marquette, natives of France, set out from the French settlements on the great lakes, in search of that wonderful river concerning which so many reports and rumors had reached them. Their company consisted of five boatmen and some Indians as guides. They passed up the Fox River, which empties into Lake Michigan, in two birch-bark canoes, and carrying them across overland to the Wisconsin, they floated down that stream until they reached the Mississippi. They passed down the Mississippi to the mouth of the Arkansas. Here they met with Indians who showed them tools of European manufacture, and they deemed it most prudent to return. On their return, when they reached the mouth of the Illinois, supposing that it would lead them to the lakes, they passed up it to its head-waters and across to Lake Michigan. Joliet immediately set out to carry the news of the discovery to Quebec, but Marquette chose to remain as a missionary among the Indians. Not long afterwards he was found dead, kneeling at the foot of a cross which he had erected in the wilderness.

5. In 1679 M. de la Salle, a French officer, in company with the celebrated Father Hennepin, a Catholic priest, and about thirty-five men, explored the shores of several of the northern lakes, and built a fort and wintered near the mouth of the Maumee River. In the spring they crossed the wilderness to the Illinois and descended it in their canoes. In their passage down the river they one day

---

4. What is said of the French priests Joliet and Marquette?
5. What is said of La Salle?

suddenly found themselves surrounded by a large body of Indian warriors, who offered battle. They, however, soon pacified them. At this place, where Peoria now stands, the adventurers built a fort and remained until the next spring, when they again set sail down the river. Arriving at the mouth of the Illinois, they turned their course up the Mississippi, which river they traversed almost to its source. On the 8th of November they set out overland for the French settlements.

6. In 1681 La Salle passed down the Illinois River the second time. He also descended the Mississippi to its mouth, which he reached on the 9th of April, 1682. He took possession of the country in the name of Louis XIV., King of France, and in his honor named it Louisiana. On the 11th he set out on his return, and arrived at Michilimackinack in September. Soon afterwards he sailed for France to make a report of his discoveries, and to solicit assistance in planting a colony at the mouth of the Mississippi. The enterprise was looked upon with favor, and a fleet of four vessels, one of them armed, was fitted out for his use. Near three hundred persons,—soldiers, volunteers, mechanics, and priests, accompanied him. In due time they entered the Gulf of Mexico, but missed the mouth of the Mississippi. La Salle soon discovered his error, but the commander of the vessels would not listen to him, and sailing due west landed on the shore of Texas.

Here they built a fort, but many of the men, becoming discouraged, when the vessels sailed for France returned in them. La Salle sought for the mouth of the Mississippi for some time, but in vain. At length he set out with sixteen companions, determined to traverse the whole breadth of the country to Canada. After travelling for two months across the prairies of Texas west of the Mississippi, he was murdered by one of his companions. The survivors passed

---

6. What did he do in 1681 and afterwards?

down a tributary of the Mississippi to its mouth. The colony planted on the shores of Texas perished, and left no trace.

7. In 1700 D'Iberville, with sixty colonists, ascended the Mississippi, the mouth of which he had discovered the previous year, about four hundred miles, and on a high bluff built a fort which he called Rosalie. This was the beginning of the town of Natchez. About the same time Mobile was settled by the French. In the year 1718 Bienville D'Iberville, brother to the one just mentioned, laid the foundation of New Orleans in a thick cane-brake, where he built a few log huts. The French found brave and determined enemies in the Chickasaws, who occupied the region around Natchez, north to the Ohio and east to the country of the Cherokees. This tribe successfully defended their country against the invaders.

In the year 1722 a settlement of industrious Germans was formed about twenty miles above New Orleans. By these colonists rice, tobacco, and indigo, and also the fig and orange, were cultivated. The Canadian settlers on the Illinois raised wheat and sent flour to the settlers below. Trading-houses were established south of Lake Erie, down the Alleghany to the Ohio, and down the Ohio to the Mississippi. It can easily be seen that the progress of the French in that quarter created the liveliest apprehensions in the minds of the English colonists east of the Alleghanies. The latter had always been accustomed to regard their possessions as extending west to the Pacific. And now to be hemmed in in this way, and confined to the slope east of the Alleghanies, was a thought they could not bear. In this state of things it seemed that the controversy in regard to the possession of the fairest portion of the North American continent could only be settled by the arbitrament of war.

---

7. When were Natchez and Mobile settled by Europeans, and by whom ? When was New Orleans settled, and by whom ? What other people made a settlement on the Mississippi River above New Orleans, in 1722 ? What did they claim ?

CHAPTER XXIII.

THE FRENCH AND INDIAN WAR OF 1754.

1754—1763.

1. The brief review of the early exploration and occupation of the Mississippi Valley, given in the last chapter, was necessary, as it was from the conflicting claims of France and England to this territory that arose what is usually called the French and Indian War of 1754, in which all the British colonies we have sketched were involved. To vindicate their claims, and to confine the English to the country east of the Alleghany Mountains, the French began the erection of a chain of forts from Nova Scotia along the lakes and down the Mississippi to the Gulf of Mexico.

2. A grant of land had been made in 1749 by the British government, to a company called the Ohio Company; and while the agents of this company were engaged in making a survey of these lands they were seized as intruders upon the territory of the French by a party of French and Indians, and carried to the French fort at Presque Isle. The Indians friendly to the English resented this treatment of their allies, and seized several French traders and sent them to Pennsylvania. Soon afterwards the French, in pursuance of their grand design, began the erection of forts south of Lake Erie, which caused serious complaints from the Ohio Company.

3. As this territory was within the original charter limits of Virginia, Governor Dinwiddie remonstrated with the French commander against these proceedings, and in-

---

CHAPTER XXIII.—**1.** What is said of the claims of the French and English to the Mississippi Valley? What was done by the French to vindicate their claims?
2. What grant had been made in 1749? What was done to the surveyors?
3. What was done by Governor Dinwiddie? Who carried his letter? What day did Washington leave Williamsburg? What day did he reach the French fort?

sisted that he should withdraw his troops. He sent a letter to the French commandant by George Washington, with the title of major, who was then only in his twenty-second year. Washington left Williamsburg, Virginia, on the last day of October, 1753, and on the 4th of December following he reached a French fort at the mouth of French Creek, which empties into the Alleghany River, sixty-five miles north of Pittsburgh. He was carried up the stream to another fort, where he met the French commandant, M. De St. Pierre.

MAJOR WASHINGTON.

He received from him a written answer to Governor Dinwiddie's letter.

4. On his return he narrowly escaped being killed by a party of hostile Indians. At another time he came very near being drowned while crossing a river on a raft, being thrown violently into the water by the floating pieces of ice striking the pole with which he was guiding the raft. However, he arrived safely at Williamsburg on the 16th of January, 1754, and delivered to the Governor the answer of the French commandant. St. Pierre refused to withdraw his troops, and informed the Governor that he was acting under instructions from his superior officer, the Governor of Canada, whom alone he was bound to obey.

5. Governor Dinwiddie immediately began to prepare to oppose the French, as their hostile intentions were plainly apparent. A party of thirty men was sent out by the Ohio Company to erect a fort at the junction of the Alleghany and Monongahela rivers, where Pittsburgh now

---

4. What happened to him on his return ? On what day did he arrive at Williamsburg ? What answer did the French commander give Governor Dinwiddie ?
5. What steps did Governor Dinwiddie then take ? What happened to the Ohio Company's men ? To the French under Jumonville ?

stands, and a body of troops, under the command of Washington, marched into the disputed territory. The Ohio Company's men were soon driven from the ground by the French, who completed the fort and called it Fort Du Quesne. A party had also been sent out under Jumonville to intercept the advance of Washington, but they were surprised in the night, and nearly all were either killed or made prisoners.

6. At this place Washington erected a fort, which he called Fort Necessity, in what is now Fayette County, Pennsylvania. He was here joined by additional troops from New York and Carolina, and with his whole force, now amounting to about four hundred men, he proceeded towards Fort Du Quesne. But, hearing of the advance of a large body of French and Indians, commanded by M. De Villiers, he returned to Fort Necessity. Soon afterwards he was attacked by about fifteen hundred of the enemy. He resisted for about ten hours, but was compelled to capitulate. He obtained advantageous terms, and was permitted to return unmolested to Virginia. This capitulation took place July 4th, 1754.

7. The British government, seeing that war with France could not be avoided, advised the colonies to unite themselves together for the purpose of general defence. Accordingly a plan was adopted by a Congress of Colonies at Albany, on the fourth day of July, 1754. The Colonies thus assembled in Congress were New Hampshire, Massachusetts, Rhode Island, Connecticut, New York, Pennsylvania, and Maryland; the others were not present. The plan of union was drawn by Dr. Franklin, a delegate from Pennsylvania. Though approved by all the delegates except those from Connecticut, it was rejected, both by the Colonial Assemblies and by the British government—by

---

6. What fort was built by Washington? What reinforcements did he receive? What was then his strength? What did he then do? What was the result?
7. What did the British government advise the colonies to do? What was the fate of the plan of union? Why was it rejected?

the Colonial Assemblies because it gave too much power to the President-General of this Confederation, and by the British government because it was thought to assume too much power on the part of the respective colonial governments. It was therefore determined to carry on the war with British troops, with such assistance as the colonies separately might freely furnish.

8. Early in the year 1755 General Braddock, commander-in-chief of all the forces in America, arrived from Ireland with two regiments of British troops. Three expeditions were agreed upon by him and the colonial Governors; one against Fort Du Quesne, to be led by Braddock; one against Niagara, and one against Crown Point, on the western shore of Lake Champlain. Meantime another enterprise, projected by the government of Massachusetts, was being prosecuted with success. Near the last of May Colonel Monckton sailed from Boston, with about three thousand troops, against the French settlements on the Bay of Fundy. The plantations of the settlers were laid waste, and several thousands of destitute people were driven from their homes and dispersed through the English colonies, for no crime and for no act of hostility against Great Britain or British subjects, but because they could not take the oath of allegiance to the British crown; and from this they had formerly been excused, on condition that they would remain neutral,—a condition not violated by them.

9. The expedition against the French on the Ohio was unsuccessful. On the 10th of June, General Braddock, at the head of about two thousand men, regulars and colonial militia, set out from Fort Cumberland. He hastened his march towards Fort Du Quesne, with about twelve hundred men, leaving Colonel Dunbar with the rest of the troops as a rear-guard with the heavy baggage. General Brad-

---

8. What expeditions were determined upon by General Braddock? What is said of the enterprise under Colonel Monckton?
9. What is said of the expedition against the French on the Ohio? Of the confidence of General Braddock? Its consequences? The advanced guard?

dock, over-confident, and paying no attention to the warning of Washington, who was acting as one of his aids, pressed forward until within a few miles of Fort Du Quesne, when he was suddenly fired upon by an unseen enemy. The advanced guard, commanded by Lieutenant-Colonel Gage, unused to savage warfare, was thrown into disorder and fell back upon the main body, causing general confusion.

10. General Braddock did everything possible to rally his troops upon the spot where first attacked. But he fell mortally wounded, after having three horses killed under him. His troops soon fled in great disorder. Washington, with his Virginians, covered the retreat of the regulars, and so saved the army from complete destruction. The loss was very heavy, more than two-thirds of all the officers and nearly half the privates being either killed or wounded.

11. The enemy made no pursuit; but the panic was so great that even Colonel Dunbar's troops fled hastily, and made no pause until they felt themselves safe in Fort Cumberland. Soon afterwards Colonel Dunbar left a few of his forces to guard Fort Cumberland, and retired to Philadelphia. The expedition against Niagara, which was commanded by Governor Shirley, of Massachusetts, commander-in-chief after the death of Braddock, accomplished nothing except the erection of two new forts on the east side of the river, in which forts suitable garrisons were left for their defence.

12. General (afterward Sir William) Johnson commanded the expedition against Crown Point. A few miles north of Fort Edward, which is about forty-five miles north of Albany, he met the enemy, and after several hours' hard

---

10. What took place after Braddock's fall? What is said of Washington's conduct?
11. Did the enemy pursue? What is said of Colonel Dunbar? Of the expedition against Niagara?
12. Who commanded against Crown Point? What is said of the battle near Fort Edward? What happened to the Baron Dieskau?

fighting, and severe loss, he completely routed and drove them from the field. The loss was heavy on both sides. Col. Williams, of the British army, and Hendricks, who commanded the Indian allies, were killed. After the retreat of the French, their commander, the Baron Dieskau, was found wounded and alone, leaning against a tree. He put his hand into his pocket, feeling for his watch, with the intention of surrendering it; but a British soldier thinking that he was searching for a pistol, fired upon him and wounded him mortally.

13. This battle was fought in the latter part of August, 1755. The British forces consisted of about six thousand men, while the French did not number more than three or four thousand.

14. Gen. Johnson built a fort near the battle-ground, which he called Fort William Henry. The French meantime strengthened their works at Crown Point, and also took possession of Ticonderoga, which they fortified. Learning these facts, Gen. Johnson did not think it advisable to make any further advances. Accordingly, late in the season, leaving garrisons at Forts William Henry and Edward, he retired to Albany. The remainder of the army he sent to their homes in the different colonies.

15. The plan of campaign for the year 1756 was similar to that of the last, the chief object being to take the posts of Crown Point, Niagara, and Fort Du Quesne. Lord Loudon was appointed, by the king of Great Britain, commander of all the forces in America, and also Governor of Virginia. But as he could not leave England immediately, Gen. Abercrombie was ordered to take command until his arrival. Up to this time there had been no declaration of war between the two countries; but in May of this year, war was formally declared by Great Britain

---

13. What was the strength of the British in this battle? Of the French?
14. What fort did General Johnson then build? What place did the French then take? What was then done by General Johnson?
15. What was the chief object of the campaign of 1756? Who was appointed commander? When was war declared?

against France, and soon afterwards by France against Great Britain.

16. General Abercrombie arrived in June, with several regiments, and proceeded to Albany, where the colonial forces were stationed. But he thought it prudent to await the arrival of the Earl of Loudon, which was delayed until the latter part of July. The French in the meantime made an attack upon Oswego. In August, the Marquis Montcalm, who now commanded the French forces, with five or six thousand men, French and Indians, and about thirty pieces of cannon, crossed Lake Ontario, and laid siege to Fort Ontario, on the Oswego River.

17. Fort Ontario was abandoned by the garrison, who retired to an old fort on the west side of the river. But at this place, on the 14th of August, their number being only about fourteen hundred, they were compelled to surrender. A large amount of military stores, provisions, small-arms, and ammunition, together with several vessels in the harbor, and about one hundred and thirty-five pieces of cannon, fell into the hands of the enemy. Montcalm destroyed the forts and returned to Canada.

18. After the defeat of Braddock, the Indians on the western frontier killed or carried into captivity more than a thousand of the inhabitants. In August, 1756, Col. John Armstrong (afterwards a major-general in the Revolutionary War), with about three hundred men, marched against Kittaning, their chief town on the Alleghany River. The principal Indian chiefs were killed; their town was destroyed, and some English prisoners were recovered. The English suffered but little. Captain Mercer, afterwards distinguished in the Revolutionary War, was wounded in this expedition. Not one of the important objects of the campaign of this year was accomplished.

16. When did Lord Loudon arrive? What was done by Marquis Montcalm?
17. What was done by the garrison of Fort Ontario? What was Montcalm's next step?
18. After Braddock's defeat, what was done by the Indians? Tell me about Colonel Armstrong. Were the objects of the campaign accomplished?

19. 1757. This year a force of about ten thousand men was sent against Louisbourg, under the command of Lord Loudon. After their arrival at Halifax, learning that the place was strongly garrisoned, and that a large French fleet was in the harbor, the expedition was abandoned. About the same time, the Marquis Montcalm, with an army of near ten thousand men, laid siege to Fort William Henry, which was defended by about twenty-five hundred men.

20. There was at Fort Edward, about fifteen miles distant, a force of four thousand men; but they were not able to send any assistance, and the defenders of Fort William Henry were compelled to surrender. Honorable terms were granted; but after the surrender, as the English were leaving the fort, the Indians fell upon them, plundered them of their luggage, and killed many of them in cold blood. It is believed that Montcalm and his officers did all they could to protect the prisoners, except that they did not fire upon the Indians.

21. 1758. The ill success of the campaigns of the two preceding years was very painful to the pride of the English, and it was therefore determined to carry on the war this year with greater vigor. A new ministry was formed, with Mr. Pitt, afterwards Lord Chatham, at the head. Larger armies were raised in America, and twelve thousand more men were promised from England. Three armies were to be sent out: one against Louisbourg; one against the French on Lake Champlain, and one against Fort Du Quesne.

22. On the 28th of May, a fleet of nearly forty armed vessels, under command of Admiral Boscawen, with twelve

---

19. Who commanded the expedition of 1757 against Louisbourg? Why was the expedition abandoned? What was done by Montcalm about the same time?
20. Upon what terms was the surrender made? What was done by the Indians? Montcalm and his officers?
21. What was the effect in England of this campaign? What was done there? In 1758?
22. Who commanded the expedition against Louisbourg? Who gave great assistance? When did the surrender take place?

thousand men under General Amherst, sailed from Halifax for Louisbourg. The troops landed on the 8th of June near Louisbourg, with little loss. General Wolfe arrived soon after and gave great assistance in the reduction of the place. Near the last of July, the city and island of Louisbourg, and St. John's, or Prince Edward's Island, were surrendered to the English.

GENERAL WOLFE.

23. But while the English were successful here, they met with a considerable reverse in the defeat of General Abercrombie. On the 5th of July he crossed Lake George, with fifteen thousand men and a great many cannon, to attack Fort Ticonderoga. On the morning of the 6th he was attacked by Montcalm. Lord Howe, in whom the troops had great confidence, was killed; but after a hard fight the French were repulsed. After Lord Howe's death the ardor of the troops abated, some confusion prevailed, and the greater part of the army fell back to Lake George. But on the 8th they again advanced in full force against Ticonderoga. The French were fully prepared to receive them; and they were defeated and driven back with great slaughter, leaving about two thousand of their number killed or wounded upon the field.

24. The army then retired to the head of Lake George, whence three thousand men, under Col. Bradstreet, were sent against Fort Frontenac, on the outlet of Lake Ontario. Bradstreet crossed, landed near the fort, and in two days compelled it to surrender. Nine armed vessels, over fifty cannon, and a large quantity of stores and ammunition, fell into the hands of the English.

---

23. What reverse did the English meet with ? Who was killed ? What took place then ? What was the final result of the contest on the 8th ?
24. To what place did the army retire ? What fort was taken by Bradstreet ?

25. The expedition against Fort Du Quesne was commanded by General Forbes, who, early in July, left Philadelphia with nine thousand men. On their approach, the French abandoned the fort and passed down the Ohio River in boats. The English army took possession, and called the place Pittsburgh, in honor of Mr. Pitt, who was then at the head of the administration in England. The place is still called Pittsburg, and is now a flourishing city in Pennsylvania. The Western Indians soon made peace with the English. The campaign closed with honor to the English arms.

26. The campaign of 1758 having been auspicious to the British arms, the ministry determined to push the war with greater vigor than ever. Gen. Amherst was made commander of all the forces in North America, and assumed the responsibility of carrying out Mr. Pitt's great project of the conquest of Canada in one campaign. This was the plan of the campaign: General Wolfe, an officer of great merit, was to go up the St. Lawrence and attack Quebec; Gen. Amherst, after taking Ticonderoga and Crown Point, was to unite his forces with those of General Wolfe; and General Prideaux, with a third army, was to take Niagara and proceed against Montreal.

27. General Amherst was so far successful as to take Ticonderoga and Crown Point, with an army of about eleven hundred men; but was not able to join General Wolfe, and went into winter quarters at Crown Poir General Prideaux in July laid siege to Niagara; but was accidentally killed soon after the commencement of the siege, when the command devolved upon Sir William Johnson. A force of French and Indians, coming to relieve the place, were routed with great slaughter, and the fort soon after

---

25. Who led the expedition against Fort Du Quesne? With what success? What is the place now called?
26. What did the British ministry determine to do? What was the plan of the campaign?
27. What success did General Amherst have? General Prideaux? Sir William Johnson?

surrendered. The French communications were thus cut off between Canada and Louisiana.

28. Meantime Wolfe was prosecuting the siege of Quebec. About the last of June, he landed his army of about eight or ten thousand men on the Isle of Orleans, a short distance below Quebec. The French, with an army of about thirteen thousand men, occupied the city, and also a strong fort between the Rivers St. Charles and Montmorenci, on the north of the St. Lawrence. General Wolfe took possession of Point Levi, on which he erected batteries. But, effecting very little against the defences of the city, he determined upon bolder measures. He determined to storm the camp between the St. Charles and the Montmorenci. The attempt failed, and his loss amounted to nearly five hundred men.

29. He soon after called a council of officers, and proposed another attack upon the French lines. They, however, proposed that an effort be made to gain the heights above the city. The plan was approved, and preparations were at once made to carry it out. On the night of the 12th of September, the troops passed down the stream in boats; landed within less than two miles of the city; ascended the precipice, and at sunrise they were drawn up in battle array on the Plains of Abraham. A general battle ensued, in which the English and French generals, Wolfe and Montcalm, were both killed.

30. General Wolfe died on the field of battle, but lived long enough to know that he had gained the victory. When in the agonies of death he heard a cry, "They run, they run." Raising his head, he asked, "Who run?" Being told it was the French, "Then," said he, "I die contented," and expired. The French general was carried into the city, and on being told that his wound was mortal, his

---

28. What was General Wolfe doing at Quebec? What was the strength of the French? What point did General Wolfe take possession of? Upon what did he then determine? With what success and loss?

29. What was the next plan adopted? With what result?

30. Who gained the victory? What were Wolfe's last words? What were Montcalm's last words?

reply was, "So much the better, for then I shall not live to witness the surrender of Quebec."

31. Five days afterwards the city surrendered, leaving Montreal the only place of importance in the possession of the French in Canada. Yet in the next year, 1760, they tried to recover Quebec, but failed. In September, 1760, Montreal and all the other French posts in Canada were surrendered to the English.

32. In the same year a war in the South broke out with the Cherokees. Governor Lyttleton, of South Carolina, invited some of their chiefs to a conference, on certain matters of difference between them and the whites; and some misunderstanding having arisen, and for some matters connected with the subjects of this conference, he put them in prison, which they considered a violation of good faith, and on their release they took up arms and incited their nation to war against the whites.

33. In April, 1760, Colonel Montgomery, with about two thousand men, was sent by General Amherst from New York to the assistance of the Carolinians. A few weeks after his arrival he was joined by the militia of the colony, and set out for the Cherokee country. Moultrie and Marion, afterwards so celebrated in the Revolutionary War, were in this expedition. Montgomery's time was limited, the grand object of the year's campaign being the conquest of Canada. He was ordered to strike a sudden blow, and return to headquarters. In pursuance of orders, he rapidly penetrated the Indian country, and burned several towns and villages, but did not remain long enough to finish the war. In his last battle, fought near the Indian town of Etchoe, he lost twenty men killed and seventy-six wounded. He was victorious, but the condition of his army rendered it imprudent to penetrate

---

31. When did the city surrender? What did the French try in 1760?
32. What war broke out in the South? What was the cause of the war?
33. Who was sent against the Cherokees? What celebrated men were in this expedition? What was the result?

further into the woods. Orders were therefore given for a retreat, which was made in good order. In August, Colonel Montgomery embarked for New York, agreeably to his orders, but left four companies to cover the frontiers. Meantime the distant garrison of Fort Loudon was compelled to surrender to the Cherokees, or perish of hunger. They surrendered on favorable terms; but after the surrender, on their way to the settlements, they were attacked by the Indians; twenty-five were slain, and the remainder, nearly two hundred in number, were kept in a miserable captivity until they could be redeemed.

34. In the next year, 1761, Colonel Grant marched into the Indian country; defeated them in battle; laid waste their fields and villages, and having driven them to the mountains, compelled them to make peace. Francis Marion accompanied this expedition, and in a letter describes very feelingly the destruction of the growing crops and the villages of the Indians. Not many years afterwards he saw much greater desolation wrought by the hands of white men against white men.

35. The war between France and England continued until 1763. In February of that year a treaty of peace was signed at Paris. France yielded to Great Britain all her possessions in North America, east of the Mississippi River, from its source to the River Iberville, one of its outlets, through Lakes Maurepas and Pontchartrain, to the Gulf of Mexico. At the same time peace was made with Spain, which nation had joined with France, a year or two before, in waging war against Great Britain. By the treaty made at this time, Spain ceded to Great Britain her possessions of East and West Florida.

---

34. In 1761 what did Colonel Grant do ? Who accompanied Colonel Grant ?
35. When did the war end ? What did France yield to Great Britain ? What possessions did Spain cede to Great Britain ?

CHAPTER XXIV.

CAUSES WHICH LED TO THE ASSUMPTION OF SOVEREIGN POWERS BY THE COLONIES.
1763—1774.

Taxation—The Stamp Act—The First Congress of the Colonies at Philadelphia—The Battles of Concord, Lexington, Ticonderoga, and Crown Point—The Appointment of Washington to Command the Armies.

1. The destruction of the French power in America, which was one of the results of the war chronicled in the last chapter, was regarded by all the colonies as a most auspicious event, and as giving them promise of long-continued peace and prosperity.

At the close of this conflict little did any suppose that troubles would so soon arise between them and Great Britain, fondly called the mother-country. The attachment to that country had never been greater, and, excepting perhaps in Massachusetts, no dissatisfaction existed anywhere. Murmurs of discontent had often arisen previous to this war; but at its close the recollections of a recent and common danger, of perils shared together, of difficulties overcome by their united efforts, all tended to kindle in the breasts of the colonists a warm and tender attachment to that country from which their ancestors came; and if a wise policy had then been pursued by the British government towards the colonies, this attachment would have deepened and become permanent. The colonies at this time were in perfect peace and harmony among themselves and with the Indian tribes. A long standing dispute between Pennsylvania and Maryland, touching their boundaries, growing out of the royal grants to Lord Baltimore, the Duke of

---

CHAPTER XXIV.—**1.** How was the result of the French war looked upon by the colonies? What was the general state of feeling at the close of the war? What is said of the dispute as to the boundary between Pennsylvania and Maryland? How was it settled?

York, and William Penn, was about this time ended by an agreement as to how the true dividing line should be established. This was to be run and marked by two distinguished English engineers, Charles Mason and Jeremiah Dixon. They entered upon their work in 1764. The line marked by them was rigidly observed by both parties, and has ever since been famous as Mason and Dixon's line.

2. The new troubles were with the mother-country, and began about taxes. The colonies had heretofore been exempt from Parliamentary exactions of any sort except a duty imposed on sugar and molasses, under a commercial regulation in 1733, which had been in a great measure evaded, and never strictly enforced.

The prevailing idea in the colonies, as well as in England, was that taxes or subsidies of every sort, for the support of government, should be the voluntary tribute of the people, through their representatives. Hence the maxim, that taxation and representation go together. In the British Parliament Lord Camden said: "Taxation and representation are inseparable—it is an eternal law of nature; for whatever is a man's own is absolutely his own; no man has a right to take it from him without his consent. Whoever attempts to do it, attempts an injury; whoever does it, commits a robbery." The colonies had also an eloquent advocate in Colonel Barré, in the House of Commons. In answer to arguments on the other side he exclaimed, "Children planted by your care! No; your oppression planted them in America. They fled from your tyranny to an uncultivated land, where they were exposed to all the hardships to which human nature is liable. They nourished by your indulgence! No; they grew by your neglect. When you began to care about them, that care was exercised in sending persons to rule over them, whose character and conduct has caused the

---

2. What did the new troubles between the colonies and the mother-country begin about? What did the colonies claim or maintain as their rights? What did Lord Camden say upon the subject? What did Colonel Barré say?

blood of those sons of liberty to recoil within them. They protected by your arms! They have nobly taken up arms in *your* defence! The people of America are loyal—but a people jealous of their liberties, and they will vindicate them."

The colonies had no representation in the British Parliament, and they maintained that no just taxes could be levied on them without their having a voice in the matter. They maintained moreover that the imposition of taxes on them by Parliament was a violation of the stipulations with the Crown, set forth in their charters. According to these stipulations, they maintained that Parliament had no governing authority over them. Their stipulations were with the King, and they insisted that the great right of local self-government was secured to them respectively under their several charters, which they severally regarded as their fundamental or constitutional law, as the principles of *Magna Charta* were regarded by all Britons as the fundamental law of England.

3. On the part of Parliament it was contended that, as the late war had greatly increased the public debt, the colonies should be made to bear a part of it. With this view the old duty on sugar and molasses was revived, or new orders given for its strict enforcement. This created considerable excitement, which was increased in 1765 by the passage of what is known as the Stamp Act. By this law of Parliament all contracts, notes, bonds, deeds, writs, and public documents were required to be on government stamped paper, which was sold by officials at a high price, and from the sales of which a large revenue was expected to be derived.

The passage of the last-named act created great excitement, especially in Virginia and Massachusetts, where a spirit of open resistance was manifested. The excitement

---

3. What did Parliament contend for? What did they do? What was the effect of these measures? What did Patrick Henry say?

was not lessened when, two months after the passage of the Stamp Act, in order to enforce it, Parliament authorized the ministry to send as many troops as they saw proper to Massachusetts and other places, which troops were to draw their supplies, not from home, but from the colonies themselves. Through the influence of Patrick Henry, strong resolutions were passed by the Virginia House of Burgesses, declaring, among other things, the exclusive right of that Assembly to tax the inhabitants of that colony. In the course of the debate on the resolutions, Henry, in a burst of eloquence, exclaimed: " Cæsar had his Brutus, Charles I. his Cromwell, and George III.—" " Treason! treason!" cried the Speaker; a few other members also joined in the cry. Henry paused for a moment, and looking with an undaunted eye upon the Speaker, continued, "may profit by their example! If that be treason, make the most of it."

4. The General Court of Massachusetts was moved by a similar spirit. They resolved that the courts should conduct their business without the use of stamps. In June, before they heard of the proceedings in Virginia, they issued a circular inviting all the colonies to send delegates to a convention, to be held in New York in October following, a short time before the day appointed for the Stamp Act to go into operation. This proposition was seconded by South Carolina. On the first Tuesday of October, 1765, the proposed convention of deputies or delegates from several of the colonies met at New York, to take into consideration the state of all the colonies, and to consult for the general welfare.

Nine colonies, to-wit: Massachusetts, New Hampshire, Rhode Island, Connecticut, New York, New Jersey, Delaware, Pennsylvania, and South Carolina, were represented

---

4. What did the General Court of Massachusetts do ? What colony seconded the proposition ? When did the convention meet ? How many colonies were represented in it ? Who was president ? What was done with the stamped paper ? What was the effect ?

in this convention by twenty-eight delegates. Timothy Ruggles, of Massachusetts, was chosen President. The convention agreed upon a declaration of principles, and asserted the right of the colonies to be exempted from all taxes not imposed by their consent.

The stamped paper, after this, in many places was either destroyed or sent back to England. Business for a time was almost suspended, as the law required stamped paper to be used, and the people had determined not to use it. Gradually, however, business revived; notes, deeds, etc., were written on unstamped paper, and things went on as before, without regard to the law of Parliament, which was regarded as usurpation.

5. About this time there arose a society known as the "Sons of Liberty," which took strong ground against the usurpations of Parliament. They exerted great influence. The merchants of New York, Boston, Philadelphia, and many other places, agreed with each other not to buy or bring any more goods from Great Britain until the Stamp Act was repealed. The British government heard of these proceedings with anger and alarm. The new ministry, at the head of which was the Marquis of Rockingham, saw that the Stamp Act must be repealed or that the colonists must be compelled by force of arms to comply with its requisitions. With him the former was preferable to the latter alternative.

6. After a long and angry debate the Act was repealed, March 19th, 1766; but at the same time it was declared that Parliament had the right and power to bind the colonies in all cases whatsoever. The news of the repeal was received with great joy by all the colonies, and the great body of the English people themselves also rejoiced. The Rockingham ministry was dissolved in July, and a

---

5. What society sprang up ? What agreement was made by the merchants ?
6. What was done with the act in Parliament ? What was the effect in America? In England ? Who became prime minister ?

new one was formed under Mr. Pitt, who was created Earl of Chatham.

7. Mr. Pitt was a friend to the colonies, and was opposed to taxing them without their consent. But while he was at home, confined by sickness, the scheme of taxation was revived, and a bill was introduced by Mr. Townsend, who was Chancellor of the Exchequer, imposing a tax on all glass, paper, painters' colors, and tea, imported into the colonies. During the absence of Mr. Pitt the bill was passed by Parliament, and approved by the King, June 29th, 1767. Other bills also in relation to the colonies were passed, one suspending the Legislative Assembly of New York from passing any act whatever, until they were willing to furnish the King's troops with certain supplies, at the expense of the colony.

8. The excitement in all the colonies was raised to the highest pitch by the passage of these acts. The different Colonial Legislatures or Assemblies passed strong resolutions against them, and associations in favor of home manufactures were entered into by the people. By the writers of the day, the assumed authority of the Parliament over the colonies was denied. In February, 1768, the General Court of Massachusetts sent a circular to the other colonies, asking their co-operation in obtaining a redress of grievances. The language of this circular gave great offence to the British ministry. The Governor of Massachusetts was instructed to require the General Court to rescind the resolution. They refused, and reaffirmed their opinions in stronger language.

9. The Governor then dissolved the Assembly, but not before they had preferred charges against him, and had petitioned the King for his removal. Soon afterwards tumults occurred in Boston, and troops were sent there

---

7. What act was passed during his sickness? What year was this?
8. What was the effect in America? What did Massachusetts propose? What was the Governor instructed to do?
9. What occurred in Boston? What did the soldiers call the people?

to overawe the citizens. About seven hundred landed on the 1st of October, with all the parade usual on coming into an enemy's country. The authorities of Boston were required to provide quarters for the soldiers; but they absolutely refused, and the Governor ordered the State-House to be opened to them. As the soldiers passed through the streets, irritating language was used, both by them and the people; the soldiers regarding the people as rebels, and the people looking on the soldiers as the instruments of tyranny.

10. In 1769 the British Parliament censured the conduct of Massachusetts, approved the employment of force to put down the rebellious, and prayed the King to direct the Governor of Massachusetts to have the traitors arrested and sent to England. The Colonial Assemblies reasserted their rights, and denied the right of the King to take offenders out of the country for trial.

11. In 1770 an affair occurred at Boston which increased the excitement in every part of the country. During a quarrel between a military guard and citizens, some soldiers fired upon the citizens, by which three were killed and several badly wounded. This is known as the Boston Massacre. The soldiers were tried for murder. Two were convicted of manslaughter, the rest were acquitted. About the same time a bill was passed by the Parliament repealing all the duties imposed by the act of 1767, except that on tea. This was the first measure of Lord North, just elevated to the premiership, 1770. But the colonists were not satisfied, because the principle of taxation without representation was not abandoned, and the non-importation agreements still continued.

12. In 1773 a bill was passed by Parliament, allowing the East India Company to carry their tea into the colonies free

---
10. What was done by the British Parliament in 1769? What was the action of the Colonial Assemblies?
11. What occurred at Boston in 1770? What duties did Parliament repeal?
12. What bill passed in 1773? What did the Americans do? What was done in New York and Philadelphia?

of duty, except the small duty to be paid in the port of entry. It was thought that the colonists would pay this small tax of three pence per pound, as, even then, they would get tea cheaper than the people of England. But they would not pay it. At the ports of New York and Philadelphia, the vessels having the tea on board were not permitted to enter, and they were obliged to go back to England without landing.

13. In Charleston, South Carolina, the tea was landed and stored away in damp cellars, where it was quietly permitted to rot. In Boston a party of men disguised as Mohawk Indians, in open day, went on board the ships containing the tea, broke open all the chests, and threw the tea into the sea.

14. In 1774 the port of Boston, for this outrage, so called, was closed by act of Parliament, and the custom-house was removed to Salem. But the people of Marblehead offered the merchants of Boston their harbor, wharves, and warehouses free of charge. The charter of Massachusetts was then subverted by act of Parliament, and the Governor was authorized to send criminals to another colony or to England for trial. The Boston Port Bill caused an excitement amounting to a fury in that city. The Assembly of Virginia, on receiving the news of the passage of this act, and sympathizing with the people of Boston, appointed the first day of June as a day of "fasting, humiliation, and prayer."

15. The royal Governor immediately dissolved the House of Burgesses, whereupon the members resolved themselves into a committee, and formed an association and passed resolutions declaring that the interests of all the colonies were equally concerned, and advising the appointment of a local committee of correspondence to consult with the other

---

13. What was done in Charleston ? in Boston ?
14. When was the port of Boston closed ? What did the Virginia Assembly do when they heard of it ?
15. What did the royal Governor of that colony do ? What did the members of the House of Burgesses then do ? What cry was then raised in Virginia

colonies on the expediency of holding a general Congress of all the colonies, to devise means for their common protection. The attack upon the chartered rights of Massachusetts might be followed by a like attack upon those of all the other colonies in turn. This was in May, 1774, and was the first step taken towards the meeting of the Congress that assembled in Philadelphia in September, 1774, and was the initiation, as we shall see, of the assumption of sovereign powers by the colonies represented. On the 1st of August a convention of delegates from various counties of Virginia met at Williamsburgh, and appointed seven delegates to represent the colony of Virginia in the general Congress to be held in September following.

It was at this time that the cry was raised in Virginia, and went through all the colonies, "The cause of Boston is the cause of us all;" for all saw that if the British Parliament could close the port of Boston and take away the charter of Massachusetts, they could do the same with all, and there was no safety for the rights of any. The maintenance of the sacred right of local self-government by each, through joint co-operation, was the object aimed at by the call for a Congress of all the colonies. The appeal of Virginia was responded to by the colonies generally, and on the 5th of September a convention of delegates from twelve of the thirteen colonies met at Philadelphia. Peyton Randolph, of Virginia, was chosen President of it, and Charles Thompson, Secretary. The first thing settled by this body was the nature of its own character and organization. It was held to be a Congress of separate and distinct political bodies. In all its deliberations each colony was to be considered as equal, and each was to have an equal vote on all questions coming before it, without regard to population or the number of delegates sent by the respective col-

which went through all the colonies? What was the object of the call of a Congress of all the colonies? When and where did it meet? Who was chosen President? What was the body held to be? How were votes taken upon all questions coming before it? What did this Congress do? What did Lord Chatham say of the addresses of this Congress?

onies; for the object of all was the defence and preservation of what was claimed to be the inestimable right of each, that is, the absolute right of local self-government. This was the substance of the instructions of the delegates.

This Congress of the colonies, so organized and so constituted, made a declaration of the indefeasible rights of all the colonies. They moreover made several recommendations to the governments of the colonies respectively, as to the course proper to be pursued. Amongst other things, they advised that there be no commercial intercourse with Great Britain until the unjust and oppressive acts of Parliament were repealed; and then dissolved, on the 26th of October, with a recommendation to the colonies to meet in Congress again, by deputies, on the 10th of May, 1775. In speaking of the papers issued by this Congress, Lord Chatham said, in the British Parliament, "that though he had studied and admired the free states of antiquity, the master-spirits of the world, yet for solidity of reasoning, force of sagacity, and wisdom of conclusion, no body of men could stand in preference to this Congress."

16. In the meantime important events were occurring elsewhere. In Massachusetts, General Gage, the Governor, had convoked the General Court to assemble at Salem on the 5th of October, but before the day appointed he issued a proclamation dissolving the Assembly. The members, however, met at Salem on the day appointed, and after waiting a day in vain for the Governor to meet them, they resolved themselves into a provisional Legislature and adjourned to Concord. Appointing John Hancock President, and addressing a communication to the Governor, they adjourned to meet at Cambridge on the 17th. Here they appointed committees of safety and supplies; voted the equipment of twelve thousand men, and the enlistment of one-fourth the militia

---

16. What did General Gage, the Governor of Massachusetts, do ? What did the Legislature or General Court do ? What did General Gage then do ? What did Lord Chatham do early in 1775 ? What did Lord North do ?

CHAP. XXIV.] ASSUMPTION OF SOVEREIGN POWERS. 169

as minute-men. Preparations of like character were made in the other colonies.

General Gage, who favored the maintenance of the rights asserted by the British government as against those claimed by the colonists, fortified Boston Neck, seized the military stores at Cambridge and Charlestown, and conveyed them to Boston.

Early in the year 1775, Lord Chatham introduced a bill in Parliament, which he hoped would bring about a reconciliation, but Parliament would listen to nothing but absolute submission on the part of the colonies. Lord North, finding that the Boston Port Bill had failed of its purpose, introduced what he called the New England Restraining Bill, which deprived the people of the privilege of fishing on the Banks of Newfoundland. Soon afterwards, learning that the Colonial Assemblies had approved and determined to support the resolutions of the Colonial Congress, he introduced a second restraining act, applicable to all the colonies except New York and North Carolina, which Parliament passed in March. These measures failed either to coerce or to divide, but tended greatly to excite and inflame all.

17. On the first of April, 1775, there were three thousand British troops in Boston. General Gage thought this force sufficient to keep down the rebellion, or to quell any sudden outbreak. On the night of the 18th of April he secretly sent eight hundred men to destroy the military stores at Concord, sixteen miles from Boston. But, although he tried to be as secret as possible, yet his troops were met at Lexington as early as five o'clock in the morning, by about seventy militia, commanded by Captain Parker.

The British troops were commanded by Colonel Smith

---

17. How many troops had General Gage in Boston early in April? What did he determine to do? Who commanded the British troops sent to Concord? Where were they met and by whom? What occurred? What did the dying militia-man say?

8

and Major Pitcairn. Major Pitcairn demanded what they meant and where they were going? The militia replied they were going to Concord. He then said, "Disperse, you rebels, disperse." They did not obey him, but replied, "We have a right to go to Concord." He then fired his pistol at them, and ordered his soldiers to fire. They immediately fired, and several of the militia were killed and the rest dispersed. The first of those who fell, in his dying agonies exclaimed, "I have a right to go to Concord." The troops then went on to Concord, and destroyed a part of the stores. But the militia rapidly assembled, a skirmish ensued, and several were killed on both sides. The British soon retreated, but the colonists pursued and kept up a constant fire.

18. At Lexington the British were met by a reinforcement of nine hundred men, under Lord Percy. They then moved rapidly to Charlestown, and on the next day crossed to Boston. In this affair the British loss was about two hundred and seventy-five in killed, wounded, and missing. The colonists lost nearly one hundred.

19. The news spread rapidly, and the excitement was very great. In a short time an army of twenty thousand colonists surrounded the city of Boston. The most active measures were taken for the public defence. Colonels Ethan Allen and Benedict Arnold, with volunteers from Connecticut and Vermont, seized upon Ticonderoga and Crown Point, on the western side of Lake Champlain. Skeenesborough, now Whitehall, in New York, was also secured. By these captures, one hundred pieces of cannon and other military stores fell into the hands of the colonists. This was on the 10th of May, 1775.

---

18. What occurred at Lexington?
19. What occurred about Boston? What did Allen and Arnold do? When was Ticonderoga taken?

CHAPTER XXV.

CONTINUATION OF THE CAUSES WHICH LED TO THE ASSUMPTION OF SOVEREIGN INDEPENDENT POWERS BY THE COLONIES.

Second Congress at Philadelphia—Battle of Bunker Hill—Canada Invaded—Boston Evacuated—Washington moves his Army to New York—Attack on Charleston, South Carolina, by the British.

1. On the same day that Ticonderoga was taken (10th of May, 1775) the second Congress of the colonies assembled at Philadelphia, according to the recommendations of the first, as we have seen. Peyton Randolph was again chosen President, and Charles Thompson, Secretary of this body. A conflict of arms had already commenced, and was actually raging.

Among the first things the Congress did, therefore, was to proclaim their reasons for an appeal to arms. They also voted to raise forces to the amount of twenty thousand men, and the means to support them, which were to be raised by the colonies, upon an equitable basis between them respectively. Other active measures of resistance were agreed upon. On the 24th of May, Mr. Randolph being called away, John Hancock, of Massachusetts, was chosen President of Congress in his stead.

One great question that engaged their attention was, who should be placed at the head of the armies. At the instance of Massachusetts, George Washington was appointed commander-in-chief. He was commissioned in the name of the United Colonies, the name of each colony being set forth in the commission. This was on the 19th of June. Only twelve colonies were then present. The delegates from Georgia did not arrive until some time afterwards.

CHAPTER XXV.—1. When did the second Congress meet ? Who were chosen President and Secretary of this body ? What was one of the first things that this Congress did ? Who was chosen President on the resignation of Mr. Randolph ? Who was appointed to command the armies ? How was he commissioned ? When was this, and how was he paid ?

Washington accepted the appointment, but refused to receive any compensation, except enough to defray his actual and necessary expenses. Four major-generals, one adjutant, and eight brigadier-generals were appointed. On the 12th of July, Washington went to Cambridge and took command of the colonial army, then amounting to about fourteen thousand men.

2. In setting forth the causes for which they took up arms, the Congress declared that they have " no wish to separate from the mother-country, but only to maintain their chartered rights." And in speaking of those rights they said, " We have not raised armies with ambitious designs of separating from Great Britain and establishing independent States. We fight not for glory or for conquest. . . . . Honor, justice, and humanity forbid us tamely to surrender that freedom which we received from our gallant ancestors, and which our innocent posterity have a right to receive from us. We cannot endure the infamy and guilt of resigning succeeding generations to that wretchedness which inevitably awaits them if we basely entail hereditary bondage upon them. . . . In our native land, and in defence of the freedom which is our birthright, and which we have ever enjoyed till the late violation of it, for the protection of our property, acquired solely by the honest industry of our forefathers and ourselves, against violence actually offered, we have taken up arms. We shall lay them down when hostilities shall cease on the part of the aggressors, and all danger of their being renewed shall be removed, and not before."

In South Carolina, the provisional Legislature of that colony, in an address to the Governor, Lord William Campbell, declared : "Impressed with the greatest apprehension of instigated insurrections, and deeply affected by the commencement of hostilities by the British troops against this

---

2. What reasons did the Congress assign for taking up arms ? What reason did the provisional Legislature of South Carolina assign to the royal Governor of that State for their conduct ?

continent, solely for the preservation and in defence of our lives, liberties, and properties, we have been impelled to associate and to take up arms. We only desire the secure enjoyment of our invaluable rights, and we wish for nothing more ardently than a speedy reconciliation with our mother-country upon constitutional principles."

3. In the meantime important events had been and were transpiring in other places. About the 25th of May, the British troops in Boston received reinforcements, commanded by Generals Howe, Clinton, and Burgoyne. The whole British force now amounted to more than ten thousand men. General Gage, on the 12th of June, issued a proclamation declaring those in arms to be rebels and traitors. He offered pardon to all that would lay down their arms and quietly go about their business, except Samuel Adams and John Hancock. The crimes of these two were considered too enormous to be pardoned.

To prevent the advance of the British into the country it was determined to fortify Bunker Hill, an eminence which commanded the neck of the peninsula of Charlestown. But by mistake the detachment under Colonel Prescott fortified Breed's Hill, an eminence nearer the city of Boston. The British were very much astonished, in the morning, to see a fort within cannon-shot, filled with armed men. This height commanded the city, and the British saw at once that a strong battery there could compel them to leave the place. They therefore determined to drive them from the height.

About 12 o'clock on the 17th of June a force of three thousand men, commanded by General Howe, crossed over to Charlestown for the purpose of attacking the fort. They formed in two columns and advanced slowly. As the troops advanced General Gage ordered the village of Charlestown

---

3. About what time did the British reinforcements reach Boston, and under whom ? What did General Gage, the Governor of the colony, do ? What did the colonists do ? What occurred the 17th of June ? What was the British loss ? What was the loss of the colonists ? What is this battle known as ?

to be set on fire. The colonists waited in silence until the British soldiers came within ten rods of the fort, when they opened such a deadly fire that the advancing column was broken and fled. Their officers rallied them and led them the second time to the attack, but the fire was so severe that they were again driven back.

At this moment General Clinton arrived with reinforcements, and a third assault was made, which proved success-

BATTLE OF BUNKER HILL.

ful. The colonists retreated across Charlestown Neck with no great loss, and fortified Prospect Hill, commanding the harbor of Boston. The British fortified Bunker Hill, but no further movements were made at that time by either army. The loss of the British in this battle was over a thousand killed and wounded; that of the colonists was about four hundred and fifty. One young officer was killed, who was greatly lamented, General Joseph Warren. This is known as the battle of Bunker Hill.

4. Upon his arrival at Cambridge, Washington found the

---

4. What did Washington find the state of the army to be on his arrival at Cambridge? Who was then commanding the British forces in Boston?

army nothing but a body of undisciplined militia, hastily collected, and destitute of tents, ammunition, and all regular supplies. His task was consequently very difficult. But with the assistance of those he called around him, he soon introduced order and discipline, and, in a short time, was able vigorously to besiege the British army, and keep it closely confined within the limits of the city. Sir William Howe at this time had command of the British forces, in place of General Gage, who had been recalled.

5. During this summer the royal authority entirely ceased in the colonies, all the Governors who held authority under the King being compelled to flee and abandon their seats of government. In all the colonies new governments, provisional in their character, were set up by the people in a peaceful manner, and based upon popular rights and representation. Lord Dunmore, Governor of Virginia, retired to a man-of-war, having first carried off about twenty barrels of gunpowder from Williamsburg, armed a few vessels, raised a regiment of several hundred negroes, to whom he offered their freedom, and attacked the Virginians near Norfolk, December 8th, but was defeated. Having the opportunity some time afterwards to gratify his revenge, he burned a portion of the town.

6. In the meantime, also, the way having been opened by the capture of Ticonderoga and Crown Point, in May, as stated, Congress, though they had previously passed resolutions to the contrary, determined on authorizing the invasion of Canada. Accordingly, a body of troops from New York and New England was put under command of Generals Schuyler and Montgomery for this enterprise. On the 10th of September they reached St. Johns, the first British post in Canada. But finding the place too strong for them, they retired and fortified Isle aux Noix, about one hundred and twenty miles north of Ticonderoga. The

---
5. What occurred in all the colonies during the summer ?
6. What did Congress resolve upon in regard to Canada ? What generals were put in command of the expedition ?

command soon afterwards devolved entirely upon General Montgomery, on account of the illness of General Schuyler, who had returned to Ticonderoga to hurry up the reinforcements.

7. In a few days General Montgomery returned to St. Johns and laid siege to it, but being short of ammunition his progress was rather slow. By a sudden move he surprised and captured, October 13th, Fort Chambly, a few miles north of St. Johns. By this capture he gained several pieces of cannon and a large quantity of powder. It was about this time that Colonel Ethan Allen, having rashly forced his way to Montreal with only eighty men, was captured and sent as a prisoner to England.

8. St. Johns surrendered on the 3d of November, and on the 13th Montgomery captured Montreal. But the Governor, Carleton, made his escape with a small force to Quebec. Montgomery left garrisons at Montreal, Forts Chambly and St. Johns, and proceeded towards Quebec with the remainder of his army, which amounted to only three or four hundred men. But he expected to meet another body of troops, which had been sent on from Cambridge to act in concert with him.

9. General Arnold, in command of this detachment of about one thousand men, ascended the Kennebec River in Maine, and crossing the mountains among which it rises, descended the Chaudiere, in Canada, and arrived at Point Levi, opposite Quebec, on the 9th of November. On the 13th he ascended the heights, and drew up his army on the Plains of Abraham. Finding the defences of Quebec too strong for his forces, he retired to Point aux Trembles, twenty miles above, to await the arrival of Montgomery.

10. Montgomery arrived on the 1st of December, but

---

7. What did General Montgomery do ? What fort was captured October 13th ? Who was taken prisoner about this time ?
8. When did St. Johns surrender ? What was Montgomery's next move ?
9. What is said of General Arnold's movements ?
10. What time did General Montgomery arrive before Quebec ? What was his strength ? Describe the siege. Who was killed ?

CHAP. XXV.] ASSUMPTION OF SOVEREIGN POWERS. 177

their whole force united amounted to only about nine hundred effective men. With these, however, they marched to Quebec, and laid siege to it. After a siege of three weeks they determined to take the place by assault. Before daybreak in the morning, on the last day of the year, the troops were put in motion. They were formed in four columns; two were sent to make a feigned attack upon the upper town, while Montgomery and Arnold, at the head of their divisions, attacked opposite sides of the lower town. Montgomery was killed at the first fire. Several of his officers, who were near him, were also killed at the same time.

11. The soldiers were intimidated by this untoward event, and the officer next in command ordered a retreat. Arnold on his side had entered the town, but was soon severely wounded, and had to be carried to the hospital. The command then devolved upon Captain Morgan, who continued the contest for several hours, but was finally compelled (after having tried in vain to retreat) to surrender the force under his command as prisoners of war.

Montgomery was much lamented, and Congress directed a monument to be erected to his memory.

12. Arnold retired with his command to a distance of three miles above Quebec, where he received some reinforcements; but he never, at any one time, had more than three thousand men, of whom it was seldom that more than one-half were fit for duty. General Thomas, Montgomery's successor, arrived early in May, 1776, and General Carleton having received reinforcements, the colonial forces were obliged to retreat. They left all their stores, and many of their sick, which fell into the hands of the British. At the mouth of the River Sorel they were joined by several regiments, but were still unable to cope with the enemy. At this place General Thomas died of the small-pox. The

---

11 What was the effect of his death? What was the final result of the assault?
12 What did Arnold do? Who was Montgomery's successor? Who retreated? What became of their stores and the sick? And what was the final result by the 18th of June?

8*

colonists continued to retreat from post to post, and by the 18th of June, 1776, they had entirely left Canada.

13. Winter had passed without any active operations around Boston; but about the 4th of March, Washington thought it was best to begin to act on the offensive. General Thomas was sent by night to throw up intrenchments on Dorchester Heights. These heights commanded the city. On discovering the colonists in the morning, General Howe determined to drive them away, but a storm prevented him until they were too strongly fortified to be dislodged. In this condition he was unable to hold the city. On the 17th of March all the British forces, both land and naval, with over a thousand loyalists, that is, Bostonians who took sides with the mother-country, left the harbor and sailed southward.

There was great rejoicing by all friends of the cause of the colonies, especially by those who had been shut up in the city. Provisions had become very scarce and dear. For firewood the people had been compelled to burn the pews of churches, the counters of stores, and, indeed, the timbers of all houses that were not used or inhabited. Congress passed a vote of thanks to the army, and caused a gold medal to be struck in commemoration of the gallantry of the troops.

14. The next active operations of the British took place near Charleston, in South Carolina. On the 4th of June, 1776, Admiral Sir Peter Parker, with a fleet having on board about twenty-five hundred men, under command of General Clinton, appeared near Charleston. The people of Carolina had made preparations for their defence. About six thousand men had collected in and near the city. A fort with walls built of palmetto logs, and filled in with sand, had been erected on Sullivan's Island. It was defended by twenty-six cannon and five hundred men, under

---

13. What took place from the 4th to the 17th of March, 1776? What was done on the last-named day? Did the inhabitants of Boston rejoice? What vote did Congress pass?
14. What were the next active operations of the British? Were the people of Carolina ready? Describe the fort.

command of Colonel Moultrie. This fort commanded the channel. There was another fort on the other side of the island held by Colonel Thompson.

15. General Charles Lee, being the superior officer present, had the general conduct of the defence. General Lee had but a poor opinion of Fort Sullivan, and told Colonel Moultrie that the British cannon would knock it to pieces in ten minutes. "In that case," replied the Colonel, "we will lie behind the ruins, and still prevent the enemy from landing." On the 28th of June the British began the attack. With all the guns at their command they fired upon the fort. But the palmetto wood being soft, and not liable to split or splinter, and all the spaces between the logs and walls being filled with sand, but little harm was done. The balls would bury themselves in the earth and logs, and the fort would remain as strong as ever.

16. Meantime the Carolinians were not idle. They kept up a rapid and very destructive fire upon the British ships. At one time the quarter-deck of Sir Peter Parker's flag-ship was cleared of every man except Sir Peter himself. During the fight General Clinton landed his force of twenty-five hundred men on Long Island, and attempted to pass to Sullivan's Island, but they were driven back by Colonel Thompson's riflemen. There were many instances of personal daring and cool bravery during the fight, but the most conspicuous was that of Sergeant Jasper.

17. Early in the action the flag-staff was cut in two by a cannon-ball, and the flag fell upon the beach outside the fort. Sergeant Jasper leaped over the wall, picked up the flag, fastened it to a staff, and again set it up, while the balls from the enemy's guns came in a perfect shower around him. For this heroic deed Governor Rutledge, of South

---

15. Who commanded at Charleston? What did he say of the fort? What was Colonel Moultrie's reply? When was the attack begun? What is said of the palmetto logs?
16. What were the Americans doing? What was the condition of Sir Peter Parker's flag-ship?
17. What is said of Sergeant Jasper's bravery? What did Governor Rutledge give him? Why did Jasper refuse the commission?

Carolina, gave him his sword and a lieutenant's commission. Sergeant Jasper accepted the sword, but refused the commission, for the reason that he could not read or write,

SERGEANT JASPER.

and did not think himself fit to be an officer. His modesty was as great as his virtue.

18. Late in the action, one of Sir Peter Parker's ships having become disabled, he ordered the crew to set it on fire and leave it. The guns were left loaded and the colors flying. As soon as the crew had left the Carolinians boarded the vessel, fired the guns at Sir Peter's ship, and carried off the flags and balls and three boat-loads of stores. For more than nine hours the British continued the battle, but made no impression upon the fort. When the firing ceased the walls were as strong and secure as at first. Ten Carolinians were killed and twenty-two wounded. The British loss in killed and wounded exceeded two hundred. The fleet lay-to a few days to refit, and then sailed northward.

18. How long did the British keep up the fight? With what result? What was the American loss?

19. Soon after the British sailed from Boston, Washington set out with the greater part of his army for New York, as that place was the object of attack by the British. Washington arrived at New York on the 14th of April, 1776. By prevailing on Congress to enlist men for three years, and offer a bounty of ten dollars for each recruit, he soon had an army of twenty-seven thousand men, though many of them were unarmed, and numbers were sick. But the whole number was not enough for the defence of the city, as it was necessary to have a line fifteen miles long.

20. Great Britain, in the meantime, had made great preparations for the subjugation of the colonies. There had been ordered to America a large fleet of ships, with seventeen thousand German soldiers and twenty-five thousand English, well supplied with provisions and all munitions of war. The people of the colonies, seeing that Great Britain showed no disposition to yield her claims, instead of thinking about submission, began to think about Sovereign Independence, though when the difficulties first began that was not the object, as we have seen.

CHAPTER XXVI.

SEPARATION FROM THE MOTHER-COUNTRY—SOVEREIGN POWERS ASSUMED BY THE COLONIES—DECLARATION OF THEIR INDEPENDENCE AS STATES—ARTICLES OF CONFEDERATION BETWEEN THEM.

1. THE manner in which the remonstrances of the colonies were received and treated by the King and Parliament,

---

19. What did Washington do when the British sailed from Boston? When did he reach New York? What was the number of his army? Was it insufficient to defend the city, and why?
20. What had Great Britain done in the meantime? What number of troops had she equipped and sent out for the subjugation of the colonies? What effect had this upon the popular mind in the colonies? Had they thought at first of sovereign independence?
CHAPTER XXVI.—**1.** What was becoming the feeling of the colonies as to independence, and what produced it? What is said of North Carolina?

as well as the formidable forces raised and sent out to reduce them to submission, extinguished all hopes they had previously entertained of an ultimate reconciliation upon the basis of right and justice. The feeling was now becoming general and almost universal for independence.

North Carolina was ahead of all her sister States on the subject of independence.

On the 20th of May, 1775, the day after receiving the news of the battle at Lexington, a convention of delegates from the several captains' companies of the militia of Mecklenburg county convened in Charlotte, and threw off all allegiance to the British crown, and declared North Carolina to be a sovereign and independent State. Her last royal Governor, Josiah Martin, was immediately afterwards compelled, by the people of Wilmington and the lower waters of the Cape Fear, to flee for safety on board his majesty's ship-of-war *The Cruiser*, whence he issued a proclamation, in which he denounced the resolutions in Mecklenburg as the most treasonable proceeding that had taken place on the continent.

On the 20th of August, 1775, she assembled a Provincial Congress at Hillsboro', which recognized the abdication of the Governor, and made an effectual organization of the militia for the public defence.

And in the autumn of that year she sent an expedition, under Colonel, afterwards General Howe, to the aid of Norfolk and lower Virginia, against the machinations of Lord Dunmore, the royal Governor of that colony, which, in conjunction with the republican troops there, defeated his lordship's army in the battle of Great Bridge, on the North Carolina frontier, and forced him to seek protection on board a man-of-war in the harbor of Norfolk.

2. The Congress continued in session, awaiting events, and, acting under the authority of their delegated powers,

---

2. When did Massachusetts instruct her delegates to vote for independence?

in providing for the general defence. In January, 1776, Massachusetts instructed her delegates to vote for independence. South Carolina gave similar instructions to her delegates in March. Georgia and North Carolina did the same in April. In May, General Washington wrote from the head of the army, at New York, "A reconciliation with Great Britain is impossible. . . . When I took command of the army I abhorred the idea of independence; but I am now fully satisfied that nothing else will save us."

In the same month, Virginia instructed her delegates in Congress to vote for independence. New Hampshire, New Jersey, and Maryland followed in giving similar instructions to their delegates, early in June. Pennsylvania and New York delayed action, still indulging hopes of an adjustment of the controversy.

The general instructions of the colonies to their delegates were to renounce all allegiance to the British crown, and to form a Confederation among themselves as independent States.

On the 7th of June, Richard Henry Lee, a delegate from Virginia, moved a resolution in Congress, "That these united colonies are and of right ought to be free and independent States. . . . . and that a plan of Confederation be prepared and transmitted to the respective colonies for their consideration and approbation."

This resolution was adopted on the 11th of June. Two committees were appointed under it, one to prepare a declaration of independence, and the other to prepare articles of union or Confederation. The committee to prepare the declaration of independence were, Thomas Jefferson of Virginia, John Adams of Massachusetts, Benjamin Frank-

---

When did South Carolina ? When did Georgia and North Carolina ? What did General Washington write in May ? When did Virginia instruct her delegates ? When did New Hampshire, New Jersey, and Maryland ? Which were the last States ? What were the general instructions of the colonies to their delegates ? Who moved the resolution for independence in Congress ? When was this ? What else did the resolution provide for ? When was it adopted ? What two committees were raised under it ?

lin of Pennsylvania, Roger Sherman of Connecticut, and Robert R. Livingston of New York.

3. On the 24th of June, 1776, the Congress declared, by resolutions, "That all persons abiding within any of the united colonies, and deriving protection from the same, owed allegiance to the said laws, and were members of such colony; and that all persons passing through or making temporary stay in any of the colonies, being entitled to the protection of the laws during the time of such passage, visitation, or temporary stay, owed, during the same, allegiance thereto."

The Committee on the Declaration of Independence reported on the 28th of June; but action was deferred on it for some days, until the delegates from Pennsylvania and New York should receive their instructions and powers to vote for it.

This celebrated paper was drawn up by Mr. Jefferson, the chairman of the committee. It came up for final action on the 4th day of July, when it received the unanimous vote, not only of all the colonies, but of all the delegates in Congress. It was voted upon by colonies, as separate and distinct political bodies.

4. After reciting the wrongs of the colonies, and the breaches of faith on the part of the British crown towards them, it concluded in the following words: "We, therefore, the representatives of the United States of America, in general Congress assembled, appealing to the Supreme Judge of all the world for the rectitude of our intentions, do, in the name and by the authority of the good people of these colonies, solemnly publish and declare that these united colonies are, and of right ought to be, free and independent States; that they are absolved from all allegiance to the British crown, and that all political connec-

---

3. What resolution did Congress pass on the 24th of June, 1776 ? When did the Committee on the Declaration report ? Who was chairman of this committee? Who drew up the Declaration ? When was it finally acted on ? How was it voted upon, and how was it carried ?

4. What is said of the Declaration of Independence ? Who signed it ? What was the title of it ? How was its announcement received ?

tion between them and the state of Great Britain is, and ought to be, totally dissolved; and that, as free and independent States, they have full power to levy war, conclude peace, contract alliances, establish commerce, and to do all other acts and things which independent States may of right do. And for the support of this declaration, with a firm reliance on the protection of a Divine Providence, we mutually pledge to each other our lives, our fortunes, and our sacred honor."

All the delegates present from all the colonies signed the declaration thus made, which was entitled "The unanimous declaration of the thirteen United States of America."

It was immediately proclaimed from the hall in which Congress met, in Philadelphia, known ever since as Inde-

INDEPENDENCE HALL.

pendence Hall. Its announcement was received with great joy everywhere, and attended in many places by the ringing of bells and the kindling of bonfires.

5. The Committee on Confederation reported articles of Union eight days afterwards.

The provisions of these articles may be divided into two classes, the first consisting of mutual covenants between the States; and the second, of mutual delegations of power by each of the States severally to all jointly. The mutual covenants, on proper analysis, may be set forth in substance as follows:

1st. The style of the Confederacy was to be "The United States of America."

2d. Each State retained its Sovereignty, freedom, and independence, and every power and right which is not expressly delegated to the United States.

3d. The object of the Confederation was for their mutual defence, the security of their liberties, and their mutual and general welfare, binding themselves to assist each other against all force offered to or attacks made upon them, or any of them, on account of religion, sovereignty, trade, or any other pretence whatever.

4th. In determining all questions in Congress each State was to have one vote.

5th. Each State was to maintain its own delegates.

6th. The free inhabitants of each State, paupers, vagabonds, and fugitives from justice excepted, were to be entitled to all privileges and immunities of free citizens in the several States.

7th. All fugitives from justice from one State into another were to be delivered up on demand.

8th. Full faith and credit were to be given to the records of each State in all the others.

9th. Congress was to grant no title of nobility.

10th. No person holding any office was to receive a present from a foreign power.

---

5. When did the Committee on Confederation report? How may the provisions of the articles of Confederation be divided? What does the first class consist of? What the second? Name some of the mutual covenants

11th. No State was to form any agreement or alliance with a foreign power, without the consent of the States in Congress assembled.

12th. No two or more States were to form any alliance between themselves without the like consent of the States in Congress assembled.

13th. No State, without the like consent of Congress, was to keep war-ships or an army in time of peace; but each was to keep a well-organized and disciplined militia, with munitions of war.

14th. No State was to lay any duty upon foreign imports which would interfere with any treaty made by Congress.

15th. No State was to issue letters of marque, or to engage in war, without the consent of the Congress, unless actually invaded or menaced with invasion.

16th. When Federal land-forces were raised, each State was to raise the quota required by Congress, arm and equip them at the expense of all the States, and to appoint all officers of and under the rank of colonel.

17th. Each State was to levy and raise the quota of tax required by Congress for Federal purposes.

18th. The faith of all the States was pledged to pay all the bills of credit emitted, or money borrowed on their joint account, by the Congress.

19th. It was agreed and covenanted that Canada might accede to the union so formed if she chose to do so.

20th (and lastly). Each State was to abide by the determination of all the States in Congress assembled, on all questions which, by the Confederation, were submitted to them. The Articles of Confederation were to be inviolably observed by every State, and the Union was to be perpetual. No article of the Confederation was to be altered without the consent of every State.

6. The delegations of power by each of the States to all

---

6. Name some of the delegations of power.

the States, in General Congress assembled, upon a like analysis, may be stated as follows:

1st. The sole and exclusive power to determine on war and peace, except in case a State should be invaded or menaced with invasion.

2d. To send and receive ambassadors.

3d. To make treaties, with a proviso, etc.

4th. To establish rules for captures.

5th. To grant letters of marque and reprisal.

6th. To appoint courts for trial of piracies and other crimes specified.

7th. To decide questions of dispute between two or more States, in a prescribed manner.

8th. The sole and exclusive power to coin money and regulate the value.

9th. To fix a standard of weights and measures.

10th. To regulate trade with the Indian tribes.

11th. To establish post-offices.

12th. To appoint all officers of the militia land-forces, when called out by Congress, except regimental.

13th. To appoint all officers of the Federal naval-forces.

14th. To make rules and regulations for the government of land and naval forces.

15th. To appropriate and apply public money for public expenses, the common defence, and general welfare.

16th. To borrow money and emit bills of credit.

17th. To build and equip a navy.

18th. To agree upon the number of land-forces, and make requisitions upon the States for their quotas, in proportion to the number of white inhabitants in each State.

7. The foregoing powers were delegated with this limitation: the war power, the treaty power, the power to coin money, the power to regulate the value thereof, the power of fixing the quotas of money to be raised by the States, the power to emit bills of credit, the power to borrow

---

7. What was the limitation on some of the powers?

money, the power to appropriate money, the power to regulate the number of land and naval forces, and the power to appoint a commander-in-chief of the army as well as the navy, were never to be exercised unless nine of the States were assenting to the same.

8. These Articles form the original basis and first Constitution of the existing Federal Union of the United States of America.

After being agreed upon by the States, voting as States through their delegates in Congress, they were also submitted to the State governments respectively for their adoption and ratification. The Congress in the meantime went on in the exercise of the powers thereby conferred. As early as 1777 all the State governments had ratified them except Maryland. It was not until 1781 that she gave her full assent to them.

This closes the history of the colonies, separately and collectively, and closes the First Book of our work, in the beginning of the seven years' conflict of arms known as the "War of the Revolution." At this time the aggregate population of the thirteen Colonies, according to the most reliable returns, was 2,803,000, about 500,000 of whom were negro-slaves, diffused throughout all the Colonies.

In the Second Book, which follows, we shall continue the history of the same Peoples during that war, and their subsequent career under the name and character, now assumed, of "The United States of America."

---

8. What do these articles form ? What was done with them after being agreed upon in Congress ? How many State governments had ratified them as early as 1777 ? When did Maryland ratify them ? With what does the First Book close ? What was the war then begun called ? What is said of the population ? How were the colonies afterwards known and how will the same peoples be treated ?

BOOK SECOND.

CHAPTER I.

THE WAR OF THE REVOLUTION FOR THE INDEPENDENCE OF THE STATES.

July, 1776—January, 1778.

Evacuation of New York—Battles of Trenton and Princeton—Connecticut Militia—Federal Flag—Miss Jane McCrea—Battle of Bennington—Defeat of Burgoyne—Battles of Brandywine and Germantown—Washington at Valley Forge.

WE now enter upon the History of the States united in a Federal Union. They had all joined, as we have seen, in a common cause for the maintenance of a separate sovereign right of local self-government on the part of each. For the maintenance of this right they had taken up arms. We proceed, therefore, first, with the bloody conflict already commenced, and which attended the achievement of this great object.

SEAL OF THE UNITED STATES.

1. On the 8th of July, the British General Howe landed

CHAPTER I.—1. What did General Howe do on the 8th of July? What was on Staten Island, near New York, nine thousand men; and a few days afterwards Admiral How arrived with reinforcements from England. Gen. Clinton also soon after arrived; so that the whole British forces now in the States amounted to about thirty thousand men. To oppose these forces, which were provided with every necessary to make effective soldiers, Washington had a badly-clothed and badly-equipped army of hardly half their number.

2. General Howe had been instructed to make an attempt at conciliation. Accordingly, soon after his arrival, he offered pardon to all who would swear allegiance to the King. The Congress caused General Howe's proclamation to be published in all the newspapers of the country, so that the people might see the extent of the submission required of them. General Howe also wrote to Washington, but directed his letter to George Washington, Esq. Washington declined to receive it. The address of the letter was then changed, " To George Washington, &c., &c., &c." Washington still declined to notice it, upon the ground that he would not receive or notice any letter from the British General, not directed to him as Commander of the Armies of the United States.

3. On the 21st of July, Lieutenant-Colonel Paterson, Adjutant of General Howe, obtained a personal interview with General Washington, on the subject of the exchange of prisoners, and during the interview brought up the subject of reconciliation. He stated that General Howe and Lord Howe, by "the benevolence of the King," had been appointed " Commissioners to accommodate this unhappy dispute;" that " they had great powers, and would derive the greatest pleasure from effecting an accommodation." Colonel Paterson, moreover, " wished to have his visit considered as making the first advance to this great object."

---

the number of the British forces about this time ? What is said of Washington's army ?
   2. What was General Howe instructed to do ? What did Congress do ? What is said of Howe's letters to Washington ?
   3. What is said of the interview between Colonel Paterson and General Washington ?

General Washington replied that he was invested with no power on the subject; "but, from what had appeared and transpired on this head, Lord Howe and General Howe were only to grant pardon; that those who had committed no faults wanted no pardons; that we were only defending what we deemed our indisputable rights."

Colonel Paterson said " that would open a very wide field of argument;" and so the matter ended.

4. General Howe now determined to push the war. Accordingly, on the 22d of August, General Clinton crossed over to the southwest point of Long Island, with ten thousand men and forty cannon. The forces of the United States, in and about Brooklyn, consisted of about nine thousand men, under command of Generals Sullivan and Stirling: General Putnam was sent over from New York to take the chief command. On the 27th a battle took place, in which the United States forces were badly defeated, with a loss of about sixteen hundred and fifty men, eleven hundred of whom were made prisoners. Generals Sullivan and Stirling were both captured. The British loss was small.

5. While the battle was at the hottest, Washington crossed over from New York to Fort Putnam, on the island. He could give no relief. The garrison in the fort was too small. Howe did not attack the fort. He camped near it, and waited for the fleet. He thought his prey was secure; but on the night of the 28th a heavy fog arose, which completely hid everything from view all the next day. On the evening of the 29th, Washington paraded his men in silence; about midnight they were embarked in boats, and in six hours the army was safe in New York. Howe had no suspicion of what was taking place until after daybreak, when the last boat was beyond his reach.

6. After this great disaster, Howe, supposing that the

---

4. What did General Howe now determine to do ? What was the result of the battle of the 27th ?
5. What did Washington do ? What took place on the night of the 29th ?
6. What was done by Howe ? With what result ?

Congress might now incline to peace, sent Sullivan on parole with a proposition to that body. But nothing was effected, as neither party was disposed to yield to the other.

7. The British army was soon ready to attack the city; and as Washington knew that he was too weak to make a successful defence, he began a retreat to the northern part of the island. But, as he was very anxious to learn something of Howe's movements, Captain Nathan Hale, of Connecticut, a promising young officer, undertook to visit the British camp as a spy. He was recognized by a Tory* relative, arrested, and on the 22d of September executed as a spy. He was treated with great harshness; no clergyman was permitted to see him; the use of a Bible was denied him; and the letters written by him to his mother and sisters were destroyed. His last words were, "I only regret that I have but one life to give to my country."

8. On the 15th of September a large detachment of the British army crossed the East River, three miles above the city, and spread out across the island, very nearly cutting off the rear-guard of four thousand men, under General Putnam. The British now held possession of the city. Washington occupied the northern part of the island, where he intrenched himself and erected Fort Washington on a rocky height overlooking the Hudson.

9. Howe determined to gain the rear of Washington's position, as the front was too strong to be attacked. He accordingly took position northeast of his camp. Washington then left three thousand men to hold the fort; crossed over to the mainland with the greater part of his army, and fixed his headquarters at White Plains. Here

---

7. What is said of Captain Nathan Hale? How did the British treat him? What was his fate? his last words?
8. About the last of September, what was the position of the opposing armies?
9. What did Howe determine? What was Washington's move? After the battle of White Plains, to what place did Washington withdraw his forces?

---

* Tory was a term applied to all who sided with the British Tory Administration. The opposite party were called Whigs in England, and in the United States all who were for independence were called Whigs; all others Tories.

a battle occurred on the 28th of October, without any very decisive results. Washington withdrew to North Castle, among the hills south of Croton River; and Howe, after a few days, returned to New York. Washington now being apprehensive that the British would attack Philadelphia, left General Charles Lee, with four thousand men, at North Castle; crossed the Hudson, and fixed his headquarters at Fort Lee, in New Jersey.

10. On the 17th of November, Fort Washington was attacked by a large force. The ammunition of the garrison failed, and they were compelled to surrender. By this disaster the United States loss amounted to nearly three thousand men. The British had nearly one thousand killed and wounded. This was a dreadful blow, and caused great depression throughout the country. Washington was blamed for trying to hold the post, and charged with want of courage in not meeting the enemy in the field.

11. On the 19th of November the British crossed the Hudson. Fort Lee was abandoned to them, and they started in pursuit of Washington's army, now amounting to only about three thousand men. Washington retreated across New Jersey, his rear being closely pressed by the British. His army suffered greatly during this retreat. Many of the men were without suitable clothes, and were barefoot. They left blood-stained tracks upon the frozen ground. After a weary and melancholy march they at last reached the Delaware River at Trenton, where they crossed into Pennsylvania. Lord Cornwallis, who was in pursuit, came up soon afterwards; but instead of building boats or a bridge across the river, he concluded to wait until the ice should be thick enough for his army to pass over on it.

12. Meantime he stationed detachments at Princeton, New Brunswick, and other places on the Jersey side of the Delaware. Washington's army seemed about to be de-

---

10. What took place November 20th? What is said of this affair?
11. Describe Washington's retreat across New Jersey.
12. What is said of Washington's army? of desertions? of Lee and Sullivan?

stroyed. Desertions were constantly taking place; and the prospect was so gloomy that many of the friends of the patriot cause now shrunk from its defence. Philadelphia was in danger, and Congress removed to Baltimore. General Charles Lee was taken prisoner by carelessly exposing himself; but General Sullivan, who had been exchanged, took command in Lee's place, and soon united his forces with those of Washington. These, with some recruits from Pennsylvania, made a force of about five thousand men.

13. Washington now planned and executed a bold enterprise. Trenton, in New Jersey, was occupied by about fifteen hundred Hessians, and a troop of British cavalry. These he determined to attack. Christmas night was dark and stormy. The Delaware River was full of ice. Washington and Sullivan, with one division of the army, crossed in the night, and at four o'clock on the morning of the 26th marched on Trenton. The surprise was complete. The Hessians were engaged in Christmas frolics, and not thinking of any danger. The officer in command, Colonel Rahl, was killed, and about a thousand Hessians at once surrendered. The remainder, with the British, escaped. All the artillery and camp-equipage were captured. Washington immediately recrossed the Delaware with his prisoners and spoils. He had lost but nine men, two of whom were frozen. This gloomy year thus closed with a brilliant victory, which gave fresh courage to the army and restored the confidence of the country.

14. On the 2d of January, 1777, Washington recrossed the Delaware and occupied Trenton. Here he received news that Cornwallis was coming to oppose him with a strong force. The opposing armies met and skirmished awhile, when the United States forces fell back, and night coming on, both parties slept on the ground where they

---

13. What was done by Washington, Christmas night? What is said of the victory at Trenton ? its effect on the country ? How many prisoners were taken in this battle ?
14. What was Washington's next move ? What did he think it better to do ?

were, with their arms by them. Washington determined not to bring on a general engagement. He thought it would be better to surprise the British at Princeton. So leaving his fires burning, he as quietly as possible moved his army in the night, and early next morning reached Princeton.

15. The surprise would have been complete, but a brigade of the enemy had just started to Trenton. An engagement ensued, in which the British were defeated; but the United States army sustained a heavy loss in the death of General Mercer, who was killed while rallying his men. The British loss was about four hundred killed, wounded, and prisoners; the United States, about one hundred. After these successes Washington continued sending out expeditions, until he recovered the greater part of New Jersey, only two posts, New Brunswick and Amboy, being at last held by the British.

16. Meantime Congress returned to Philadelphia, where they were employed in measures for supplying the army and for obtaining aid from foreign countries. As early as March, 1776, Mr. Silas Deane, of Connecticut, had been sent to France to solicit aid. He was afterwards joined by Benjamin Franklin and Arthur Lee. No open encouragement to the American cause was given at first, but help was secretly furnished. More than twenty thousand stand of arms and one thousand barrels of powder were sent to the United States in the course of the year 1777.

17. The nobility of France were, in general, opposed to the American cause, as they thought the people were rebels against their King. But there was one young Noble, the Marquis de La Fayette, who was filled with an ardent enthusiasm in favor of the cause of those struggling for the right of self-government on this continent. On hearing

---

15. What is said of the battle of Princeton? What general was killed? What was the British loss? the American?
16. How was Congress employed? What envoys were sent to France?
17. What is said of the nobility of France? What is said of La Fayette?

the Declaration of Independence read, he was completely convinced of the justice of their cause, and he determined to give them all the assistance in his power. In opposition to the wishes of his family, and without permission of the King of France, he came to this country. Immediately after his arrival, in July, 1777, he received the commission of Major-General in the army, which had been promised him by Mr. Deane. His acquaintance with Washington, which took place in a few days after his arrival, soon ripened into a warm and life-long friendship.

18. In March, General Howe sent a force up the Hudson to destroy the "rebel" stores at Peekskill. The garrison there, seeing the approach of the British, set fire to the stores and left the place. On the 25th of April several thousand of the enemy, under General Tryon, the last royal Governor of Connecticut, made a raid into that State. On the 26th they burned the town of Danbury, and all the supplies collected there. They committed many other atrocities. On their retreat they were assailed by the militia, who harassed them so sharply that they lost nearly three hundred men. The loss sustained by the militia was much less; but among the number was General Wooster, an old man, then in his seventieth year.

19. By way of retaliation, Colonel Meigs crossed over from Connecticut, and burnt twelve British vessels and a large quantity of supplies, near Sag Harbor, on Long Island. He took about ninety prisoners; lost none. About this time, also, July 10th, Major Barton, of Providence, achieved a very daring exploit. With about forty men, he captured the British General Prescott and carried him off a prisoner. Congress immediately gave him a sword and a colonel's commission.

20. In July of this year, Congress adopted a flag, con-

---

18. When did La Fayette arrive in the United States ? What office was given him ? What happened on the 25th and 26th of April in Connecticut ?
19. What did Colonel Meigs do ? What is said of Colonel Barton's exploit ?
20. Describe the flag adopted by Congress. What do the stars represent ? How did the stripes originate ?

sisting of thirteen stripes, red and white alternately, with thirteen white stars on a blue ground; each star representing a State.

FLAG AND SHIELD.

The stripes came from the six sections of the shield, which formed part of the original device of a seal proposed for the United States. These six sections, or quarterings of the escutcheon, were intended to designate the six European countries from which the United States had been chiefly peopled, to wit, England, Scotland, Ireland, France, Germany, and Holland. In drawing these six sections on the shield-figure, seven spaces of the original color were, of course, left, which gave to the whole the appearance of thirteen bars, or stripes. The motto on the seal, finally adopted in 1782, was "E PLURIBUS UNUM"— that is, "one of many;" or "one Federal Government by several Independent States."

21. All this time the British were preparing to invade the United States from Canada. General Burgoyne, with ten thousand men, was approaching the upper part of the Hudson River. His object was to get in between Washington and New England. On the 21st of June he gave a great "war-feast" to the Indians. The chiefs promised to help him; and when they saw his fine, large army, they thought that he would be able to whip the rebels in a short time. He soon reached Ticonderoga with his army. St. Clair was there with about three thousand men. He thought at first that he could hold the place, but he soon found himself compelled to beat a hasty retreat.

22. The British pursued, defeated his rear-guard, took

---

21. What were the British preparing to do all this time? What was Burgoyne's object? What did the Indian chiefs think?
22. What proclamation did Burgoyne issue? How did General Schuyler reply?

Skeenesborough, and destroyed the supplies there collected. General Burgoyne then issued a proclamation, promising pardon and protection to all who would return to their allegiance. General Schuyler immediately published a proclamation in answer, in which he made appear what kind of protection had been given to the people of New Jersey, and warned the people against listening to the promises of the enemy. After the loss of so many strong forts in the north, the country became very much alarmed and despondent; and, as is usual in such cases, Generals Schuyler and St. Clair were blamed without cause.

23. Other officers were ordered to the north to their assistance,—Lincoln, Arnold, and Morgan. Burgoyne came on slowly. On the 30th of July he reached Fort Edward. The United States army fell back to Saratoga, Stillwater, and to the Mohawk River, near where it empties into the Hudson.

24. It was during the advance of Burgoyne, about this time, that the Indians murdered a young lady, whose fate has always been much pitied, and around which a sad and tender interest has always hung. The name of the young lady was Jane McCrea. She lived near Fort Edward with her brother. She had become acquainted with Lieutenant Jones, of the British army; had fallen in love with him, and was engaged to be married to him. Jane's brother was a Whig, and on the approach of the British army he left home and went to Albany.

25. The young lady, wishing to see her lover, remained with a friend and neighbor, Mrs. McNeil, who was a loyalist, and a near relative of the British General Frazer. All her friends thought that she would be entirely safe. On the 27th of July the house was surrounded by Indians, and Mrs. McNeil and Jane were both seized, but by different parties, and were carried off in different directions. The

---

23. What officers were sent north to the assistance of Schuyler and St. Clair?
24. What young lady was murdered about this time?
25. What is said of Jane McCrea?

house being near where some of the United States forces were camped, the alarm was given, and the Indians were pursued and fired upon; but the captives were not rescued. The Indians carried Mrs. McNeil to the British camp, but Miss McCrea was never again seen alive.

Mrs. McNeil recognized her scalp in the hands of some of the party who had seized her, and they were charged with her murder. But they declared that she had been killed by the soldiers, who pursued and fired upon them as they were carrying her off; and that they scalped her to obtain the bounty which the British were in the habit of paying. Lieutenant Jones, heart-broken at his loss, resigned his commission in the army. His resignation was not accepted, and he deserted. We are told that for more than fifty years he lived the life of a hermit, mourning with unavailing regret the cruel loss of his beloved Jane.

26. General Burgoyne, finding his army greatly in need of provisions, and it being a very difficult task to bring them from Ticonderoga, sent Colonel Baum, a German officer, from Fort Edward, with five hundred men, to seize some stores which had been collected by the patriots at Bennington. They were met and entirely defeated near Bennington, by Colonel Stark, in command of the Green Mountain Boys, as they were called; they were Vermont militia-men. Soon after this battle another party of the British arrived, and the militia, in turn, would very probably have been defeated, had not Colonel Warner fortunately come up with a regiment at this critical moment. The battle was renewed with great spirit, and the enemy was entirely defeated. The British loss in the two engagements was about seven hundred men, mostly prisoners; the United States loss not more than one hundred.

27. By the battle of Bennington, Burgoyne was delayed

---

26. What is said of Burgoyne's army at this time ? Describe the battle of Bennington. Who commanded the Americans ? What was the British loss ? the American ?
27. What was the effect of the battle of Bennington ? What news was received from Fort Schuyler ? of Herkimer's defeat etc. ?

at Fort Edward nearly a month. At this time news was received from Fort Schuyler. This fort being besieged by the British, General Herkimer collected the militia and marched to its relief; but he was defeated and slain. Soon after a sally was made from the fort, which damaged the enemy greatly. On the approach of Arnold the Indian allies left the British army, and St. Leger, who was in command, was forced to give up the siege.

28. About the middle of September, General Burgoyne crossed the Hudson and took position at Saratoga. General Gates, who had superseded Schuyler in command of the United States forces in that section, was in camp near Stillwater. On the 18th of September, Burgoyne was within two miles of Gates's camp. On the 19th a general battle was fought, which continued three hours. Night put an end to the contest. Gates withdrew to his camp; the British remained upon the field of battle. Both parties claimed the victory, which really belonged to neither, for neither was defeated. Burgoyne intrenched himself, to wait for assistance from New York.

29. The Canadians and Indians now began to desert him, and being cut off from the means of obtaining supplies, he was obliged to shorten his soldiers' rations. On the 7th of October another general battle occurred, on nearly the same ground as the former, which was fought with desperate bravery on both sides. But the British were defeated with heavy loss. Some of their best officers were killed, among them General Frazer, one of the noblest and most efficient, slain by General Morgan's riflemen. The United States loss was not great. The night after the battle the British fell back to a better position, and Gates occupied his former camp.

---

28. What was the position of Burgoyne and of Gates about the middle of September? What is said of the battle of Stillwater? Was a victory claimed by either party?
29. What was now done by the Canadians and Indians? What is said of the battle of October 7th?

30. Burgoyne's next move was to retire to Saratoga, in the effort to reach Fort Edward. But he was not able to accomplish his purpose; pressed on all sides by Gates, reduced to a three days' supply of provisions, and losing all hope of assistance from New York, he was compelled to propose terms of surrender. On the 17th of October he surrendered his army prisoners of war. This great victory was soon followed by the capture of Forts Clinton and Montgomery, and the re-occupation of Ticonderoga and all the forts on the northern frontier by the United States forces. In the latter part of October, four thousand of these victorious troops proceeded to join Washington, in the neighborhood of Philadelphia, where he had been sorely pressed for several months, as we shall now state.

31. In the month of July, while the operations were going on northward, as related, General Howe, with sixteen thousand men, sailed from New York with the intention of attacking Philadelphia. Washington, with little more than half the number, hastened to front him. The two armies met at Shad's Ford, on the Brandywine Creek. Here, on the 11th of September, was fought a desperate battle, in which La Fayette and Count Pulaski, a noble Pole, who had also espoused the cause of the States, greatly distinguished themselves. In this engagement La Fayette received a wound, but was not disabled by it.

Washington was at length compelled to yield the ground to superior forces. He retreated, and took position about eight miles above Philadelphia. That city fell into the hands of the British, and the Congress retired to York, in Pennsylvania.

On the 4th of October, Washington made an attack on the British at Germantown. His plans were well laid, and would, perhaps, have been successful if his orders had been

---

30. What was Burgoyne's next move? When did he surrender? What followed this great victory?
31. What is said of the battles of Brandywine, Germantown, and Red Bank? What of Forts Mifflin and Mercer?

promptly executed; but as they were not, nothing was effected by it.

Soon after, the British made an attack on part of Washington's forces, stationed at Red Bank, on the east side of the Delaware. In this the British were defeated, with the loss of General Donop, who commanded this movement.

Forts Mifflin and Mercer, a short distance below Philadelphia, on opposite sides of the river, were then both attacked by the enemy, on the 22d of October. After a series of attacks Fort Mifflin was captured, the garrison retiring to Fort Mercer; but in a few days, being pressed by the enemy, this fort was also abandoned, and the Delaware was thus opened to the British shipping. Soon afterwards Washington advanced to White Marsh, where the British General Howe frequently tried to draw him into a general engagement, but failed.

32. On the approach of winter the British retired to Philadelphia, where, surrounded by plenty and all the comforts of life, they passed the cold season of winter. Washington encamped at Valley Forge, in rude huts. Here he was daily compelled, through a long and rigorous season, to witness sufferings that he could not relieve, and to hear murmurs and complaints it was impossible to still. But his exertions to save his country never relaxed. Calumny did its worst. His enemies spared no efforts to supplant him, to have him removed from the chief command, and to put General Gates in his place. But their malicious efforts failed, and they finally received the deserved contempt of the army and of the people.

---

32. Where did the British take up winter quarters? Describe the condition of Washington's army at Valley Forge. What is said of the efforts to remove Washington from the command?

CHAPTER II.

WAR OF THE REVOLUTION, CONTINUED.

1778—1779.

Treaty with France—Battle of Monmouth—Massacre of Wyoming—Capture of Savannah, etc.—Count D'Estaing—Paul Jones.

1. Soon after the defeat and surrender of Burgoyne, commissioners were sent from Great Britain to America to see if the difficulties could not be settled in a friendly manner without a separation of the Colonies from the mother-country. But their proposals were rejected by Congress, who refused to treat unless Great Britain would withdraw her armies, or acknowledge the independence of the United States. About this time news was received that France had acknowledged the independence of the several thirteen States at war with England, and had entered into a treaty with them under their articles of Confederation.

2. The treaty was signed on the 6th day of February, 1778. The commissioners on the part of the United States were Benjamin Franklin, Silas Deane, and Arthur Lee. Congress ratified the treaty on the 4th of May following. The making of this treaty was considered by Great Britain as a declaration of war on the part of France against her, and the two nations immediately prepared for the contest. A French fleet, under Count D'Estaing, was sent over to blockade the British fleet in the Delaware, while Washington operated by land in New Jersey. But Lord Howe, being informed of what was going on, before the arrival of the French fleet, sailed for New York, at which place all the British forces were ordered to concentrate.

3. On the 18th of June, General Clinton, in command of

CHAPTER II.—**1.** Just after Burgoyne's surrender, what was done? On what terms was Congress willing to treat? What news was received from France?
2. What was the consequence of this treaty?
3. What move did General Clinton make? What was Washington anxious to do? What order did he give?

the British land-forces, began his march from Philadelphia to New York. His force consisted of about eleven thousand men, with a great amount of baggage and provisions. Washington, with the main body of his army, followed cautiously. At the same time he sent forward detachments to operate with the Jersey militia in harassing the enemy and retarding his march. He was anxious to bring on a general engagement; but did not do it in opposition to the views of his officers, as expressed in a council of war. When, however, the British had arrived at Monmouth, Washington was so unwilling for them to reach the heights of Middletown without a battle, that he ordered General Charles Lee (who had been exchanged for General Prescott) to attack their rear.

4. On the morning of the 28th, La Fayette, with his light-horse, attacked a body of the enemy, but was forced to retire before them. Lee, surprised by the sudden onset of the enemy, ordered his troops to fall back, in order, as he maintained afterwards, to gain a better position. Part of his men, misunderstanding the order, continued to retreat, and Lee followed, pursued by the enemy. Washington came up at this moment, and seeing the disastrous retreat of General Lee, addressed him in a sharp and cutting manner. Some writers blame General Lee very much for this whole affair, and say that he entirely deserved the reproaches of Washington.

LA FAYETTE.

---

4. Who made the attack? With what result? How did Washington address Lee?

5. Whether he really deserved them or not, (with his subsequent explanation,) it is yet true that after the arrival of Washington on the ground, the troops were soon rallied; order was restored, and as the main body of the army came up the battle became general, and was continued until night. The victory was not decisive either way, but the Americans kept possession of the field. They expected to renew the battle in the morning; but General Clinton quietly withdrew during the night, moving on towards New York. The total loss of the British in this battle was about five hundred; that of the United States, about two hundred and thirty.

6. General Lee, angry at the reproaches of Washington, wrote to him on the next day in an insulting manner. Washington immediately had him arrested for disobedience of orders and for improper conduct in the presence of the enemy. He was tried by court-martial, and the sentence of the court was that he be suspended from his command for one year. This eccentric genius and soldier of fortune was a native of Wales. He had served in the British army in Portugal, under Burgoyne. He afterwards had served in the army of Poland. When the dispute arose between England and the Colonies he offered his services to the latter, and was one of the five Major-Generals appointed by Congress in 1775. He never returned to the army after his suspension, but died in Philadelphia in 1782.

7. After the battle of Monmouth the British proceeded without molestation to Sandy Hook, whence they were conveyed on the fleet to New York. Washington took position at White Plains, where he remained until he went into winter quarters at Middlebrook, in New Jersey.

8. In July a French fleet, under Count D'Estaing, ap-

---

5. What took place after Washington came up? What was the British loss? the United States?
6. How did Lee write to Washington? What was the result? What is said of this eccentric genius?
7. Where did Washington go into winter quarters?
8. What happened in July?

peared off the coast of Virginia. Measures being concerted for the siege of Newport, in Rhode Island, D'Estaing entered that harbor early in August. Soon after operations began a British fleet approached. D'Estaing went out to meet the enemy; but a great storm arose, which prevented an engagement, and damaged both fleets considerably. The French returned to Newport, and the British sailed for New York.

9. Meantime General Sullivan, with the land-forces, had begun the siege, confidently expecting the co-operation of the fleet. In this he was disappointed. Against the urgent entreaties of La Fayette and Greene, D'Estaing soon sailed for Boston, for the purpose of refitting his vessels, and Sullivan was then compelled to abandon the siege. On his retreat he came near being cut off by General Clinton, who had arrived on the 31st of August, with four thousand men and a light squadron, for the relief of Newport.

10. In this year occurred the massacre of Wyoming, in Pennsylvania, which has become so celebrated in song and story. Early in the summer this lovely valley was invaded by a party of about fifteen hundred Iroquois Indians and Tories, led by Colonel John Butler. On the 3d of July Colonel Zebulon Butler, with about four hundred men and boys, advanced to meet the invading party. He was defeated, and lost nearly the whole of his men, killed, wounded, or prisoners. The next day the fort of Wyoming was laid siege to by the Indians and Tories. It was surrendered on condition that the survivors might be allowed to go to their homes in security.

11. This promise of security was soon broken. No sooner was the fort thrown open, and its occupants scattered on the way to their several homes, than the work of butchery began. At night the Indians and Tories spread themselves

---

9. Meantime what did General Sullivan do? D'Estaing? What was the result?
10. What terrible massacre took place this year? Go on and tell all about it.

over the valley; burned the houses of the inhabitants, and slaughtered, without mercy, men, women, and children. Only a very few escaped the dreadful massacre. The tortures inflicted on the unfortunate victims were cruel in the extreme. One, a Captain Bidlack, was thrown alive on burning coals, and kept there with pitchforks until he died. Six others were placed near a stone on the river-bank, and held by six savages, while Queen Esther, an old Indian woman, walked round them in a circle, singing their death-song, and striking them on the head with a club until they died. The desolation of Wyoming was complete.

12. In November a like scene was enacted in Cherry Valley, New York. Brant, a noted Mohawk chief, at the head of a band of Indians and Tories, suddenly entered the valley, and killed and carried off most of the inhabitants. There seemed to be a race between the Indians and Tories, as to which could excel in deeds of ferocious bloodthirstiness.

13. With these events, or soon after, active operations by large armies closed in the northern and middle sections of the country. The scene now shifts to the South, and, until the close of the war, the principal operations were confined to that section.

In November, 1778, General Clinton sent Lieutenant-Colonel Campbell, with two thousand men, and a fleet under Admiral Hyde Parker, against Savannah, in Georgia. That place was held by General Robert Howe, with about nine hundred United States troops. An engagement ensued, in which the British were successful in getting possession of the place; the United States forces crossed over into South Carolina.

14. The whole of the lower part of eastern Georgia was thereafter soon overrun, and left to the mercy of the British and Tories. This conquest of Savannah and inroad

---
12. What is said of the massacre of Cherry Valley?
13. What was the result of the British attack on Savannah?
14. What was the consequence of this defeat? How much had the British gained after two years' fighting?

into Georgia were the only advantages gained by the enemy during the year. Indeed, after two years of fighting at the North, the British had, in fact, accomplished nothing; and the positions of the opposing armies were, at the close of 1778, almost the same as at the beginning of 1777.

15. In the beginning of the year 1779, the British force in the South consisted of about three thousand effective men, under the command of General Prevost. General Lincoln, a brave and skillful officer, had at this time the command of the United States army in this section; but his forces were inferior in number to the British, and consisted chiefly of militia. The first attempt of the British General was the conquest of South Carolina and the upper part of Georgia, on the Savannah River. He sent a body of regulars to take possession of Port Royal Island; but they were met by General Moultrie and driven back with severe loss.

Soon afterwards Colonel Boyd, an English officer, who commanded a regiment of loyalists, or Tories, at a place known as Ninety-Six, in the upper part of South Carolina, was ordered to join the British army near the city of Savannah. He crossed over into Georgia, intending to take Augusta in his route; but was met by Colonel Andrew Pickens and Lieutenant-Colonel Elijah Clarke, commanding Carolina and Georgia militia respectively, and defeated, in a battle fought the 14th of February, on Kettle Creek, in Wilkes county, Georgia. Colonel Boyd received a mortal wound in the action. After the fighting was over, Colonel Pickens went to him, and tendered him any service which his situation authorized. Boyd thanked him for his kindness, and asked what was the result of the battle. Upon being informed that it was against him, he said it would have been otherwise if he had not fallen. He then requested Colonel Pickens, as he had but a few hours to live, to leave two men with him to furnish him water, and to

---

15. What was the British strength, early in 1779, in the South ? What is said of General Lincoln ? What was the first attempt of the British this year ? What is said of the battle of Kettle Creek ?

bury his body; also to write to his wife, in England, informing her of his fate; and with the letter to send her a few articles he had about his person. He died very soon afterwards, and Colonel Pickens complied faithfully with his requests. Seventy of Boyd's regiment were taken prisoners, quite a number were left dead on the field, while the remainder of his command was utterly routed. Pickens and Clarke also encountered and defeated several other squads of the enemy, on both sides of the river. Clarke was the great Georgia partisan leader.

16. General Lincoln, being encouraged by these successes, sent General Ashe to take position at the mouth of Brier Creek, which empties into the Savannah River, on the Georgia side, some distance above the city of Savannah. His force was about two thousand strong. On the 3d of March he was surprised by General Prevost, and defeated, with the loss of nearly the whole of his army.

17. By this defeat of General Ashe the subjugation of Georgia below Augusta was made complete for the time. The United States loss by this affair was very heavy; but, by the middle of April, General Lincoln was again able to take the field at the head of five thousand men. With these troops he began his march up the Savannah River, intending to enter Georgia at Augusta. But the march of Prevost upon the city of Charleston, before which he appeared on the 11th of May, compelled Lincoln to abandon this enterprise and hasten back to oppose the British general. On Lincoln's approach Prevost gave up the siege and retired.

18. On the 20th of June, the Carolinians attacked a British force at Stono Ferry, ten miles west of Charleston, but were defeated, with considerable loss. Shortly afterwards the British established a post at Beaufort, in South Caro-

---

16. What did General Lincoln then do ? What happened to General Ashe ?
17. What resulted from the defeat of General Ashe? What was Lincoln's next move ? What caused him to give up the enterprise ?
18. What was done June 20th ?

lina, but the main body retired to Savannah. The weather now being very hot, and the season unhealthy, active operations were suspended by both armies until October.

19. During this year the British forces at the North were chiefly employed in marauding expeditions. In February, Governor Tryon (last royal Governor of Connecticut), commanding a body of about fifteen hundred men, destroyed the salt-works at Horse Neck, in Connecticut, and plundered the town. It was at this place that General Putnam made his escape from the enemy by riding down a steep precipice, over which they dared not follow.

20. In May the enemy made an expedition into Virginia, in which they destroyed public and private property to a large amount in Norfolk, Portsmouth, and all the neighboring country. General Clinton himself conducted an expedition up the Hudson from the city of New York. On the 31st of May he captured Stony Point, and on June 1st Verplanck's Point, and made the garrison prisoners of war. He then left garrisons of British troops in both forts. In July, Governor Tryon burnt East Haven, Fairfield, and Norwalk, plundered New Haven, and desolated the coasts of Connecticut generally.

21. But all this time the United States forces at the North were not entirely idle. About the middle of July was performed one of the most brilliant achievements of the whole war. This was the recapture, by General Anthony Wayne, of Stony Point, on the Hudson. On the evening of the 15th he arrived, with his command, near the fort, without having been perceived by the enemy. About midnight on the night of the 15th, with unloaded muskets and fixed bayonets, they rushed up the height on which the fort was situated, scaled the walls, and in a few minutes were masters of the place. The British loss was about six hundred

---

19. How were the British forces employed at the North ? What was the remarkable feat of General Putnam ?
20. In May what was done in Virginia ? on the Hudson ?
21. What were the Americans doing ? Describe the capture of Stony Point by General Wayne.

killed, wounded, and prisoners; the loss of Wayne was about one hundred. He thought it best, however, not to try to hold the fort, and therefore retired after destroying it.

22. On the 19th of July, Major Henry Lee surprised a British garrison at Paulus Hook. Thirty were killed, and one hundred and sixty were made prisoners. In August, General Sullivan, with near five thousand men, was sent against the Indians in Pennsylvania and New York. He proceeded up the Susquehanna River, and on the 29th of August found a force of Indians and Tories strongly posted at Elmira. Here a battle was fought, in which the Indians were so completely defeated that they gave up all thoughts of further war. General Sullivan laid waste the Indian country to the Genesee River, which empties into Lake Ontario, seven miles from Rochester, New York. This was a terrible blow to the Iroquois, from which they never recovered.

23. Let us now return to the South. On the 9th of September, Count D'Estaing, returning from the West Indies, appeared near Savannah with his fleet. Soon afterwards, General Lincoln, in concert with the French, laid siege to Savannah. After continuing the siege a month, they made an assault upon the enemy's works, but were repulsed with great slaughter, losing nearly a thousand men, killed and wounded. Count Pulaski, a noble Pole, was mortally wounded. The brave Sergeant Jasper, the hero of Fort Moultrie, was also mortally wounded in this assault.

General Lincoln wished to renew the attack; but the Count D'Estaing refusing to co-operate with him, he was compelled to abandon the enterprise. The next day the siege was raised; the French returned home; Lincoln withdrew into South Carolina, and moved his army to Charleston.

---

22. Describe the events of July and August.
23. What is said of the siege and defeat at Savannah? What two remarkable men were killed there?

24. On the 23d of September of this year was fought, near the coast of Scotland, a very severe and bloody naval battle, between some United States vessels commanded by Paul Jones, and two English ships of war that were conducting a fleet of merchantmen. At half-past seven o'clock P.M. the battle began by the attack of Jones's ship, the *Bon Homme Richard*, carrying forty guns, upon the *Serapis*, a British frigate of forty-four guns, commanded by Captain Pearson. Jones moved his ship close to the side of the British vessel, and fastened them together. In this position they fought for two hours, neither having any thought of surrender.

25. Both vessels took fire, and when Jones's ship was almost at the point of sinking, the American frigate *Alliance* came up, and, by mistake in the dark, discharged a broadside into the *Richard*. The mistake being discovered directly, she fell with great fury upon the *Serapis*, which soon surrendered. Jones immediately took possession of the English vessel, and had scarcely time to do so before his own sank. The other English frigate was also captured. Out of three hundred and seventy-five men on board the *Bon Homme Richard*, three hundred were either killed or wounded. Such terrible loss shows the desperate nature of the conflict.

26. With these events the military operations of the year 1779 closed. The hopes of the people, founded upon the alliance with France, had not been realized. The schemes of co-operation had in great measure failed, and general despondency of mind was the result. The winter was the severest ever experienced on the continent. All the Atlantic harbors were frozen as far south as Virginia. Long Island Sound was frozen to a solid highway. The snow was four feet deep for three months. The army was badly

---

24. What severe battle was fought near the coast of Scotland? Who commanded the United States vessels?
25. Go on and describe the fight, and tell the number of killed and wounded.
26. What is said of the condition of the country and of the United States army at the close of the year 1779? What of the severity of this winter?

clothed, and suffered greatly. Its numbers were also greatly reduced. There was no money in the treasury, and the credit of the country was so low that it was impossible to borrow. But Great Britain seemed to be greater than ever. Though Spain had declared war against her, yet her resources seemed equal to the emergency, and she determined on still greater efforts for the conquest of the Colonies. For the year 1780, Parliament determined to enlist eighty-five thousand seamen and thirty-five thousand land troops, in addition to those already in service. They voted also a sum amounting to one hundred millions of dollars for the same year.

CHAPTER III.

THE WAR OF THE REVOLUTION—CONTINUED.
1780.

Fall of Charleston—Battle of Camden—Battle of King's Mountain—Treason of Arnold.

1. As soon as Sir Henry Clinton heard that Count D'Estaing had left the American coast, he determined on the conquest of South Carolina; and with this object sailed from New York, with a large land and naval force, under convoy of Admiral Arbuthnot. He landed at John's Island, thirty miles below Charleston, on the 11th day of February, 1780. At that time the State was badly provided for defence; there was little or no money; the Indians and Tories on the borders and in the interior excited continual alarm and commotion; Lincoln's army was a mere handful.

2. When Clinton landed, Lincoln's first impulse was to abandon the city and retire into the interior; but learning that the British General was preparing for a regular siege, and being urged by the inhabitants to remain, he deter-

---

CHAPTER III.—**1.** What did Sir Henry Clinton resolve on? What was the condition of South Carolina at the time?
2. What was Lincoln's first impulse? Why did he change? Did the reinforcements ever arrive?

mined to risk a siege, relying upon the arrival of reinforcements which had been promised him. The reinforcements never arrived, and at a time when his army ought to have numbered ten thousand men, it did not exceed the third of that number. Clinton invested the city on the 29th of March, and on the 9th of April the fleet, under Admiral Arbuthnot, favored by a strong wind, passed Fort Moultrie with little damage, and anchored in Charleston harbor within cannon shot of the city.

3. The siege lasted about eight weeks. In that time the city was completely surrounded, without hope of succor, either by land or sea. A corps which had assembled at Monk's Corner, under command of General Hugher, for the relief of the city, had been surprised, defeated, and dispersed by a detachment of fourteen hundred men, under Webster, Tarleton, and Ferguson; so that there now being no hope of relief, Fort Moultrie surrendered on the 6th of May, and Charleston on the 12th. General Lincoln and the whole army under his command at this place became prisoners of war. To add to the gloom which this disaster cast upon the country, there occurred a few days afterwards a most remarkable natural phenomenon, that filled the minds of the timid and superstitious with great apprehension and alarm.

It was what was long known as the dark days. About 10 o'clock on the 19th of May, the heavens became darkened by a dense vapor or smoke, of a yellow color. It was so dark that lights had to be kindled in the houses for all business purposes, and the fowls went to roost. The Legislature of Connecticut was in session at the time, and the House adjourned in consequence of the darkness. It was the opinion of some that the day of judgment was at hand. A motion was also made in the Council to adjourn. Colonel Davenport, a bold leader of the patriot cause, opposed it, saying: "The day of judgment is either approaching or it

---

3. How long did the siege last? What was the result? What is said of the dark days?

is not. If it is not, there is no cause for an adjournment; if it is, I desire to be found doing my duty. I move, therefore, that candles may be brought."

This strange and extraordinary phenomenon continued all the next day; but the unusual vapor, or whatever it was, passed off on the night of the 20th; the firmament after that was as bright as ever. Hope again revived in the breasts of the desponding.

4. After the fall of Charleston, Clinton, to extend his conquests, sent out three detachments into the interior; one, under Lord Cornwallis, toward Camden; one, under Colonel Cruger, toward Ninety-Six; and one, under Colonel Brown, to Augusta. A truce in South Carolina was also proclaimed, and a pardon offered to all who would take British protection. Great numbers accepted the terms, and the country appeared so quiet that Clinton, thinking the subjugation complete, sailed for New York, leaving Cornwallis in command. At this time they might have accomplished their object, if those in authority had pursued a different and more politic course.

5. Instead of conciliating, the British General pursued the opposite course; and the Whigs, who, in despair, had yielded for a moment, were soon roused to resistance by the cruel exactions of the British. They flocked to the standards of Sumter, Marion, Pickens, of South Carolina, and Clarke, of Georgia, who began a partisan warfare, which finally resulted, as we shall see, in the expulsion of the British from the State. At this time, also, another event occurred, which for awhile revived the hopes of the people. This was the appointment of General Gates to the command of the Southern army. While Sumter, on the Catawba; Marion, in the swamps of the Pedee; Pickens, on the Saluda, and Clarke, on the Savannah, were keeping the

---

4. What was the action of Clinton after the fall of Charleston? What is said of the proclamation of the truce and its effect?
5. What roused the Whigs to resistance? What gave great encouragement to the Whigs?

Tories in check, Gates was approaching with a strong army from the North.

6. The most brilliant hopes are often most suddenly blasted; so they were now. Gates, blinded by his great success at Saratoga, disregarded the warnings and suggestions of his officers, and pushed rapidly on, confident of victory. On the approach of Gates, the British General, Lord Rawdon, concentrated his strength at Camden, where he was joined, August 13th, by Lord Cornwallis, from Charleston. On the night of the 15th, Gates set out from his camp at Clermont, about ten miles north of Camden, with the purpose of surprising the British camp. Cornwallis and Rawdon left Camden about the same hour, intending to surprise Gates. The vanguards of the two armies soon met, when some skirmishing took place.

7. On the morning of August 16th, there was a general engagement. Gates was defeated with heavy loss. At the first onset the Virginia and Carolina militia began to waver, when the British charged with fixed bayonets, and put them to flight. The regulars stood their ground bravely; in fact, soldiers never behaved better; but, being abandoned by the militia, they were at length overpowered and driven from the field. Gates, with the remnant of his army, retired to Hillsborough, North Carolina. His loss in this battle was about one thousand, killed, wounded, and prisoners, besides all his artillery, ammunition, and supplies. Among the slain was the brave Baron De Kalb. The British loss was only a little over three hundred.

BARON DE KALB.

---

6. How did General Gates conduct himself? What took place on the night of August 15th?
7. Describe the battle of August 16th. What was the American loss?

8. Soon after Gates's defeat, Sumter was surprised at Fishing Creek, by Colonel Tarleton, August 18th, and defeated with great slaughter. For a time immediately succeeding these disastrous events, there were very few Whigs in arms in South Carolina, except Marion and his men, on the Pedee. Lord Cornwallis, in order to secure the submission of the inhabitants, thought it necessary to adopt severe measures. He gave orders to hang every militia-man who, once having served with the British, had afterwards joined the cause of the States. Those who had once submitted and then revolted were imprisoned, and their property either taken from them or destroyed. But these severe measures failed to accomplish the intended purpose. They rather increased in the breasts of the people a spirit of resistance, which only wanted opportunity to burst forth.

9. After the battle of Camden, Cornwallis proceeded to Charlotte. He sent Tarleton to operate east of the Catawba River, and Major Ferguson to embody the Tories among the mountains of North and South Carolina. Ferguson crossed Broad River, at the Cherokee Ford, on the 1st of October. A considerable number of Tories joined him, and with a body of about fifteen hundred men he encamped on King's Mountain. The atrocities he committed soon roused the Whigs to action; and on the 7th of October, under the leadership of Colonels Campbell, Cleveland, Shelby, Sevier, and Williams, they attacked him with great fury. The Whig forces consisted chiefly of Carolina and Georgia militia.

10. The defence was very obstinate; but after a desperate engagement Ferguson himself was slain, and his army, after a loss of three hundred killed and wounded, was entirely routed. Eight hundred prisoners were taken, and about fifteen hundred stand of arms. The Carolinians and

---

8. What took place at Fishing Creek ? What measures did Lord Cornwallis adopt ? Did these severe measures accomplish their purpose?
9-10. After the battle of Camden, what was done by Cornwallis ? What took place October 7th ? Who commanded the Americans ? Who gained the victory? What was the British loss ?

Georgians lost about twenty killed. After the battle, ten of the captives, Tories, who had been notorious for their cruelty to the Whigs, were hung.

11. Sumter did not remain idle after his defeat. He soon collected a band of volunteers, with whom he continued to harass the enemy. His activity and energy were so great that he well deserved the title of "Game-Cock," which was given to him. On the 12th of November he was attacked at the Fishdam Ferry, on Broad River, by a detachment of the enemy, commanded by Major Wemys. The British were defeated, and Major Wemys was taken prisoner. On the 20th he was again attacked at Blackstocks, in Marion District, South Carolina, by Colonel Tarleton, the most active, energetic, and dangerous of all the British partisan officers of the time. Again Sumter's star was in the ascendant. Tarleton was obliged to retreat, severely worsted, leaving Sumter in possession of the field.

12. General Francis Marion, who gained the title of "Swamp-Fox," distinguished himself greatly in the partisan warfare of this period. He did much service by keeping the Tories in check, and by cutting off straggling parties of the enemy. He bore with unflinching fortitude and hope the reverses of the darkest period of the war, and infused into his brigade a spirit which was willing to bear all things and to suffer all, but never to surrender.

GENERAL FRANCIS MARION.

13. We must now take a brief glance at some events that occurred at the North during this year. On the 7th of June, five

---

11. What was the result of the battles of Fishdam Creek and Blackstocks?
12. What is said of General Francis Marion?
13. What is said of General Knyphausen? What is said of the poverty of the Americans at this time?

thousand men, under General Knyphausen, invaded New Jersey, and plundered the country, but withdrew on the advance of United States forces from Morristown. On the 10th of July a French fleet arrived at Newport, Rhode Island, having on board five thousand men, commanded by Count de Rochambeau; but so greatly reduced were the resources of Washington that he had neither men nor supplies sufficient to enable him to co-operate with the French. For this reason active operations were mostly suspended for the remainder of the season.

14. At this dark and gloomy period there was found one man, Benedict Arnold, a Major-General in the United States army, weak enough and base enough to offer to betray his country. He had been distinguished for his bravery and good conduct, and had been appointed by Congress commandant at Philadelphia, on the evacuation of that post by the British. He became haughty and arrogant; lived very extravagantly, and having squandered his own fortune by gambling, he appropriated the public funds to his private use. For this misconduct he was tried by court-martial, and having been convicted, was reprimanded by Washington. Dissembling his feelings of revenge, he afterwards obtained command of the important fortress of West Point, which he then privately engaged to deliver into the hands of the enemy for ten thousand pounds sterling and a commission of Brigadier-General in the British army.

15. Sir Henry Clinton agreed to his proposition, and sent Major André, a young officer of great merit, to see him. On his return to the British camp, Major André was stopped, September 23d, by three New York militia-men— John Paulding, David Williams, and Isaac Van Wert. They searched him, and found in his boots papers containing evidence of the treason. They carried him to Colonel

---

14. What is here said of the Major-General who offered to become a traitor? What was his price?
15. Was his offer accepted? What is said of Major André and his capture? What was the final fate of the traitor? What was done with Major André?

Jameson, their commanding officer, who incautiously permitted him to write to the traitor at West Point. Arnold at once went on board the *Vulture*, a British ship-of-war, then lying in the river, and so made his escape. He afterwards received the reward promised him, the gold and the commission of Brigadier-General in the British army, in which capacity he fought against his countrymen. But he lived contemned and despised by his new friends as much as he was hated by his old ones. He died in England in the year 1801; obscure, unnoticed, unloved, unhonored. Major André was tried by court-martial, by order of Washington. He denied none of the charges alleged against him; but, upon his own confession, he was adjudged to be a *spy*, and condemned to be hung. He died regretted by both friends and foes.

16. On the 20th of December of this year England declared war against Holland. The Hollanders had been giving encouragement and protection to the United States privateers, and had also actually begun to negotiate a treaty with Congress; when England, making the discovery, at once declared war. It would seem that by this time Great Britain might be considered as having her hands full. It was certainly no child's-play to carry on war at once with the United States, France, Spain, and Holland. But as yet Great Britain showed no sign or indication of having any disposition to yield. On the contrary, Parliament, under the lead of Lord North, the Tory Prime Minister, voted large amounts of money for the coming year, and also great armaments to operate both by sea and land.

---

16. Why did England declare war against Holland ? How many countries was she now at war with ?

CHAPTER IV.

WAR OF THE REVOLUTION, CONTINUED AND CONCLUDED.
1781—1783.

Meeting of the Pennsylvania Line—Battle of the Cowpens—Retreat of General Greene—Battle of Guilford—Siege of Ninety-Six—Battle of Eutaw—Siege of Yorktown—Surrender of Lord Cornwallis—Peace.

1. THE distresses of Washington's army had become so great that on the 1st of January, 1781, the whole Pennsylvania line of troops, numbering thirteen hundred, left their camp at Morristown, determined to seek directly from Congress a redress of grievances. They were met at Princeton, New Jersey, by emissaries from Sir Henry Clinton, who tried to induce them to enter the British service. They seized the emissaries and delivered them to General Wayne to be treated as spies. A committee from Congress, and one also from the Pennsylvania authorities, met them at Trenton, and induced them to return to the service after a short furlough. They were offered a reward for seizing the British agents, but refused it, saying that they desired no reward for doing their duty.

2. The Congress consummated as promptly as possible the measures of relief in which they had been engaged for some time. Taxes were levied; and money and clothing were obtained from Europe. Robert Morris, who was placed at the head of the Treasury Department of the Government, freely used his own money and credit to furnish supplies. Being very wealthy, he was able to do a great deal.

3. In January of this year the traitor Arnold, now a brigadier in the British army, invaded Virginia, and did an immense deal of mischief along the coasts. He destroyed

---

CHAPTER IV.—**1**. What is said of Washington's army at this time ?
2. What measures were adopted for its relief? What is said of Robert Morris ?
3. What of Arnold, the traitor? Were efforts made to capture him ? What result ?

a large amount of property, both public and private, in the neighborhood of Richmond, and finally made his headquarters at Portsmouth, which he fortified. While he was at Portsmouth, Washington laid a plan to capture him. La Fayette, with a considerable force, was sent into Virginia, while the French fleet was to co-operate with him. But the British fleet attacked that of the French, and compelled it to return to Rhode Island. So the plan failed, and Arnold escaped.

4. On the 25th of March the British General Phillips arrived in the Chesapeake with two thousand men. He joined Arnold, took command of their united forces, and, having but little opposition, laid waste the country extensively.

5. After the battle of Camden, in which Gates was so badly defeated, Congress appointed General Greene commander of the Southern army in his place. Greene took command at Charlotte, North Carolina, December 3d, 1780, and although his army was only about two thousand strong, yet he dispatched General Morgan with one division to the relief of the district about Ninety-Six, which was then held by the British and overrun by the Tories. He himself took post at Cheraw, South Carolina. This placed Cornwallis, who had returned to South Carolina after Ferguson's defeat at King's Mountain, between the two divisions of Greene's army.

GENERAL GREENE.

6. As he was about to march into North Carolina, and not

---

4. What is said of General Phillips?
5. Who was appointed to command the Southern patriot army? What was his first move? How did this place Cornwallis?
6. Who was defeated at the battle of the Cowpens? With what loss?

being willing to leave Morgan in his rear, he sent Tarleton against him with instructions to push him. Morgan retreated to the Cowpens in Spartanburg District, where a battle ensued between him and Tarleton, in which the latter was defeated with the loss of three hundred killed and wounded, five hundred prisoners, and a large quantity of ammunition and stores. Tarleton himself narrowly escaped being captured by Colonel William Washington, who pursued him very closely, and wounded him slightly in the hand with his sword. Colonel Washington might have shot him, but he did not want to kill him: his object was to take him prisoner.

7. An amusing story is told of Tarleton in this connection. Some time after the battle, he remarked to a witty Carolina lady, Mrs. Willie Jones, "I have been told that Colonel Washington is very illiterate and can scarcely write his name." "Ah, Colonel," replied the lady, "at least he can *make his mark.*" Tarleton said he should like very much to see Colonel Washington. A sister of Mrs. Jones instantly replied, "Had you looked behind you at the battle of Cowpens, Colonel, you might have had that pleasure." Tarleton bit his lip, and said no more about Colonel Washington in that company.

8. After Tarleton's defeat, Lord Cornwallis hastened to meet General Morgan, hoping to intercept and defeat him before he could cross the Catawba. In this he failed; Morgan crossed in safety, but only two hours later Cornwallis appeared on the opposite bank. It was then near night, and Cornwallis encamped, having no doubt of being able to overtake Morgan in the morning. Heavy rains in the night raised the river so that it was impossible to cross for two days, during which time Morgan continued his retreat in safety. On the 31st of January, General Greene, having left the main body of his army on the Pedee, arrived and took

---

7. Relate the anecdote about Colonel Tarleton.
8. What prevented Lord Cornwallis from overtaking Morgan at the Catawba? When did General Greene take command?

command of Morgan's division. He continued the retreat, still followed by Cornwallis.

9. Greene reached and crossed the Yadkin River, but so closely pursued by the British that his forces were attacked in rear and were compelled to abandon part of their baggage. Cornwallis again encamped with only a river between him and the retreating army; and again a sudden rise in the river prevented his crossing. General Greene proceeded to Guilford Court-House, where he was joined by the main body of his army, 7th February. He still felt too weak to face Cornwallis, and continued his retreat towards Virginia, closely pursued. On the 15th of February he had just succeeded in crossing the River Dan, in Virginia, when Cornwallis appeared on the opposite bank. At this point his lordship gave up the pursuit, and turning to the south, established himself at Hillsboro, North Carolina.

10. General Greene, having received reinforcements, so that his army now amounted to nearly five thousand men, and feeling himself strong enough to oppose Lord Cornwallis, marched back into North Carolina and sought an engagement. The armies met at Guilford Court-House on the 25th of March. A battle ensued, and after a severe contest General Greene was obliged to fall back several miles. Cornwallis kept possession of the field of battle, and that was all. He derived no further benefit from the victory. Greene's loss in killed and wounded was about four hundred. The loss of the British was fully equal, and perhaps greater.

11. A few days after this battle Cornwallis moved to Wilmington, North Carolina, pursued as far as Deep River by Greene, who then discontinued the pursuit and marched into South Carolina. After entering South Carolina he changed his position several times, but finally encamped on

---

9. What happened at the Yadkin River? Do you not think these are very remarkable facts?
10. Where did the armies meet at last? Which kept possession of the field? What was the loss on both sides?
11. Where did the next battle occur? Who retreated?

Hobkirk's Hill, near Rawdon's post at Camden. Lord Rawdon attacked him on the 25th of April. Victory for some time inclined to the side of Greene. At last, however, a vigorous charge of the enemy decided the contest, and Greene was forced to retreat. The loss on both sides was nearly equal.

12. On the 10th of May, Lord Rawdon left Camden and retired beyond the Santee. Hearing that Fort Watson had been captured by the Carolina partisan chieftains, and that Forts Mott, Granby, and Orangeburg would probably soon fall, he retreated to Eutaw Springs. By the 5th of June the British held in the Carolinas but the three posts of Ninety-Six, Eutaw Springs, and Charleston. After Lord Rawdon retreated from Camden, General Greene proceeded to Ninety-Six by way of Granby. Ninety-Six was a place of great natural strength, and was also strongly fortified. General Greene besieged it for about four weeks, when, learning that Rawdon was approaching with reinforcements, an assault was determined upon. On the 18th of June the assault was made, but the assailants were beaten off with heavy loss, and were compelled to raise the siege and retire.

13. Rawdon pursued for a while, but finding pursuit vain, he retired and took post at Orangeburg, pursued in turn by Greene. At Orangeburg, Colonel Stewart joined the British with reinforcements from Charleston. The enemy now being too strong for Greene to make an attack with any hope of success, he withdrew and retired beyond the Santee, to pass the sickly season in a healthier region of country. Lord Rawdon soon after left Colonel Stewart in command.

14. Early in September, General Greene again advanced upon the enemy, then commanded by Colonel Stewart.

---

12. By the 5th of June, what places were held by the British in the Carolinas ? What was the result of the siege of Ninety-Six ?
13. Mention the movements of the armies after the siege of Ninety-Six.
14. What is said of the battle of Eutaw Springs ? What is said of the execution of Isaac Hayne ? At the close of the year, what places were held in the Carolinas and Georgia ?

Stewart retreated to Eutaw Springs. On the morning of September 8th the battle began. At first Greene was completely successful, and drove the British from the field; but they rallied, and, after a contest of four hours, he was compelled to retreat. During the night the British withdrew, and soon afterwards retired to Charleston. Shortly after this battle the British entirely abandoned all the up-country. About this time Lord Rawdon, commanding the British forces at Charleston, committed a great outrage upon the usages of civilized warfare, which, while it was intended to overawe the people, only tended to intensify their determination to resist to the last. The outrage was this: On the surrender of Charleston, in May, 1780, Isaac Hayne, who was fighting in the line as a private soldier, though he was a man of distinction in the State, fell into the hands of the British, as a prisoner of war, and was with others discharged on subscribing a declaration of allegiance to the king. This he and the others did on condition that they should not be required to take up arms against their country. But Lord Rawdon now ordered him and others in his position to join the British army. Hayne made his escape, and joined the Carolina forces. Soon after, he was taken prisoner again, and was ordered to be hung, which sentence was carried into execution the 4th of August. This caused, as it was well calculated to do, the most desperate efforts everywhere to rid the country of the presence of the enemy. At the close of the year they held no places in the Carolinas or Georgia except Charleston and Savannah, and to these they were closely confined. With these events the campaign of 1781, and, indeed, the active operations of the war, closed in the Carolinas.

15. To return to Lord Cornwallis. He left Wilmington on the 25th of April, and marched northward, purposing to conquer Virginia. About the last of May he reached

---

15. Mention the movements of Lord Cornwallis. How was Virginia defended?

Petersburg, where he considerably increased the strength of his army by adding to it the forces stationed at that place. Virginia, at that time, was defended by the Marquis de La Fayette, whose army consisted of only about three thousand men, mostly militia. La Fayette would not risk an engagement, feeling himself too weak to cope with his adversary. Cornwallis, taking advantage of his weakness, overran the country, and destroyed a great deal of property, both public and private. An expedition penetrated as far as to Charlottesville, and succeeded in capturing several members of the Virginia House of Delegates, and came very near taking the Governor, Thomas Jefferson.

16. In June, Cornwallis received orders from Sir Henry Clinton to take post near the sea, so that he might be able to send assistance to New York, if it should become necessary. Cornwallis proceeded to Yorktown, at which place he concentrated his forces, and immediately began fortifying it. Colonel Tarleton, with a small body of troops, held Gloucester Point, on the opposite side of the river. General Washington had intended, in combination with the French troops and fleet, to attack Sir Henry Clinton in New York, but the intention was abandoned in August, for Clinton had received reinforcements, and the situation of Cornwallis offered a fairer prospect of success.

17. Clinton, however, remained impressed with the belief that New York would be the point of attack, until Washington suddenly drew up the combined French and United States forces. On the 30th of September he appeared before Yorktown. The French fleet blockaded the James and York rivers, and thus prevented the escape of Cornwallis by sea, while a French land-force of two thousand men joined La Fayette at Williamsburg to prevent his

---

16. What orders did Cornwallis receive in June? To what did he go? What did Washington now resolve upon?
17. When did he appear before Yorktown? In what position did Cornwallis now find himself?

retreat upon the Southern States. Cornwallis found himself hemmed in on all sides, with little prospect of relief.

18. On the evening of October 9th, Washington, who had moved rapidly from the North, opened his batteries on the fortifications of Cornwallis at Yorktown. On the 14th two redoubts were carried by assault. On the 16th nearly a hundred pieces of artillery were brought to bear on their works

SURRENDER OF CORNWALLIS.

with such effect that the walls were beaten down and nearly every gun was silenced. On the 19th Lord Cornwallis surrendered to Washington his army of more than seven thousand men. The shipping in the harbor was surrendered to the commander of the French fleet. Five days afterwards Sir Henry Clinton arrived at the mouth of the Chesapeake with an army of seven thousand men,—too late. Cornwallis and his army were prisoners of war, and Sir Henry returned to New York.

19. By this great success the whole country was, in fact, recovered from the power of the British. The war was virtually at an end. All hope of subduing the States and holding them as colonies was gone. The British troops, after this, were principally confined to the cities of New York, Charleston, and Savannah. The British government no longer pursued active measures.

---

18. When did the surrender take place?
19. What was in fact the consequence of this great success?

20. It was in the middle of the night that the news of the surrender of Cornwallis reached Philadelphia. A watchman in the street called out, "Twelve o'clock, and a cloudy morning,—*Cornwallis is taken!*"

Soon the whole city was aroused with the cry, which went up in every street and alley. The hope that peace with liberty would now come at last was strong and buoyant. The wildest enthusiasm prevailed. The same news was received with like joy everywhere in the States.

21. In England the effect was decisive against any further prosecution of the war. The Whigs there immediately gained the ascendency, and Lord North, who for twelve years had governed the country, was compelled to resign the lead of the ministry. Negotiations for peace were entered into. Five commissioners, John Adams, John Jay, Dr. Franklin, Thomas Jefferson, and Henry Laurens, were appointed by the United States. Five were appointed by the British Government. They met at Paris, and on the 30th of November, 1782, signed a Provisional treaty of peace. A final treaty was signed at the same place September the 3d, 1783. The first article of the latter was in these words:

"His Britannic Majesty acknowledges the said United States, viz.: New Hampshire, Massachusetts Bay, Rhode Island and Providence Plantations, Connecticut, New York, New Jersey, Pennsylvania, Delaware, Maryland, Virginia, North Carolina, South Carolina, and Georgia, to be free, sovereign, and independent States; that he treats with them as such; and for himself, his heirs and successors, relinquishes all claim to the government, propriety, and territorial rights of the same, and every part thereof."

Thus, after a bloody war of seven years, each of the original separate thirteen Colonies was acknowledged by Great Britain to be an independent sovereign State. This grand achievement of independence and sovereign right of self-government, on the part of each of the States, was

---

20. Can you describe how the news was received in Philadelphia, and in the States generally?
21. What was the effect in England? When was peace made? When was a final cessation of hostilities proclaimed?

effected through the joint action of all, under their articles of Federal Union.

At the same time, England made treaties of peace with all the other countries with whom she had so lately been at war.

On the 19th of April, 1783, just eight years after the battle of Lexington, a final cessation of hostilities between Great Britain and the United States was proclaimed.

By the treaty with Spain, England restored to that country East and West Florida, which had been ceded to her by Spain in 1763.

22. The preamble to the Provisional treaty of peace between Great Britain and the United States deserves special notice. It sets forth a great truth, which all statesmen would do well to study; and presents a moral lesson which forms a fitting conclusion to this chapter, closing, as it does, a brief outline sketch of the first great war for the sovereign right of local self-government by the States of this continent. The preamble referred to is in these words:

"Whereas, reciprocal advantages and mutual convenience have been found by experience to form the only permanent foundation for peace and friendship between States; it is agreed to form the articles of the proposed treaty on such principles of liberal equity and reciprocity as that," etc.

Had England acted towards the Colonies from the beginning on these principles, she might have saved herself all the blood and treasure expended in this unholy crusade against the essential principle in issue, and might have secured inestimable advantages to her own commerce, trade, and renown, for centuries to come.

---

22. What is said of the preamble to the Provisional treaty of peace ?

CHAPTER V.

PROGRESS OF EVENTS.

1783—1787.

Destitution of the Country—Attempted Mutiny in the Army at Newburg—Washington's Greatest Display in Suppressing it—Shay's Rebellion in Massachusetts—Washington's Retirement from the Army—Proposed Amendments to the Constitution—The "three-fifths" Ratio of Federal Population—Regulation of Foreign Trade—The Call of a General Convention to consider and propose Amendments to the Federal Constitution.

1. THE long struggle was now over. The popular joy at the success of the cause of Liberty, and of the Independence of the States, was unbounded everywhere. But the fruition of the long hoped for and newly acquired blessings came far short of the fondly cherished anticipations. This arose from several causes. New troubles soon presented themselves, which disquieted the minds of those who had been the most hopeful and sanguine during the darkest hours of the conflict.

One of these troubles grew out of the state of the army, and the destitute condition of the public treasury, as well as the country generally. Congress was largely in arrears, not only with the officers, but with the men. Money to pay could not be raised by taxation, and the public credit was exhausted. Would the army consent to be disbanded without a settlement of their dues? This was a perplexing question. Washington still continued his headquarters at Newburg, New York, patiently and anxiously waiting the action of Congress, and hoping that some satisfactory provision would be made in due season for the exigency.

2. At this time, too, it is sad to relate, there were many

CHAPTER V.—**1.** What is said of the popular feeling when liberty with the independence of the States was secured?
2. What was one of the new troubles that arose? What is said of the designs of some of the restless spirits in the army? What is said of Washington on this occasion?

restless spirits in the army, such as all great or long wars usually give rise to; men of ambitious views and projects, who, even to the most daring and gallant deeds, are often moved much more by the selfish motives of personal distinction and fame than by a true love of liberty. Many of this class had been engaged in the cause of the States from the beginning. They had little sympathy with the real cause for which arms had been taken up, which was the great right of self-government on the part of the people of each Colony. But the establishment of free institutions and republican governments were not the controlling objects which induced this class to take the field, and a military government was what they now looked to, as the only hope of securing their personal aggrandizement.

Some of these restless spirits sought to make the patriotic and self-sacrificing army of Washington the instrument of their unhallowed purpose. The wants and needs of the army; the destitution of the country, and the utter inability of Congress to make immediate adequate provision for these wants, and even to deal justly by them by making prompt, full payment for past dues, were seized upon as the means to inflame the passions of the soldiers, in hopes, by appeals to their misguided impulses, they might be influenced not to disband, but, under the claim and demand of their rights, to overthrow Congress and all the civil authorities.

These designing men knew that this would lead to a military government of some sort, in which they hoped to be the chief actors. They knew that Washington was too true and patriotic to countenance their object; hence their design was most insidiously to weaken the influence of the Commander-in-chief by instilling into the minds of the soldiers that he, by not favoring their appeal to Congress for redress by arms, was himself not in real sympathy with their wants. This was the most critical period of all in the history of the United States. It was the turning point of the liberties of the country. It was now more than on any other single occasion that Washington showed those principles and qualities which so distinguished him throughout his life, and exhibited those transcendent powers, intellectual and moral, which mark him as one of the greatest men the world has ever produced.

3. On the 10th of March, 1783 (after the preliminary articles of peace were signed), an anonymous address of great point and force, but most guileful in its character, was issued and circulated through the army. Its tenor and object will be seen from the following extracts:

" *To the Officers of the Army:*

" A fellow-soldier, whose interests and affections bind him strongly to you, whose past sufferings have been as great and whose fortune may be as desperate as yours, would beg leave to address you.

" Age has its claims, and rank is not without its pretensions, to advise; but though unsupported by both, he flatters himself that the plain language of sincerity and experience will neither be unheard nor unregarded.

" After a pursuit of seven long years, the object for which we set out is at length brought within our reach. Yes, my friends, that suffering courage of yours was active once—it has conducted the United States of America through a doubtful and a bloody war, and peace returns again to bless—whom? a country willing to redress your wrongs, cherish your worth, and reward your services? A country courting your return to private life, with tears of gratitude and smiles of admiration—longing to divide with you that independency which your gallantry has given, and those riches which your wounds have preserved? Is this the case? Or is it rather a country that tramples upon your rights, disdains your cries, and insults your distresses?

" Have you not more than once suggested your wishes and made known your wants to Congress? Wants and wishes which gratitude and policy would have anticipated rather than evaded; and have you not lately, in the meek language of entreating memorials, begged from their justice what you could no longer expect from their favor? How have you been answered? Let the letter, which you are called to consider to-morrow, reply. If this, then, be your treatment while the swords you wear are necessary for the defence of America, what have you to expect from peace when your voice shall sink, and your strength dissipate by division? When those very swords, the instruments and companions of your glory, shall be taken from your sides, and no remaining mark of military distinction left, but your wants, infirmities and scars. Can you, then, consent to be the only sufferers by this Revolution, and, retiring from the field, grow old in poverty, wretchedness, and contempt? Can you

---

3. What is said of the seditious circular issued the 10th of March?

consent to wade through the vile mire of dependency, and owe the miserable remnant of that life to charity which has hitherto been spent in honor? If you can—go! and carry with you the jest of Tories and the scorn of Whigs;—the ridicule, and what is worse, the pity of the world. Go! starve, and be forgotten!

"But if your spirit should revolt at this; if you have sense enough to discover, and spirit enough to oppose, tyranny under whatever garb it may assume, whether it be the plain coat of republicanism, or the splendid robe of royalty; if you have yet learned to discriminate between a people and a cause, between men and principles, awake! attend to your situation, and redress yourselves. If the present moment be lost, every future effort is in vain, and your threats then will be as empty as your entreaties now."

4. This address, with these and other like sentiments, invoked a general meeting to be held next day. Its inflammatory character was well calculated to arouse the passions of all the army, officers as well as men. It was put forth and circulated without the knowledge of Washington. He immediately, on getting notice of it, by general orders, condemned the spirit of the address, and invited a meeting of all the general and field officers to take place on the 15th. It was on this occasion, in this meeting of the general officers, of which General Gates was chairman, that Washington performed one of the greatest, if not the greatest, act of his life. It was the matchless speech which he then and there made, and by which this grand mutiny, so well schemed and artfully planned, was suppressed. Among other things in that speech, which should never be forgotten, he said to the war-worn patriot veterans around him:

"This dreadful alternative of either deserting our country in the extremest hour of her distress, or turning our arms against it, which is the apparent object, unless Congress can be compelled to instant compliance, has something so shocking in it that humanity revolts at the idea. My God! what can this writer have in view by recommending such measures? Can he be a friend to the army? Can he be a friend to this country? Rather is he not an insidious foe; some emissary, plotting the ruin of both by sowing the seeds of discord and separation between the civil and military powers? And what a compliment does he pay to our understandings when he recommends measures in either alternative impracticable in their nature!

"With respect to the advice given by the author to suspect the man who shall recommend moderate measures and longer forbear-

---

4. What did Washington do when he got notice of it? What did he say of it in the meeting of the officers?

ance, I spurn it, as every man who regards that liberty and reveres that justice for which we contend, undoubtedly must; for if men are to be precluded from offering their sentiments on a matter which may involve the most serious and alarming consequences that can invite the consideration of mankind, reason is of no use to us. The freedom of speech may be taken away, and dumb and silent we may be led like sheep to the slaughter."

He assured them in this speech that he believed that Congress intended to do justice to the army, and would do it; that they would meet all their engagements with the army as speedily and promptly as they were able; and after these assurances he concluded this ever-memorable speech in these words:

"While I give these assurances and pledge myself in the most unequivocal manner to exert whatever abilities I am possessed of in your favor, let me entreat you, gentlemen, on your part, not to take any measures which, viewed in the calm light of reason, will lessen the dignity and sully the glory you have hitherto maintained. Let me conjure you in the name of our common country, if you value your own honor as you respect the rights of humanity, to express your utmost horror and detestation of the man who wishes, under any specious pretences, to overthrow the liberties of our country. By thus determining and thus acting you will pursue the plain and direct road to the attainment of your wishes; you will defeat the insidious designs of our enemies, who are compelled to resort from open force to secret artifice; you will give one more distinguished proof of unexampled patriotism and patient virtue, rising superior to the pressure of the most complicated sufferings; and you will, by the dignity of your conduct, afford occasion for posterity to say, when speaking of the glorious example you have exhibited to mankind, had this day been wanting the world had never seen the last stage of perfection to which human nature is capable of attaining."

5. The effect of this speech was never surpassed by anything uttered by the greatest orators of the world; and yet oratory was not one of Washington's chief excellencies. In him seemed to be combined all the elements which constitute true greatness. His appeal on this occasion was not to the passion of his hearers, but to their reason, their virtue, and their patriotism. His sentiments were pure, unselfish, elevating, and ennobling! They saved public liberty at the time.

---

5. What is said of Washington's speech on this occasion? What effect had it upon the concocted conspiracy?

6. The Congress did the best they could in providing for the immediate wants and needs of both the men and officers of the army. They were still kept together, and not disbanded until after the British evacuated the city of New York, which was on the 25th of November, 1783. The

WASHINGTON RESIGNING HIS COMMISSION.

same day a portion of the United States army entered the garrison there. On the 4th of December, Washington took his leave of the officers, and went to Annapolis, Maryland, where the Congress of the States was in session, and to them, on the 23d of December, 1783, when peace, quiet, and order prevailed everywhere, resigned his commission.

7. Another trouble, which was severely felt everywhere, arose from the general indebtedness of the country and the scarcity of money. The public debt, domestic and for-

6. What did Congress do? What was done with the army? When did the British evacuate New York? When did the United States army take possession? When did Washington take his final leave of the officers? When and where and to whom did he resign his commission?
7. What was another trouble felt at this time? What is said of Shay's rebellion in Massachusetts?

eign, had swelled to near one hundred millions. The war had been carried on by the issue of paper of some sort or other, as a circulating medium. The currency had depreciated until it ceased to have even a nominal value. The Congress had borrowed from Holland and France several million dollars. To meet the interest on this required heavy taxation. Some of the States were unable to raise their quotas under the Articles of Union. In several of them, to meet the wants of their own governments a tax to be paid in produce, instead of money, was resorted to. In many instances strong appeals were made to the Legislatures of the several States for measures of relief, and for laws staying the collection of debts. The evil of the times bore most heavily upon the laboring classes. In Massachusetts a strong party arose on the part of those who had borne the brunt of the fight, against those who had become rich during the war. This ended in what is known as Shay's rebellion in that State. It was an organized resistance to the collection of debts.

8. In the mean time it was discovered that the basis fixed upon in their Articles of Union for the quotas of the States respectively was not a just one. That basis was the relative value of real estate in the several States. This value was by no means uniform. The proper basis, it was thought, was the relative population of the States.

In April, 1783, therefore, Congress proposed to the States to amend the Constitution in this particular, by making population the basis of the States' quotas. This was the original idea in 1776 when the Articles of Union were first brought forward. But a difficulty soon arose in the discussion, which caused its abandonment at that time. The difficulty sprung from the fact that there were more negro slave laborers in some of the States than in others, and it was insisted that negro laborers were not as efficient in the

---

8. What is said of the basis fixed upon in the Articles of Union for the quotas of the States ? What amendment did Congress propose in April, 1783 ? What is the origin of the three-fifths ratio of Federal population ?

production of wealth, the proper subject of taxation, as free, intelligent, white men. Some insisted that one white man was as efficient as four negroes, some put the ratio at three, and some at two. As this difficult question could not be satisfactorily adjusted at first, the basis then adopted was the one stated; but after years of discussion it was agreed that *five* negro-slaves should be rated as *three* white persons in establishing a proper basis for taxation, taking relative population as the best standard of relative production. This was known as the ratio of Federal population. Accordingly in April, 1783, as stated, the Congress passed a resolution recommending to the States a change of the Constitution in this particular. The change was that the quota of each State should be—

"In proportion to the whole population of white and other citizens, and inhabitants of every age, sex and condition, including those bound to servitude for a term of years, and *three-fifths* of all other persons not comprehended in the foregoing description, except Indians not paying taxes in each State."

This change the States were slow in agreeing to.

9. Another trouble was, that each State, under the Constitution, had its own regulations of foreign commerce. Different States had different rates of duties on foreign imports, which worked badly for the common interest.

A considerable foreign trade had also commenced. The exports as well as imports of the United States were greatly increased. The imports consisted of manufactured goods of various kinds, sugar, coffee, tea, etc. The exports from Virginia and the more Southern States consisted largely of tobacco and rice. The cultivation of cotton was not yet introduced. From the Northern and Eastern were exported articles of greater variety, but not of equal value to those from the Southern States. The Congress, therefore, during the same year, 1783, proposed that the Constitution should

---

9. What was another one of the troubles of the times? What is said of the general prosperity? What did the imports consist chiefly of? what the exports? What other amendment to the constitution did Congress propose the same year? What advice did Washington give?

be changed so as to allow them to resort to the system of *indirect taxes*, that is, of levying duties upon imports, which would bear less heavily upon the people, and enable them to meet the interest on the foreign debt. During the same year, and before he retired from the army, Washington addressed a circular letter to the Governors of the States, in which he urged several changes in "the Constitution." While the proposed amendments, however, were pending before the States, it was further moved in Congress, that that body be invested with power to regulate trade with foreign nations.

10. Before any of these propositions were finally acted upon by the States, to wit, in January, 1786, the Virginia Legislature, at the instance of James Madison, passed a resolution inviting all the States to send commissioners to meet at some place to be agreed upon—

"To take into consideration the trade of the United States; to examine the relative situation and trade of the said States, and to consider how far a uniform system, in their commercial regulations, may be necessary to their common interest and their permanent harmony."

Four other States responded to this call, to wit, New York, New Jersey, Pennsylvania, and Delaware. Commissioners from these met Commissioners from Virginia in Annapolis, the 11th September, 1786. They did nothing, however, but pass a resolution recommending the calling of

"A general convention of all the States, to meet at Philadelphia, in May, 1787, to take into consideration the situation of the United States; to devise such further provisions as shall appear to them necessary, to render the Constitution of the Federal Government adequate to the exigencies of the Union."

This resolution, with an address, urging the importance of the Convention, was sent to the Governors of all the States, and to the States in Congress assembled.

11. On the 21st of February, 1787, the Congress took the same into consideration, and

---

10. What did the Virginia Legislature do in January, 1786, and at whose instance? How many and what States responded? When and where did the Commissioners meet? What did they do?

11. What did Congress do in February, 1787? How many States responded to the call for a General Convention of the States?

"Resolved, That in the opinion of Congress, it is expedient that on the second Monday in May next a Convention of Delegates who shall have been appointed by the several States, be held at Philadelphia, for the sole and express purpose of revising the Articles of Confederation, and reporting to Congress, and to the several Legislatures, such alteration and provisions therein, as shall, when agreed to in Congress, and confirmed by the States, render the Federal Constitution adequate to the exigencies of Government and the preservation of the Union."

All the States except Rhode Island responded to this call for a General Convention of the States, and sent Delegates clothed with powers, under this resolution of Congress. The action of the Convention thus called will be the subject of the next chapter.

12. In the mean time Congress passed an Ordinance for the government of the Territory of the United States northwest of the Ohio River. To this Territory several of the States had claims, as parts of it lay within the original chartered limits of those States; much the larger portion lay within the limits of Virginia. This State and the others had ceded their rights to the land or soil, to the United States as a common fund for the use and benefit of all.

This Ordinance was in the nature of a compact between the States and the settlers of this Territory, providing a system of self-government for them, while in the condition of inchoate States, and for their future admission into the Union when the population of its respective parts, particularly designated, should reach the number of sixty thousand inhabitants.

By the 6th section of this celebrated Ordinance, "slavery, or involuntary servitude, except for crime," was to be forever prohibited from this portion of the public domain.

---

12. What celebrated Ordinance did Congress pass in 1787? What was the nature of it?

CHAPTER VI.

THE FEDERAL CONVENTION OF 1787.

1787—1789.

The New Constitution—Its Formation and Ratification—Election of Washington as President.

1. THE General Convention for a revision of the Articles of Union between the States, called as related in the last chapter, met in Philadelphia on the 14th of May, 1787. It was unquestionably the ablest body of jurists, legislators, and statesmen that had ever assembled on the continent of America.

Among the more prominent of these may be named— Samuel Johnson, Roger Sherman, and Oliver Ellsworth, of Ct.; Dunning Bedford and George Read, of Del.; William Few, George Walton, and Abraham Baldwin, of Ga.; Daniel Carrol, James McHenry, and Luther Martin, of Md.; Nathaniel Gorham, Caleb Strong, Elbridge Gerry, and Rufus King, of Mass.; John Langdon and Nicholas Gilman, of N. H.; Jonathan Dayton, William Livingston, and William Patterson, of N. J.; John Lansing, Robert Yates, and Alexander Hamilton, of N. Y.; Alexander Martin, Richard D. Spaight, and William R. Davie, of N. C.; Robert Morris, Gouverneur Morris, James Wilson, and Benjamin Franklin, of Pa.; John Rutledge, Pierce Butler, Charles Pinckney, and Charles Cotesworth Pinckney, of S. C.; Edmund Randolph, George Mason, James Madison, and George Washington, of Va. Patrick Henry was opposed to the general objects of the Convention, and therefore declined any participation in its action. Mr. Jefferson was Minister to France, and not in the country at the time.

CHAPTER VI.—**1.** When and where did the General Convention for the revision of the Articles of Union between the States meet? What is said of it? Can you name some of the more prominent members of it? What is said of Patrick Henry and Mr. Jefferson?

2. Washington was unanimously chosen President of the body, and William Jackson, Secretary. On all questions, as in the Congress, the vote was taken by States, without regard to the number of Deputies or Delegates from each respectively.

3. It was soon discovered that a considerable number were in favor of disregarding the specific objects for which the Convention had been called, and instead of revising the Articles of Union, were in favor of presenting an entirely new plan of government for public consideration. The leading spirits of this class were Hamilton, of N. Y.; King, of Mass.; the two Morrises and Wilson, of Penn.; Randolph and Madison, of Va. The controlling idea of this class was to do away with the Federative feature in the Constitution, and to merge the separate sovereignties of the several States into one Incorporate Union; and thus to form, of all the States, one single National Republic, instead of a Federal Republic of distinct States.

4. The great vice or evil under the Constitution as it then existed, which was generally admitted, was, that many of the laws of the Union applied only to States, in their corporate capacity, and did not act directly upon the people on the subjects constitutionally embraced in them. As the Constitution then stood, many of the Acts of the Congress were binding primarily only on the States, and required the subsequent action of the State Legislatures to carry them into effect. Thus, when all the States "in Congress assembled" enacted that certain quotas of money should be raised by the States respectively, the collection of the amount required of each depended upon the subsequent action of its Legislature. This was a very serious evil, as some of the States were slow in raising their quotas.

---

2. Who was chosen President? who Secretary? How was the vote taken on all questions?
3. What was soon discovered? Who were the leading spirits of this class? What was their controlling idea?
4. What was the great vice or evil under the old Constitution? What was the problem which few seemed to understand?

How it could be avoided with the preservation of a Federal system was a problem which few seemed to understand. History afforded no light upon the subject.

5. To remedy this evil, and still preserve the Federal system, Mr. Jefferson, the Minister to France, had suggested a new idea to Mr. Madison in a letter from Paris on the 16th of December, 1786.

This idea was, that the " Federal Head " could, by proper changes in the Constitution, be enabled to exercise its functions efficiently, by a division of the powers conferred on it into three departments—" Legislative, Executive, and Judiciary "—and with an organized Federal machinery for their direct execution on individuals, within a prescribed sphere, similar to the like organizations of the State Governments in their more general spheres.

In this way the States would continue to be " one Nation as to all foreign concerns," and still remain " distinct as to all domestic ones."

The idea of a division of the powers of government into the three departments named, in any changes that might be proposed, was very generally entertained on all sides at the time of the meeting of the Convention; but on what basis, National or Federal, was the vexed question.

6. Four general propositions or plans were submitted, two on the National basis, and two on the Federal. The first of the former was by Mr. Randolph, and known as the Virginia plan. It was founded upon the principle of doing away with the Federal system entirely, and providing for the establishment of a National Government upon the model of a single Representative Republic, with a division of the powers of government into three departments.

The other proposition on the National line was submitted by Col. Hamilton. His plan embodied the same general

---

5. What new idea did Mr. Jefferson suggest for its solution ? What was the vexed question at the time of the meeting of the Convention ?
6. How many general propositions were submitted ? By whom were they submitted, and what was their character ?

ideas as that of Mr. Randolph. It differed from it only in details.

On the Federal side, two propositions were also submitted. One by Mr. Patterson, of New Jersey, which proposed only to make a few additional delegations of power to Congress, without any other change; and the other by Mr. Charles Pinckney.

7. Mr. Pinckney's plan provided not only for the delegation of additional powers, such as to levy duties on foreign imports, and to regulate commerce with foreign nations, and for a division of the powers delegated into the three departments named; but it also provided a complete machinery for the execution of all the Federal powers conferred, by a Federal organization, similar to that of the States, and by which the Federal character of the Government would be retained, as suggested by Mr. Jefferson.

8. The Convention, with closed doors in all their proceedings, first took up the Virginia plan, as it was called. They considered it in Committee of the Whole.

The first of the series of the resolutions setting forth this plan which came to a vote, was in these words:

"Resolved, That it is the opinion of this Committee that a National Government ought to be established, consisting of a Supreme Legislative, Judiciary, and Executive."

This was on the 30th of May. The resolution was adopted by the Committee, voting by States. Only eight States were present at the time. The Convention then went through with the Virginia plan, and perfected it on the basis of a National Government, or a single Republic, in contradistinction to a Federal Union of separate States.

9. Afterwards, on the 20th of June, when the report from the Committee of the Whole came up for considera-

---

7. What is said of Mr. Pinckney's plan?
8. Which did the Convention first take up? How did they consider it? What was the first resolution agreed to in committee of the whole? When was this, and how many States were present? What did the committee then do?
9. What was done on the 20th of June, on motion of Mr. Ellsworth? What did this vote indicate? What followed? How was the Congress under Mr. Pinckney's plan to be divided?

tion in the House, and when eleven States were present (the New Hampshire delegation still being absent), this resolution was disagreed to, and on motion of Mr. Ellsworth the word "National" was stricken out, and the words "Government of the United States" substituted in its place.

This indicated clearly that a majority of the States did not intend to depart from the Federal system. The whole of Mr. Randolph's plan was then gone through with in the House, and the word "National" was stricken out, with a substitution of the words "Government of the United States" in its place, wherever it occurred. It was now found that Mr. Pinckney's plan in the main was the only one that could be adopted. By his plan all Federal Legislative power delegated was still to be vested in the Congress of the United States; but this Congress itself was to be divided into two branches, an upper and a lower House; the concurrence of both of which was to be necessary to the passage of any law, or public measure.

10. The great contest between the Nationals and Federals was now on the question of the suffrage of the States in the two proposed Houses of Congress. By many of the Federals it was insisted that the vote in each should be as it was in the old Constitution; that is, that the vote in each House on all questions should be by States, and without regard to the number of their Representatives in either. On the National side it was most persistently maintained, that, in view of the great disparity in population and wealth between the smaller and larger States, this equality of political power should not be retained in either House.

11. A majority of the Federals finally yielded the point as to the House, but would not yield an equal voice on the part of the several States in the Senate. They were deter-

---

10. What was the great contest between the Nationals and Federals now on ?
11. What point did the Federals finally yield ? On what vote did the States stand five for and five against ? What did Mr. Bedford declare at this time ? What did Dr. Franklin propose ?

mined to maintain an equality of political power in the States severally, in whatever form the Constitution might be amended. On the first test vote on the motion to allow each State an equal vote in the Senate, the States stood five for it, and five against it, with one divided. Eleven States only then, as before, were present. New Hampshire was still absent. This was on the 2d of July, and it was at this stage of the proceedings that Mr. Bedford announced the position of the Federals in these words:

"That all the States at present are equally sovereign and independent, has been asserted from every quarter in this House." "The small States never can agree to the Virginia plan, and why, then, is it still urged?" "Let us then do what is in our power—amend and enlarge the Confederation, but not alter the Federal System."

It was at this period of their deliberations, when they had come to a dead-lock on this vital point, and it seemed likely that nothing would be done in the then temper of the Convention, that Dr. Franklin moved for prayers.

12. A grand committee was now raised, consisting of one from each State. This effected nothing. Another grand committee was raised. The final result was, that on the 16th of July a majority of the States then present decided to let the vote in the lower House be taken upon a representation by the States respectively, on the "three-fifths" basis of Federal population, which had been fixed for taxation; thus carrying out the principle of "taxation and representation going together" in this branch; while in the upper House, or Senate, each State was to continue to have an equal voice; so that no law or public measure could pass against the vote of a majority of the States; and so this matter was ended. The new Constitution did not differ from the old one in this particular. But before this final agreement was reached, Mr. Lansing and Mr. Yates, of New York, and Mr. Martin, of Maryland, had left, be-

---

12. What was now raised? How many States were now present? What was the result? What is said of Mr. Lansing and Mr. Yates, of N. Y., and Mr. Martin, of Md.?

lieving that no satisfactory adjustment would be made on a Federal basis.

13. Most of the Nationals, after this, with a patriotism seldom exhibited, gracefully yielded their opposition, and devoted all their powers in perfecting a plan conforming to the outlines submitted by Mr. Pinckney. This was especially the case with Mr. Madison, Mr. Wilson, and Col. Hamilton. All the essential features of the old Constitution were preserved. Some very important changes in detail were made. These consisted chiefly in the new organization, and new machinery introduced for the execution of the Federal powers. The new delegations of power were also of an important character, but few in number.

14. The following are the principal ones of these:

1st. The power to raise revenue by duties upon imports, etc.; and to lay taxes directly upon the people of the several States, to be apportioned on the "three-fifths" basis of population;

2d. The power to make uniform rules, to be observed in all the States, for the admission of aliens to citizenship in the several States, and like uniform rules regulating bankruptcy;

3d. The power to regulate commerce with foreign nations, and among the several States;

4th. The power to promote the progress of science and useful arts by securing, for limited times, to authors and inventors, the exclusive right to their writings and discoveries.

Besides these four, there is hardly a new power delegated in the new Constitution of sufficient importance to need special notice.

15. The covenants between the States, imposing re-

---

13. What is said of most of the Nationals ? What of the features of the old Constitution ? What of the changes introduced ?
14. What are the principal new delegations of power ?
15. What is said of the covenants between the States ? Which was the most important ? What other change needs special notice ? What was further covenanted ? What is said of the whole ? What of Mr. Randolph and other individual members ?

straints and assuming obligations, run almost in the same language throughout both instruments. Amongst the new restraints the most important are:

1st. That no State shall emit bills of credit, or make anything but gold and silver a legal tender in the payment of debts; pass any bill of attainder; or *ex post facto* law; or law impairing the obligation of contracts; or grant any title of nobility.

2d. No State shall, without the consent of Congress, lay any imposts, or duty upon imports, exports, etc.

Of all the new obligations assumed by the States, the most important, and one without which it was universally admitted the amended Constitution would not have been agreed to, is that which provides for the rendition of fugitives from service from one State to another. This was on the same principle as the rendition of fugitives from justice, in the original articles of Confederation.

One other change in the mutual covenants needs special notice. This relates to the manner in which the Constitution thereafter should be amended. Unanimity on the part of the States was no longer to be necessary to carry an amendment, but this could be effected by a vote of three-fourths of the States, with a *proviso*, that no amendment should ever be made which would deprive any State of its equal suffrage in the Senate. On the principle thus agreed to, as to future changes in the organic law of the Union, it was further covenanted that

" The ratification of the Conventions of nine States shall be sufficient for the establishment of this Constitution between the States so ratifying the same."

The great object in framing the new Constitution, as the old, was to secure not only the general welfare, but the inestimable right of local self-government by the people of the several States, which was the controlling object in their common struggle for, and achievement of, their independence.

The Constitution so formed finally received the unanimous consent of all the twelve States present in the Convention, on the 17th of September, 1787.

Mr. Randolph refused to sign the plan adopted, because the Federative feature was retained.

Some other individual members refused to sign for different reasons.

16. The result of the four months' work of this most eminent body—the proposed new Constitution—was then sent, with a letter prepared by the Convention and signed by Washington as its President, to the Congress then in session at New York; and by them it was submitted to the States severally for their separate consideration and action, as had been provided in the call for the Convention.

17. Mr. Madison, and Col. Hamilton and Mr. John Jay of New York, distinguished Nationals at first, now entered upon a most zealous advocacy of the amended Federal system as proposed. They wrote a series of very able articles explaining its provisions, over the signature of "Federalist," which were afterwards collected and printed in book-form. In one of these papers, Mr. Madison, with great point and truth, said of the new Constitution,

" The change consists much less in the addition of new powers to the Union than in the invigoration of its original powers."

18. By the terms of the plan proposed, it was to go into operation on the 4th of March, 1789, between any nine of the States which should ratify it by that time. In point of fact, it was adopted and ratified by conventions duly called in all the States, except North Carolina and Rhode Island, before the close of the year 1788.

19. In Virginia, Pennsylvania, New York, and Massa-

---

16. What was done with the proposed new Constitution?
17. What is said of Mr. Madison, Col. Hamilton, and Mr. Jay?
18. When was the plan proposed to go into operation? What is said of the ratification in point of fact?
19. What is said of the opposition? Who headed the opposition in Virginia? What did seven of the States insist upon in their ratifications? What is one of these amendments? What did Mr. Samuel Adams say of it? What is further stated about it?

chusetts, it was strongly opposed upon various grounds; chiefly, however, because it was thought that in none of its provisions was there a sufficient guard against the assumption of undelegated power, on the part of Federal functionaries, by construction and implication. This was the position of Patrick Henry, who headed the opposition in the Virginia Convention. In seven of the States ratifying it, Massachusetts leading, and Virginia following, several important amendments, covering this alleged defect, were insisted upon; and the ratification was carried in these State Conventions, with the assurance that these amendments would soon be incorporated in the instrument. One of these was, that

"The powers not delegated to the United States by the Constitution, nor prohibited by it to the States, are reserved to the States respectively, or to the people."

In the Massachusetts Convention, Mr. Samuel Adams said of this amendment,

"It is consonant with the second Article in the present Confederation, that each State retains its Sovereignty, Freedom, and Independence, and every power, jurisdiction, and right, which is not, by this Confederation, expressly delegated to the United States in Congress assembled."

It may be proper to state here, that this amendment, with some others insisted on in like manner, was soon afterwards unanimously adopted by the States, and thus became part of the Constitution.

20. The system, as a whole, presented the most perfect model of a "Confederated Republic," as Washington styled it, ever before established by the wisdom of men. Its new features and striking peculiarities were without example or a parallel in the annals of History. Its wonderful and matchless framework in these particulars has attracted the attention and excited the admiration of men of the greatest learning and highest statesmanship throughout the civilized world. M. de Tocqueville, a French philosopher of great

---

20. What is said of the new Constitution as a whole? What did M. de Tocqueville say of it? What did Lord Brougham say of it?

research, after a thorough study of its nature, character, and workings, said of it, many years ago,

"This Constitution, which may at first be confounded with Federal Constitutions which have preceded it, rests, in truth, upon a wholly novel theory, which may be considered as a great discovery in modern political science. In all the Confederations which preceded the American Constitution of 1789, the allied States, for a common object, agreed to obey the injunctions of a Federal Government; but they reserved to themselves the right of ordaining and enforcing the execution of the laws of the Union. The American States, which combined in 1789, agreed that the Federal Government should not only dictate, but should execute its own enactments. In both cases the right is the same, but the exercise of the right is different; and this difference produced the most momentous consequences."

The novel theory here referred to, is that indicated by Mr. Jefferson, of a division of the delegated powers into Legislative, Executive, and Judiciary Departments, with an organization and machinery in the Conventional Government thus formed, for the full exercise of all its delegated and limited powers, similar to those of the States creating it. This is the peculiar specific difference between the Federal Republic of the United States and all others of similar general type, to which Lord Brougham also alludes in his Political Philosophy, when he says, in speaking of the Government of the United States,

"It is not at all a refinement that a Federal Union should be formed; this is the natural result of men's joint operations in a very rude state of society. But the regulation of such a union upon pre-established principles, the formation of a system of Government and Legislation in which the different subjects shall be not individuals but States; the application of Legislative principles to such a body of States, and the devising means for keeping its integrity as a Federacy, while the rights and powers of the individual States are maintained entire, is the very greatest refinement in social policy to which any state of circumstances has ever given rise, or to which any age has ever given birth!"

21. According to the provisions of the new Constitution, the Chief Executive designated as President, and an alternative designated as Vice-President, were to be elected by Colleges of Electors, to be chosen in the several States re-

---

21. What is said of the election of President and Vice-President under the new Constitution? Who were first chosen?

spectively. The number of the College in each State was to be equal to the number of Senators and members of the House to which each State was entitled in the Congress of the States under the new organization.

As soon, therefore, as the Congress under the old organization received official notice of the ratification of the new Constitution by the requisite number of States, they immediately proceeded to provide for its going into operation at the time designated.

All the necessary elections, State and Federal, were ordered, and held in every ratifying State except New York. Washington received every electoral vote cast, in all the Colleges of the States thus voting, for the office of President; and John Adams was chosen for the office of Vice-President by a majority of the votes cast in the Colleges.

The United States now entered upon a new and a more brilliant career under their new Constitution.

CHAPTER VII.

ADMINISTRATION OF WASHINGTON.

1789—1797.

1. THE 4th of March, 1789, was the time appointed for the Government of the United States to begin its operations under its new organization; but several weeks elapsed after this time before quorums of both the newly constituted Houses of the Congress were assembled. The city of New York was the place where the Congress then met.

2. Washington, having been duly notified of his elec-

CHAPTER VII.—**1.** When was the Government under the new organizations to go into operation?
2. What is said of Washington and his travels to New York? What occurred at Trenton?

tion, left his home at Mount Vernon, on the 16th of April, to enter upon the discharge of his new duties. He set out with a purpose of travelling privately, and without attracting any public attention; but this was impossible. Everywhere on his way he was met by thronging crowds eager to see the man whom they regarded as the chief defender of their liberties; and everywhere he was hailed with those public manifestations of joy, regard, and love, which spring spontaneously from the hearts of an affectionate and grateful people. At Trenton a grand display was made. A triumphal arch had been erected on the bridge spanning the Assumpink. This arch was highly decorated with flowers and laurels, and bore an inscription in large letters: "DECEMBER THE 26th, 1776." This was in commemoration of the noted surprise at that place. Beyond the bridge the road was literally strewn with flowers, spread by the hands of little girls dressed in white, who greeted him by chanting in their silvery voices the following and other like stanzas:

PRESIDENT WASHINGTON.

> "Welcome, mighty chief, once more;
> Welcome to this grateful shore;
> Now, no mercenary foe
> Aims again the fatal blow.
>
> . . . .
>
> Virgins fair and matrons grave
> (These thy conquering arms did save)
> Build for thee triumphal bowers;
> Strew, ye fair, his way with flowers!"

3. A Committee of Congress met him on the way, and

---

3. By whom was he met on the way? What is said of the barge in which he embarked? What of his reception in New York? What of his inauguration?

conducted him to New York. On leaving the Jersey line, "they embarked in an elegant barge of *thirteen* oars, manned by *thirteen* Branch pilots." These *thirteen* oars and *thirteen* pilots were symbolical of the *thirteen* States, over the Government established by which, or to be established by all of which (the accession of two of them only still being wanted), the great Chief was called upon to preside. His reception in New York was marked by a grandeur and an enthusiasm never before witnessed in that metropolis. The inauguration took place on the 30th of April, in the presence of an immense multitude, who had assembled to witness the new and imposing ceremony. The oath of office was administered by Robert R. Livingston, Chancellor of the State. When this sacred pledge was given in the presence of his fellow-citizens, with an appeal to Heaven, "to the best of his ability," in the execution of the office of President, "to preserve, protect, and defend the Constitution of the United States," he retired with the other officials into the Senate chamber, where he delivered his Inaugural Address to both Houses of the newly constituted Congress in joint assembly.

4. The first session of this first Congress of the States under the new organization, continued nearly six months. It was occupied chiefly in the consideration and enactment of laws necessary to put the new Federal machinery into successful operation; and in the adoption of measures for raising revenue from duties on tonnage and imports, which the new Constitution authorized. Among the first things which thus engaged their attention were the amendments to the Constitution, which had been insisted on by a majority of the States at the time of its ratification. All the important amendments so insisted on were agreed to, and sent back to the States for their approval. Ten of these were soon adopted, and became parts of the organic

---

4. What is said of the first session of Congress under the new Constitution? What of the amendments agreed to? What of the judiciary? What executive offices were established?

law. The Federal Judiciary was also organized. Several necessary subordinate executive offices were likewise established. These were the office of Secretary of State, of the Treasury, of War, and of Attorney-General.

5. In the discussion of these questions, the nature and character of the Government necessarily came under review. On no one of them did any decided antagonism of opinion arise. All held it to be a limited Government, clothed only with specific powers conferred by delegation by the States. Those who had advocated a National Government, now warmly defended the Federal system as it had been amended and enlarged. All friends of the new organization now assumed the name of "Federalists." To fill the office of Secretary of State, Washington nominated Thomas Jefferson; that of Secretary of the Treasury, Colonel Alexander Hamilton; that of Secretary of War, General Henry Knox. Edmund Randolph, the great leader of the "Nationals" in the Philadelphia Convention, was nominated to fill the office of Attorney-General. These were all confirmed by the Senate, and constituted what is known as the "President's Cabinet." John Jay, of New York, was in like manner appointed Chief-Justice of the Supreme Court, with John Rutledge of South Carolina, James Wilson of Pennsylvania, Robert H. Harrison of Maryland, and John Blair of Virginia, Associate Judges. Nearly all of these distinguished personages belonged to that class who, before the formation of the new Constitution, had been known as "Nationals," which awakened the anxiety of many of the opposite party, and caused them to fear that, notwithstanding professions of attachment to the new system, an attempt would be made by them to exercise powers by "construction," which the States had uniformly refused in positive language to confer.

---

5. Did any antagonism of party arise on the discussion of questions at this session? How did all hold the Government to be? What party-name did the friends of the new organization assume? Who were nominated as Secretaries to fill the executive offices? Who was Chief-Justice? Who the Associate Judges? What is said of all these appointments? What fears did it cause?

CHAP. VII.]   ADMINISTRATION OF WASHINGTON.   257

6. These apprehensions became realities at the next session. On the 12th of February, 1790, a petition invoking the Federal authorities to adopt measures with a view to the ultimate abolition of African slavery, as it then existed in the respective States, was sent to the Congress, headed by Dr. Franklin, who had been a very distinguished though not a very active leader, owing to his age, in the ranks of the "Nationals," in the Philadelphia Convention. There were then in the United States 697,897 negro-slaves. They had been introduced into all the States, as we have seen, but most of them were at this time in the Southern States.

This movement was looked upon with alarm everywhere by the true friends of the Federal system, as it involved the exercise of powers not delegated by the States to the Congress. After a thorough discussion in the House of Representatives, the question was quieted for the time by the passage of a resolution—

"That Congress have no authority to interfere in the emancipation of slaves, or in the treatment of them within any of the States; it remaining with the several States alone to provide any regulations therein which humanity and true policy may require."

7. Soon after this, the general principles of the Government, with the nature and extent of its powers, came up in discussion on the apportionment of the number of members to the House of Representatives, to which each State was entitled under the census of population, according to the "three-fifths" basis of the Constitution; and on the system of funding the public debt, and other financial measures, including a Bank of the United States, recommended by Colonel Hamilton. On these latter measures party

---

6. Did these fears prove to be well founded? What occurred at the next session? Who headed the petition? What is said of him? What was the number of negro-slaves in the United States at that time? How was this movement looked upon? How was the question quieted?

7. What new questions arose after this on which party lines became clearly marked? What was the difference between the parties so formed? What names did they assume? Who was recognized as the chief of each? What position did Washington hold between them? What is said of the first apportionment bill? What became of it? With which party did Washington side on this measure? What was the result of the veto?

lines became very clearly marked between those known as "strict constructionists" and those known as "latitudinarian constructionists." The former were for confining the action of the Government strictly within its specific and limited sphere, as clearly defined by the language of the Constitution, while the others were for enlarging its powers by inference and implication. The latter still adhered to the popular name of "Federalists," while the former took the name of "Republicans" in some places, and of "Democrats" in others. Col. Hamilton and Mr. Jefferson were soon recognized as the chief leaders respectively of these opposing ranks. Gen. Washington was regarded as holding a neutral position between them; though after mature deliberation he vetoed the first apportionment bill passed by the party headed by Col. Hamilton, which was based upon a principle constructively leading to centralization or consolidation. This principle was manifested in applying the ratio of representation under it to the entire population of all the States as one mass, instead of applying it to the population of each State severally. The latter was the only way in which it could be made upon correct Federal principles, as was insisted upon by Mr. Jefferson in a written Cabinet opinion, notwithstanding large fractions of population in several of the States were left out by this mode of apportionment. This was the first exercise of the veto power under the present Constitution. It created considerable excitement at the time. The veto, however, was sustained by a majority of the House. Another bill was passed in pursuance of Mr. Jefferson's views, which has been adhered to in principle in every apportionment bill which has been passed since.

8. At the second session of the new Congress, Washington announced the gratifying fact of "the accession of

---

8. What announcement did Washington make at the second session of the new Congress? What was done at this session about the seat of government? What name was given to the ten miles square? What to the seat of government itself?

North Carolina" to the Constitution of 1787; and on the first of June, the same year, by special message, he announced the like " accession of the State of Rhode Island," with his congratulations on the happy event which " united under the General Government all the States which were originally Confederated." At this session of the Congress an act was also passed changing the seat of the Federal Government. The law provided that after the year 1790 the Government should be located for ten years at Philadelphia; and that after the first Monday in December, 1800, it should be permanently established on the eastern bank of the Potomac, near Georgetown, within a district of territory not exceeding ten miles square. This territory, subsequently ceded and accepted for this purpose, became known as the " District of Columbia," and to the seat of government itself the name of " Washington " was given.

9. The post-office establishment, and the seal, as well as the flag, of the United States, under the old organization, were continued under the new.

10. During the year 1790, Indian troubles manifested themselves among the Creeks in Georgia, as well as among the tribes west of the Ohio. The chiefs of the Creeks were induced to visit New York, and a treaty with them was made by Washington. But in the Northwest, depredations continued until open war broke out. General Harmer was sent with about fifteen hundred men to repel these hostile incursions. He burned several Indian towns, and destroyed a large quantity of provisions; but at the junction of the rivers St. Joseph's and St. Mary's, in Indiana, he was defeated in two battles—one fought on the 17th and the other on the 22d of October. After these defeats he was removed, and General St. Clair, Governor of the Northwestern Terri-

---

9. What is said of the post-office establishment, seal, and flag of the United States?
10. What is said of the Indian troubles in 1790? Who succeeded Harmer in the Northwest? What is said of his campaign?

tory, was appointed to succeed him. In September, 1791, with about two thousand men, he left Fort Washington, and after proceeding northward for a considerable distance into the Indian country, on the 4th of November he was surprised in camp, and his army was routed with great slaughter; nearly half of his men were killed.

11. In 1791, two new States were admitted into the Union on an equal footing with the original thirteen. These were Kentucky and Vermont.

COAT OF ARMS OF KENTUCKY.   COAT OF ARMS OF VERMONT.

Kentucky was admitted on the 4th of February, and Vermont on the 18th of the same month. In October of the same year an Act was passed by the Congress providing for the general organization and discipline of the militia of the several States under the Constitution.

An Act was also passed at the same session imposing an excise on distilled spirits. This caused great discontent in several quarters, and especially in Pennsylvania. In the western part of this State public meetings were held by which the measure was not only denounced, but the revenue officers were threatened with violence if they proceeded with the collection of the tax. In May, 1792, an Act was passed, authorizing the President to call out the militia, if, in his judgment, it should be necessary, in aid of the execution

---

11. What two new States were admitted into the Union in 1791, and when? What two Acts of Congress were passed the same year? What Act passed in 1792? What is said of the "Whiskey Insurrection"?

of the laws. Washington at first issued a proclamation, urging the people to desist from violence. This proving ineffectual, he subsequently called out fifteen thousand men, volunteers and militia, by which imposing military force all disorders were quelled without bloodshed. In this way was ended what was known as "The Whiskey Insurrection."

12. In 1792 another Presidential Election took place. Washington was very desirous to retire; but yielded to the general wishes of the country, and was again chosen President by the unanimous vote of the Electoral Colleges of the States. He was again duly inaugurated for a second term on the 4th of March, 1793. Mr. Adams was re-elected Vice-President. About this time the French Revolution, and the wars growing out of it, had an important bearing on the politics of the United States. A large majority of the people throughout the Union deeply sympathized with the French people in their struggle for liberty and the right of self-government against the combined efforts of surrounding nations to impose a monarchical dynasty upon them. This sympathy prompted a strong desire for the United States to take part in the conflict in aid of France. But the policy of Washington, in which he was sustained by Mr. Jefferson, still Secretary of State, was to remain neutral among all the contending powers of Europe. As early as April, 1793, M. Genét, Minister of the French Republic to the United States, under the title of "Citizen Genét," arrived at Charleston, South Carolina; and taking advantage of the feeling of the people in favor of France, endeavored to excite them to hostile acts against Great Britain. He issued commissions to vessels-of-war for fitting out privateers to sail from ports of the United States to cruise against the enemies of France. Upon this, Washing-

---

12. What election took place in 1792? Who was chosen President, and who Vice-President? Did Washington receive the unanimous vote of the Colleges? When was he inaugurated for a second term? What occurred about this time having an important bearing on the politics of the United States? What is said of it? What is said of M. Genét? What of Washington's proclamation? What was the result of M. Genét's course?

ton issued his celebrated proclamation of neutrality. M. Genét disregarded the Proclamation of the President, and persisted in his course, with threats of an appeal from the President to the people. For this violation of international law, Washington demanded his recall. M. Genét's commission was withdrawn, and M. Fauchét was appointed Minister in his stead.

13. Early in the first session of the third Congress, in 1793, an important amendment to the Constitution in arrest of centralizing tendencies through the exercise of power by construction was proposed and adopted, with only two dissentient votes in the Senate and one in the House. It is in these words:

> "The judicial power of the United States shall not be construed to extend to any suit in law or equity commenced or prosecuted against one of the United States by citizens of another State, or by citizens or subjects of any foreign State."

This was soon unanimously ratified by the States. It constituted the Eleventh Amendment. What called forth this amendment was the action of the Federal Judiciary in assuming, by a construction of their powers, jurisdiction of a suit brought against one of the States. This was deemed by all the States in derogation of the separate sovereignty of each under the Constitution.

14. On the 16th of December, 1793, Mr. Jefferson, the Secretary of State, made his celebrated report on the relations of the United States with foreign nations. This is one of the ablest state papers penned by him or any other man in this or any other country. On the 31st of the same month, much to the regret of Washington as well as that of his own party friends, he resigned his office, and retired to his home at Monticello, Virginia.

15. In the Fall of 1793, General Wayne, who had been

---

13. What occurred at the first session of the third Congress? Give the words of the Amendment. Why was it adopted?
14. What is said of Mr. Jefferson's report? What of his resignation?
15. What is said of General Wayne? What forts did he build? What is said of his battle with the Indians? When and where did it occur? What was the number of his army? What was the result of the treaty?

CHAP. VII.]   ADMINISTRATION OF WASHINGTON.   263

appointed to conduct the war against the Indians of the Northwest, after St. Clair's disaster, built Fort Recovery, near the scene of that celebrated surprise. He there passed the winter, and during the next spring and summer he advanced further into the interior and built Fort Defiance. Leaving this Fort, he moved down the Maumee River, and on the 20th of August met the enemy in battle. The Indians were signally defeated. Wayne then laid waste their country, and compelled them to make peace. His whole army amounted to about three thousand men. By the treaty finally made, the Indian title was extinguished to extensive tracts of country west of the Ohio River.

GENERAL WAYNE.

16. During the year 1794, the popular feeling in favor of France became still stronger than it had been before. Many persons of high distinction insisted on a war against Great Britain. While Washington was desirous to preserve peace if possible, yet the conduct of the British Government greatly embarrassed the execution of his purpose. In disregard of the Treaty of Peace of 1783, the forts on Lake Erie and vicinity were still occupied by British troops, and merchant vessels of the United States on their way to French ports were seized, and United States seamen were violently impressed by commanders of British ships. To avert so great a calamity as war with England, which now seemed so imminent, Washington concluded to send a special envoy to that country, and to spare no effort con-

16. What is said of popular feeling in 1794? What did many insist on? What was Washington's position? How was it embarrassed? What did he do? What was the result? Was Jay's treaty universally approved? What provision in it was most bitterly assailed?

sistent with honor for the attainment of his great end. For this high and extraordinary mission, John Jay, Chief-Justice of the United States, was selected. Mr. Jay assumed the responsibilities of the great trust. He proved himself equal to them all. In November following a treaty was signed. The provisions of this treaty met the approval of Washington; it was ratified on the 14th of August, 1795. By it a war with Great Britain at this critical period was avoided, and the honor and dignity of the United States fully maintained, though some of the provisions of the treaty met with violent opposition in several quarters. The provision of it which met the bitterest assaults was the one that secured payment to British creditors of debts which were due to them by citizens of the Colonies before the war of the Revolution.

17. A treaty was also concluded with Spain, by which the boundaries between Louisiana and Florida and the United States were definitely settled. The right to navigate the Mississippi was granted by Spain, and the privilege of using New Orleans as a place of deposit for ten years. Peace was also made with Algiers, one of the Barbary States of Africa, and the captive citizens of the United States held by that country were redeemed.

18. The financial report of the Secretary of the Treasury, in November, 1794, was the last official act of Colonel Hamilton. It was one of the ablest state papers of his life. It recommended the establishment of a sinking fund for the gradual extinction of the public debt. His recommendation in this particular was carried out by the Congress, and from it the public credit was greatly improved. On the 31st of January, 1795, Col. Hamilton resigned his position as Secretary of the Treasury, and retired to private life.

---

17. What other treaties were made about this time?
18. What is said of Colonel Hamilton's financial report in November, 1794? When did he resign?

19. In January, 1795, M. Adét succeeded M. Fauchét as Minister to the United States from the Republic of France. The object of his mission seems to have been to embroil the United States with the European Powers with which France was engaged in war. He brought with him a flag of the French Republic, which he presented to Washington, accompanying the presentation with an address which was doubtless intended more for the public than for the Executive ear. A suitable response to this artful address imposed a difficult and delicate duty on Washington, who had at all times proved himself fully equal to the requirements of the occasion. No one sympathized more deeply than he did with the French people in their struggles; and yet no one could be more determined than he was to pursue that course in regard to it which duty to his own country demanded. In reply, therefore, under these embarrassments, he said:

"Born, sir, in a land of liberty; having early learned its value; having engaged in a perilous conflict to defend it; having, in a word, devoted the best years of my life to secure its permanent establishment in my own country; my anxious recollections, my sympathetic feelings, and my best wishes, are irresistibly attracted whensoever, in any country, I see an oppressed nation unfurl the banners of freedom. But, above all, the events of the French Revolution have produced the deepest solicitude, as well as the highest admiration. To call your nation brave, were but to pronounce but common praise. Wonderful people! Ages to come will read with astonishment the history of your brilliant exploits. I rejoice that the period of your toils and of your immense sacrifices is approaching. I rejoice that the interesting revolutionary movements of so many years have issued in the formation of a Constitution designed to give permanency to the great object for which you have contended. I rejoice that liberty, which you have so long embraced with enthusiasm—liberty, of which you have been the invincible defenders, now finds an asylum in the bosom of a regularly organized Government; a Government which, being formed to secure the happiness of the French people, corresponds with the ardent wishes of my heart, while it gratifies the pride of every citizen of the United States by its resemblance to their own. On these glorious events, accept, sir, my sincere congratulations."

In this, there was the fullest assurance of the profoundest

---

19. What is said of M. Adét, and his mission to the United States? What of his address to the President? What of Washington's reply?

sympathy; but not the slightest intimation of a purpose to render the United States a party to the war.

20. The address, so timely and prudent, checked the designs of M. Adét of alienating the people from confidence in Washington, by representing his course as proceeding from a want of sympathy for France in her struggle. M. Adét afterwards behaved worse than "Citizen Genét" had done. He issued an address to the people of the United States, charging the Federal Administration with a breach of faith to their former allies, the French. His efforts, however, availed nothing. Washington had the confidence of the people.

TENNESSEE COAT OF ARMS.

21. On the 1st of June, 1796, Tennessee was admitted into the Union.

22. The time was now approaching for another Presidential Election. The country being at peace with the world, and in a prosperous condition, Washington, against all entreaties to the contrary, positively determined to retire. In September, 1796, he gave to his countrymen his memorable "Farewell Address." This was a fitting and crowning glory of his illustrious life.

23. The candidates of the Federal party for President and Vice-President were John Adams of Massachusetts, and Thomas Pinckney of South Carolina. The Republican or Democratic candidate for President was Thomas Jefferson; for Vice-President, the party was divided between Col. Aaron Burr of New York, and others. The contest

---

20. What effect had the reply of Washington on Adét's designs? What is said of Adét's course afterwards? What did he do? What is said of his efforts?
21. When was Tennessee admitted into the Union?
22. What memorable paper did Washington issue in September, 1796, before the Presidential Election in that year?
23. Who were the candidates of the Federal party for President and Vice-President at that election? Who were the Republican or Democratic candidates? What was the result?

resulted in the choice of John Adams for President, and Thomas Jefferson for Vice-President. The votes of the Electoral Colleges of the several States for the office of President were, seventy-one for John Adams, and sixty-eight for Thomas Jefferson. This, as the Constitution then stood, conferred the office of President upon Mr. Adams—he having the highest vote, and the office of Vice-President on Mr. Jefferson—he having the next highest.

MOUNT VERNON.

24. At the opening of the session on the 7th December, 1796, Washington delivered his Annual Communication upon the state of the country to both Houses in joint assembly in the Representative Hall. His custom from the beginning, was thus to meet the Congress in joint assembly on the opening of each session, and give his views on public matters, not in a written message, but in an oral speech. The answer of the two Houses in their separate action to this

---

24. When did Washington last meet Congress? How did he make his annual address—by written message or by speech? What is said of the answers of the Houses of Congress to his last speech?

his last Presidential speech, expressed the grateful sense of Congress of his eminent services to his country, their deep regret at his retiring from office, and ardent wish for his future personal happiness. These answers, in spirit and substance throughout, showed the high estimation in which the retiring chief was held by men of all parties. After the 4th of March, 1797, he retired to Mount Vernon.

25. The administration of the Government during Washington's two terms had been successful and prosperous beyond the expectations and hopes of even the most sanguine of its friends. The finances of the country were no longer in an embarrassed condition; the public credit was fully restored; life was given to every department of industry. The workings of the new system of allowing Congress to raise revenue from duties on imports, proved to be not only harmonious in its Federal action, but astonishing in its results upon the trade and commerce of all the States. The exports from the Union increased from nineteen million to over fifty-six million dollars; while the imports increased in about the same proportion. Three new members had been added to the Union. The progress of the States in their new career, under their new organization, thus far was exceedingly encouraging, not only to the friends of liberty within their own limits, but their sympathizing allies in all climes and countries.

CHAPTER VIII.

ADMINISTRATION OF JOHN ADAMS.

4th March, 1797—4th March, 1801.

1. On the 4th of March, 1797, John Adams, of Massachusetts, the second President of the United States, was duly inaugurated at Philadelphia, in the presence of both Houses of Congress, and a large concourse of distinguished persons. He was then in the 62d year of his age. He was dressed in a full suit of pearl-colored broadcloth, and wore his hair powdered. His Inaugural Address was delivered before his oath of office was taken. This was administered by Oliver Ellsworth, then Chief-Justice of the Supreme Court of the United States, he having been elevated to that position on the resignation of Chief-Justice Jay.

PRESIDENT JOHN ADAMS.

2. The new President continued in office the same members of the Executive Cabinet left by Washington. These were, Timothy Pickering, Secretary of State; Oliver Wolcott, Secretary of the Treasury; and James McHenry, Secretary of War.

3. The relations existing between France and the United States were now becoming not only complicated, but decidedly unfriendly. They occupied the earliest attention of the new Administration. The conduct of M. Adét had

---

CHAPTER VIII.—**1.** Who was the second President? When and where was he inaugurated?
2. What is said of his Cabinet?
3. What is said of the relations existing between the United States and France at that time? What did Congress do in view of these relations? What is said of the Stamp Act? What of Mr. Adams?

led to a suspension of diplomatic intercourse between the two Republics. France had issued orders quite injurious to the commerce of the United States. In this emergency, Mr. Adams thought the immediate attention of Congress necessary, and therefore called an extra session of the two Houses, to take place on the 15th of May. The course pursued by the Revolutionary Government of France towards all nations was so violent and offensive, that the observance of a strict neutrality, in the opinion of the President, seemed to be impossible with a due regard to the interests of the United States. A majority of Congress, still wishing to maintain a neutral position, and to preserve peace with France as well as England, passed an Act to prevent the fitting out of Privateers, and also to prohibit the exportation of arms and ammunition. Moreover, the President was authorized, if he deemed it necessary, to call out the militia and volunteers to the number of eighty thousand men. To provide means to meet and defray expenses which might be thus incurred, duties by way of stamps were imposed upon paper and parchment used for the various purposes of business. This measure, carried chiefly by the party still styling themselves "Federalists," proved to be very unpopular. It revived the old feeling of hostility to the Stamp Acts of England; and the more so from the fact that Mr. Adams' sympathies were generally believed to be with England, and against France, in the contest then waging between them.

4. In obedience to the popular sentiment, Mr. Adams resolved to make another attempt for an amicable adjustment of the controversy with France. In pursuance of this policy, by and with the consent of the Senate, he appointed Charles Cotesworth Pinckney, of South Carolina; Elbridge Gerry, of Massachusetts; and John Marshall, of Virginia, Special Envoys to that Republic. These Ministers Extraor-

---

4. What did Mr. Adams do in obedience to the popular sentiment? What did Mr. Pinckney say in reply to the X. Y. Z. Junto?

dinary met at Paris, in October, 1797, and at once attempted to execute the duties assigned them. M. de Talleyrand, the French Minister for Foreign Affairs, refused to receive them in their public capacity, but employed unofficial individuals to confer with them, using, instead of their proper names (which were then unknown), the letters X. Y. Z., and in this way the intercourse with the Ministers of the United States was attempted to be carried on. The object was to detach the Envoys from each other, and to learn the several views of each by secret interviews. It was soon disclosed that the payment of the sum of two hundred and fifty thousand dollars would secure the official recognition of the Ministers, with a settlement of all matters in dispute. It was on this occasion that Mr. Pinckney gave expression to the sentiment, " Millions for defence, but not a cent for tribute !"—which met with a hearty response from the people of the United States. Two of the Envoys, Mr. Pinckney and Mr. Marshall, requested the President to send them permission to return home. They were shortly afterwards ordered by the French Government to quit the territories of that Republic. Mr. Gerry was invited to remain, and did so; but effected nothing.

5. At the session of Congress which began on the 13th of November, 1797, and continued over eight months, Acts were passed for the protection of navigation ; for the defence of the sea-coast, by fortifying Boston, Newport, New York, Baltimore, Norfolk, Charleston, and Savannah; for an additional land and naval force; for a loan, which was negotiated at eight per cent., and for a direct tax on real estate. All treaties with France were declared abrogated, and all commercial intercourse between her and the United States was declared suspended. A new Executive Office was created, known as the " Navy Department," the chief

---

5. Mention some of the Acts of Congress passed at its session beginning November, 1797? How were most of these Acts received? What is said of some others? Which were the leading ones that were unpopular? What is said of the Alien Acts? What of the Sedition Act? How did the Republican party regard them? What is said of Mr. Jefferson in regard to them ?

officer of which was to be known as the "Secretary of the Navy," and constitute one of the President's Cabinet Councillors. Under this Act, Benjamin Stoddert, of Maryland, was appointed Secretary of the Navy. A Provisional Army was also ordered to be raised, the President being authorized to organize twelve regiments of infantry, one regiment of cavalry, and one of artillery, with engineers, to serve during the difficulty with France. He was also empowered to have built, purchased, or hired, twelve vessels of twenty guns each. These Acts met with the general approbation of the people.

But during the same session, some other Acts were passed which created great discontent and indignation. The leading ones of this character were what are known as the "Alien and Sedition Acts."

"By one of the Alien Acts (there were two on this subject) the President at his pleasure was authorized to order any foreigner, whom he might believe to be dangerous to the peace and safety of the United States, to depart out of the country, under very heavy penalty for refusing to obey the order. By the Sedition Act it was made a crime, with a very heavy penalty, for any one to ' write, print, utter, or publish ' ' any false, scandalous, and malicious writing,' against ' either House of the Congress of the United States, or the President of the United States, with intent to defame, or to bring them, or either of them, into contempt or disrepute.' "

These Acts were looked upon by the Republican party everywhere as greatly transcending the power of the Congress under the Federal compact. Not only so, they were regarded as a palpable violation of the Amendments to that compact, which guaranteed the liberty of speech, and the freedom of the press, with the right of trial by jury in all cases. The Legislatures of Kentucky and Virginia declared these Acts to be direct and gross violations of the Constitution, and appealed to the other States to join in opposition to them. Numerous petitions for their repeal were presented to the Congress at its next session; but without avail. This increased the popular excitement and alarm. Mr. Jefferson, in his retirement, looked upon these Acts of the Federal party, and the principles upon which they were

CHAP. VIII.] ADMINISTRATION OF JOHN ADAMS. 273

based and defended, as leading inevitably to a centralized empire. These views he expressed in strong and earnest language in his extensive correspondence.

6. In the event of a war with France, which seemed imminent, all eyes were turned to Washington, as a proper person to be placed at the head of the armies. He was therefore appointed Commander-in-chief of all the United States forces, with the rank of Lieutenant-General. This he accepted conditionally. But, fortunately for humanity, it never became necessary for him to take the field in the discharge of the duties of this responsible position. No declaration of actual war was made either by France or the United States against the other, although for some time a state of *quasi* war existed between them upon the high seas, and several engagements took place between their ships-of-war. On the 9th of February, 1799, the United States frigate *Constellation* of thirty-eight guns, commanded by Commodore Truxton, captured the French frigate *L'Insurgent*, of forty guns. This French vessel had previously taken the United States schooner *Retaliation*. The *Constellation*, after refitting in the United States, subsequently met at sea the French frigate *La Vengeance* of fifty-four guns, and in an engagement of about five hours, silenced her batteries; though she succeeded in making her escape, with the loss of one hundred and fifty-six men, in killed and wounded.

7. At the opening of the session of Congress in December, 1798, Washington was present in the Hall of the House of Representatives for the last time; this was also his last visit to Philadelphia. Acting upon the principle of one of his favorite maxims, "In time of peace, prepare for war," he was there actively conferring with the President and Cabinet officers upon matters connected with the organization of

---

6. What new duty was assigned General Washington? What is said of his acceptance of the office of Lieutenant-General? Did he ever take the field in the discharge of the duties of his office? Why not? What is said of the naval engagements of the ships-of-war of the United States and France?
7. What is said of Washington? What of the preparations for war?

12*

the military forces ordered to be raised. Preparations for war were vigorously pushed forward. Several necessary Acts of Congress were passed. The President was authorized to contract for building six additional ships-of-war of seventy-four guns each, and six sloops-of-war of eighteen guns each. To meet the expenditures, one million of dollars was appropriated.

8. But in the midst of these active movements, a new turn was given to affairs. Intimations having been given, though in an indirect and informal way, through Mr. Van Murray, United States Minister in Holland, that the French officials were now willing to renew diplomatic intercourse with this country, Mr. Adams determined to make another attempt at negotiation. He therefore appointed three other Envoys Extraordinary to France, clothed with ample powers to adjust all existing difficulties between the two countries. This high commission consisted of Oliver Ellsworth, then Chief-Justice of the United States, William R. Davie, one of the most distinguished statesmen of North Carolina, and William Van Murray, through whom the informal intimation had been given. In this most important act, Mr. Adams did not consult his Cabinet. When Mr. Pickering and Mr. McHenry were informed of it, they expressed their very decided and earnest opposition to it. Most of those who had so far supported Mr. Adams' measures considered it inconsistent with the honor and dignity of the United States to adopt the course resolved upon by him. They insisted that proposals to treat should come directly from France. The breach between the President and several of the leaders of his party on this question became irreparable. The reasons which governed him at the time have never been clearly explained. But the most rational

---

8. What occurred amidst these active movements? What was the cause of it? What did Mr. Adams do? Who constituted the second high commission? How was this conduct of Mr. Adams looked upon by his Cabinet and several of the leaders of his party? Were his reasons ever clearly explained? What is the most probable solution of his conduct? What is said of the act itself? What was the final result?

probable solution of it, in the absence of direct proof, is, that he acted under the urgent private advice of Washington. Be that as it may, it proved to be one of the wisest and most beneficent deeds of his life. On the arrival of the Envoys at Paris, they found that a great change had taken place in the Government there. The Directory had been overthrown, and Napoleon Bonaparte was First Consul. They were favorably received. Commissioners were appointed to meet them: one of these was Joseph Bonaparte. Negotiations were entered into, and articles of a treaty were agreed upon, which were afterwards confirmed and ratified by both Governments.

9. But in the mean time, while negotiations were pending, and before the conclusion of peace, the illustrious character who was again acting so conspicuous a part in the drama of national affairs, passed from the public stage forever. Washington died at Mount Vernon, on the 14th of December, 1799, in the sixty-eighth year of his age. He was born the 22d of February, 1732.

The announcement of the afflicting event of his death was made in the House of Representatives as soon as the news of it reached Philadelphia, by John Marshall, then a member of Congress from Virginia. Both Houses immediately adjourned. The whole country was filled with gloom by the intelligence. Men of all parties in politics and creeds in religion united with Congress in "paying honor to the memory of the MAN first in war, first in peace, and first in the hearts of his fellow-citizens." These manifestations were no mere outward semblance of grief, but the natural outbursts of the hearts of the people, prompted by the loss of a father. He was, indeed, regarded everywhere as "the Father of his Country." His remains

---

9. What great event happened pending the negotiations? When and where and at what age did Washington die? When was he born? Who announced his death in Congress? What effect did it produce in the whole country? How was he regarded by men of all parties and creeds? Where were his remains deposited?

TOMB OF WASHINGTON.

were deposited in a family vault on his own estate, on the banks of the Potomac, where they still lie entombed.

10. The country, in the midst of its grief for the loss of Washington, early in 1800, received the gratifying news of the opening of negotiations which led to the amicable and honorable settlement of the French controversy. During the summer of this year the seat of government was moved from Philadelphia to the then new City of Washington, where President Adams met Congress at its next session, on the 22d of November.

During this year also occurred another Presidential election. The contest became very exciting and heated between the opposing parties. The candidate of the party styling itself "Federal," for the office of President, was Mr. Adams, the then incumbent; and for the office of Vice-President, Charles Cotesworth Pinckney, of South Carolina. The candidate of the Republican or Democratic party for President was Mr. Jefferson; and for Vice-President, Col. Burr, of New York. The chief issues in the contest were the principles involved in the Alien and Sedition Acts, and other like centralizing measures, with which Mr. Adams and his supporters had become identified.

---

10. What gratifying news was received early in 1800? When was the seat of government removed from Philadelphia to the City of Washington? When did Congress hold its first session there? When did the next Presidential election take place? Who were the candidates of the opposing parties? What were the chief issues involved in the contest? What is said of the "Alien and Sedition" Acts? What of Matthew Lyon? What offences was he charged with? Before whom was he tried? What was the result? How was it proposed to raise the amount of the fine? What was done with the printer who published the lottery scheme? What effect had these proceedings upon the people in the election which took place while he was in jail? What is said of the case of Thomas Cooper? What is said of Callender's case? What of Peck's?

These measures were odious to the great mass of the common people. They became more so from the manner in which they were executed.

Under the Sedition Act several persons of high character and known integrity were prosecuted, condemned, and punished. Matthew Lyon, of Vermont, was selected as the first victim. He was an Irishman by birth, an extreme Republican, and a man who did not mince phrases. He had given offence to the Federal members of the House by styling the President's address " the King's speech." It was the custom of Mr. Adams, as it had been of General Washington, to make his annual communication to Congress on the state of the country in an oral address to both Houses in joint assembly. It was to this Presidential speech or address Mr. Lyon referred. The offences for which he was indicted, however, were his having declared, in a letter published in a Vermont newspaper, that with the Federal Executive, " every consideration of the public welfare was swallowed up in a continual grasp for power, an unbounded thirst for ridiculous pomp, foolish adulation, and selfish avarice ;" and in regard to the Fast-Day, he had said, " the sacred name of religion had been used as a state engine to make mankind hate and persecute each other." These utterances were charged to have been " false, scandalous, and malicious," and made with an intent " to bring the President into contempt and disrepute," in violation of the Sedition Act. He was tried before Judge Patterson, of the Supreme Court, and found guilty. The Judge, after a severe reprimand, sentenced him to four months' imprisonment and a fine of a thousand dollars. Lyon was poor, and unable to pay the fine. A private lottery was made of his property, to raise the amount; but the printer of the paper in which the plan of the lottery was published, was indicted and found guilty under the same Act. While Lyon was still in prison, he was again triumphantly elected to Congress.

Thomas Cooper was found guilty and sentenced to fine and imprisonment for speaking of the act of President Adams in the case of "Jonathan Robbins" as being "without precedent, without law, and against mercy," and as an act "which the Monarch of Great Britain would have shrunk from."

In the trial of James T. Callender, the question of the constitutionality of the law was raised by the defendant's counsel before Judge Chase. He refused to hear them on the question. They threw up their briefs, and left the court. Callender was found guilty, and sentenced to fine and imprisonment.

Jared Peck, an eminent citizen of the State of New York, was indicted under the Act for circulating a petition to Congress for the repeal of the "Alien and Sedition Laws," in which the odious features of those Acts were severely handled. The indictment was found by a Grand Jury in the city of New York; a bench-warrant was issued; Peck was arrested in the midst of his family, and taken to the city for trial. A political historian of New York, speaking of this case, says:

"A hundred missionaries in the cause of Democracy, stationed between New York and Cooperstown, could not have done so much for the Republican cause as the journey of Judge Peck, as a prisoner, from Otsego to the capital of the State. It was nothing less than the public exhibition of a suffering martyr for the freedom of speech and the press and the right of petitioning, to the view of the citizens of the various places through which the Marshal travelled with his prisoner."

11. It was in this state of popular feeling, and excitement and alarm for public liberty, that the Presidential election of 1800 took place. The doctrines and principles of the Virginia and Kentucky resolutions of 1798, and Mr. Madison's matchless Report on those of Virginia in 1799, embodied the general views of the Republican party everywhere. Mr. Jefferson was regarded as the master-spirit

---

11. What is said of the Virginia and Kentucky resolutions of 1798, and Mr. Madison's report of 1799? Who was regarded as the master-spirit from whom the doctrines and principles therein embodied essentially emanated? Against what odds did the Republican party contend?

from whom they all essentially emanated. The Republican party was, however, contending against great odds; all three Departments of the Federal Government—the Executive, Legislative, and Judicial—were decidedly against them, with all the power and influence of public patronage. The Legislatures of all the States, also, except those of Kentucky and Virginia, were against them. Of the two hundred newspapers then published in the United States, all but about twenty were enlisted by preference or patronage on the Federal side.

12. The result of the votes of the Electoral Colleges was, for Jefferson, 73; Burr, 73; Adams, 65; Pinckney, 64, and John Jay, 1. The States that cast the Electoral votes of their Colleges for Mr. Jefferson and Col. Burr were nine; to wit, New York, Pennsylvania, Maryland, Virginia, Kentucky, North Carolina, Tennessee, South Carolina, and Georgia. Those that cast the Electoral votes of their Colleges for Mr. Adams and Mr. Pinckney, were seven; to wit, New Hampshire, Massachusetts, Rhode Island, Connecticut, Vermont, New Jersey, and Delaware. Rhode Island cast one vote for Mr. Jay, to prevent that equality of votes on the Federal ticket, which, for the want of a like precaution, resulted on the Republican side, and which caused so much excitement and confusion. Mr. Jefferson and Col. Burr having received an equal number of votes, there was no election by the Colleges, as the Constitution then stood. It then devolved upon the House of Representatives, voting by States, to choose for President and Vice-President between Mr. Jefferson and Colonel Burr—the two having the highest number of the Electoral votes.

On the 11th of February, 1801, the House proceeded to make this choice by ballot. It was well known that Mr.

---

12. What was the result of the votes of the Electoral Colleges? How many States voted the Republican ticket? How many for the Federal ticket? Which State cast one vote for Mr. Jay, and why? What was the effect of the want of a like caution on the part of the Republican party? On whom did the election devolve under the circumstances? How many ballotings were had? What was the result of the first and of all to the last? How many days were occupied in these ballotings?

Jefferson was the popular choice for President, and Col. Burr for Vice-President; but a majority of the States at that time having a "centralist" majority in the House, there was for some time a strong determination to defeat the popular will, if possible. On the first ballot for President, the vote by States stood: for Jefferson, eight; for Burr, six, with two divided. There were then sixteen States in the Union; so there was no choice, as eight was not a majority of all. The States proceeded to ballot nineteen times on that day, with the same result. The States remained in session all night, and proceeded to the twenty-eighth ballot next day, when the result was the same. On the 13th they proceeded to the twenty-ninth ballot. On the 14th they proceeded to the thirty-third ballot. On the 16th they proceeded to the thirty-fourth ballot, when the result was the same. On the 17th they proceeded to the thirty-fifth ballot, with the same result; then to the thirty-sixth ballot, the result of which was—10 votes for Mr. Jefferson; 4 for Col. Burr, and 2 in blank. Mr. Jefferson was, thereupon, declared duly elected President for four years from and after the 4th of March, 1801. Col. Burr became the Vice-President for the same term.

13. During the Administration of Mr. Adams the progress of the prosperity of the States was considerably retarded. The taxes were greatly increased, and foreign trade and commerce were seriously injured by the difficulties with France. From these causes the industrial pursuits throughout the country were more or less affected. Foreign immigration was also checked by the Alien Acts. By one of these the period required for naturalization was extended to 14 years. Discontent prevailed everywhere, and the country was brought to the verge of civil war by the tyrannical execution of those measures of the party in power, calling

---

13. What is said of the state of the country during Mr. Adams' Administration? What produced the discontent? To what period was naturalization extended? How were the measures of the party in power regarded by a majority of the people?

itself Federal, which were looked upon by a majority of the people as unconstitutional and tending to centralism and despotism.

CHAPTER IX.

ADMINISTRATION OF JEFFERSON.

4th of March, 1801—4th of March, 1809.

1. MR. JEFFERSON, the third President, was inaugurated the 4th of March, 1801, at the new Capitol, in the City of Washington. He was then in the fifty-eighth year of his age. His accession to office was regarded as a complete revolution in the politics of the country, effected through the peaceful and constitutional instrumentality of the elective franchise. The doctrines as taught by him and advocated by his friends during the canvass, were looked upon by many as not only tending to weaken the bonds of union between the States, but partaking of the licentious character of those which marked the Jacobins of France. In his thorough devotion to the cause of the right of every separate people to govern themselves as they pleased, according to the principles set forth in the Declaration of Independence, of which he was well known to be the author, it was supposed by many that he lost sight of those elements of power which were necessary in all governments to make them strong enough for their own preservation. Intense interest, therefore, was felt everywhere as to the line of policy which would be indicated in his

PRESIDENT JEFFERSON.

CHAPTER IX.—1. When and where was Mr. Jefferson inaugurated? What was his age? What is said of his accession to office? How were his doctrines looked upon by many? How was his Inaugural Address looked to? What is said of it?

Inaugural Address. This was delivered before both Houses of Congress, the Foreign Ministers, and a large concourse of citizens. It was clear, pointed, and bold. Speaking of the Federal system, he said:

> "Some honest men fear that a Republican Government cannot be strong; that this Government is not strong enough."

On the contrary, he declared it in his opinion to be

> "The strongest Government on earth"—"the world's best hope." In his opinion, the real strength of all Governments is in the affections of the people. "Some," said he, "think that man cannot be trusted with the government of himself. Can he then be trusted with the government of others? or have we angels, in the form of kings, to govern him? Let history answer this question."

He then announced what he deemed the essential principles of our Government, and those upon which its Federal administration should be conducted. These he summed up as follows:

> "Equal and exact justice to all men, of whatever state or persuasion, religious or political; peace, commerce, and honest friendship with all nations—entangling alliances with none; the support of the State Governments in all their rights, as the most competent administrations for our domestic concerns, and the surest bulwarks against anti-republican tendencies; the preservation of the General Government in its whole constitutional vigor, as the sheet-anchor of our peace at home and safety abroad; a jealous care of the right of election by the people—a mild and safe corrective of abuses, which are lopped off by the sword of revolution where peaceable remedies are unprovided; absolute acquiescence in the decisions of the majority—the vital principle of republics, from which there is no appeal but to force, the vital principle and immediate parent of despotism; a well-disciplined militia—our best reliance in peace, and for the first moments of war, till regulars may relieve them; the supremacy of the civil over the military authority; economy in the public expense, that labor may be lightly burdened; the honest payment of our debts, and sacred preservation of the public faith; encouragement of agriculture, and of commerce, its handmaid; the diffusion of information, and the arraignment of all abuses at the bar of public reason; freedom of religion; freedom of the press; freedom of person under the protection of the *Habeas Corpus;* and trial by juries impartially selected—these principles form the bright constellation which has gone before us, and guided our steps through an age of revolution and reformation. The wisdom of our sages and the blood of our heroes have been devoted to their attainment. They should be the creed of our political faith—the text of civil instruction—the touchstone by which to try the services of those we trust; and should we wander from them in moments of error or alarm, let us hasten to retrace our steps, and to regain the road which alone leads to peace, liberty, and safety."

In conclusion he said:

"Relying, then, on the patronage of your good-will, I advance with obedience to the work, ready to retire from it whenever you become sensible how much better choice it is in your power to make. And may that Infinite Power, which rules the destinies of the universe, lead our councils to what is best, and give them a favorable issue for your peace and prosperity."

The oath of office was then administered to him in the Senate Chamber by John Marshall, the newly-appointed Chief-Justice of the United States.

2. In the organization of the new Cabinet, James Madison was appointed to the office of Secretary of State; Henry Dearborn, of Massachusetts, to the office of Secretary of War; Levi Lincoln, of Massachusetts, to the office of Attorney-General. Samuel Dexter, Secretary of the Treasury, and Benjamin Stoddert, Secretary of the Navy, under Mr. Adams, were continued in their offices for a time. After some months of this continuance, Mr. Dexter was succeeded in the Treasury Department by Albert Gallatin, of Pennsylvania; and Mr. Stoddert, in the Navy Department, by Robert Smith, of Maryland.

3. The Sedition Act of 1798 was by its terms limited to the 3d of March, 1801; with a proviso, however, that the limitation was not to affect any prosecutions commenced before that period, or thereafter to be commenced, for violations of it during its existence. At the time of Mr. Jefferson's inauguration, there were quite a number then suffering the penalty of the Act in various jails. These prisoners he immediately ordered to be discharged, as he held the Act to be "unconstitutional, null and void." The discharge was ordered without hesitation under the pardoning power; though he held that the three departments of Government—the Executive, Legislative, and Judicial—are co-ordinate; and each in its sphere is equally authorized to judge for itself of what is and what is not constitutional in cases properly before it; and that no one of the three is

---
2. Who constituted his Cabinet?
3. What is said of the Sedition Act? What was done with the prisoners in jail under it, when Mr. Jefferson came into office?

bound by the decision of either, or both of the others, on any constitutional question, either in the same case or any other similar to it. No other prosecutions, however, for past violations of the Sedition Act, were commenced.

4. At the meeting of the first session of the Seventh Congress, in December, 1801, in pursuance of an announcement before made, of his intention to discontinue the mode of addressing Congress on their assembling in what was known as "the Presidential Speech," he simply sent to each House a Message in writing, giving his views on public affairs and the situation of the country. His example thus set has been uniformly followed since.

5. The State elections of 1801 resulted in favor of the Republican or Democratic party. Mr. Jefferson's principles and policy were so popular with the masses of the people, that his Administration was cordially sustained by decided majorities in both Houses of this Congress. They repealed all the obnoxious measures of their immediate predecessors. Among these were the internal taxes, the taxes on stills, distilled spirits, refined sugar, carriages, and stamped paper, etc. They also repealed the Act extending the period of naturalization to fourteen years; reducing it to five, in conformity with Mr. Jefferson's suggestion. They passed an Act for redeeming the public debt, by which it was provided to appropriate annually seven millions three hundred thousand dollars as a Sinking Fund for that purpose. An Act was also passed reducing the army with its expenditures.

6. An object which occupied the early attention of Mr. Jefferson, was the securing to the people of the United States from Spain of the free navigation of the Mississippi

---

4. What change did Mr. Jefferson introduce in making his annual communications to Congress?

5. How did the elections of 1801 result? What Acts did the Republicans repeal when they came into power? What was done to sustain the public credit?

6. What was the object which occupied the early attention of Mr. Jefferson? Who was sent as a Special Minister to accomplish this service? What was the result? What was the purchase-price of Louisiana? What was the number of the inhabitants? Of what classes did it consist? What influenced Napoleon in making the cession? What was his remark at the conclusion of the treaty? What was the extent of the territory acquired by the United States by this purchase, and what did Mr. Jefferson say of it?

River, with a dépôt of trade at its mouth. In 1802 he received information of the cession of Louisiana to France by Spain, in a secret treaty in 1800. He immediately instituted a commission to treat with France upon the subject. For this purpose Mr. Monroe was sent out as Special Minister, to act in conjunction with Mr. Livingston, the United States Resident Minister at Paris. The mission was more successful than had been even hoped for. Napoleon was ready, not only to negotiate upon the object sought, but for a cession of the entire territory. A treaty to this effect was made on the 30th of April, 1803, by which the United States were to pay fifteen million dollars, with a guaranty to the then inhabitants of all their rights of person and property. The population consisted of about 90,000. Nearly half of these were negro-slaves; the others were French and Spanish colonists. In this negotiation Napoleon was governed both by necessity and policy. He wanted money for his European wars, and knew that an attempt to hold Louisiana would be but an incumbrance. His remark on this occasion was characteristic of the man. "This accession of territory strengthens forever the power of the United States, and I have just given to England a maritime rival that will sooner or later humble her pride." The treaty was received in the United States in July, and added greatly to the popularity of the Administration. It was opposed by a few of the old Federal party leaders; but was ratified by the Senate in the October following, by 24 for it, to 7 against it. In the House, an Act for carrying the treaty into effect, was adopted by a vote of 90 to 25. This acquisition added over a million of square miles to the territory of the United States, and more than doubled the extent of their original limits. In relation to it, Mr. Jefferson, in a letter to Dr. Priestley, said:

"The *dénouement* has been happy, and I confess I look to this duplication of area for the extending a Government so free and economical as ours, as a great achievement to the mass of happiness which is to ensue. Whether we remain in our Confederacy, or form into Atlantic and Mississippi Confederacies, I believe not very important to the happiness of either part. Those of the Western Confederacy will be as much our children and descendants as those of the Eastern, and I feel myself as much identified with that country in future time as with this; and did I now foresee a separation at some future day, yet I should feel the duty and the desire to promote the Western interests as zealously as the Eastern, doing all the good for both portions of our future family which should fall within my power."

7. In 1803 was consummated the cession by Georgia (in 1802), to the United States, of nearly 100,000 square miles of territory between the Chattahoochee and Mississippi Rivers; and on the 19th of February, of the same year, the State of Ohio was admitted into the Union.

COAT OF ARMS OF OHIO.

At the same session of Congress, another important Amendment to the Constitution was proposed. It now stands as the Twelfth Amendment to that instrument. It is that which regulates the present mode of electing the President and Vice-President, requiring the Electors in the several colleges of the States to designate the person voted for, for President, and the one voted for, for Vice-President. It was to prevent the recurrence of such a state of things as took place between Mr. Jefferson and Colonel Burr at the last election. This Amendment was opposed by the old Federal leaders; but was passed by two-thirds of both Houses of Congress, and speedily ratified by all the States except three, to wit, Connecticut, Delaware, and Massachusetts.

8. The Barbary Powers on the coast of Africa still continued to obstruct the commerce of the United States in the Mediterranean. This led to a war with Tripoli, one of them. A considerable naval force was sent against that power in 1803, under command of Commodore Preble.

---

7. What other cession of territory was consummated to the United States in 1803? When was the State of Ohio admitted into the Union? What Amendment to the Constitution was proposed at this session? What is said of its ratification?

8. What is said of the Barbary Powers? Who was sent with a naval force against Tripoli? What is said of Lieutenant Decatur's exploit? Who succeeded Preble? When was peace made? What was accomplished by it?

The *Philadelphia*, a ship of his squadron, ran aground near the harbor of Tripoli, and was taken by the enemy. The retaking and burning of this ship by Stephen Decatur, then a lieutenant, was one of the most brilliant naval achievements on record. This feat was accomplished by him with but seventy-six men, in a small schooner, and under a constant fire of the guns of the Tripolitan fleet, as well as their land-batteries. The war, however, lasted for some time. Commodore Preble was succeeded by Commodore Barron, who succeeded in bringing the Bashaw to terms. A treaty was finally made for the future security of commerce, and by which several citizens of the United States, who had been held by the Tripolitan pirates as slaves, were ransomed and restored to their homes and liberty. This was in the summer of 1805.

9. In the mean time another Presidential election had taken place. The Republicans, or Democrats, voted for Mr. Jefferson for the office of President, and for George Clinton, of New York, for the office of Vice-President. The Federals supported Charles Cotesworth Pinckney for President, and Rufus King, then of New York, for Vice-President. The result was one hundred and sixty-two electoral votes for Mr. Jefferson and Mr. Clinton, and fourteen only for Mr. Pinckney and Mr. King. By States the vote stood: fifteen States for the Democratic ticket, and only two for the Federal. These two were Connecticut and Delaware. So popular was Mr. Jefferson's Administration, that the centralizing party, styling itself "Federal," had become almost extinct. He was inaugurated for a second term on the 4th of March, 1805.

10. In 1804, Col. Burr, the then Vice-President, was a candidate for the office of Governor in the State of New York, and was supported by many of the old Federalists. Col. Hamilton, who had no confidence in his integrity, op-

---

9. Who were candidates for President and Vice-President in 1804? What was the result of the election?
10. What is said of Colonel Burr?

posed his election, and he was defeated. Some remarks made by Hamilton during the canvass against Col. Burr led to a correspondence between them, which ended in a challenge from Burr. The parties met, and Hamilton was mortally wounded. This fatal duel occasioned general regret, and after that Burr lost caste with all parties. He subsequently was engaged in planning a military organization of some sort; which, from the great secrecy and mystery in which it was conducted, caused a suspicion that his designs were against the United States. He was arrested, indicted, and tried for treason; but no case being made against him, he was acquitted.

11. The course of France and England in conducting the war then fiercely raging between them, was highly injurious to the commerce of the United States. The British Government, by its "Orders in Council," declared all vessels engaged in conveying West India produce from the United States to Europe legal prizes. This was intended as a blow to cripple France; but it fell heavily upon the interests of the United States, and excited great indignation throughout the country. In May, 1806, further "Orders in Council" were passed, declaring several European ports, under control of the French, in a state of blockade. This, of course, authorized a seizure of the United States vessels with their cargoes bound for these ports. These "Orders in Council" by the British Government were met by Napoleon in what is known as his "Berlin Decree." This forbade the introduction of any English goods in any port of Europe, even by the vessels of neutral powers. This decree closed the harbors of France against any vessel which should touch at any English port. This was followed by further "Orders in Council," declaring the whole coast of Europe in a state of blockade. This measure was

---

11. What is said of the effect of the course of France and England in their wars on the commerce of the United States? What of the "Orders in Council?" What of the "Berlin Decree?" What of the further "Orders in Council?" What of the "Milan Decree?" Who were the chief sufferers from these extreme measures? How were their expostulations answered?

further met by Napoleon by his famous "Milan Decree," confiscating not only the vessels and cargoes that should violate the "Berlin Decree," but also all such as should submit to be searched by the English. The United States were the chief sufferers by these extreme measures on both sides; but it was in vain that they expostulated with the contending powers, in insisting upon the indefeasible rights of neutrals. "Join me in bringing England to reason," was the substance of the reply of Napoleon; "join us in putting down the disturber of the world," was the substance of the reply of England. The United States, therefore, was left to choose which of the belligerents she would take for an enemy. War against both was too great an undertaking; continued neutrality between them seemed to be out of the question—it involved all the disadvantages, without any of the advantages, of open war. Other events happened which turned the scale of choice in the popular mind against England.

12. In June, 1807, the British man-of-war *Leopard* fired into the United States frigate *Chesapeake*, and killed three of her men, wounding eighteen more. This was near the coast of the United States, and without provocation. The *Chesapeake* was not in condition for action, and immediately struck her colors. The pretence for this outrage was the capture of certain British seamen alleged to be on board the *Chesapeake.* It greatly increased the existing indignation in all the States. Meetings were held in all sections, without distinction of party, at which resolutions were passed to support the Administration in any measures of retaliation or redress which might be adopted. A proclamation was issued by the President forbidding British ships-of-war to enter the waters of the United States. Satisfaction for the insult was demanded of the British

---

12. What turned the scale of popular opinion against England? What was the result? What did the President do? What did the British Government do? What was the temporary effect of this? What did Congress do in December, 1807? What was the object of the embargo? What was its effect?

Government. Congress was also convened in Extra Session to take the subject into consideration. The British Government promptly disavowed the act of the officer in command of the *Leopard*, and also disclaimed the right of search to be extended to ships-of-war. This allayed the excitement for a time, but no redress could be obtained from either party for the violation of the neutral rights of the United States.

In December, 1807, the Congress, as a last resort, by way of retaliation, as well as an initiative step towards war with England, passed the celebrated " Embargo Act," by which all the United States trading-vessels were prohibited from leaving their ports. This measure operated much more to the disadvantage of England than of France. But it operated also very injuriously, as was believed, upon the shipping interests of this country. It caused great distress and much murmuring, especially in the New England States, where most of the shipping was owned. The political effect in that section was decidedly adverse to the Republican party.

13. In 1808 another Presidential election took place. Mr. Jefferson had signified his determination to retire from office at the expiration of his second term. Notwithstanding the disaffection in New England, on account of his policy in the matter of the Embargo, he was yet sustained by larger Republican majorities in both Houses of Congress. In the elections for this year the anti-Administration, or old Federal party revived, supported the same ticket for the offices of President and Vice-President that they did in 1804; that is, Charles Cotesworth Pinckney for President, and Rufus King for Vice-President; while the Administration or Republican party supported James Madison for President, and George Clinton, of New York, for

---

13. When did the next Presidential election take place? What had Mr. Jefferson signified his determination to do? Who were the Republican candidates? Who the Federal? How were Presidential candidates then put forth? What was the result of the election?

CHAP. IX.] ADMINISTRATION OF JEFFERSON. 291

Vice-President. Candidates for these offices were then put forth by Congressional caucuses of the respective parties. The result of the election was, 122 electoral votes for Madison, and 47 for Pinckney, and 113 for Clinton for Vice-President, and 47 for King. By States, the vote stood: 12 for the Republican ticket, and 5 for the Federal. These five were New Hampshire, Massachusetts, Rhode Island, Connecticut, and Delaware.

14. Shortly before the expiration of Mr. Jefferson's second term of office, information was given to him from a quarter which he believed to be reliable, that the disaffection to the Embargo was so great in some of the New England States, that they would withdraw from the Union, if it were persisted in. He,

MONTICELLO.

therefore, without any change of views as to the propriety of the policy, but with a view to harmony between the States, recommended its repeal. This recommendation was carried out by the Congress, and Mr. Jefferson left for his successor the settlement of the many difficult and perplexing questions then pending between the United States, England, and France. After the 4th of March, 1809, he retired forever from public office, and returned to his residence at Monticello, with a reputation for integrity and statesmanship unsurpassed even by Washington. His popularity was greater at the close than at the beginning of his Adminis-

---

14. What induced Mr. Jefferson to recommend a repeal of the Embargo Act? Was the recommendation carried out by Congress? What is said of Mr. Jefferson after the 4th of March, 1809? What of his statesmanship and popularity? How was he everywhere regarded? Which are said to be the two most important acts of his life?

tration, which seldom happens to the ablest, wisest, and best of rulers. He was everywhere regarded by the masses of the people, not only as the true expounder of our Federal system, but the great apostle of Liberty on this continent. The two most important acts of his life, in their immediate as well as their remote bearings upon the destinies of the country, were those connected with the Declaration of Independence, and the acquisition of Louisiana. The three which seemed to be the most fondly cherished in his own memory, were his draft of the Declaration of Independence, the part he took in securing the Statute of his State for freedom in religious worship, and the establishment of the University of Virginia.

CHAPTER X.

ADMINISTRATION OF MADISON.

First Term, 4th of March, 1809—4th of March, 1813.

1. JAMES MADISON, the fourth President of the United States, was inaugurated on the 4th of March, 1809, in the fifty-eighth year of his age. The oath of office was administered by Chief-Justice Marshall, in the presence of a large concourse of people. The new Cabinet consisted of Robert Smith, of Maryland, Secretary of State; Albert Gallatin continued in the office of Secretary of the Treasury; William Eustis, of Massachusetts, Secretary of War; Paul Hamilton, of S. C., Secretary of the Navy, and Cæsar A. Rodney, of Delaware, continued Attorney-General.

PRESIDENT MADISON.

CHAPTER X.—**1.** Who was the fourth President of the United States? When was he inaugurated? Who constituted his Cabinet?

2. In politics, Mr. Madison was at this time a recognized leader of the Republican or Democratic party. He had been Secretary of State during Mr. Jefferson's entire Administration, and was a cordial supporter of his principles and measures. He has been styled "the Father of the Constitution." This was because he was the author of the Virginia Resolution in 1786, that proposed the call of a Convention of the States, which finally resulted in the adopted modification of the Articles of the union between them; and not from his having originated or suggested any of the leading features of the new Constitution so formed and adopted. On this score no man of that day was less entitled to such an appellation; for he was one of the most prominent leaders of the National Party in the Philadelphia Convention, and with Randolph, Hamilton, Wilson, Morris, and King, endeavored to effect a consolidation of the States by a merger of their separate sovereignties into one; and thus out of the whole to form one single, centralized Republic. It was on his violent speech against the adoption of the first report of the Grand Committee of Compromise, that Mr. Lansing and Judge Yates, of New York, retired from that body, believing that no plan would be adopted which would not do away with the Federal System. After the Nationals in that Convention found that they could not succeed in remodelling the Union on their line of a single, centralized Republic, then Mr. Madison, as we have said before, with Hamilton and Wilson, came into a cordial support of the amended Federal System, as it was finally agreed to and adopted; and he united with Hamilton and Jay in earnestly recommending the adoption of the New Constitution by the States, in a series of very able articles, known as "The Federalist," as we have stated.

3. When the Government, under the new organization,

---

2. What is said of Mr. Madison's political position at the time? What has he been styled? Why so styled? What was his position in the Philadelphia Convention that formed the new Constitution?
3. What was Mr. Madison's position when the Government first went into operation under the new organization? How did he subsequently lean? What

went into operation, Mr. Madison was a member of the House of Representatives, and at first held a prominent position with those then styling themselves "Federalists." He co-operated thoroughly with Hamilton, while the latter was Secretary of the Treasury, in several of his financial measures. But before the end of General Washington's Administration, he leaned very strongly towards the views of Mr. Jefferson; and when party lines became clearly defined, in Mr. Adams' Administration, on the constructive and centralizing doctrines of that period, he became one of the ablest champions of the "Strict Construction" or Republican side. Mr. Jefferson was on most intimate terms with him during life, and had no small influence over him, as he had over all men of intellect with whom he came in personal and social contact. Mr. Jefferson drew the celebrated Resolutions of Kentucky, of 1798, which fact, though not generally known at the time, was most probably known to Mr. Madison, as well as to all his intimate political friends; and it is not improbable that the Resolutions of Virginia, of 1798, if not drawn by him, at least received their inspiration from the same master brain.

Mr. Madison also, most probably, received aid from the same source when he wrote his famous Report upon the latter, in 1799, which set forth the principles on which the revolution of parties in 1800 was effected. This celebrated Report is one of the ablest papers and clearest expositions of the Constitution of the United States that has ever been penned in the same compass. It utterly annihilated the positions assumed by the consolidating and centralizing party of that day.

4. Such is a brief sketch of the antecedents of the man who succeeded Mr. Jefferson in 1809, and on whom devolved the administration of Federal affairs, with the management and adjustment of the difficult questions then disturbing

---

was his final course? What great paper did he write in 1799? Who was the author of the Kentucky resolutions of 1798?

CHAP. X.] ADMINISTRATION OF MADISON. 295

the foreign relations of the States with the two greatest powers on earth.

5. The Embargo had been abandoned, as we have seen, by Mr. Jefferson, in order to preserve peace and harmony between the sections of the Union. In lieu of this, however, in accordance with his views, an Act of Congress was passed just before his retirement, substituting for the Embargo what was called a "Non-intercourse Act." This left United States shipping free to trade with all countries except England and France; and the prohibition as to these was to cease, as to them or either of them, on the repeal of their "Orders in Council" or "Decrees" respectively, affecting the commerce of the United States.

6. Very soon after Mr. Madison's accession to office, Mr. Erskine, the British Minister at Washington, gave assurance that the "Orders in Council" of England would be annulled. Whereupon a proclamation was issued on the 19th of April, by the President, suspending the Non-intercourse Act as to England after the 10th of June following. This good news had hardly reached the most distant parts of the country, before the President was informed by the British Government that Mr. Erskine had exceeded his powers, and his act in the assurance given was disavowed. Another proclamation was immediately issued countermanding the first. So matters remained for some time. Mr. Erskine was recalled, and another Minister sent out by England. This was a Mr. Jackson. The tone and style of his correspondence with the Secretary of State was of such a character that Mr. Madison ceased to hold communication with him, and demanded his recall. In the mean time Congress had convened. The prevailing sentiment was for war. The President, however, and a majority of his Cabinet, were for adjusting the questions by peaceable

---

5. What Act was passed in lieu of the Embargo ? What was its effect ?
6. What occurred soon after Mr. Madison's accession to office? What became of Mr. Erskine ? Who succeeded him ? What became of Mr. Jackson's mission ? What was the prevailing sentiment in Congress? How did the President and a majority of the Cabinet stand?

negotiations if possible. An extension with a modification of the Non-intercourse Act was adopted.

7. In 1810, the United States Minister at Paris was informed "that the Berlin and Milan Decrees were revoked, and would cease to have effect after the 1st of November of that year." The President accordingly issued a proclamation on the 1st of November, 1810, declaring that the French "Decrees" were revoked, and that the Non-intercourse Act would be continued as to Great Britain unless her "Orders in Council" should be revoked in three months after that date. He also urged upon the British Government a revocation of its "Orders in Council," upon the ground that the French "Decrees," upon which they were based, had been repealed. The British Government objected on the pretext that no sufficient evidence was furnished that the Berlin and Milan Decrees had actually been repealed, and that the President's proclamation and the Non-intercourse Acts of Congress were partial and unjust. The enforcement of their "Orders in Council" was still persisted in; and for this purpose, ships-of-war were stationed before the principal harbors of the United States. The course of England at the time greatly increased the war feeling in the United States against her. This feeling too was inflamed by an event similar to that of the attack of the *Leopard* upon the *Chesapeake*. Commodore Rodgers, commanding the United States frigate *President*, met off the coast of Virginia, in the dusk of the evening of the 16th of May, 1811, a vessel which he hailed, but from which he received no answer. In a short time he was hailed in turn by a shot from the vessel he had hailed, which struck his mainmast. He accepted the mode offered of exchanging salutations, and answered with a broadside from his own deck, which he kept up in quick succession, until he found his adversary was disabled; and then, on hailing again as at

---

7. What occurred in 1810? What is said of the war feeling in the United States against England? What event inflamed this feeling? What was the cry of the period?

first, he was informed that it was the British sloop-of-war *Little Belt*. She was put *hors de combat* in the encounter, and lost thirty-two men in killed and wounded. This prompt chastisement of overbearing insolence was highly gratifying to the popular sentiment throughout the United States, and gave new life to the cry of the period, " Free Trade and Sailors' Rights."

8. The Twelfth Congress was called together by the President on the 4th of November, 1811, in advance of the regular time of meeting. This was done in view of the still more embarrassing aspect of the relations of the United States with Great Britain. This Congress, as all since 1801 had been, was largely Republican in both Houses; and while the measures of the Administration were generally sustained by considerable majorities in both Houses, yet there was a strong feeling rising up among the younger leaders of the party against what they considered the weak and timid course of the President. This class was for immediate war against England. The leaders of the class were Henry Clay, of Kentucky, and John C. Calhoun, Langdon Cheves, and William Lowndes, of South Carolina.

Another Presidential election was approaching, and Mr. Madison was given to understand, that if he did not yield to an active war policy, he would not receive the Republican nomination. His Cabinet at this time was divided upon that question. Mr. Monroe, who was then Secretary of State, instead of Mr. Robert Smith, favored the war policy; Mr. Gallatin, in the Treasury Department, was decidedly opposed to it; Mr. William Pinkney, who was then Attorney General, instead of Mr. Rodney, was of opinion that the country was entirely unprepared for a declaration of war at that time. The other members of the Cabinet seemed to have no very decided opinions on the subject. But all the

---

8. When was the Twelfth Congress convened? What was the party character of this Congress? What was said of the new Republican leaders? Who were these? What is said of the Cabinet at this time?

members of the Administration, with the President at the head, were perfectly willing to commit themselves to, and endeavor to carry out, any policy that might be determined upon by the Congress, as the wisest and the best for the maintenance of the safety, interests, rights, and honor of the country.

9. The feeling of hostility against England about this time was increased by Indian outbreaks in the Northwest, which were attributed to her instigation. Just before the meeting of Congress, General William Henry Harrison, Governor of the Territory of Indiana, had been sent against the tribes on the Wabash with a body of Kentucky and Indiana militia, with one regiment of regular troops. On the 6th of November, he encamped at Tippecanoe, near the town in which Elkswatawa, the famous "Prophet," and the triplet brother of the celebrated Tecumseh, resided. Harrison was here met by the principal chiefs with offers of peace and submission. But having no faith in their professions, and apprehending an attack in the night, he caused his troops to sleep on their arms and in the order of battle. At four o'clock on the morning of the 7th of November, 1811, the camp was furiously assaulted, and a bloody contest ensued. The issue was doubtful for some time; but the Indians were finally repulsed. Harrison lost sixty-two killed and one hundred and twenty-six wounded. The loss sustained by the Indians was much greater. General Harrison destroyed the Prophet's town, built some forts, and returned to Vincennes.

10. Under the influence of the war spirit thus excited, the Congress voted an increase to the regular army of thirty-five thousand men, and authorized the President to accept the services of fifty thousand volunteers, as well as to call out the militia as occasion might require. They also provided for a large increase of the navy. To meet the ex-

---

9. What increased the hostility against England? When and by whom was the battle of Tippecanoe fought? What was the result?
10. What measures did Congress adopt?

penses of these measures, they authorized a loan of eleven million dollars. The policy of Mr. Jefferson and Mr. Madison heretofore had been to keep the military establishments, army and naval, on as small a footing as possible consistent with the public necessities. This policy was considered by them as most consonant with the spirit of a free people. The army, before the increase now ordered, consisted of only about three thousand men. The navy consisted of less than twenty frigates and sloops-of-war in commission, and about one hundred and fifty gun-boats, with officers and men to man them. The gun-boats were suited only for harbor defence.

11. During the same session of Congress, the President, by Special Message, sent to that body certain documents, from which it appeared that one John Henry, a British subject, had been employed by his Government as a secret agent in certain intrigues, with a view to produce a disaffection in the New England States, that might result in their political connection with Great Britain. A Committee in the House, to whom the matter was referred, reported that—

"The transaction disclosed by the President's Message presents to the mind of the Committee conclusive evidence that the British Government, at a period of peace, and during the most friendly professions, have been deliberately and perfidiously pursuing measures to divide these States, and to involve our citizens in all the guilt of treason and the horrors of civil war."

Meantime preparations for war went actively on.

12. During this winter occurred two events of a different character, each of which produced a great sensation everywhere at the time, and both of which deserve to be noted in giving a general history of the country. One was the accidental burning of a theatre in the city of Richmond, Virginia, during a play which had attracted an unusually crowded audience, in which several of the most prominent citizens of the State, with their families, including the Governor, perished. This took place on the 26th of December,

---
11. What is said of the John Henry plot?
12. What two notable events occurred in the winter of 1811-12? What is said of them?

1811. The other was a frightful earthquake in the Valley of the Mississippi River, which exhibited its greatest force and most terrific effects in the vicinity of New Madrid. This was on the 11th of February, 1812.

13. On the 8th of April, 1812, the State of Louisiana was admitted into the Union. Soon after an Act was passed organizing a Territorial Government for all that portion of the Louisiana Purchase lying outside of the then limits of the State of Louisiana. To this territory the name of Missouri was given.

COAT OF ARMS OF LOUISIANA

14. On the 20th of April, the venerable George Clinton, Vice-President of the United States, died in Washington, at the age of seventy-three. His place was filled by William H. Crawford, of Georgia, who had previously been elected by the Senate President *pro tempore* of that body.

15. We turn again to the progress of events involving the peace of the country. On the 30th of May, Mr. Foster, the new British Minister, resident at Washington, gave the *ultimatum* of his Government upon all the questions in controversy between the two countries. This Mr. Madison communicated to Congress on the 1st of June, and the question was submitted to them: Whether the wrongs justly complained of should continue to be borne, or whether the United States should resort to war. The subject was referred to the Committee of Foreign Relations, of which Mr. Calhoun was Chairman. They reported in favor of a declaration of war. This was discussed in the House for

---

13. When was the State of Louisiana admitted into the Union? What new Territorial Government was established soon after?

14. What occurred on the 20th of April, 1812? Who filled the place of Mr. Clinton?

15. What occurred on the 30th of May? What did the President do? Who was Chairman of the Committee on Foreign Relations? What report did he make? How was it discussed? What was the vote in the House and Senate on the Declaration of War? When did the Act receive the President's approval, and become a law?

several days with closed doors. An Act making a declaration of war was finally passed in that body, by a vote of 79 to 49. It went to the Senate, where it likewise passed, by a vote of 19 to 13, and was approved by the President on the 18th of June, 1812.

16. Such was the state of public affairs when the Presidential Election of that year took place. Mr. Madison received the Republican or Democratic caucus nomination for re-election, and Elbridge Gerry, of Massachusetts, received the like nomination for the office of Vice-President. Some of the more violent War Democrats, who looked upon Mr. Madison's course as too dilatory in avenging public wrongs, put in nomination for the Presidency, De Witt Clinton, an eminent statesman of New York, and a nephew of the late Vice-President. Mr. Clinton was generally supported by the anti-Administration party, with Jared Ingersoll, of Pennsylvania, who had belonged to the old Federal party, for Vice-President, instead of Mr. Gerry. The result of the Election was, 128 of the Electoral votes for Mr. Madison, and 89 for Mr. Clinton; for Vice-President, the Election by the Colleges stood: 131 for Mr. Gerry, and 86 for Mr. Ingersoll. By States, the vote stood: for the regular Democratic candidates, 11; and for the Opposition candidates, 7. The eleven States that voted for Mr. Madison were: Vermont, Pennsylvania, Maryland, Virginia, North Carolina, South Carolina, Georgia, Kentucky, Tennessee, Ohio, and Louisiana; and the seven that voted for Mr. Clinton were: New Hampshire, Massachusetts, Rhode Island, Connecticut, New York, New Jersey, and Delaware.

17. The active scenes and stirring events which took place immediately after the declaration of war, will be set forth in the next chapter.

---

16. Who were the candidates of the respective parties for the offices of President and Vice-President in the Fall of 1812? What was the result of the election? How did it stand as to the electoral votes, and how by States?
17. What is said of the active scenes which immediately took place after the declaration of war? What is here said of the position of John Randolph, of Roanoke, upon the declaration of war?

It may be proper to state here, that notwithstanding the declaration of war was a Republican or Democratic measure, yet it was not sustained with unanimity by that party. The Act declaring war was opposed in the House of Representatives by the celebrated " John Randolph of Roanoke," a member from Virginia (long a leader of the Republican side in that body), with great ability, vehemence, and eloquence. He saw no practical good that would be likely to be accomplished by it, but many serious ills that would attend it, and many more serious that might result from it. While he was by no means insensible of the British wrongs complained of, yet he was disposed to be more forbearing in exactions for an immediate redress of them, in view of the desperate necessities of " Mother Country," from which the essential principles of our own liberty had been derived, in her then perilous struggle with Napoleon, whom he regarded as the public enemy of all free institutions. With that directness and boldness which marked every act of his life, he did not hesitate to aver, without regard to personal considerations or popular favor, that whatever might be her faults and short-comings, his sympathies in the terrible struggle then in its crisis for national existence, between England and France, were with the country from which his own ancestry had descended, and with " the land which had given birth to Shakespeare and Milton, to Coke, Hampden, Sidney, and Chatham."

18. It may be proper here, also, to notice the fact, that soon after the declaration of war, England renewed her overtures for a settlement of the controversy by negotiation. This was done through Admiral Warren, of the British Navy, who wrote from Halifax, in September, 1812, to Mr. Monroe, Secretary of State, informing him that he was authorized to enter into stipulations for a cessation of

---

18. What is further said in this chapter about the British overtures for a cessation of hostilities? What is further said of Mr. Randolph's position, and his views of the probable success of obtaining the main object of the controversy by war?

hostilities upon the basis of a revocation of the "Orders in Council." Mr. Monroe replied that the President was willing to agree to an armistice, provided Admiral Warren was authorized and was willing to negotiate terms by which impressment of seamen from vessels of the United States should be suspended and discontinued, as experience had proved that no peace could be durable until that question was definitely and finally adjusted. The correspondence here closed, as Great Britain refused to relinquish the right of search and impressment. The rejection of this overture at the time was, perhaps, the greatest error of Mr. Madison's Administration. That was the main point in the controversy, which Mr. Randolph did not believe it was in the power of the United States to have settled according to their liking.

The doctrine of the right of expatriation, with the accompanying rights of naturalization under the laws of the United States, as held in this country, he did not believe that England could be brought to accede to. The other questions he thought might be adjusted by negotiation, and that the time was near at hand for their being thus adjusted, when war, as he thought, was too hastily declared. This overture of England, to some extent, confirmed the correctness of his opinion. But being rejected, however, the war went on, and with what results we shall see.

CHAPTER XI.

ADMINISTRATION OF MADISON—CONTINUED.

Second Term, 4th March, 1813—4th March, 1817.

WAR WITH GREAT BRITAIN.

1. MR. MADISON was inaugurated President for a second term, on the 4th of March, 1813. There were now

---

CHAPTER XI.—1. When was Mr. Madison inaugurated for a second term? What changes were made in his Cabinet?

two changes in his Cabinet. William Jones, of Pennsylvania, filled the office of Secretary of the Navy, instead of Paul Hamilton, resigned, and General John Armstrong filled the office of Secretary of War, instead of Dr. Eustes, resigned.

2. War against Great Britain had been declared, as we have seen, on the 18th day of June before. This war was then going on, and it is now proper to bring up the events connected with it, which had transpired in the mean time.

3. In bringing up these events it is also proper to premise by stating that at the time the war was declared, the prevailing idea was that England was to be brought to terms by the seizure of her neighboring Provinces on the northern boundary of the United States. This was the only vital point at which it was expected that the United States could deal telling blows. Little or nothing was expected from any contest on the ocean. The United States navy, of less than thirty frigates and sloops-of-war in commission, even with the new additions ordered, could not, it was supposed, cope with England's fleets of a thousand sail. All that was expected of these was to aid the gun-boats in coast defence, and in preventing a land invasion; while they might, also, in conjunction with privateers put in commission, cripple the enemy to some extent by the destruction of their commerce on the high seas. But the capture of the Canadas was looked upon as an easy prize. It was with this view that the army was organized, and active preparations made. The chief command of all the forces was assigned to General Henry Dearborn, of Massachusetts. His position was to be on the eastern end of the line; the forces on the west end were assigned to General William Hull, then Governor of Michigan; those in the centre, or middle of the line, were assigned to General Stephen Van Rensselaer. They were all to co-op-

---
2. What is said of the war?
3. What was the prevailing idea of the time? Who was put in chief command? Who were his subordinates, and where were they stationed?

erate in their movements, with a view to Montreal as an ultimate objective point.

4. On this line of policy, General Hull had, early in July, 1812, concentrated an army of about 2,500 at Detroit. On the 12th of that month he crossed over and took possession of the village of Sandwich. Here he issued a very famous proclamation, and remained until the 8th of August, when, upon hearing that Fort Mackinaw, on the river above Detroit, had been taken by the British and Indians, he recrossed the river and again took position at Detroit. A few days after this, General Brock, Governor of Upper Canada, who had called out a force, took his position at Malden. On the 15th of August he erected batteries on the opposite side of the river, but in such position as to bring the town of Detroit within the range of his guns, and demanded of Hull a surrender of the place. Colonel McCarter and Colonel Lewis Cass had been sent off on detached service with a small force on the River Raisin, a few days before, by General Hull. Captain Brush, of the Ohio Volunteers, had also, with a small force, been sent off on similar detached service. These detachments were recalled by General Hull on the 15th. On the 16th, General Brock commenced crossing the river with his forces, three miles below the position occupied by General Hull. When the British had advanced within about five hundred yards of Hull's line, to their surprise they saw the display of a white flag. An officer rode up to inquire the cause. It was the signal for a parley. A correspondence was opened between the commanding generals, which speedily terminated in a capitulation on the part of Hull. The fortress of Detroit, with the garrison and munitions of war, was surrendered. The forces under Cass and McCarter, and other troops, at the River Raisin, were included in the surrender. Captain Brush, however, not considering himself bound by Hull's engagement, broke up his camp and retreated towards Ohio. The army sur-

---

4. What is said of General Hull?

rendered by Hull amounted to 2,500 men. General Brock's entire command consisted of about 700 British and Canadians, with 600 Indians. This unaccountable conduct of Hull filled the whole country with indignation. As soon as he was exchanged he was brought to trial by court martial. He was charged with treason, cowardice, and neglect of duty, but found guilty only of the two latter charges. He was sentenced to be shot, but his life was spared in consideration of gallant services in his younger days.

5. By the surrender of Hull, the whole Northwestern frontier was exposed, not only to British invasion, but Indian depredations of the most savage character. Great alarm spread through all the neighboring States. Not less than ten thousand volunteers tendered their services to the Government for defence. These were accepted and placed under command of General William Henry Harrison, who succeeded Hull.

6. After Hull's disaster, General Van Rensselaer, who had command, according to the original plan, of the centre of the invading line, made a movement over the Canada border. His forces consisted of regulars and militia, and were assembled at Lewistown, on the Niagara River. On the opposite side was Queenstown, a fortified British post. This was the first object of his attack. On the 13th of October, he sent a detachment of a thousand men over the river, who succeeded in landing under a heavy fire from the British. The troops were led to the assault of the fortress by Colonels Christie and Scott. They succeeded in capturing it. General Brock came up with a reinforcement of 600 men, and made a desperate effort to regain the fort, but was defeated, and lost his life in the engagement. General Van Rensselaer was now at Queenstown, and returned to carry over reinforcements, but his troops refused to obey the order. Soon after, another British re-

---

5. What was the effect of Hull's surrender? Who succeeded him?
6. Who made the next movement over the Canada border? What is said of it, and how did it end?

inforcement was rallied, which recaptured the fort after a bloody engagement, in which the greater part of the thousand men who had first taken it were killed. General Van Rensselaer immediately resigned.

7. The command of the Army of the Centre was then assigned to General Alexander Smyth. He was soon at the head of an army of 4,500 men. On the 28th of November he was ready to move. That was the day fixed for crossing the river. The troops were embarked, but the enemy appearing on the opposite side in considerable force and battle array, a council of war was held, which resulted in a recall of the troops in motion, and a postponement of the enterprise till the 1st of December. On that day another council of war was held, at which the invasion from that quarter was indefinitely postponed. General Smyth in turn immediately resigned. So ended the third and last attempt at an invasion of Canada, during the Fall and Winter of 1812.

8. While the military operations on land, from which so much had been expected, bore so gloomy an aspect, quite as much to the surprise as to the joy of the country, the exploits of the gallant little navy, in its operations on sea, from which very little had been looked for or hoped for, were sending in the most cheering tidings. These may be thus stated: First. On the 19th of August, 1812, three days after the disastrous surrender of Detroit by General William Hull of the army, a most brilliant victory was achieved off the Gulf of St. Lawrence by Captain Isaac Hull of the navy. The latter was in command of the United States frigate *Constitution*, and coming up with the British man-of-war *Guerriere*, under the command of Captain Dacres, at the time and place stated, an engagement immediately ensued. The fight was a desperate one, and lasted for some time. But the result was the triumph of

---

7. Who succeeded Van Rensselaer? What is said of Smyth's projected movement?
8. What is said of the naval operations in the Fall of 1812?

Hull and his gallant men. Dacres surrendered; but the *Guerriere* was too much disabled to be brought into port, and was blown up at sea. The loss of the *Constitution* in men was seven killed and seven wounded; the loss of the *Guerriere* was fifty killed and sixty-four wounded; among the latter was Captain Dacres himself.

About the same time, Captain Porter, in command of the United States frigate *Essex*, met and captured the British sloop-of-war *Alert*, after an action of only eight minutes.

Second. On the 18th of October, Captain Jones, in command of the United States sloop-of-war *Wasp*, of eighteen guns, met and captured the British sloop-of-war *Frolic*, of twenty-two guns, after a hard fought battle of forty-five minutes, losing but eight men, while the loss of his enemy, in a vessel one-third his superior, was eighty men.

Third. On the 25th of October, Captain Decatur, in command of the frigate *United States*, of forty-four guns, met and captured the British frigate *Macedonian*, mounting forty-nine guns and manned by three hundred men. The action continued an hour and a half. The loss of the *Macedonian* was thirty-six killed and sixty-eight wounded; while the loss on the *United States* was only seven killed and five wounded. The *Macedonian* was brought into New York, and the gallant Decatur, who when lieutenant had so signally distinguished himself at Tripoli, was welcomed with the applause and honors which he had so nobly won.

Fourth. On the 29th of December, the *Constitution*, familiarly called by the sailors *Old Ironsides*, then in command of Commodore Bainbridge, had another encounter at sea. This was with the British frigate *Java*, of thirty-eight guns. The action was fought off San Salvador, and lasted three hours. The *Java* was dismasted, and reduced to a wreck, losing one hundred and sixty-one killed and wounded, while the loss of the *Constitution*, in killed and wounded, was but thirty-four.

Fifth. In addition to these victories of the public vessels, United States privateers, fitted out under letters of marque, succeeded in severely distressing the enemy's commerce, capturing about five hundred of their merchantmen, and taking three thousand prisoners, during the first seven months of the war. England, as Napoleon had predicted, had found an enemy which was ably contesting her supremacy as mistress of the sea.

9. Such was the aspect of affairs on land and sea in the progress of the war up to the time of Mr. Madison's inauguration for a second Presidential term. Soon after this, on the 8th of March, 1813, the Russian Minister at Washington, Mr. Daschkoff, communicated to the President of the United States an offer from the Emperor Alexander of his mediation between the United States and Great Britain, with a view to bring about peace between them. Mr. Madison promptly and formally accepted the Russian mediation, and appointed Mr. Gallatin, John Quincy Adams, and James A. Bayard Commissioners to negotiate a treaty of peace with Great Britain under the auspices of the tendered mediation. Messrs. Gallatin and Bayard soon set out on the mission to join Mr. Adams at St. Petersburg, where he was then Resident Minister of the United States. The British Government declined the mediation, and nothing came of this commission.

10. The first session of the Thirteenth Congress met on the 24th of May, 1813. The principal business of this Congress was to provide means to carry on the war and to sustain the public credit. Direct taxes and internal duties were again resorted to. The expenditures of the war had greatly exceeded the estimates. New loans had to be made and provided for. The public finances were in a state of much embarrassment; Treasury notes issued according to Act

---

9. Who proposed mediation early in March, 1813 ? How was the offer treated by Mr. Madison ? Who were the Commissioners appointed ? What was the result, and why ?
10. When did the Thirteenth Congress meet ? What was the principal business of this Congress ? What is said of the public finances ? What is said of the war spirit ?

of Congress were at a great discount; the loans authorized by the Government were paid in depreciated currency; all the banks in the Union had suspended specie payments, except some in the New England States. Proper arms and clothing for the militia when called into the field were both wanting. Already the war spirit was beginning to abate in several quarters, especially in New England.

11. Still the invasion of Canada was the leading object of the Administration. The campaign planned for this purpose in 1813 was similar to that of 1812. The operations extended along the whole northern frontier of the United States. The Army of the West, under General Harrison, was stationed at the head of Lake Erie; that of the East end of the line, under the command of General Hampton, on the shore of Lake Champlain; while that of the Centre, under Dearborn, the Commander-in-chief, was placed between the Lakes Ontario and Erie. The result of this campaign, in view of its main object, the conquest of Canada, was very little more successful than that of the year before. There were many movements and counter-movements of forces, advances, retreats, and sieges, with some pitched battles, in which great valor was displayed, but no one of them was attended with any decisive results.

12. The most noted events of this campaign may be thus briefly stated: First. The slaughter of United States prisoners at Frenchtown, in Canada, on the 22d of January, 1813. Colonel Proctor, the British officer to whom General Winchester had surrendered a force of several hundred men, in violation of his pledge turned the prisoners over to the vengeance of the Indians; or at least did not restrain his allies, the savages, in their most atrocious acts of barbarity upon their unarmed victims. Second. The battle of York, or Toronto, in Upper Canada, on the 27th of April, in which

---

11. What of the invasion of Canada? What is said of the campaign planned for this purpose in 1813? How were the forces placed, and under the command of whom? What is said of the result of the campaign?
12. What are the most noted events of this campaign?

the young and gallant United States officer, General Zebulon M. Pike, was killed. He expired in the midst of victory. Third. The siege of Fort Meigs by Proctor, and its successful defence by Harrison, in the month of May. Fourth. The subsequent siege of Fort Sandusky by Proctor in the same month, and its like gallant defence by Major Croghan. Fifth. The battle of Sackett's Harbor, on the 29th of May, in which the British General Prevost was signally repulsed. Sixth. The capture on the same day of the British Fort George by the United States troops. Seventh. The battle of Lake Erie, fought on the 10th of September. This was a naval engagement, planned and executed by Commodore Perry. Its results stand briefly chronicled in his report of it to General Harrison, in these words: "We have met the enemy, and they are ours!—two ships, two brigs, one schooner, and one sloop." Eighth. The battle of the Thames, as it is called, fought by Harrison on the 5th of October, and in which he gained a complete victory. It was in this battle that the famous Indian warrior Tecumseh was killed. Soon after this, General Harrison resigned his commission and retired from the service. General Dearborn had previously resigned, when the chief command had been conferred upon General James Wilkinson.

13. In the mean time the Creek Indians in Georgia and Alabama had taken up arms. On the 30th of August they had surprised Fort Mims on the Chattahoochee River, and massacred nearly three hundred persons, men, women, and children. The militia of Georgia and Tennessee were called out. Those of Georgia were under the command of General John Floyd; the whole were under the direction of Andrew Jackson, of Tennessee, with the commission of Major General. Floyd had two engagements with the

---

13. What is said of the Creek Indians? How was their outbreak met? To whom was the Georgia militia assigned? To whom the Tennessee? Who had the direction of the whole? What is said of the battles of Callebee, Antossee, Tallushatchee, Talladega, Emuckfau, and Tohopeka? What was the result? What of Witherford's speech?

enemy; one at Callebee, the other at Autossee. Both were successful. The Indian town of Autossee was burned by him on the 29th of November. A detachment of the Tennessee forces, under General Coffee, had an engagement at Tallushatchee on the 3d of November, in which two hundred Indians were killed. His success was complete. On the 8th of November the battle of Talladega was fought, under the immediate direction of Jackson himself. This was another complete victory. Soon after, another fight was had at Emuckfau, with like result. The Indians rallied again, and made their last stand at a place known as "The Horseshoe Bend," or, as they called it, "Tohopeka," on the Tallapoosa River. Here they were completely crushed by Jackson in his great victory of the 27th of March following. A treaty of peace with them was soon after made. The speech of their chief prophet and warrior, Witherford, on the occasion of his surrender to General Jackson, and as reported by him at the time, deserves perpetuation:

"I am," said he, "in your power. Do with me as you please. I am a soldier. I have done the white people all the harm I could. I have fought them, and fought them bravely. If I had an army I would yet fight, and contend to the last. But I have none. My people are all gone. I can now do no more than weep over the misfortunes of my nation. Once I could animate my warriors to battle; but I cannot animate the dead. My warriors can no longer hear my voice. Their bones are at Talladega, Tallushatchee, Emuckfau, and Tohopeka. I have not surrendered myself thoughtlessly. Whilst there were chances for success I never left my post, nor supplicated peace. But my people are gone; and I now ask it for my nation and for myself."

14. The operations on the sea in 1813 continued, upon the whole, to add lustre to the "infant navy" of the United States. The most noted of these, the successful as well as adverse, were as follows:

First. Captain Lawrence, of the United States sloop-of-war *Hornet*, on the 24th of February, met and captured the British brig *Peacock*, in a conflict that lasted only fifteen

---

14. What is said of the operations on the sea in 1813? What is said of Admiral Cockburn's operations on the waters of the Delaware and the Chesapeake? What of the ports north to the limits of the New England coast?

minutes. The *Peacock*, in striking her colors, displayed at the same time a signal of distress. Captain Lawrence made the greatest exertions to save her crew, but she went down before all of them could be gotten off, carrying with her three brave and generous United States seamen, who were extending their aid.

Second. On the 1st of June, the British frigate *Shannon* captured the United States frigate *Chesapeake*. The *Chesapeake* at this time was in the command of Lawrence. Every officer on board of her was either killed or wounded. Lawrence, as he was carried below, weltering in blood, and just before expiring, issued his last heroic order—"*Don't give up the ship!*" But the fortunes of battle decided otherwise.

Third. The British met with another like success on the 14th of August, in the capture of the United States brig *Argus* by the *Pelican*. The *Argus* had carried Mr. Crawford, United States Minister to France, in the month of May; after which she had made a brilliant cruise, capturing more than twenty of the enemy's ships, when she was in turn captured, as stated. Her colors, however, were not struck in her last engagement until after Captain Allen, in command, had fallen mortally wounded.

Fourth. In September, the United States brig *Enterprise* met the British brig *Boxer* on the coast of Maine, and after an engagement of forty minutes the *Boxer* surrendered. The commanders of both vessels fell in the action, and were buried beside each other in Portland, with military honors.

Fifth. During the summer, Commodore Porter, of the frigate *Essex*, after making many captures of British merchantmen in the Atlantic, visited the Pacific Ocean, where he was no less signally successful.

Sixth. During the same summer, British fleets entered the waters of the Delaware and Chesapeake bays, under the command of Admiral George Cockburn. All small merchant ships within their reach were destroyed, and much damage done to many of the towns on the coast. Frenchtown, Georgetown, Havre de Grace, and Fredericktown were burned. An attack was made upon Norfolk, which was repulsed with heavy loss. After committing many barbarities at Hampton, Cockburn with his command sailed south. All the ports north, to the limits of the New England coast, were kept in close blockade.

15. During the session of the Congress which convened in December, 1813, a communication was received from the British Government, of the purport, that although they had declined to treat under the mediation of Russia, yet they were willing to enter into direct negotiations either in London or Gottenburg. The offer was immediately acceded to, and the latter place appointed for the meeting. Henry Clay and Jonathan Russell were added to the Commissioners who had already been sent to Europe. The place of meeting was afterwards changed from Gottenburg to Ghent. The country at this time was feeling sorely the ills of war everywhere. New loans had to be made; increased taxes had to be levied; more troops had to be raised. The conquest of Canada was still the chief object of the Administration.

16. The plan of the campaign of 1814 was projected by General Armstrong, the Secretary of War. The Department of War was temporarily removed to the frontier, and established at the headquarters of the army on the Canada line. The operations in this quarter during this year, as those of 1813, were attended with many marches and countermarches, and much gallant fighting on both sides; but without any decisive results on either. The most

---

15. What communication was made from the British Government, and when? What was done with the offer? What new Commissioners were added to the Embassy? Where was the place finally agreed upon for the negotiators to meet? What is said of the state of the country? What was still the chief object of the Administration?

16. Who projected the campaign of 1814? Where was the Department of War temporarily established? What is said of the operations on the Canada line during this year? What are the most noted events of it? What is said of the battle of Plattsburg?

noted events connected with them may be thus summed up:

First. The general advance of Wilkinson into Canada commenced in March, and ended with the affair at La Cole Mill on the 31st of that month, in which he was defeated with heavy loss. Soon after this he was superseded, and the chief command given to General Izard.

Second. The battle of Chippewa, which was fought on the 5th of July by General Brown, and in which the United States forces won the day.

Third. The battle of Bridgewater, or Lundy's Lane, which was fought on the 25th of July. It was here that General Scott so signally distinguished himself.

Fourth. The battle of Fort Erie, fought on the 15th of August, in which the British General Drummond was repulsed with great loss.

Fifth. The battle of Plattsburg, which was fought on the 11th of October. This was a joint land and naval action. General Macomb commanded the United States land forces at this place; General Prevost commanded those on the British side. The United States naval forces were commanded by Commodore McDonough; the British fleet was commanded by Commodore Downie. The assault was commenced by Prevost with his land forces. As Commodore Downie moved up to assist with his fleet, he was met and engaged by McDonough with his small flotilla. The chief interest of both armies was now diverted from the action on land to that on the water, while the conflict between the fleet and flotilla lasted. It continued for upwards of two hours, and was fierce as well as bloody. It ended in the surrender of the British fleet to Commodore McDonough. Commodore Downie was killed in the fight, and when his flag-ship struck her colors the results of the day were decided, on land as well as on the water. Prevost immediately retreated. This victory ended all active operations in that quarter.

17. Meantime, during the Summer of 1814, a fleet of fifty or sixty vessels arrived in the Chesapeake Bay under Admirals Cockburn and Cochrane, bringing a large land force under General Ross. The design was the capture of the City of Washington. Ross landed five thousand men on the 19th of August, at the head of the Patuxent, and commenced his march overland. There were at the time no forces for defence near the Capital. The raw militia were hastily got together, and put under General Winder, who met the enemy at Bladensburg. The President and Cabinet left the city. Winder with his militia was barely able to retard the advance of Ross. He entered Washington the 24th of August, and burned most of the public buildings, including the President's house and the Capitol. The troops then returned to their shipping and proceeded up the Chesapeake. Landing at North Point, they advanced on Baltimore. This place was defended by General Striker with a force consisting mostly of raw militia and volunteers. In an action which took place on the 12th of September, Ross was killed, and his forces retired. After an unsuccessful attack of the British fleet under Cockburn upon Fort McHenry, which commanded the entrance to the city, the whole army re-embarked and left the Bay.

During this bombardment of Fort McHenry by Cockburn, which lasted a night and whole day, without effect upon the garrison or fort, Francis Key, of Baltimore, then detained on board one of the British vessels, whither he had gone on some public mission, as he gazed most anxiously upon the flag of his country, still floating triumphantly on the ramparts in the midst of the heavy cannonading, composed his soul-stirring song, in which occur the famous lines:

---

17. What is said of General Ross's movement during the summer of 1814? What was the design of the movement? What was the result? When was the City of Washington taken? What outrages were committed? After these, what did Ross do? Who defended Baltimore? When was the battle fought near that place? What became of Ross? What of his forces? What is said of Francis Key during the bombardment of Fort McHenry?

"The Star-spangled Banner! oh, long may it wave
O'er the land of the free and the home of the brave."

18. The New England States suffered much in the same way during the same Summer. Stonington was bombarded with similar unsuccess. Attempts were made to land an invading force at several places, which were repulsed by the militia.

19. The operations of the respective navies on the ocean during the entire year of 1814 resulted about as they did in 1813. The United States lost two war-ships and captured five of like character, besides many British merchantmen.

Mr. Gerry, the Vice-President, died suddenly in Washington, on the 23d of November of this year. He expired in his carriage as he was going to the Capitol. His death was universally regretted. John Gaillard, of South Carolina, succeeded him.

20. While these events were occurring on land and water, during the Summer of 1814, the hostility in the New England States to the Federal Administration had ripened into a determination to take decisive steps for the maintenance of their own rights in their own way. A majority of the people of these States were strongly opposed to the conquest of Canada. Massachusetts and Connecticut, throwing themselves upon their Reserved Rights under the Constitution, refused to allow their militia to be sent out of their States in what they deemed a war of aggression, especially when they were needed for their own defence in repelling an invasion. For this course they were very severely censured by most of their sister States, and the more so from the fact that the war had been entered upon

---

18. What is said of New England during this Summer?
19. What of the naval operations during the year 1814? What is said of Mr. Gerry and Mr. Gaillard?
20. What is said of the conduct of the New England States during the year 1814? What determination had they come to? What was the alleged cause of their hostility to the Federal Administration? How was their course looked upon by most of their sister States? What increased the opposition of the New England States? What did it result in? Where did the Convention meet? How were their deliberations held? What is said of their ultimate designs? What was the result of their positive action?

for the joint maintenance of the rights of their seamen and commerce. Moreover, it was insisted upon by the friends of the Administration that the mode of warfare adopted was the surest for the attainment of the objects aimed at. But what increased the opposition of the New England States at this time, was the refusal of the Administration to pay the expenses of their militia, called out by the Governors of these respective States for their own local defence. This refusal was based upon the ground that these States had refused to send their militia out of their limits upon a Federal call. To this may be added the new scheme of the Administration for forcing the militia of the respective States outside of their limits, not by a call on the Governors of the States for them, but by a general Act of Federal Conscription. It was in this condition of things that the Legislature of Massachusetts invited the neighboring States to meet in convention for mutual consultation. Accordingly, a Convention of delegates from Massachusetts, Rhode Island, New Hampshire, Vermont, and Connecticut met at Hartford, in the latter State, on the 15th day of December, 1814. The deliberations of this famous body were with closed doors. What the real ultimate designs of the leading members of it were, have never been fully disclosed. Some mystery has ever hung over it. But the resolutions adopted by it, and the public address put forth by it at the time, very clearly indicate that the purpose was, either to effect a change of policy on the part of the Federal Administration in the conduct of the war, or for these States, in the exercise of their Sovereign rights, to provide for their own well-being as they thought best by withdrawing from the Union. The only positive results of the Convention were, the appointment of a deputation of the body to wait upon the Federal authorities at Washington, to whom in person their views were to be presented, and the call of another Convention, to which this deputation was to report, before any further decisive action should be taken.

CHAP. XI.] ADMINISTRATION OF MADISON. 319

21. In the mean time it became known that a large British force of at least twelve thousand men had been land-

BATTLE OF NEW ORLEANS.

ed at or near the mouth of the Mississippi River, under Sir Edward Pakenham. The country everywhere was in the greatest alarm for the safety of New Orleans. The command of this Department was now in charge of General Jackson, with such forces as he could collect, consisting mostly of volunteers and militia, amounting in all to not more than half the numbers of the approaching foe. He went vigorously to work to repel this most formidable invasion. With such means of resistance as the genius of "a born general" only can improvise, he was soon in an attitude of defence. The result was the ever-memorable heroic charge and bloody repulse of the 8th of January, 1815. This was the most brilliant victory achieved by the arms of the United States during the war. Two thousand British soldiers, led in a charge on Jackson's breastworks, were left dead or wounded upon the field. Pakenham him-

21. What was occurring in the mean time in the Southwest? Who was in charge of this Department at this time? What is said of Jackson and what he did? What was the result? How was the news of Jackson's victory received? What other intelligence soon followed? What seemed to be forgotten in the general joy?

self was killed. Major-Generals Gibbs and Keane, the two officers next in command, were both wounded, the former mortally; while Jackson's loss was only seven killed and six wounded.

Upon the heel of the news of this splendid achievement, which electrified the country with joy, came the still more gratifying intelligence of a Treaty of Peace, which the Commissioners had effected at Ghent on the 24th of December, 1814, fifteen days before this great battle was fought. All discontents ceased, and in the general joy at this close of the bloody scenes of two years and over, it seemed to be entirely forgotten or overlooked that not one word was said in the treaty about the right of search and of impressment by Great Britain, which was the main point in issue at the commencement of the war.

22. The Treaty of Peace with England was promptly ratified, and all necessary steps for a disbandment of the army were immediately taken by Congress. But further work was in store for the navy. The Dey of Algiers had recently, in violation of the treaty of 1795, been committing outrages upon American commerce within his waters. Another war against him was soon afterwards declared. The gallant Decatur was sent with a fleet to the Mediterranean for the chastisement of this piratical power. He in a short time captured two Algerine ships of war, and brought the Dey to terms. A treaty of peace was made on the 30th of June, by which the United States obtained not only security for the future, but indemnity for the past.

23. William H. Crawford, on his return from Paris, where he had been resident United States Minister for some time, was appointed Secretary of War, 1st of August, 1815.

24. The charter of the first Bank of the United States

---
22. What further work was left for the navy to do? Who was sent out to wage the war which was declared against the Dey of Algiers? What was the result of this short war?
23. What is said of Mr. Crawford?
24. What of the second Bank of the United States?

having expired in 1811, and an Act for its renewal having failed to pass, several attempts afterwards were made to obtain a charter for a similar institution, which likewise failed. A bill for this purpose, which had passed both Houses of Congress, was vetoed by Mr. Madison, in January, 1814. But on the 10th of April, 1816, another bill of like character received his approval, by which a new Bank of the United States was incorporated for twenty years, with a capital of thirty-five million dollars.

25. On the 19th of April, 1816, an Act was passed for the admission of Indiana into the Union as a State.

26. During the Fall of 1816 another Presidential election took place. There was at this time considerable division among the Republicans as to whom the successor should be. Mr. Madison had positively declined standing for re-election. The choice of candidates finally made by the Democratic members of Congress in caucus was, Mr. Monroe for President, and Governor Daniel D. Tompkins, of New York, for Vice-President. The Federal party, still so called, nominated Rufus King, of New York, for President, and John Howard, of Maryland, for Vice-President. The result of the vote of the Electoral Colleges was 183 for Mr. Monroe, and 34 for Mr. King; 183 for Governor Tompkins, and 22 for Mr. Howard. The vote by States between the Democratic and Federal tickets at this election stood: 16 for the Democratic, and 3 for the Federal. The 16 States that voted for Mr. Monroe and Mr. Tompkins were: New Hampshire, Rhode Island, Vermont, New York, New Jersey, Pennsylvania, Maryland, Virginia, North Carolina, South Carolina, Georgia, Ken-

COAT OF ARMS OF INDIANA.

---

25. When was Indiana admitted as a State into the Union?
26. What is said of the Presidential election in the Fall of 1812?

tucky, Tennessee, Ohio, Louisiana, and Indiana. The 3 that voted for Mr. King were: Massachusetts, Connecticut, and Delaware.

27. After the 4th of March, 1817, Mr. Madison retired from office, leaving the country at peace with the world, and rapidly recovering from the injurious effects of the late war. He returned to his home at Montpelier, Virginia, where he enjoyed the society of his friends and the general esteem of his countrymen. The most distinguishing feature of his Administration was the war with Great Britain. Whatever may be thought of the wisdom or the policy of that war, or of its general conduct, the result unquestionably added greatly to the public character of the United States in the estimation of foreign powers. The price at which this had been purchased was in round numbers about one hundred million dollars in public expenditures, and the loss of about thirty thousand men, including those who fell in battle as well as those who died of disease contracted in the service. Of the amount of private or individual losses and suffering no approximate estimate can be made; and though in the Treaty of Peace nothing was said about the main cause for which the war was prosecuted, yet Great Britain afterwards refrained from giving any offence in the practical assertion of her theoretic right of search and impressment. Whether the same ends could have been attained by any other course which would not have involved a like sacrifice of treasure and blood, is a problem that can never be satisfactorily solved by human speculation.

27. What is said of Mr. Madison after the 4th of March, 1817 ? What was the most distinguishing feature of his Administration ? What is said of the results of the war ?

CHAPTER XII.

ADMINISTRATION OF MONROE.

4th of March, 1817—4th of March, 1825.

1. JAMES MONROE, of Virginia, fifth President of the United States, was inaugurated on the 4th of March, 1817, in the 59th year of his age His Inaugural Address gave general satisfaction to all parties. The oath of office was administered by Chief-Justice Marshall. His Cabinet were: John Quincy Adams, of Mass., Secretary of State; William H. Crawford, of Ga., Secretary of the Treasury; John C. Calhoun, of S. C., Secretary of War; and William Wirt, of Va., Attorney General. Benjamin W. Crowninshield, of Mass., who was in office during the latter part of Mr. Madison's Administration, was continued Secretary of the Navy until November 30th, 1818, when Smith Thompson, of New York, received the appointment. These were all men of distinguished ability, and thoroughly identified with the Democratic Party at the time.

PRESIDENT MONROE.

2. The first session of the Fifteenth Congress began on the 1st of December, 1817. The recommendations of the President met with cordial approval. The internal taxes which had been imposed during the war, were abolished. A Pension Act was passed, which gave great satisfaction to the country at large, and relief to not less than thirteen thousand soldiers who had served in the war of the Revolu-

---

CHAPTER XII.—1. Who was the fifth President of the United States? When was he inaugurated? Who were his Cabinet? What is said of them?
2. When did the first session of the Fifteenth Congress begin? What Acts did they pass? What new State was admitted into the Union, and when?

tion, and in the late war with Great Britain. On the 10th day of December, 1817, a joint resolution was approved by the President for the admission of Mississippi as a State into the Union. This was the dawn of a period known in the history of the United States as "the era of good feeling." Old party lines were nearly extinct.

COAT OF ARMS OF MISSISSIPPI.

3. War having broken out with the Seminole Indians in 1818, Gen. Jackson was ordered to take the field, and to call upon the Governors of the adjoining States for as many troops of the militia as he might think necessary to subdue them. He soon raised a force of a thousand men, with whom he marched into the Indian country. Believing that the hostile Indians fled to the Spanish commandants for protection, that they were encouraged by them, and that the safety of the inhabitants of that part of the United States required such proceedings, he invaded the province of Florida; seized the post of St. Mark's, and sent the Spanish authorities and troops to Pensacola. At St. Mark's he found two English traders, named Ambrister and Arbuthnot; and believing that they were supplying the Indians with arms and ammunition, and inciting them to hostilities against the citizens of the United States, he had them arrested and tried by court martial. They were found guilty, and executed.

The Governor of Pensacola continuing to give shelter and assistance to the Indians, Jackson took possession of that place on the 14th of May. The Governor escaped and fled to Barancas. Jackson took possession of that place on the 27th, and sent the Governor and troops to Havana. His conduct in this matter was made a subject of inquiry in both Houses of Congress; but upon investigation his course was

---

3. What is said of the war with the Seminole Indians? What two English traders did Jackson hang? When did Jackson take possession of Pensacola? What became of the Spanish Governor?

approved by a large majority in each. Don Onis, the Spanish Minister resident at Washington, protested against his arbitrary proceedings; but as negotiations were then pending for the cession of Florida to the United States, the matter was not pressed.

4. The people of Illinois were admitted as a separate State into the Union by joint resolution of Congress, approved by the President on the 3d of December, 1818.

COAT OF ARMS OF ILLINOIS.

5. An event occurred in the year 1819, which deserves to be noted, not only in the history of the United States, but in the annals of the world. It was the passage of the first steamship across the Atlantic Ocean. This exploit, so wonderful at the time, was performed by the steamer *Savannah*, projected and owned in Savannah, Ga., though built in the city of New York. She left the port of Savannah in May, 1819, for Liverpool; and after making a successful voyage to that place, proceeded with equal success to St. Petersburg. She was the object of great curiosity wherever she went.

6. On the 14th of December, 1819, the people of Alabama were admitted as a separate State into the Union.

7. The most important and distinguishing measure of Mr. Monroe's Administration up to this time was what has been called the "Missouri Compromise of 1820." Under it the people of Maine were admitted as a separate State into the Union, on the 15th day of March,

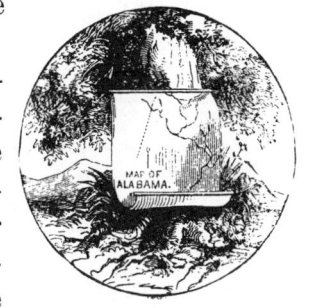
COAT OF ARMS OF ALABAMA.

---

4. When were the people of Illinois admitted as a separate State into the Union?
5. When did the first steamship cross the Atlantic? What was her name? From what port did she make her voyage?
6. When were the people of Alabama admitted as a separate State into the Union?

1820. Missouri, however, was not admitted under that measure, as is generally supposed.*

8. During the Fall of 1820, came off another Presidential election. Mr. Monroe and Governor Tompkins received the Democratic nomination for re-election to the respective offices of President and Vice-President; and at the election Mr. Monroe received the vote of every State in the Union, and every elective vote of all the Colleges except one. One vote in the College of New Hampshire was cast for John Quincy Adams for President. Governor Tompkins received every electoral vote for the office of Vice-President except fourteen. The vote of Missouri,

COAT OF ARMS OF MAINE.

---

7. What is said of the Missouri Compromise of 1820? When was the State of Maine admitted into the Union?
8. What is said of the Presidential election of 1820?

---

* The following is a brief, but accurate, history of the nature and character of this "solemn compact, or covenant," as it has been styled:
A Bill for the admission of the State of Missouri into the Union, came up in the Lower House of Congress for action, on the 13th of February, 1819. To this Bill, Mr. Tallmadge, of N. Y., moved an amendment in these words:
"And *Provided*, That the further introduction of slavery, or involuntary servitude, be prohibited, except for the punishment of crimes whereof the party shall have been fully convicted; and that all children born in said State after the admission thereof into the Union, shall be free at the age of twenty-five years."
The announcement of this Amendment produced a great sensation in the House, which soon extended to the country everywhere. It opened anew the question of the powers of the Federal Government over Negro slavery in the States ; which had been considered as put at rest by the Resolution of the House of Representatives of 1790, upon the first petition presented upon the subject. From that day to this movement no attempt had been made in the Congress to bring the subject of Negro slavery, as it existed in the States or Territories, within the sphere of Federal legislation, under the new Constitution. Territorial Governments had been instituted in Tennessee, Mississippi, Louisiana, Alabama, and Missouri, without any such claim of power. The States of Kentucky, Tennessee, Louisiana, and Alabama, all tolerating Slavery, had been admitted, without any such claim of powers. The right to impose the restriction, moved by the Amendment upon the State of Missouri, was denied by the Strict Constructionists everywhere, North as well as South.
A bitter debate arose. Although an overwhelming majority of the House claimed to be Republicans, or Democrats, yet, during "the era of good feeling," party lines had not been closely drawn in the late State elections; many, therefore, who had been returned to the Fifteenth Congress as Democrats, or Strict Constructionists, sided on this question with those who held the Centralizing principles which had marked the Administration of the elder Adams. The question on the Amendment was divided in the House. On the first branch the vote was 87 for it, and 76 against it; on the second branch, 82 for it, and 78 against it. The Bill, with the restrictive Amendment, passed the House. The Senate disagreed to the Amendment. The House adhered. So this Bill was lost between the two Houses.
The application of the people of Missouri was renewed on the 9th of December, 1819, on the opening of the First Session of the Sixteenth Congress. To a Bill, offered in the usual form for this purpose, the same restriction in effect, but not in the same words, was renewed by Mr. Taylor, of N. Y. This gave rise to a renewal of the conflict of the Session before, with increased spirit and vigor. Never had any discussion shaken the foundations of the Government from its beginning as this then did. It was a conflict of principle. The friends of the Constitution and Union under it everywhere became alarmed.
Mr. Jefferson, in his retirement, said the news of this Amendment fell upon his ear as the sound of a fire-bell at night. He was well known to be opposed to Slavery, as it existed in the States, and was anxious for the adoption, by each State for itself, of suitable measures for

CHAP. XII.]   ADMINISTRATION OF MONROE.   327

which was cast for Mr. Monroe and Governor Tompkins, was not counted, because of a refusal of a majority of the House to recognize her as a State of the Union under the celebrated " Compromise," so called.

9. On the 22d of February, 1821, the President issued a proclamation announcing the ratification of a treaty with Spain; by which East and West Florida were ceded to the United States, and all claims of Spain to territory on the Pacific Coast north of 42° of North latitude. This included all the Spanish claims to any portion of Oregon. For the entire cession the United States were to pay five

---

9. What is said of the treaty with Spain in 1821?

---

emancipation. But he held that it was a subject on which Congress had no constitutional power to act ; and believed that the whole movement of its introduction into that body was instigated by the arch-leaders of the old Centralizing party by an artful appeal to the passions of the people on a popular issue, to revive their principles, on which they had been so utterly defeated for years. To Mr. Pinkney, he wrote :

"The Missouri question is a mere party trick. The leaders of Federalism, defeated in their schemes of obtaining power by rallying partisans to the principle of Monarchism—a principle of personal, not of local division—have changed their tack, and thrown out another barrel to the whale. They are taking advantage of the virtuous feelings of the people to effect a division of the parties by a geographical line; they expect this will insure them, on local principles the majority which they could never obtain on principles of Federalism."

While the discussion was going on, in the House, on the Missouri Bill, an Act passed that body, on the 3d of January, for the admission of the State of Maine, in the usual form, without any Restriction. When this House Bill went to the Senate, a motion was made and carried in that body, to tack on to it a Bill for the like admission of Missouri, in the usual form, without any Restriction. To the Amendment thus made, by tacking a Bill for the admission of Missouri to the Bill for the admission of Maine, Mr. Thomas, of Ill., moved another Amendment in these words

"*And be it further enacted*, That in all the territory ceded by France to the United States under the name of Louisiana, which lies north of thirty-six degrees and thirty minutes north latitude, excepting only such part thereof as is included within the limits of the State contemplated by this Act, slavery and involuntary servitude, otherwise than in the punishment of crimes, whereof the party shall have been duly convicted, shall be, and is hereby, forever prohibited: *Provided always*, That any person escaping into the same from whom labor or service is lawfully claimed in any State or Territory of the United States, such fugitive may be lawfully reclaimed, and conveyed to the person claiming his or her labor or service as aforesaid."

This Amendment passed the Senate on the 17th of February, by a vote of 34 to 10. The Maine Bill, with these two Senate Amendments so put upon it, came back to the House on the 19th of February. Its consideration was there postponed. The House went on discussing its own separate Bill for the admission of Missouri. Before coming to a final vote on that, however, they, on the 22d of February, took up the Maine Bill, with the Senate Amendments. They disagreed to both the Amendments of the Senate ; the one tacking on the Missouri Bill to the Maine Bill, as well as the Thomas Amendment to the Missouri Bill. On agreeing to the Thomas Amendment to the Missouri Bill, the vote in the House was only 18 in favor of it, while there were 159 against it. They then took up, and went on with, their own Bill for the admission of Missouri, with the restriction on the State in it. Pending this discussion, still going on in the House, a message was received from the Senate, on the 28th of February, stating that that body insisted on their Amendments to the Maine Bill. This message was taken up, and by a vote of 160 to 14 the House adhered to their disagreement to the Thomas Provision. The House, meantime, went on with their own separate Bill as to Missouri. The Senate asked a Committee of Conference on the disagreeing votes of the two Houses on the Maine Bill. This was granted on the 29th of February. But on the same day, the House adopted Mr. Taylor's restriction in their own Bill, by a vote of 94 to 86 ; and, with this restriction, passed and sent to the Senate their separate Bill for the admission of Missouri, on the next day (1st of March), by a vote of 91 to 82.

On the 2d of March, Mr. Holmes, of Mass., from the Committee of Conference, on the part of the House, on the disagreeing votes of the two Houses, upon the Bill for the admission of Maine, reported. Their recommendation was, that the Senate should recede from its Amendments to the House Bill for the admission of Maine, and that the House should strike out the Restriction as to the State in their separate Bill for the admission of Missouri, and insert in lieu of it the Thomas Provision, imposing the Territorial Restriction proposed. This was the "Compromise" reported. By it Maine and Missouri were both to be admitted under the separate Bills which had passed the House without any Restriction as to either State; but with the Territorial Thomas Restriction, so to be incorporated in the Missouri Bill.

millions of dollars. The territory thus acquired by them amounted to 367,320 square miles.

10. On the 10th day of August, 1821, the State of Missouri was admitted into the Union, under a proclamation of the President, in pursuance of a joint resolution emanating from a Grand Joint-Committee of the two Houses of Congress, at the instance of Mr. Clay, approved of by the President on the 2d of March before.

COAT OF ARMS OF MISSOURI.

11. The 4th of March this year coming on Sunday, Mr. Monroe was inaugurated for the Second Term on the succeeding day, Monday, the 5th of that month. The oath of office was

---

10. When was Missouri admitted, and how?
11. What is said of Mr. Monroe's second inauguration?

A similar report was made to the Senate on the 3d of March. which was agreed to in that body without a count; but in the House the yeas and nays were taken on both propositions of the report. The test vote was on striking out the Restriction on the State as it then stood in the House Bill for the admission of Missouri. On this question the vote was 90 in favor of striking out, and 87 against it; so the Restriction on the State was stricken out by a majority of 3. The question then came up on concurring with the Senate, in the insertion of the Thomas Provision for the future line of division on thirty-six degrees and thirty minutes, north latitude. This was passed by a vote of 134 to 42.

The eighty-seven votes which had been given against striking out the Restriction on the State, were on the last question given in favor of inserting the Restriction on the Territory—not as a "Compromise" for the admission of the State without Restriction. but as the next best thing that could be accomplished on their unyielded line. as results showed. The forty-two votes against the insertion of the Territorial Restriction, were given by Strict Constructionists. upon the ground that Congress had no more right, under the Constitution, to impose a Territorial Restriction than a State Restriction. Many others, of the Strict Construction Party, however, viewing the question in a different light, accepted the Thomas Proposition, and voted for it, upon the principle of a fair division of the public domain between the two great sections of the Union. By them, in this view, it was agreed to as a "Compromise," under the belief that it would be an end of the agitation of the subject; but in this they were greatly mistaken. The result was, that the separate Act for the admission of Maine received the approval of the President on the 3d of March, 1820, and that State was admitted into the Union under it on the 15th day of that month. The separate Act in relation to Missouri also received the President's approval, on the 6th of March, 1820. It was entitled, "An Act to authorize the People of Missouri Territory to form a Constitution and State Government, and for the admission of such State into the Union on an equal footing with the original States, and to prohibit Slavery in certain Territories."

But *Missouri was not admitted under this Act.* She was denied representation in the Senate and in the House, as a State of the Union, at the next Session of Congress, though her people had formed a State Constitution and organized a State Government, under the provisions of the Act so passed, and in pursuance of the understanding upon which these provisions were based. They had, as Maine had, elected Senators and members to Congress, and had voted in the Presidential election of that year. But on a resolution to allow her representation, on the 13th of December, 1820, the vote was 79 for it, and 93 against it. Of these ninety-three votes against it, seventy-two were given by the identical men who, on the 2d of March, had voted against striking out the State Restriction, on the test vote in the House, on the Compromise reported by the Committee of Conference, as before stated; and sixty-seven of them were the identical men who voted immediately afterwards for the insertion of the Territorial Restriction, which was carried by 134 to 42, as stated. This shows that they, and the Centralizing party with which they acted, never considered the adoption of the Thomas Provision as a "Compromise" for the admission of Missouri, without any Restriction upon the State. *So, Missouri, in point of fact, was not admitted into the Union as a State under the so-called "Compromise."* The conflict for her admission after its adoption, and her organization under it, was fiercer at the Session of December, 1820, than it ever had been before.

CHAP. XII.] ADMINISTRATION OF MONROE. 329

administered by Chief-Justice Marshall. No immediate changes took place in his Cabinet.

12. The 17th Congress held its first session from the 3d of December, 1821, to the 8th of May, 1822. On the organization of the House at this Session a marked division among the Republicans or Democrats manifested itself, upon the question of the limitations and powers of the Federal Government. Those who favored the policy of levying duties upon foreign imports, with a view spe-

---

12. What two questions did the Democrats divide on in December, 1821? What is said of the Speakership at this session? Who was finally elected Speaker?

It was at this stage of the proceedings that Mr. Clay threw himself into the breach, and exerted his transcendent powers in efforts at conciliation and harmony. He moved, on the 2d of February, 1821, that a Committee of Thirteen be appointed to report such action as should properly be taken in view of the situation. A committee was raised, and reported on the 20th of February.

The pretext for the opposition to the recognition of the State in December, 1820, was, that a clause of the Constitution of Missouri, about the immigration of Free Negroes and Mulattoes into that State, was in violation of the Constitution of the United States. This, however, was nothing but a pretext; for if the State Constitution contained anything inconsistent with the Constitution of the United States, it was, of course, inoperative, null and void.

The report of Mr. Clay's Committee of Thirteen was in substance: That Missouri should be recognized as a State of the Union upon the "Fundamental Condition" that her Legislature should pass no law in violation of the rights of the citizens of other States; and that the Legislature should also, by proper Act, give its assent to this "Fundamental Condition," before the 4th Monday in November next ensuing; and that the President of the United States, upon the receipt of this assent of the Legislature, should announce the fact by Proclamation, and then the State was to be considered in the Union. This report was rejected by a vote of 80 for it, and 83 against it. This shows very conclusively what was the real objection to Missouri at that time, and that the Restrictionists had not agreed to any compromise of their views upon the subject of Slavery, either in the State or Territory, by which they considered themselves bound, or intended to abide. The parties, in the mean time, continued to stand as they stood at the Session before. The passions on both sides waxed warmer as the conflict was prolonged. The strife was really one between Centralism and Confederation. The rejection of Mr. Clay's resolution was reconsidered next day; but when it was again put on its passage, it was again lost, by a vote of 82 for it, and 88 against it. Discordant opinions now prevailed as to what was the actual *status* of the people of Missouri, in their relations to the Federal Government. Some held that they were still in a Territorial condition, subject to Federal authority; while others maintained that they constituted an independent State, out of the Union. The withdrawal of other States seemed imminent.

Mr. Clay, undaunted by his previous failure, again came to the rescue of the Union. On the 22d of February, he moved that a Grand Joint-Committee, consisting of members of the House and Senate, should be raised to propose "suitable action for the alarming crisis." The Committee, on the part of the House, was to consist of twenty-three members. This was agreed to, and the twenty-three members were elected by the House. The Senate concurred. The Grand Joint-Committee was raised. Mr. Clay, as Chairman of this Grand Joint-Committee, on the part of the House, made the report from it on the 26th of February. It was a joint resolution, substantially the same as that reported by him before from the Committee of Thirteen. This resolution passed the House the same day, by a vote of 87 to 81. It was sent to the Senate, and passed that body the next day, by a vote of 26 to 15; and was approved by the President on the 2d of March, 1821. The Legislature of Missouri readily passed the indicated Act, on the 26th of June thereafter; and on the 10th day of August, 1821, the President issued his Proclamation accordingly, declaring the admission of Missouri into the Union as being complete.

This is the true history of "The Missouri Compromise," so called, of 1820, from the beginning to the end, so far as related to the admission of Missouri. A general idea prevails very extensively at this time, that Missouri was admitted as a Slave State in 1820, under an agreement with the Restrictionists or Centralists, proposed by Mr. Clay, that she should be so admitted upon condition that Negro slavery should be forever prohibited thereafter in the public domain north of thirty-six degrees, and thirty minutes north latitude. No greater error on any important historical event ever existed. The truth is, Mr. Clay was not the author of the Territorial line of thirty-six thirty degrees, incorporated in the Act of 1820; nor was Missouri admitted under the provisions of that Act. On the contrary, she was admitted on the 10th of August, 1821, by Presidential proclamation, upon the "Fundamental Condition," in substance, that the State Government, in all its departments, should be subject to the Constitution of the United States, as all the State Governments were, and are.—AUTHOR.

cially to protect domestic manufactures in the United States, and also of entering into a system of internal improvements throughout the States by the Federal Government, put in nomination for the Speakership John W. Taylor, of N. Y., who had been the mover of the Missouri Restriction. They who constituted the "straightest sect" of Strict Constructionists put in nomination Philip P. Barbour, of Va., who was decidedly opposed to a protective tariff, and to any system of general internal improvements to be carried on by the Federal Government; he had also opposed the Missouri Restriction. Mr. Barbour was elected by a majority of four votes.

13. During this session the subjects of a Protective Tariff and Internal Improvements constituted the chief topics of discussion; nothing of importance, however, was done upon them. The Tariff movement ended with the report of the committee having that subject in charge, that any additional legislation on that subject was inexpedient. A bill was passed by Congress making an appropriation for continuing the Cumberland Road, which contained clauses unconstitutional in the opinion of the President, and was returned by him with his veto. On the 4th of May he sent to Congress a message on the subject of Internal Improvements; which was one of the ablest State Papers ever issued from the Executive Department, on the general nature, character, and powers of the Federal Government under the Constitution.

14. During the same session of Congress, in accordance with the recommendation of the President, a resolution was passed recognizing the independence of Mexico and five new States in South America, formerly under the dominion of Spain as Provinces; and one hundred thousand

---

13. Did any Protective Tariff Bill pass this session? What was done with the Bill for continuing the Cumberland Road? What is said of Mr. Monroe's message of the 4th of May?
14. When was the independence of Mexico and the other Spanish Provinces on the Western Continent recognized as States? What is said of the "Monroe Doctrine?"

CHAP. XII.] ADMINISTRATION OF MONROE. 331

dollars were appropriated to defray the expenses of Envoys to those Republics. It was about this time that the President, in a message to Congress, declared that, "as a principle, the American Continents, by the free and independent position which they have assumed and maintained, are henceforth not to be considered as subjects for future colonization by any European power." This principle is what has since been known as "The Monroe Doctrine."

15. The 18th Congress met the 1st day of December, 1823, and continued in session until the 26th of May, 1824. Mr. Clay, being again returned as a member of the House from Kentucky, was again chosen with great unanimity as the Republican or Democratic Speaker. The most important subjects which engaged the attention of this Congress, as that of the last, were those relating to internal improvements and domestic manufactures. An Act finally passed ordering certain surveys, on the first of these subjects, which received the President's approval. An Act also was passed imposing a duty or tariff upon several articles of foreign importation, with a direct view thereby of affording protection to manufactures of like articles in the United States. The passage of this Act was strongly opposed, and its discussion called into exercise the first talent of Congress. This, as well as the internal improvement measure, was carried mainly by the eloquence, influence, and popularity of Mr. Clay. This policy of building up home manufactures by a protective tariff, and of carrying on internal improvements by the Federal Government, is what at the time was called the "American System," the authorship of which was attributed to Mr. Clay. It soon made a wide and permanent split in the Democratic party.

16. The year 1824 was signalized by the visit of La Fayette to the United States, on the express invitation of

---

15. Who was Speaker of the 18th Congress ? What questions now agitated the public councils ? What is said of the "American System ?" What effect had it on the Democratic party ?
16. What was the year 1824 signalized by ? What is said of La Fayette's visit? What grants did Congress make him ?

Congress. He arrived at New York the 13th of August, and became the guest of Daniel D. Tompkins, the Vice-President, who resided on Staten Island. Here he was waited upon by a committee of the State of New York and many distinguished citizens, to welcome him to this great metropolis. The escort of steamboats, decorated with the flags of every nation, brought him to the view of the assembled multitudes in the city, who manifested their joy at beholding him. He was waited upon by deputations from Philadelphia, Baltimore, New Haven, and many other cities, with invitations to visit them. He travelled through all the States, and was everywhere received with the warmest demonstrations of respect and affection. He returned to Washington during the session of Congress, and remained there several weeks. In token of their gratitude, and as a part payment of the debt due him by the country, Congress voted him the sum of two hundred thousand dollars and a township of land. At the time of his visit to the United States he was nearly seventy years of age.

17. Another Presidential election came off during the Fall of the same year (1824). Mr. Monroe declining a re-election, the division in the Republican party in their nomination for the succession became very marked. The usual Congressional caucus selected William H. Crawford, of Ga., for President, and Albert Gallatin, of Penn., for Vice-President. Mr. Gallatin declining, John C. Calhoun, of S. C., was subsequently run in his place. Mr. Crawford, before the election, was stricken with paralysis, from which it was supposed, in some of the States, he never would sufficiently recover to perform the duties of the office. The consequence was, the caucus nomination, so far as Mr. Crawford was concerned, was not conformed to by the Electoral Col-

---

17. When did the next Presidential election take place? Who received the Democratic caucus nominations? What affliction fell upon Mr. Crawford, the nominee for President? What was the result of this affliction? What was the result of the Electoral vote for President? What for Vice-President? Who was chosen by the States in the House of Representatives? What effect did the election of Mr. Adams produce in the country? How did it affect Mr. Clay's popularity, and why?

leges throughout the Union. Other distinguished Republicans were voted for instead of Mr. Crawford. The general result of the Electoral vote was 99 for Andrew Jackson, 84 for John Quincy Adams, 41 for William H. Crawford, and 37 for Henry Clay, for President; and 182 for John C. Calhoun for Vice-President, with some scattering votes for others. The States that voted for Gen. Jackson were: New Jersey, Pennsylvania, Maryland, North Carolina, South Carolina, Tennessee, Louisiana, Mississippi, Indiana, Illinois, and Alabama—eleven in all. Those which voted for John Quincy Adams were: Maine, New Hampshire, Massachusetts, Rhode Island, Connecticut, Vermont, and New York—seven in all. Those that voted for Mr. Crawford were: Delaware, Virginia, and Georgia—only three. While those which voted for Mr. Clay were: Kentucky, Ohio, and Missouri—being also only three.

Mr. Calhoun, having received a large majority of the Electoral votes, was duly declared Vice-President; but neither of the candidates voted for for President having received a majority of the votes of the Electoral Colleges the choice of one of the three having the highest vote devolved, under the Constitution, upon the House of Representatives, voting by States. This choice was made on the 9th of February, 1825; when, upon counting the ballots, it was found that John Quincy Adams received the votes of thirteen States, Andrew Jackson the votes of seven States, and Mr. Crawford the votes of four States. Mr. Adams having received, therefore, a majority of the States so cast under the Constitution, was declared duly elected to succeed Mr. Monroe.

This election produced great discontent throughout the country, and most seriously affected the popularity of Mr. Clay, as the election of Mr. Adams was attributed mainly to his agency, which had been exerted, as was supposed by many, with a view to defeat the election of Gen. Jackson, who by the returns seemed to stand highest in popular favor.

CHAPTER XIII.

ADMINISTRATION OF JOHN QUINCY ADAMS.

4th of March, 1825—4th of March, 1829.

1. JOHN QUINCY ADAMS, the 6th President of the United States, was inaugurated on the 4th of March, 1825, in the 58th year of his age. He was the son of John Adams, the 2d President. He was a man of very great natural ability; and by education and thorough training had acquired a vast deal of varied knowledge. After having been United States Minister to the Netherlands and to Portugal, under Washington; and to Berlin, during his father's Administration, he was elected in 1803 by the Legislature of Massachusetts to the Senate of the United States. In this body he soon gave a cordial support to the Administration of Mr. Jefferson, and became thoroughly identified with the Republican or Democratic party of that period. His support of the Embargo gave great offence to the Federalists of Massachusetts, who censured his course. He thereupon resigned, and was called to the Chair of Rhetoric and Oratory in Harvard College. This position, however, he did not continue to hold long; for soon after the accession of Mr. Madison to the Presidency, he was nominated and confirmed as Minister Plenipotentiary to Russia. This position he held for a number of years, and was one of the Commissioners who negotiated the treaty

JOHN QUINCY ADAMS.

CHAPTER XIII.—1. Who was the sixth President of the United States? When was he inaugurated? What is said of him? How did he stand on the Missouri question?

of peace at Ghent. After this, Mr. Madison (in 1815), appointed him Minister to Great Britain, where he remained until Mr. Monroe's accession in 1817, when he was appointed Secretary of State; which office he continued to hold until his own accession to the Presidency, as we have seen. In the agitation of the Missouri question, his influence was exerted for conciliation. Though an ardent Anti-Slavery man, he did not believe that under the Constitution and the Treaty of Cession by which Louisiana was acquired, Congress had the rightful power to adopt the proposed restrictions on the admission of that State; but on the new question now dividing the Democratic party, he sided with those who favored what was called the "American System."

2. In the organization of his Cabinet, Mr. Adams appointed Henry Clay, of Kentucky, Secretary of State; Richard Rush, of Pennsylvania, Secretary of the Treasury; and James Barbour, of Virginia, Secretary of War. Mr. Samuel L. Southard, of New Jersey, was continued Secretary of the Navy, and Mr. Wirt was retained as Attorney-General.

3. One of the first questions that produced considerable agitation in the country, soon after Mr. Adams's accession to office, was a controversy with the State of Georgia, growing out of a treaty with the Creek Indians. On the 12th of February, 1825, two United States Commissioners, Duncan G. Campbell and James Meriwether, had made a treaty with the principal chiefs of this tribe, at what was known as the "Indian Springs;" by which the United States had procured the extinguishment of the Indian title to a large extent of Indian territory, in pursuance of the agreement with Georgia in her cession of 1802 of the Territories of

---

2. Who constituted the new Cabinet?
3. What was the first question which produced agitation under the new Administration? What was the cause of the controversy? Who negotiated the treaty at the Indian Springs? When was this treaty made and ratified? What did some of the factious Indian leaders do? What did the Administration do? Who was Governor of Georgia at the time? What did he do? What became of the land ceded by the "old treaty"?

Alabama and Mississippi. This treaty was ratified by the Senate just before the close of Mr. Monroe's Administration; but, under the instigation of certain white men, it was very strongly opposed by a few factious leaders of the tribe. They set upon Mackintosh, the principal chief, who had signed it, and assassinated him in the night, with another, who had also signed it, and then called upon the Federal Government to repudiate the treaty so made and ratified. This was done by the Administration, and a new treaty was made by new Commissioners on the 24th of January, 1826. In the mean time, the Governor of Georgia, George M. Troup, proceeded to take possession of the territory ceded by the first or "old treaty," as it was called. He utterly refused to be controlled by the proceedings of the Federal authorities under the second, or what was called the "new treaty." He caused the boundary line between Georgia and Alabama to be run according to the terms of the cession of 1802, and the lands embraced in the "old treaty" to be surveyed and disposed of according to an Act of the Legislature of the State. This was done in open disregard of orders from Washington. The arrest of the Commissioners making the surveys was threatened. But upon the announcement of Troup, in effect, that force would be met by force, the surveys were permitted to go on, and the lands were occupied by Georgia under the "old treaty." Mr. Adams submitted the subject to Congress; but no further steps were taken to arrest the action of the authorities of Georgia in the matter.

4. The opposition to the Administration, which had thus early manifested itself, continued to gain strength and make new developments. In October, 1825, General Jackson was nominated by the Legislature of Tennessee for the next Presidency. He accepted the nomination in an address delivered before that body, and resigned a seat which he then held in the United States Senate.

---

4. What is said of General Jackson?

5. The first session of the 19th Congress convened the 5th of December, 1825, and continued to the 22d of May, 1826. The debates became very bitter. Mr. McDuffie, of South Carolina, upon one occasion censured in strong terms the course of Mr. Clay and his friends in the matter of the late Presidential election. Mr. Trimble, of Kentucky, and others, replied in like spirited language, and a scene of considerable excitement ensued. An imputation affecting Mr. Clay's integrity having been made in this debate, an investigation followed. A mass of testimony was produced by Mr. Clay, which was thought by his friends amply sufficient to rebut the accusations, and to justify him in voting for Mr. Adams. The object of the testimony was to show that any other course on his part would have rendered him liable to the charge of gross violation of principle.

6. Another cause of opposition to the Administration was what was known as the "Panama Mission." On an invitation from Peru, Chili, Colombia, Mexico, and the States of Central America, to meet in a general Congress at Panama, on the 22d of June, 1826, Mr. Adams appointed Richard C. Anderson and John Sergeant, United States Commissioners, with William B. Rochester, Secretary. Mr. Anderson, who was then Minister to the Republic of Colombia, died of a malignant fever at Carthagena, on his way to Panama. Mr. Sergeant not being able to attend, the United States had no representative at this celebrated assembly. Peru, Colombia, Mexico, and the States of Central America, were represented. They entered into a treaty of friendship and perpetual Confederation, to which all the other American powers or States were invited to accede. The Congress then adjourned to re-assemble in February, 1827, at Tocubaza, a village near the City of Mexico. Mr. Poinsett, United States Minister to Mexico, was ap-

---

5. When did the first session of Congress meet after Mr. Adams's election? What is said of the debates; of Mr. McDuffie; of Mr. Clay, and the charges against him?
6. What was another cause of opposition to the Administration? What is said of the "Panama Mission," and the United States Commissioners sent on it?

pointed Commissioner, in place of Mr. Anderson, to meet this body on its re-assembly. Mr. Sergeant also repaired to Mexico for the same purpose; but the Congress never met again: so that matter ended.

7. During the same session of the Congress of the United States the subject of internal improvements gave rise to warm and heated debate. Party lines on the new division became more distinctly marked.

8. The 4th of July of the year 1826 was memorable from the fact of its being the semi-centennial anniversary of the independence of the States; but it became more so from the fact that two of the most prominent men connected with the movement which brought about that independence, departed this life on that day. These were John Adams and Thomas Jefferson. They expired within a few hours of each other; the one at Monticello, Virginia, the other at Quincy, Massachusetts; Mr. Jefferson in the 84th and Mr. Adams in the 91st year of his age. The news of the death of these two distinguished statesmen filled the whole country with mourning. The impression upon the public mind thereby was increased from the wonderful coincidences taken all together. In every town and village nearly, as well as in the cities, funeral ceremonies, by processions and orations, were performed in memory of the honored dead.

9. The elections to the 20th Congress showed an increase in the strength of the Opposition. The Administration gained somewhat in the New England States, in Delaware, New Jersey, Ohio, Indiana, and Louisiana; but lost largely in all the other States. The first session of this Congress commenced on the 3d of December, 1827, and continued to May 26th, 1828. The absorbing topic of this period was the Protective policy. A convention of manufacturers had been held in Harrisburg, Pennsylvania,

---

7. What other subject excited warm and heated debates at the same session?
8. What is said of the 4th of July, 1826?
9. What was the general result of the elections to the 20th Congress? When did this Congress first meet? What was the absorbing topic? What was the Tariff Act of 1828 called? On what ground was it opposed?

which memorialized Congress on the subject. A committee on manufactures in the House was empowered to send for persons and papers. They reported a new Tariff Bill, based upon the Protective policy. The discussions on this Bill lasted from the 12th of February, 1828, to the 15th of April, when, after having received various amendments, it finally passed the House by a vote of 109 to 91. This tariff was opposed upon the ground, as it was insisted, that it was clearly unconstitutional, and also partial in its operation, being highly injurious to the interests of the Southern States, as they were producers of staples for export, and it was to their interest to get manufactures for their consumption in the cheapest markets. Duties under the Protective policy, their representatives contended, were not only bounties to the manufacturers, but a heavy tax, levied upon their constituents, and a great majority of the consumers in all the States, which never went into the public treasury.

10. During the excitement produced by the discussions and passage of the Tariff Act of this year, which was called the "Bill of Abominations," and the various projected schemes of internal improvement, involving the appropriation of many millions of dollars, the Presidential election of 1828 took place. The contest between the two parties, the Administration and Opposition, over the powers and limitations of the Federal Government, became almost as hot and fierce as it was in 1800, between the Federalists and Republicans of that day. General Jackson, without any caucus nomination, was supported by the Opposition everywhere for President, and Mr. Calhoun for Vice-President. The friends of the Administration put forth the utmost of their exertions for the re-election of Mr.

---

10. Who were the candidates for President and Vice-President in the election which took place in the Fall of 1828? What was the result of the vote of the Electoral Colleges? What by States? What was General Jackson's party position? What new distinctive names did parties take? Who was regarded as the head of the Democratic party? Who was recognized as the leader of the National Republicans? What had been Mr. Clay's previous position?

Adams to the office of President, and Richard Rush to the office of Vice-President. The result of the vote of the Electoral Colleges was, 178 for Jackson, and 83 for Adams; 171 for Mr. Calhoun, and 83 for Mr. Rush. Seven of the Electoral votes of Georgia were cast for William Smith, of South Carolina, instead of Mr. Calhoun. The vote for President by States stood: 15 for Jackson and 9 for Adams. The 15 States that voted for Jackson were: New York, Pennsylvania, Virginia, North Carolina, South Carolina, Georgia, Kentucky, Tennessee, Ohio, Louisiana, Indiana, Mississippi, Illinois, Alabama, and Missouri; the 9 that voted for Mr. Adams were: Maine, New Hampshire, Massachusetts, Rhode Island, Connecticut, Vermont, New Jersey, Delaware, and Maryland.

From this time the political parties in the United States took the distinctive names of Democratic and National Republican. General Jackson, belonging to the strict-construction Jeffersonian school, was now regarded as the head of the Democratic party. Mr. Clay, who had also heretofore belonged to the same school, was now recognized as the great leader of the National Republicans.

CHAPTER XIV.

ADMINISTRATION OF JACKSON.

4th of March, 1829—4th of March, 1837.

1. ANDREW JACKSON, the 7th President of the United States, was inaugurated the 4th of March, 1829, in the 62d year of his age. His Inaugural Address was delivered at the Capitol before the largest audience that had ever assembled on a similar occasion, since the inauguration of Washington in New York, on the 30th of April, 1790. The oath of office was administered by Chief-Justice Marshall.

CHAPTER XIV.—**1.** What is said of Gen. Jackson's inauguration? What of his address on the occasion? What is further said of him?

The tone of his Inaugural, as well as its sentiments, was highly gratifying to a large majority of the people in all sections. The new President was one of the most remarkable men of the age in which he lived. He possessed a combination of qualities seldom met with in any one person. Education had done but little for him; but by nature he was fitted for the government of men both in the field and in the Cabinet. During the Administration of the elder Adams he had occupied a seat in the United States Senate from Tennessee, and gave a most cordial support to the principles of Mr. Jefferson. Resigning his place in that body, he was afterwards elected one of the judges of the Supreme Court of his State. His military achievements in the wars against the Creek and the Seminole Indians, and his victory over the British at New Orleans, have been stated. Being now elevated to the Presidency, a great anxiety was felt everywhere as to the course or policy which he should adopt. While he was the popular favorite, many entertained apprehensions from his well-known imperiousness of will. The first indication of his administrative purposes was manifested in the selection of his Cabinet, as all the members of the late Cabinet had resigned upon his accession to office.

PRESIDENT JACKSON.

2. The persons selected to fill their places were: Martin Van Buren, of N. Y., Secretary of State; Samuel D. Ingham, of Penn., Secretary of the Treasury; John H. Eaton, of Tenn., Secretary of War; John Branch, of N. C., Secretary of the Navy; John M. Berrien, of Ga., Attorney-

---

2. Who were selected for his Cabinet? What new Cabinet office was now created? What is said of the new Cabinet?

General; and it having been determined to make the Postmaster-General a Cabinet officer for the future, William T. Barry, of Ky., was appointed to that position. Mr. Van Buren, Mr. Branch, and Mr. Berrien had been leading supporters of Mr. Crawford in the Presidential contest of 1824. Mr. Ingham was appointed through the influence of Mr. Calhoun, the Vice-President; and Messrs. Eaton and Barry were among the original supporters of Gen. Jackson.

3. The first leading feature of the new Administration was the policy of removing all the Indian tribes east of the Mississippi to a region of country west of that river, where they would be better provided with the means of sustaining themselves according to their modes and habits of life; and where they would cease to be either the source or subject of border troubles and depredations. At the first session of the 21st Congress, which commenced the 7th of December, 1829, and continued to the 31st of May, 1830, an Act was passed with the view of carrying this policy fully into effect, which was finally accomplished some years afterwards. The President also recommended to this Congress a revision and modification of the Tariff of 1828, and expressed very decided opinions against the Protective policy.

4. During the same session of Congress in 1830, came off the great debate in the Senate between Robert Y. Hayne, of S. C., and Daniel Webster, of Mass., in which what was known as "the peculiar doctrines of South Carolina" on State Rights, came in review. South Carolina held, with several other States, that the Protective policy was unconstitutional; but she also held, as they did not, that it was within the reserved rights of the States to have the question of constitutionality on this subject rightfully determined by the judiciary of the States severally, each for itself, in-

---

3. What was the first leading feature of the new Administration? What is said of it? What other subject did the President recommend to Congress at its first session after his coming into office?

4. What great debate took place in the Senate in 1830? What was the subject of it? What is said of "the peculiar doctrine" of South Carolina?

stead of exclusively by the Federal judiciary. This "peculiar doctrine" is what was known at the time as "Nullification," and this is the doctrine which Mr. Hayne in that debate sustained with so much ability, and which Mr. Webster assailed with so much eloquence.

5. During the same session, the question of Internal Improvements by the Federal Government was revived. The Maysville Road Bill, as it was called, passed both Houses of Congress. This the President vetoed, upon the ground that it was unconstitutional. The veto was sustained by the House where the Bill originated. Several other similar bills, passed at the same session, were arrested by a like veto. These acts of the President greatly gratified the strict constructionists everywhere.

6. About this time, or near the close of the first session of the 21st Congress, occurred the memorable alienation between Gen. Jackson and Mr. Calhoun. It was occasioned by a disclosure to Gen. Jackson, that Mr. Calhoun, in Mr. Monroe's Cabinet, had taken part against him in his conduct in Florida during the Seminole campaign of 1818. The rupture thus occasioned became bitter and permanent.

7. Early in 1831, the question of the succession was agitated. The Legislature of Pennsylvania had put Gen. Jackson in nomination for re-election, and he had consented to be a candidate. About the same time the members of his Cabinet, for various reasons, had ceased to be harmonious. The result of this was an entire reorganization of that body, in April, 1831, with the exception of Mr. Barry, who was retained as Postmaster-General. In this course Jackson acted upon the principle that his Cabinet should be a unit. In the new organization, Edw'd Livingston, of La., was made Secretary of State; Louis McLane, of Del., Secretary of the

---

5. What other question was revived at the same session? What is said of the Maysville Road Bill? What of other similar bills?
6. What memorable event occurred about the close of this session of Congress?
7. What question was agitated early in 1831? What is said of it? What changes took place in the Cabinet about this time? When and where did Mr. Monroe die?

Treasury; Lewis Cass, of O., Secretary of War; Levi Woodbury, of N. H., Secretary of the Navy; and Roger B. Taney, of Md., Attorney-General.

On the 4th day of July of this year ex-President Monroe died, in the 74th year of his age. He was at the time in New York, with his daughter, Mrs. Samuel L. Gouverneur.

8. In the meantime a Convention of the "National Republicans" was called to meet on the 12th of December, 1831, in the city of New York. At this Convention Mr. Clay was nominated for the Presidency, and John Sergeant, of Penn., for the Vice-Presidency. During the same year, a new party, styling itself "Anti-Masonic," put in nomination for the same offices Mr. Wirt, late Attorney-General, and Amos Ellmaker, of Penn.

The year 1831 is also memorable for the election of John Quincy Adams, from Mass., late President, as a member of the House to the 22d Congress, and the election to the Senate of Mr. Clay, from Ky., and also the election to the same body of Mr. Calhoun, of S. C., he having resigned the office of Vice-President.

9. Among the most noted subjects which were agitated during the 1st session of the 22d Congress, which commenced the 5th of December, 1831, and lasted to the 16th of July, 1832, were the re-charter of the Bank of the United States, and a modification of the Tariff of 1828. A Bill for the re-charter of the Bank passed both Houses, and was vetoed by the President upon constitutional and other grounds. The veto was sustained, but lost Jackson many friends, as it brought most of the moneyed power then in the Democratic party into decided opposition to his re-election. The Tariff Bill of this session rather increased than diminished the opposition to the Protective policy; for although

---

8. Who else were nominated for President and Vice-President during the same year, and by what parties? What was the year 1831 memorable for?
9. What two topics chiefly engrossed the attention of the first session of the 22d Congress? What became of the Bill for the re-charter of the U. States Bank? What effect had the veto upon Jackson's popularity? What is said of the Tariff Bill of this session?

it reduced the duties on many imported articles, it was yet based upon the principle of Federal Protection to local interests in several States, to the injury of the general interests of the country, as was maintained by its opponents.

10. It was on the 21st of June, 1832, that the Eastern Plague, known as the Asiatic Cholera, made its first appearance in the United States, in the city of New York. Its rapid spread produced universal panic, though it was less fatal in the South Atlantic States than in the North and in the Valley of the Mississippi. Thousands of persons of all ages and conditions died of it within a few months. The most robust constitutions in many instances became victims of its malignancy within 24 hours from its first attack.

During the same year, 1832, a war broke out with the Winnebagoes and several other Western and Northwestern tribes of Indians. General Scott was put in command of the forces sent against them. The war was soon terminated by the capture, on the 27th of August, of " Black Hawk," the chief, and several subordinate warriors of note.

11. During the Fall of this year, also, came off another Presidential election. The party canvass against Gen. Jackson was very bitter, on account of his opposition to the Protective policy, and his vetoes of the bills for internal improvements and the re-charter of the Bank.

The first general Convention of the Democratic party ever held in the United States met this year, in the month of May, in Baltimore, for the purpose of nominating a candidate for Vice-President, to run on the ticket with Jackson for the Presidency. Martin Van Buren, of N. Y., received the nomination of this Convention. The general result of the election, under all the nominations made as stated, was: 219 electoral votes for Jackson; 49 for Clay; and 7 for

---

10. What is said of the cholera? What war broke out in 1832, and what is said of it?
11. What is said of the party canvass of this year? When and where was the first General Convention of the Democratic party held, and for what purpose? Who was nominated for the office of Vice-President to be run on the Jackson ticket? What was the result of the election? What was the vote by States?

Wirt. For Vice-President, the electoral votes stood: for Martin Van Buren, 189; for John Sergeant, 49; for Amos Ellmaker, 7. The vote by States for the candidates for the Presidency, stood: 16 for Jackson; 6 for Clay; and 1 for Wirt. The 16 States that voted for Jackson were: Maine, New Hampshire, New York, New Jersey, Pennsylvania, Virginia, North Carolina, Georgia, Tennessee, Ohio, Louisiana, Mississippi, Indiana, Illinois, Alabama, and Missouri; the 6 States that voted for Mr. Clay were: Massachusetts, Rhode Island, Connecticut, Delaware, Maryland, and Kentucky; the State that voted for Mr. Wirt was: Vermont; South Carolina cast her vote for John Floyd, of Va., for President, and Henry Lee, of Mass., for Vice-President.

12. In the meantime a Sovereign Convention of the people of South Carolina was called, which adopted what was known as the "Nullification Ordinance." The leading features of this were a declaration that the Tariff Act of 1832, being based upon the principle of Protection to manufacturers, and not upon the principle of raising revenue, was unconstitutional, and therefore null and void; and a provision for testing the constitutionality of this Act before the courts of the State; with a further provision that in case the measures thus adopted for the purpose stated should be forcibly resisted by the Federal authorities, then the State of South Carolina was declared to be no longer a member of the Federal Union. This measure was to take effect on the 12th of February, 1833, if before that time the principle of levying duties upon imports, not with a view to revenue, but for the protection of domestic manufactures, should not be abandoned by the Congress of the States.

13. It was in this state of things, after the elections of

---

12. What occurred in the meantime? What was the object of the Nullification Ordinance? What were its leading features?

13. What did the President recommend on the meeting of Congress in December, 1832? What other paper did he issue a few days afterwards? What is said of the Proclamation? What explanation did Gen. Jackson make about it?

this Fall were concluded, that the 2d session of the 22d Congress was held, in December, 1832. The President in his annual Message urged upon Congress a reduction of the Tariff. The Message gave satisfaction to the anti-Protectionists everywhere. This was followed a few days afterwards by his celebrated Proclamation against "Nullification." In this he urged the people of South Carolina not to persist in the enforcement of their Ordinance, as it would necessarily bring the Federal and State authorities in conflict, so long as the State retained her place in the Union, and her citizens, who should take up arms against the United States in such conflict, would be guilty of treason against the United States.

In speaking of the action of the Convention of that State he said:

"The Ordinance is founded, not on the indefeasible right of resisting acts which are plainly unconstitutional, and too oppressive to be endured; but on the strange position that any one State may not only declare an Act of Congress void, but prohibit its execution; that they may do this consistently with the Constitution; that the true construction of that instrument permits a State to retain its place in the Union, and yet be bound by no other of its laws than those it may choose to consider as constitutional."

This Proclamation produced great excitement in South Carolina and other States. Its principles in some parts were thought to be inconsistent with the doctrines taught by Jefferson upon the subject of the rights of the several States; and by many who did not approve of the course of South Carolina, the Proclamation, taken as a whole, was looked upon as amounting in substance to a denial of the right of secession on the part of any State for any cause whatever. This was the view taken generally by the old Federalists and the extreme advocates of State Rights; but the President afterwards maintained that an erroneous construction had been put upon those parts of the Proclamation referred to, and in a full explanation he declared his adherence to the principles of Mr. Jefferson as set forth in the Kentucky and Virginia Resolutions of 1798 and 1799.

14. Soon after this Proclamation was issued, Mr. Verplanck, an Administration member from N. Y., introduced a Bill for the further reduction of the Tariff, and Virginia sent Benjamin Watkins Leigh, one of her most distinguished statesmen, as a Commissioner of Peace to South Carolina, urging her to suspend the execution of her Ordinance, at least until the 4th of March, as there was some prospect of having the Tariff policy rightly adjusted before that time. This overture was acceded to by South Carolina, and the Ordinance suspended until the time stated.

15. It was now that Mr. Clay, in the Senate, came forward with his celebrated "Tariff Compromise" of 1833. This was based upon the principle of an abandonment of the Protective policy, which had been with him a cherished object for a number of years, and constituted the basis of his "American System." The Bill provided for a gradual reduction of all duties then above the revenue standard. One-tenth of one-half of all duties for protection above that standard was to be taken off annually for ten years, at the end of which period the whole of the other half was to be taken off, and thereafter all duties were to be levied mainly with a view to revenue, and not for protection.

It was on this occasion that Mr. Clay displayed the highest qualities of his heart and head. His Bill, in the main, was promptly accepted by Mr. Calhoun, and declared by him to be entirely satisfactory to the people of South Carolina as well as the friends of free trade generally. This measure, with some modifications, satisfactory to both sides, soon passed the Senate, and went to the House, where it also passed, and afterwards received the Executive approval, on the 2d day of March, 1833. The Convention of South Carolina was re-assembled and their famous Ordinance was promptly rescinded. So ended the Nullification *imbroglio*.

---

14. What soon after occurred? Did South Carolina suspend the execution of her Ordinance, and to what time?
15. What is said of Mr. Clay, and the "Tariff Compromise" of 1833? What was done in South Carolina in reference to the Nullification Ordinance?

16. Pending this adjustment of the threatening troubles between the State of South Carolina and the Federal authorities, occurred the great debate between Mr. Calhoun and Mr. Webster upon the nature and character of the Federal Government. Mr. Calhoun in this Senatorial conflict held, with Mr. Jefferson, that the Constitution was "a compact" between the several States as sovereign parties to it; while Mr. Webster maintained that it was in the nature of a social compact, entered into by the people of all the States consolidated in one mass or political community. The debate was on a series of resolutions introduced into the Senate by Mr. Calhoun. Different opinions were entertained at the time as to the merits of the debate; but no one thoroughly informed upon the subject can, it would seem, at this day, after reading the speeches, which will remain forever as a monument of American eloquence, feel much embarrassment in deciding as to which one of the contestants should be justly awarded the mastery in the argument. The proceedings and debates of the Convention that framed the Constitution, which were held with closed doors, had not up to that time been published. Since then they have been given to the public, and they throw a flood of light upon the question, in support of the position of Mr. Calhoun. The subject which gave rise to the discussion having been disposed of, no vote was taken in the Senate upon the resolutions.

17. On the 4th of March, 1833, Gen. Jackson was duly inaugurated President for another four years. The oath of office was administered by Chief-Justice Marshall. The

---

16. What is said of the debate in the Senate pending the adjustment of the Tariff question?
17. When was Gen. Jackson inaugurated for a second term? What is said of the state of public opinion and the auspices under which he entered upon this term? What of his tour through New York and the New England States? What is said of the temporary lull? What act of the President gave rise to the renewal of party excitement? Who was then Secretary of the Treasury? What was done with him? Who was put in his place? What is said of Calhoun. Clay, and Webster at this time? Who stood against 'hem? What was done in the Senate? What new party name was now taken by the combined Opposition? How did Jackson treat the resolution of the Senate? What is said of his protest on this occasion? What was the final result of the contest?

country was again in perfect repose. The late adjustment of the Tariff question had not only been the source of gratification, but had given general joy throughout the Southern States; while the centralizing principles, as they were considered, of the late Proclamation, had won for Gen. Jackson "golden opinions" from many of his former bitterest opponents. He therefore entered upon his second term under apparently most propitious auspices. In the Spring of 1833 he made a tour through New York and the New England States. He was everywhere received with manifestations of the highest esteem and enthusiasm. The flattering compliment of the scholarly distinction of Doctor of Laws was conferred upon him by Harvard University.

This, however, was but a deceptive and "weather-breeding" lull in the political elements. The storm soon burst forth with greater fury and violence than ever before.

Soon after his return to the capital, Jackson ordered the deposits of public money to be removed from the Bank of the United States, and to be put in certain State Banks. William J. Duane, who had recently been appointed Secretary of the Treasury in place of Mr. McLane (promoted), declined to execute the order. Duane was promptly removed, and Roger B. Taney made Secretary of the Treasury. This action of the President produced great sensation and excitement in the country. It was the cause of an open war between the President and the Senate. In this war, Calhoun, Clay, and Webster, "the Great Trio," as they were called, for the first time in their lives were cordially united in their assaults upon the Administration. Against this array of talent stood the indomitable Benton, of Mo., and the accomplished Forsyth, of Ga. A resolution severely censuring the President, and declaring this act of his unconstitutional, passed that body. It was now that the United Opposition assumed the party name of "Whig." Jackson replied to this resolution of censure by the Senate in a paper known as "The Protest." This was one of the ablest documents ever produced by him. The result of this contest was a complete triumph of Jackson. The resolution

JOHN C. CALHOUN.   HENRY CLAY.   DANIEL WEBSTER.

of censure was finally expunged from the Journal of the Senate by its own order to have black lines drawn around it. The whole force of the Opposition at this time was exerted in favor of a re-charter of the Bank; but every effort on this line signally failed.

18. During the Fall of 1833 occurred a natural phenomenon of a most wonderful character. This was on the night of the 13th of November. It was what was known as the "Meteoric Shower," or the "Falling of the Stars." It was witnessed with amazement and astonishment throughout the entire limits of the United States.

19. On the 20th of May, 1835, the second General Convention of the Democratic party of the United States, for the purpose of nominating candidates for the office of President and Vice-President, convened in the city of Baltimore. It was understood that Gen. Jackson intended to retire at the expiration of his second term. By this Convention, Martin Van Buren, of N. Y., was put in nomination for the Presidency, and Col. Richard M. Johnson, of Ky., for the Vice-Presidency. In the same month William T.

---

18. What great natural phenomenon occurred on the 13th of November, 1833?
19. When and where did the second General Convention of the Democratic party assemble, and for what purpose? Who were nominated?

Barry was appointed Minister to Spain, and Amos Kendall succeeded him as Postmaster-General.

20. On the 6th day of July thereafter the venerable Chief-Justice Marshall died, in the 80th year of his age, and Roger B. Taney succeeded him in office.

21. The Winter of 1834–1835 was noted for its great severity throughout the United States. On the 4th of January, 1835, mercury congealed at Lebanon, N. Y., and several other places. The Chesapeake Bay was frozen from its head to Capes Charles and Henry. On the 8th of February the thermometer fell to 8 degrees below zero, as far south as 34° north latitude. The day before, the 7th, is remembered as "the cold Saturday" to this day. The Savannah River was coated with ice at Augusta. Orange-trees were killed as far south as St. Augustine, Fla., and fig-trees, nearly a hundred years old, were killed on the coast of Georgia. The ground in the interior of this State was covered with snow for several weeks. The falls of snow in Georgia on the 14th of January and 2d and 3d of March averaged from 11 to 13 inches deep.

22. On the night of the 16th of December, 1835, occurred the great fire in the city of New York, by which in fourteen hours were consumed over seventeen million dollars' worth of property. The burnt district covered several acres of ground in the most business part of the city.

23. On the 28th of the same month another war broke out with the remaining Seminole Indians in Florida, who refused to go West, which continued for several years. It commenced by the murder of Hon. Wiley Thompson, U. S. Agent to the tribe, by a party of Indians led by Osceola, their great chief. On the 28th of December, Major Dade, of the U. S. army, and his command of about a hundred men, were massacred near Wahoo Swamp, on their march

---

20. When did Chief-Justice Marshall die? At what age? Who succeeded him in office?
21. What is said of the Winter of 1835?
22. What of the fire in New York?
23. What of the Seminole War?

from Fort Brook to join Gen. Clinch near the Withlacoochee.

24. On the 15th day of June, 1836, Acts were passed for the admission of two new States into the Union: these were Arkansas and Michigan.

COAT OF ARMS OF ARKANSAS.

COAT OF ARMS OF MICHIGAN.

25. On the 28th day of June of the same year (1836), ex-President James Madison died at Montpelier, his residence in Virginia, in the 86th year of his age.

26. In the Presidential election which came off in the Fall of the same year, the Opposition, which at one time was so formidable to the Administration of Gen. Jackson, had been so completely discomfited by him, that, in their disorganized condition, they were unable to concentrate upon any regular candidates. The result of the election was: 170 electoral votes for Martin Van Buren for President, 14 for Daniel Webster, 73 for William H. Harrison, 11 for Willie P. Mangum, of N. C., and 26 for H. L. White, of Tenn. Mr. Van Buren, having received a majority, was duly declared President for the next term. The vote by States in this election was: 15 for Mr. Van Buren, 7 for Gen. Harrison, 2 for Mr. White, and 1 for Mr. Webster. The 15 States that voted for Mr. Van Buren were: Maine, New Hampshire, Rhode Island, Connecticut, New York, Penn-

---

24 What two new States were admitted into the Union in 1836?
25. When did ex-President Madison die, where, and at what age?
26. What is said of the Presidential election of 1836? What was the result of this election? On whom did the duty devolve to make a choice of Vice-President? What was the vote in the Senate on making the choice?

sylvania, Virginia, North Carolina, Louisiana, Mississippi, Illinois, Alabama, Missouri, Arkansas, and Michigan; the 7 that voted for Gen. Harrison were: Vermont, New Jersey, Delaware, Maryland, Kentucky, Ohio, and Indiana; the 2 that voted for Mr. White were: Georgia and Tennessee; the 1 that voted for Mr. Webster was Massachusetts.

The votes of the Electoral Colleges for Vice-President were: 147 for Richard M. Johnson, of Ky.; 77 for Francis Granger, of New York; 47 for John Tyler, of Va.; and 23 for William Smith, of Ala. Neither one of the persons voted for for Vice-President having received a majority of the votes of the colleges, the choice of that officer devolved, under the Constitution, upon the Senate. In the discharge of this duty the Senate chose Col. Johnson by a vote of 33, against 16 cast for Mr. Granger.

27. The Administration of Gen. Jackson was distinguished for many acts of foreign as well as domestic policy which cannot be embraced in this brief sketch. Taken all together, it made a deep and lasting impression upon the policy and history of the States. On his retirement, following the example of Washington, he issued a Farewell Address, in which he evinced the most ardent patriotism and the most earnest devotion to the cause of constitutional liberty. In view of the dangerous centralizing tendencies of the times, he said in this Address—

"It is well known that there have always been those among us who wished to enlarge the powers of the General Government, and experience would seem to indicate that there is a tendency on the part of this Government to overstep the boundaries marked out for it by the Constitution. Its legitimate authority is abundantly sufficient for the purposes for which it was created; and its powers being expressly enumerated, there can be no justification for claiming anything beyond them. Every attempt to exercise power beyond these limits should be promptly and firmly opposed. For one evil example will lead to others

---

27. What is said of the Administration of Gen. Jackson? What of his retirement?

still more mischievous; and if the principle of constructive powers, or supposed advantages, or temporary circumstances, should ever be permitted to justify the assumption of a power not given by the Constitution, the General Government will, before long, absorb all the powers of legislation, and you will have, in effect, but one consolidated Government. From the extent of our country, its diversified interests, different pursuits, and different habits, it is too obvious for argument, that a single consolidated Government would be wholly inadequate to watch over and protect its interests. And every friend of our free institutions should be always prepared to maintain unimpaired, and in full vigor, the rights and sovereignty of the States, and to confine the action of the General Government strictly to the sphere of its appropriate duties."

At the expiration of his second term he retired from the Executive chair to his home, near Nashville, Tenn., where he spent the remnant of his days with the continued confidence and affection of the people, who took pleasure in honoring him as the "Hero of New Orleans" and the "Sage of the Hermitage."

CHAPTER XV.

ADMINISTRATION OF VAN BUREN.

4th of March, 1837—4th of March, 1841.

1. MARTIN VAN BUREN, the 8th President of the United States, was inaugurated on the 4th of March, 1837, in the 55th year of his age. "At 12 o'clock on that day, the weather being remarkably pleasant, the President elect took his seat, with his venerable predecessor, Gen. Jackson, in a beautiful phaeton, made from the wood of the frigate *Constitution*, and presented to Gen. Jackson by the Democracy of the city of New York. In this they proceeded from the President's house to the Capitol. After

---

CHAPTER XV.—**1.** Who was the 8th President ? What is said of him, and his inauguration ?

reaching the Senate Chamber a procession was formed, and Mr. Van Buren, attended by the ex-President, the members of the Senate and of the Cabinet, and the diplomatic corps, led the way to the rostrum erected on the ascent to the eastern portico. There the Inaugural Address was delivered in clear and impressive tones, and in an easy and eloquent manner. At the close of the Address the oath of office was administered by Chief-Justice Taney."

PRESIDENT VAN BUREN.

2. In the Address Mr. Van Buren indicated his purpose, on all matters of public policy, to follow in the " footsteps of his illustrious predecessor."

His Cabinet consisted of John Forsyth, of Ga., Sec'y of State; Levi Woodbury, of N. H., Sec'y of the Treasury; Joel R. Poinsett, of S. C., Sec'y of War; Mahlon Dickerson, of N. J., Sec'y of the Navy; Amos Kendall, of Ky., Postmaster-General; and Benjamin F. Butler, of N. Y., Attorney-General. All these gentlemen were in these offices respectively at the time under Gen. Jackson, except Mr. Poinsett, who took the place of Gen. Cass in the War Department, as he had lately before been appointed Minister to France.

3. Soon after Mr. Van Buren became President occurred a great commercial crisis. This was in April, 1837, and was occasioned by a reckless spirit of speculation, which

---

2. What is said of his Inaugural? What of his Cabinet?
3. What occurred soon after Mr. Van Buren came into office? What is said of it? What reply did the President make to the delegation from New York? What did the banks do? What did the President do? What did Congress do? What is said of the Sub-Treasury? What of Mr. Calhoun?

had for the two or three preceding years been fostered and encouraged by excessive banking, and the consequent expansion of paper currency beyond all the legitimate wants of the country. During the months of March and April, of this year, the failures in New York city alone amounted to over one hundred millions of dollars. The state of affairs became so distressing, that petitions were sent to the President from several quarters, and a deputation of merchants and bankers of New York waited upon him in person, and solicited him to defer the immediate collection of duties for which bonds had been given, and to rescind the Treasury Orders requiring dues to the Government to be paid in specie. They also asked that an extra session of Congress should be called to adopt measures of relief. He granted their request so far only as to suspend suit on bonds which had been given for the collection of duties. In a few days after his response to this deputation was known in New York, all the banks in that city stopped specie payments, and their example was soon followed by nearly all the banks in all the States. In this emergency Mr. Van Buren was compelled to convene an extra session of Congress to provide for meeting demands on the Treasury with legal currency. He accordingly summoned the 25th Congress to meet at the Capitol on the 4th day of September, 1837. The session lasted five or six weeks. In his Message to Congress, Mr. Van Buren assigned as the causes of the unhappy condition of the country the excessive issues of bank paper; the great fire in New York in December, 1835; the large investments that had been made in unproductive lands, and other speculative enterprises. To meet the exigencies of the Treasury, as well as to provide for the public relief, as far as to them seemed proper, Congress passed an Act authorizing the issue of Treasury Notes to the amount of ten millions of dollars.

The policy of the Administration now adopted, for the collection and transmission of the public funds, was known as the "Sub-Treasury System." It was all done by and through officers of the Government, without the agency of any banking institution. On this financial system, characterized as a divorce of the Government from the banks, Mr. Calhoun separated from Messrs. Clay and Webster in their opposition to the Democratic party. He advocated this divorce with all his ability; while they, in like manner, opposed it.

4. The war with the small remnant of the Seminole Indians still remaining in Florida was not yet closed. Col. Zachary Taylor, being chief in command at that time in that quarter, on the 5th of December, 1837, with a small force completely routed their warriors at Okee Chobee, by which he acquired considerable distinction; but the retreating foe sought refuge in the Everglades, where they remained some time longer. Before this, Osceola, their chief, had been seized by Gen. Jessup, with some of his subordinates, who visited Jessup's camp under the protection of a flag of truce. They were all retained as prisoners, and Osceola himself was sent to Fort Moultrie, near Charleston, S. C., where he died of a fever, in 1838. This act of Gen. Jessup can hardly be excused, though he was dealing with foes known to be treacherous. A flag of truce should ever be held sacred, even when presented by the lowest type of savages. Osceola himself was not of this grade, whatever some of his allies may have been.

5. The two questions which produced the greatest excitement and agitation of the public mind during Mr. Van Buren's Administration were, the Sub-Treasury system and the abolition of Negro slavery, as it then existed in the District of Columbia. The Opposition to the financial

---

4. What is said of the Seminole War? What of the treatment of Osceola?
5. What two questions produced the greatest excitement at this time? Who led the Opposition in the Senate? By whom and how was the Administration sustained in that body? What is said of Mr. Adams and the Anti-Slavery agitation? What is said of Mr. Calhoun in the Senate? Can you give the substance of Mr. Calhoun's resolutions? What was the vote in the Senate taken *per capita* on the adoption of Mr. Calhoun's first resolution? What by States? What was the vote on the others? What is said of Mr. Clay?

policy of the Administration was led in the Senate by Mr. Clay and Mr. Webster, and conducted with a great deal of ability, power, and eloquence. It was successfully sustained in the same body by Mr. Calhoun, Mr. Benton, and Mr. Silas Wright, of N. Y.

The agitation of the Slavery question in the District was led by ex-President John Quincy Adams in the House. He became the great Agitator on this subject soon after his entrance in the House, in December, 1831. He commenced it by presenting memorials and petitions. At first very little attention was paid to them; but his course soon produced considerable excitement. This continued to increase, and, in 1837, it became an absorbing topic, not only in Congress, but throughout the States. The petitions at first presented by him related to the District; but at this time embraced not only the District, but the States. It was pending this agitation, so produced, that Mr. Calhoun, on the 28th of December, 1837, introduced into the Senate another series of resolutions, similar in substance to those submitted by him in 1833, upon the nature and character of the Federal Government. At this time he pressed a vote; and, after an exciting debate, it passed that body early in January, 1838. These are the resolutions then adopted by the Senate:

"I. *Resolved*, That in the adoption of the Federal Constitution, the States adopting the same acted, severally, as free, independent, and sovereign States; and that each, for itself, by its own voluntary assent, entered the Union with the view to its increased security against all dangers, *domestic* as well as foreign, and the more perfect and secure enjoyment of its advantages, natural, political, and social.

"II. *Resolved*, That in delegating a portion of their powers, to be exercised by the Federal Government, the States retained, severally, the exclusive and sole right over their own domestic institutions and police, to the full extent to which those powers were not thus delegated, and are alone responsible for them; and that any intermeddling of one or more States, or a combination of their citizens, with the domestic institutions and police of the others, on any ground, political, moral, or religious, or under any pretext whatever, with a view to their alteration or subversion, is not warranted by the Constitution, tending to endanger the domestic peace and tranquillity of the States interfered with, subversive of the objects for which the

Constitution was formed, and, by necessary consequence, tending to weaken and destroy the Union itself.

"III. *Resolved*, That this Government was instituted and adopted by the several States of this Union as a common agent, in order to carry into effect the powers which they had delegated by the Constitution for their mutual security and prosperity ; and that, in fulfilment of this high and sacred trust, this Government is bound so to exercise its powers as not to interfere with the stability and security of the domestic institutions of the States that compose this Union ; and that it is the solemn duty of the Government to resist, to the extent of its constitutional power, all attempts by one portion of the Union to use it as an instrument to attack the domestic institutions of another, or to weaken or destroy such institutions.

"IV. *Resolved*, That domestic slavery, as it exists in the Southern and Western States of this Union, composes an important part of their domestic institutions, inherited from their ancestors, and existing at the adoption of the Constitution, by which it is recognized as constituting an important element in the apportionment of powers among the States, and that no change of opinion or feeling, on the part of the other States of the Union in relation to it, can justify them or their citizens in open and systematic attacks thereon, with the view to its overthrow, and that all such attacks are in manifest violation of the mutual and solemn pledge to protect and defend each other, given by the States respectively, on entering into the constitutional compact which formed the Union, and, as such, are a manifest breach of faith, and a violation of the most solemn obligations.

"V. *Resolved*, That the interference by the citizens of any of the States, with the view to the abolition of Slavery in this District, is endangering the rights and security of the people of the District; and that any act or measure of Congress designed to abolish slavery in this District, would be a violation of the faith implied in the cessions of the States of Virginia and Maryland, and just cause of alarm to the people of the slaveholding States, and have a direct and inevitable tendency to disturb and endanger the Union.

"*And Resolved*, That any attempt of Congress to abolish slavery in any territory of the United States in which it exists, would create serious alarm and just apprehension in the States sustaining that domestic institution ; would be a violation of good faith towards the inhabitants of any such territory who have been permitted to settle with and hold slaves therein, because the people of any such territory have not asked for the abolition of slavery therein ; and because when any such territory shall be admitted into the Union as a State, the people thereof will be entitled to decide that question exclusively for themselves."

The vote on the adoption of the First of these resolutions was 32 to 13. By States, the vote stood, in the Senate, 18 for it, and 6 against it ; one State was divided, and one did not vote.* The vote on the Second of these resolutions

---

* The following is the vote by States: *Ayes*—Alabama, Arkansas, Connecticut, Georgia, Illinois, Kentucky, Louisiana, Mississippi, Missouri, Michigan, Maine, North Carolina, New

stood 31 in favor of it, to 9 against it. By States, the vote on this resolution was 20 *for it, and only* 4 *against it;* one divided, and one not voting. The vote on the Third resolution was 31 in favor, and 11 against it. By States, the vote on this resolution was 16 in favor, and only 4 against it; 3 were divided, and 3 did not vote. On the Fourth resolution the vote stood, 34 for it, and only 5 against it. By States, on this the vote was 18 for it, and only 2 against it; 2 were divided, and 4 did not vote. On the Fifth resolution the vote was 36 in favor, and 8 against it. On the second clause of it, the vote by States was 19 for it, and 3 against it; 3 were divided, and 1 did not vote.

The adoption by the Senate of these resolutions, to which he had given a cordial support, Mr. Clay thought would quiet agitation upon the subject. In this, however, he was mistaken.

6. On the 1st of September of this year (1838), the United States, by their agent, received the liberal donation which was bequeathed to them in trust for the "general diffusion of knowledge among men," by James Smithson, an Englishman, which constitutes the endowment of the Institute in Washington City that bears his name. The amount of the legacy received, in American coin, was $575,169.

7. The agitation of the subject of Slavery in the House was renewed by the Abolitionists with increased bitterness at the next session of Congress, which commenced in December, 1838. Early in this session, Mr. Atherton, of New Hampshire, introduced a series of resolutions in that body covering the whole subject, especially the powers of the Federal Government over it, which became quite famous at

---

6. What is said of the Smithsonian Institute ?
7. What is said of the renewal of the agitation of slavery ? What of Mr. Atherton's resolutions ? What is said of the vote on the First ? What is said of the votes on the other resolutions offered by Mr. Atherton ? What effect did the votes produce upon the public mind ? Did the expected result ensue ? What is said of the Abolition agitators ? What was openly proclaimed by one of their chief leaders ?

Hampshire, New York, South Carolina, Pennsylvania, Tennessee, and Virginia, 18. *Nays*—Delaware, Indiana, Massachusetts, New Jersey, Rhode Island, and Vermont, 6. *Divided*—Ohio. *Not voting*—Maryland.

the time. The First of his resolutions was in these words:

"*Resolved*, That this Government is a Government of limited powers, and that, by the Constitution of the United States, Congress has no jurisdiction whatever over the institution of Slavery in the several States of the Confederacy."

This resolution passed the House by a vote of 194 to 6. The six votes against it were: Mr. Adams, of Mass., Mr. Evans, of Me., Mr. Everett, of Vt., Mr. Potts, of Penn., Mr. Russell, of N. Y., and Mr. Slade, of Vt.

The vote on this resolution, viewed in reference to the States, shows that it received the sanction, by their duly appointed representatives, of every member of the "Confederated Republic," a "Confederacy," as they then styled the Federal Union.

The Second of Mr. Atherton's resolutions was in these words:

"*Resolved*, That petitions for the abolition of Slavery in the District of Columbia and the Territories of the United States, and against the removal of Slaves from one State to another, are a part of a plan of operations set on foot to affect the institution of Slavery in the Southern States, and thus indirectly to destroy that institution within their limits."

On this resolution the vote stood: 136 for it, and 65 against it.

The Third resolution was in these words:

"*Resolved*, That Congress has no right to do that indirectly which it cannot do directly; and that the agitation of the subject of Slavery in the District of Columbia, or the Territories, as a means, and with a view, of disturbing or overthrowing that institution in the several States, is against the true spirit and meaning of the Constitution, an infringement of the rights of the States affected, and a breach of the public faith upon which they entered into the Confederacy."

The vote on this resolution was: 164 in favor of it, and 40 against it.

The Fourth of this series was in these words:

"*Resolved*, That the Constitution rests on the broad principle of equality among the members of this Confederacy, and that Congress, in the exercise of its acknowledged powers, has no right to discriminate between the institutions of one portion of the States and another, with a view of abolishing the one and promoting the other.'

The vote on this resolution was: 174 in favor of it, and 24 against it.

The Fifth and last of Mr. Atherton's resolutions was in these words:

"*Resolved*, That all attempts on the part of Congress to abolish Slavery in the District of Columbia or the Territories, or to prohibit the removal of Slaves from State to State, or to discriminate between the institutions of one portion of the Confederacy and another, with the view aforesaid, are in violation of the Constitution, destructive of the fundamental principle on which the Union of these States rests, and beyond the jurisdiction of Congress; and that every petition, memorial, resolution, proposition, or paper, touching or relating in any way, or to any extent whatever, to Slavery, as aforesaid, or the abolition thereof, shall, on the presentation thereof, without any further action thereon, be laid upon the table, without being debated, printed, or referred."

The vote on the first branch of this resolution was, 146 in favor, and 52 against it; on the second branch of the resolution the vote stood, 126 for it, and 78 against it.

After this clear and explicit declaration by the unanimous voice of the States in the House, as to the powers of Congress over the subject, and after the equally explicit declaration of so overwhelming a majority of that body as to the future policy to be pursued by them in reference to it, it was again thought, not only by Mr. Clay, but by most of the public men of the country, that this exciting agitation, so materially affecting the harmony, peace, and permanency of the Union, would be abandoned. But the Anti-Slavery or Abolition party, which was organized a few years before, and which, by its affiliated associations in several of the Northern States, stirred up the agitation, cared nothing for constitutional restraints; they did not wish to preserve any Union of the States under any such Constitution. The Constitution as it was, the chief of their leaders openly proclaimed to be nothing but "a covenant with death, and an agreement with hell." The agitation, therefore, did not cease, as we shall see.

8. Another Presidential election came off in the Fall of 1840. The principal issues in this contest were, the Sub-

---

8. What is said of the candidates for the Presidency in 1840? What was the

Treasury system, extravagant appropriations, defalcations, and profligacy of numerous subordinate officers. The "gold spoons" furnished the Executive mansion figured prominently in the canvass. Neither of the two great parties at that time had any avowed connection with the Anti-Slavery or Abolition agitators. The contest was an exciting one over the leading measures and practices of the Administration. All the opposing elements united under the Whig banner. This party had held a general Convention at Harrisburg, Penn., on the 4th of December, the year before, for the purpose of nominating candidates for President and Vice-President. It was generally supposed that Mr. Clay would receive the nomination of this body for President. But his course on the Tariff Compromise of 1833 had greatly weakened him with the Protectionists. When he adopted that course he was told it would lose him the Presidency. His reply at the time was, "I would rather be right than be President." The result of the Convention's action was the nomination of Gen. William H. Harrison, of Ohio, for President, and John Tyler, of Virginia, for Vice-President. The Democratic party held their General Convention in Baltimore, on the 5th of May, 1840. Mr. Van Buren was unanimously nominated by that body for President; but as the Convention could not agree upon any candidate for Vice-President, the nomination of this officer was left to the party in each State severally. The result of the election, after a heated canvass, was, 234 Electoral votes for Harrison for President, and 234 for John Tyler for Vice-President. Mr. Van Buren received 60 Electoral votes for President, Richard M. Johnson, of Ky., received 48 for Vice-President; Littleton W. Tazewell, of Va., 11, and James K. Polk, of Tenn., 1. The vote for President by States stood, 19 for Gen. Harrison and 7 for Mr. Van Buren. The 19 States

---

result of the election by the Colleges and by the States? What is said of Mr. Van Buren after the expiration of his term of office? What has a writer of note said of his Administration as a whole?

that voted for Gen. Harrison were: Maine, Massachusetts, Rhode Island, Connecticut, Vermont, New York, New Jersey, Pennsylvania, Delaware, Maryland, North Carolina, Georgia, Kentucky, Tennessee, Ohio, Louisiana, Mississippi, Indiana, and Michigan; the 7 that voted for Mr. Van Buren were: New Hampshire, Virginia, South Carolina, Illinois, Alabama, Missouri, and Arkansas.

Mr. Van Buren having lost his re-election, at the close of his term, on the 4th of March, 1841, retired to his home, at Kinderhook, N. Y. One remarkable feature of his Administration was, that the veto-power was not exercised by him in a single instance. A writer of note, in speaking of his Administration, as a whole, says:

"The great event of Gen. Jackson's Administration was the contest with the Bank of the United States, and its destruction as a Federal institution—that of Madison's was the war—while Jefferson's was a general revolution of the anti-Democratic spirit and policy of the preceding Administration. The great event of Mr. Van Buren's Administration, by which it will hereafter be known and designated, is, the divorce of Bank and State in the fiscal affairs of the Federal Government, and the return, after half a century of deviation, to the original design of the Constitution."

CHAPTER XVI.

ADMINISTRATIONS OF HARRISON AND TYLER.

4th of March, 1841—4th of March, 1845.

1. WILLIAM H. HARRISON, the 9th President of the United States, was inaugurated on the 4th of March, 1841, in the 69th year of his age. The City of Washington was thronged with people, many of whom were from the most distant States of the Union. A procession was formed

---

CHAPTER XVI.—**1.** What is said of Gen. Harrison and his inauguration as President?

from his quarters to the Capitol. The President elect was mounted on a white charger, accompanied by several personal friends, but his immediate escort were the officers and soldiers who had fought under him. The Inaugural Address was delivered on a platform erected over the front steps of the portico of the east front of the Capitol. The oath of office was administered by Chief-Justice Taney, before an audience estimated by many at sixty thousand.

PRESIDENT HARRISON.

2. Harrison had been a warm supporter of Mr. Jefferson in 1800, though he had received and held office under the elder Adams. He belonged to the Strict Construction school of politics of that day. Great anxiety, therefore, was felt as to what line of policy he would pursue in the Executive chair on the disturbing questions which were agitating the public mind at the time of his elevation to the Chief Magistracy. Its indication was looked for in his Inaugural Address. This was written and read by him: it was long, and went into a full review of all subjects of general public interest. In its delivery

"His voice never flagged, but to the end retained its full and commanding tone. As he touched on successive topics lying near the hearts of the people, their sympathy with his sentiments was manifested by shouts which broke forth involuntarily from time to time; and when the reading of the address was concluded, they were renewed and prolonged without restraint."

Among other things in this address, which was particularly gratifying to the friends of the Union under the Constitution everywhere, was the following:

"Our Confederacy, fellow-citizens, can only be preserved by the

---

2. To what party did he belong in early life? What is said of his Inaugural Address?

same forbearance. Our citizens must be content with the exercise of the powers with which the Constitution clothes them. The attempt of those of one State to control the domestic institutions of another, can only result in feelings of distrust and jealousy, and are certain harbingers of disunion, violence, civil war, and the ultimate destruction of our free institutions. Our Confederacy is perfectly illustrated by the terms and principles governing a common copartnership. There, a fund of power is to be exercised, under the direction of the joint counsels of the allied members; but that which has been reserved by the individuals is intangible by the common government, or the individual members composing it. To attempt it finds no support in the principles of our Constitution."

3. The new Cabinet consisted of Daniel Webster, of Mass., Secretary of State; Thomas Ewing, of Ohio, Secretary of the Treasury; George E. Badger, of N. C., Secretary of the Navy; Francis Granger, of N. Y., Postmaster-General; and John J. Crittenden, of Ky., Attorney-General.

4. On the 17th of March, the President issued his proclamation calling an Extra Session of Congress, to meet on Monday, the last day of May ensuing. He, however, did not live to meet them. On the 27th of March he was seized with a violent attack of pneumonia, or bilious pleurisy, which, baffling all medical skill, terminated fatally on the 4th of April—just one month from the day of his inauguration.

The office of President now, for the first time under the Constitution, devolved upon the Vice-President.

5. John Tyler, the Vice-President, on whom now devolved the duties of President, and who, by the death of Gen. Harrison, became the 10th President of the United States, was not in the City of Washington at the time of the demise of his predecessor. But immediately upon receiving intelligence of that sad event, which filled the whole country with gloom and mourning, he repaired thither as soon as possible; and, after taking the oath of office prescribed by the Constitution for the President before Judge

---

3. Who constituted his Cabinet?
4. What was done on the 17th of March? When did Harrison die, and what was the consequence?
5. Who became the 10th President of the United States? What is said of him, and his Inaugural? How old was he?

Cranch, Chief-Justice of the District of Columbia, he issued, through the public prints, on the 9th of April, an Address to the People of the United States, in the form of a usual Presidential Inaugural.

PRESIDENT TYLER.

President Tyler at the time was in the 52d year of his age. In this address there was no indication of a different line of policy from that announced in the Inaugural of Gen. Harrison. The same members of the Cabinet appointed by Gen. Harrison were retained in their respective positions.

6. The 27th, which became memorable as the "Whig Congress," convened on the 31st of May, under the proclamation which had been issued by Gen. Harrison. The discordant elements of which it was composed, that had combined against the late Administration of Mr. Van Buren, though largely in the majority when united, yet from opposing views among themselves upon many questions of public policy, soon came to open rupture. Mr. Tyler himself, who had always been a Strict Constructionist, soon found himself at variance in principle with a majority of both Houses of Congress, upon many matters of public interest then brought forward. A Bill was passed for the creation of an institution known as "The Fiscal Bank of the United States." This he vetoed. The veto was sustained for lack of a two-thirds majority in favor of the

---

6. When did the 27th Congress meet? What did it become memorable as? What is said of the opposing elements which composed it? What of Mr. Tyler? What of the Acts of this Congress at this session? What was the result as to the Cabinet?

Bill. Another bill of like character was passed under the title of "The Fiscal Corporation of the United States;" this was likewise vetoed, and in like manner failed to become a law. These vetoes were sustained generally by the Strict Constructionists, irrespective of party, in all sections of the country. But they led to an immediate re-organization of the Cabinet. All the members appointed by Gen. Harrison resigned, except Mr. Webster. The persons appointed to fill their places were: Walter Forward, of Penn., Secretary of the Treasury; John C. Spencer, of N. Y., Secretary of War; Abel P. Upshur, of Va., Secretary of the Navy, and Hugh S. Legaré, of S. C., Attorney-General. These new members were all prominent Whigs of the Strict Construction school, who sustained the President. The party was now completely divided, not only in Congress, but throughout the country. The session was brought to a close on the 13th day of September, after passing an Act for the repeal of the Sub-Treasury, and an Act providing uniform rules of Bankruptcy in the United States. This latter Act was very unpopular in many places, on account of some of its features which were held by many to be unconstitutional.

7. The 2d session of the 27th Congress met in December, 1841, and continued in session until August, 1842. It was the longest session ever before held, and became notable for many things. The opposing wings of the Whigs met in no good temper towards each other. Mr. Clay, of the Senate, was the recognized leader of the majority portion. The minority were called "Tyler Whigs," and were led in the Senate by William C. Rives, of Va., and in the House by Henry A. Wise, of the same State. There was no renewal of an effort to establish a Bank; but the Tariff was again agitated. This was the year when, according to the Compromise Act of 1833, the duties were to be regulated

---

7. What is said of the second session of the "Whig Congress"? What of Mr. Clay? What of the Tariff Bills? What is said of the "Treaty of Washington"?

on a revenue standard. The Protectionists, however, made a new rally. On the 31st of March, 1842, Mr. Clay resigned his seat in the Senate, and retired to his home at Ashland, near Lexington, Ky. A new Tariff Bill, highly protective in its objects and character, passed both Houses of Congress. It was vetoed by the President. Another Bill of like character, though with some modifications, was passed. It was vetoed in like manner. After that the celebrated "Tariff of 1842" was passed, and received the Executive signature on the 30th of August. In this the Compromise of 1833 was utterly abandoned, against the urgent protest of the opponents of the principle of levying duties with a view, not of revenue, but protection. The debates during all this session were animating and exciting. The Democrats and "Tyler Whigs" upon most questions acted together. In the mean time a very important treaty was made with Great Britain. It was effected under the auspices of Mr. Webster, Secretary of State, and Lord Ashburton. It is known as the "Treaty of Washington," and was ratified by the Senate on the 22d of August, 1842. By this, for the first time, the Northeastern Boundary between the United States and the neighboring British Possessions was definitely settled.

8. The 3d and last session of the "Whig Congress" met in December, 1842. Their term of office was to expire on the 4th of March following, and nothing of special note was done by them, except the repeal of the Bankruptcy Act of their first session. In May, 1843, Mr. Webster resigned the office of Secretary of State, and Mr. Upshur, of Va., was promoted to his place. Some other changes took place in the Cabinet: George M. Bibb, of Ky., became Secretary of the Treasury; William Wilkins, of Penn., Secretary of War; Thomas W. Gilmer, of Va., Secretary of the Navy; Charles A. Wickliffe, of Ky., Postmas-

---

8. What is said of the third and last session of the "Whig Congress"? What changes in the Cabinet took place in 1843?

ter-General, and John Nelson, of Maryland, Attorney-General.

9. The 28th Congress commenced its 1st session on the 4th of December, 1843, and continued it to the 17th of June, 1844. The House at this session was largely Democratic. On the 28th of February, 1844, occurred the lamentable accident by which Mr. Upshur and Mr. Gilmer of the Cabinet, and a number of other prominent citizens of the country, lost their lives. The President and his Cabinet, with a number of Senators and members of the House, and officers of high rank in the army and the navy, and many distinguished citizens, went as a party to visit the U. S. steamship-of-war *Princeton*, lying in the Potomac River, to witness the experimental firings of a very large new gun on that ship, which had been named the "Peacemaker." At one of the firings the gun exploded, causing the instant death of these Secretaries, besides a gallant officer of the navy and several prominent members of the party. This great calamity produced a profound sensation throughout the country.

After this, Mr. Calhoun, who was still in the Senate, was made Secretary of State, and John Y. Mason, of Va., Secretary of the Navy. Very soon after Mr. Calhoun's accession to the State Department, a treaty was negotiated between the United States and the Republic of Texas, for the cession of that country to the United States. This treaty was rejected by the Senate on the 8th of June following.

10. Another Presidential election came off in the Fall of 1844. The Whigs held their General Nominating Convention in Baltimore, on the 1st of May. Mr. Clay was their unanimous choice for President, and Theodore Freling-

---

9. What is said of the first session of the 28th Congress? What great accident occurred on the 28th of February, 1844? What new members were appointed to Cabinet offices? What is said of the treaty negotiated soon afterwards?
10. What is said of the candidates for President and Vice-President in the Fall of 1844? What of the main issues between the Whigs and Democrats? What is said of Mr. Clay's position on the Texas question? What of that of the majority of his supporters? What was the result of the election by the Colleges and by the States? What of the vote given to Mr. Birney?

huysen, formerly of New Jersey, but then of New York, was selected as the candidate for Vice-President.

The like General Convention of the Democratic party met at Baltimore on the 27th of the same month. The candidates nominated by this body were James K. Polk, of Tenn., for President, and George M. Dallas, of Penn., for Vice-President. This Convention also passed resolutions strongly in favor of the immediate annexation of Texas, and the occupation of the whole of Oregon, up to 54° 40' north latitude, without regard to any claim of England to any portion of it.

At this election the Abolitionists, for the first time as a regularly organized party, put in nomination James G. Birney, of Mich., for the office of President.

The prominent issues presented in the contest by the Whigs and the Democrats, were the Texas and Oregon questions. While Mr. Clay himself was in favor of the acquisition of Texas, upon proper principles and under suitable circumstances that would not involve the United States in a war with Mexico, which he deprecated, yet an overwhelming majority of his supporters were utterly opposed to the measure, in any and every form. The result of the Election by the Colleges was: 170 Electoral votes for James K. Polk, for President, and 170 for George M. Dallas, for Vice-President; 105 for Henry Clay, for President, and 105 for Theodore Frelinghuysen, for Vice-President. By States the vote stood: 15 for the Democratic ticket, and 11 for the Whig ticket. Mr. Birney received no Electoral vote; but local returns showed that out of the popular vote of upwards of two and a half millions, there were polled for him 64,653. The 15 States that voted for Mr. Polk were: Maine, New Hampshire, New York, Pennsylvania, Virginia, South Carolina, Georgia, Louisiana, Mississippi, Indiana, Illinois, Alabama, Missouri, Arkansas, and Michigan; the 11 that voted for Mr. Clay were: Massachusetts, Rhode Island, Connecticut, Vermont, New Jersey, Delaware, Maryland, North Carolina, Kentucky, Tennessee, and Ohio.

11. On the meeting, in their 2d session, of the 28th Congress in December, 1844, various plans for the "Annexation of Texas," as it was called, were introduced into the House of Representatives. A few Strict Construction Whigs held the balance of power in that body on this question at the time, as a considerable number of Democrats in the Northern States were opposed to it, because of the extension of slavery, which they maintained would attend it. It was in this state of things, and on the 13th of January, 1845, that Mr. Milton Brown, of Tenn., of the class of Whigs stated, introduced in the House his celebrated joint resolutions* authorizing the President to make a proposition to Texas for the introduction of that Republic into the Federal Union as a separate State, on certain terms specifically set forth, providing for the settlement of all questions pertaining to slavery, so as to avoid all future agitation of that subject, and guarding against any difficulty that might arise with Mexico, growing out of matters of boundary, by leaving that subject to be amicably adjusted between Mexico and the United States. These resolutions were violently opposed by the Slavery Restrictionists, though they were based upon a distinct recognition of the dividing line of 36° 30′, known as "the Missouri Compromise," so called. But when all other plans failed, Mr. Brown's resolutions were taken up in the House, and finally passed that body on the 25th of January, by a vote of 120 in favor, to 98 against them. They were sent to the Senate, where, on

---

11. What is said of the 2d session of the 28th Congress? Who held the balance of power on the Texas question? What is said of Mr. Milton Brown, of Tenn., and his resolutions upon the Texas question? Who opposed these resolutions? Upon what principle in regard to the Slavery question were they based? What became of them in the House? What in the Senate? What is said of Mr. Benton's Alternate Proposition in the Senate? What was the final result in the two Houses upon this subject? Which of the alternate propositions did Mr. Tyler elect?

---

* "Resolved by the Senate and House of Representatives of the United States of America in Congress assembled, That Congress doth consent that the territory properly included within and rightfully belonging to the Republic of Texas, may be erected into a new State, to be called the State of Texas, with a Republican form of Government, to be adopted by the people of said Republic, by deputies in Convention assembled, with the consent of the existing Government, in order that the same may be admitted as one of the States of this Union.

"SEC. 2. And be it further Resolved, That the foregoing consent of Congress is given upon the following conditions, and with the following guarantees, to wit:

"FIRST. Said State to be formed, subject to the adjustment of this Government of all ques-

motion of Mr. Benton, of Mo., they were amended by adding an Alternate Proposition to be submitted to Texas, which, however, did not close the door against future agitation of the Slavery Question. His proposition provided that the President should choose between the House measure and his Alternate, in submitting the action of Congress to Texas. This was on the 27th of February. It was Mr. Benton's expectation at the time that the execution of the resolutions would devolve upon the new President. His amendment for an alternate proposition was agreed to in the House, and the whole measure approved by Mr. Tyler on the 1st of March, and he immediately elected the House Proposition, and despatched a messenger with it to Texas before the expiration of his term of office.

12. On the 3d of March, 1845, an Act of Congress was approved by the President admitting the people of Iowa and the people of Florida, as separate States, into the Union.

COAT OF ARMS OF IOWA.

COAT OF ARMS OF FLORIDA.

13. After the expiration of his term of office, Mr. Tyler retired from the seat of Government to his residence in

---

12. When were Iowa and Florida admitted into the Union as separate States?
13. What is said of Mr. Tyler after the close of his term of office? What of his Administration?

---

tions of boundary that may arise with other Governments; and the Constitution thereof, with the proper evidence of its adoption by the people of said Republic of Texas, shall be transmitted to the President of the United States, to be laid before Congress for its final action, on or before the first day of January, one thousand eight hundred and forty-six.

"SECOND. Said State, when admitted into the Union, after ceding to the United States all public edifices, fortifications, barracks, ports and harbors, navy and navy-yards, docks, magazines, arms, armaments, and all other property and means pertaining to the public defence belonging to said Republic of Texas, shall retain all the public funds, debts, taxes, and dues of every kind, which may belong to or be due and owing said Republic; and shall also retain all the vacant and unappropriated lands lying within its limits, to be applied to the payment of the debts and liabilities of said Republic of Texas; and the residue of said lands, after discharging

Virginia. His Administration was a stormy one, but signalized by many important events. It was during this period that the electro-telegraphic system was established by Morse. A room was furnished him at the Capitol for his experimental operations in extending his wires to Baltimore; and among the first messages ever transmitted over them was the announcement of the nomination of Mr. Polk for the Presidency. It was during his Administration that diplomatic communications were opened with China, the first that that ancient empire ever held with any Christian state. The settlement of the Northeastern Boundary with Great Britain was an epoch in the history of both countries. During his Administration two new States were admitted into the Union; and to Mr. Tyler is chiefly due the addition of the great State of Texas, with its 237,504 square miles of territory, to the Union; the admission of which soon followed. His Administration, as a whole, was distinguished, not only for its unpopularity, while its integrity was unassailable, but for the great ability of the many eminent men who filled his Cabinet throughout his term in the various changes that were made in it at different times. His own State Papers compare favorably in point of ability with those of any of his predecessors. In reference to the aspersions of the extreme partisans of the day, who denounced him as a "traitor to the Whig cause," it is but due to his memory to give his own words: "I appeal from the vituperation of the present day to the pen of impartial history, in the full confidence that neither my motives nor my acts will bear the interpretation which has, for sinister purposes, been placed upon them."

---

said debts and liabilities, to be disposed of as said State may direct ; but in no event are said debts and liabilities to become a charge upon the Government of the United States.

"THIRD. New States, of convenient size, not exceeding four in number, in addition to said State of Texas, and having sufficient population, may hereafter, by the consent of said State, be formed out of the territory thereof, which shall be entitled to admission under the provisions of the Federal Constitution. And such States as may be formed out of that portion of said territory lying south of thirty-six degrees thirty minutes north latitude, commonly known as the Missouri Compromise line, shall be admitted into the Union with or without slavery, as the people of each State asking admission may desire. And in such State or States as shall be formed out of said territory north of said Missouri Compromise line, slavery or involuntary servitude (except for crimes) shall be prohibited."

CHAPTER XVII.

THE REPUBLIC OF TEXAS.

Its Colonization and Progress to Independence, and Union with the United States, 1714–1845.

1. ANTERIOR to 1714, numerous unsuccessful efforts had been made by the Jesuits to establish missionary settlements among the Indians at several places included in the present boundary of Texas. It was about this time, however, that the Government of Spain, which claimed the territory by right of discovery, determined to hold it against apprehended advancements of the French, by the erection of a chain of forts from Florida to New Mexico, directly through the interior of Texas. At each of these forts religious missions, with settlements under their direction, were securely established. The priests labored diligently in their pious efforts to convert and civilize the Indians; in which efforts, however, they met with poor success.

TEXAS COAT OF ARMS.

2. About the beginning of the present century pioneers from the United States began to find their way to these settlements. To Moses Austin, a native of Durham, Conn., one of these adventurers, Texas owes its origin—first as a Spanish colony, and afterwards as an independent State. He first conceived the idea of planting a large colony of emigrants from the United States in that country. He obtained an extensive grant of land from the Government of Spain in 1820 for this purpose and on this condition. He died, however, before he effected his contemplated settlement. His son, Stephen F. Austin, succeeded to the rights

---

CHAPTER XVII.—**1.** What is said of the early colonization of Texas? How and when were settlements first securely established? With what success did the priests meet?
2. What is said of Moses and Stephen F. Austin?

of his father under his grant, and, with a small party of emigrants from the United States, carefully explored the country, and selected, as the most desirable territory for their Colony, the region lying between the Brazos and Colorado rivers, and the place for their town the site of the present City of Austin, named in honor of the founder of the Colony. Austin himself, leaving the settlers in their new home, returned to the United States for other emigrants to join in the enterprise.

3. Meantime Mexico, and other Spanish Provinces, had become independent of Spain, and on Austin's return he found that it was necessary for him to visit the City of Mexico, and obtain from the new Government a confirmation of the grant made to his father, before he could proceed in the distribution of his lands. This he succeeded in effecting. His Colony soon consisted of about three hundred families. They were governed by such laws as they imposed upon themselves under rules drawn up by Austin.

4. The political condition of Texas during her colonial existence, without going into a minute detail of Mexican history, may be briefly thus set forth: The General Government, located in the City of Mexico, in order to encourage settlements in the Colony of Texas, declared by an Act of the *Cortes*, or Congress, of the Republic, dated May 2d, 1824,

"That Texas is to be annexed to the Mexican *Province* of Cohahuila, until it is of sufficient importance to form a separate State, when it is to become an independent State of the Mexican Republic, equal to the other States of which the same is composed, free, sovereign, and independent, in whatever exclusively relates to its internal government and administration."

On the faith of this Act or Decree, adventurers went to Texas from all countries, especially from the United States, not only to Austin's Colony, but to other settlements es-

3. What is further said of Stephen F. Austin? How was his Colony at first governed?
4. What did the Congress of Mexico do in 1824 to encourage the colonization of Texas? What checked it in 1830? What is said of Bustamente? What of the conduct of the Colonists against his outrages?

tablished in like manner. Austin's Colony increased rapidly in prosperity until 1830, when it met with a sudden check. Bustamente, having contrived, by intrigue and violence, to become President or Emperor of the Mexican Republic, so called, prohibited the ingress of foreigners, and made several decrees in conflict with the Constitution of 1824. To carry out his measures and execute his oppressive edicts, he introduced a considerable force of Mexican soldiers into the country, and thus placed Texas almost entirely under military rule. The Texans were roused to resistance to many outrages of this tyrant, and his mercenaries were soon forced to leave the province. Bustamente's rule closed in the year 1832. Early in 1832, Santa Anna was proclaimed President.

5. Soon after the accession of Santa Anna to the Chief Magistracy, Texas petitioned to be separated from Cohahuila, and for a separate State Government, according to the Constitution and Act of the Cortes of 1824. The petition set forth the condition and prospects of the Province; and that it was necessary for the prosperity and protection of the inhabitants that they should be permitted to exercise the exclusive powers of local self-government. Austin was selected by the Texans as their Agent to proceed to Mexico, and present their petition to the Congress. He remained there nearly a year without being able to obtain any reply to the application. He then wrote to the authorities of Texas, recommending them to organize a State Government, without waiting for the action of the Mexican Congress. This proceeding was considered treasonable by the authorities of Mexico; and shortly afterwards, Austin, returning to Texas, was arrested at Saltillo, and carried back to that city, where he was imprisoned, and held in close confinement for over a year. In the mean time, Santa Anna had overthrown the Constitution of 1824, and had

---

5. What did the Colonists petition for in 1832? Who was their Agent? What was the result of the petition? What became of their Agent? What is said of Santa Anna?

established a central consolidated Government; and had, in fact, become Military Dictator of the "Republic of Mexico," so called.

6. Some of the Departments, styled States, were opposed to this change, and resorted to arms, but were overcome by the Dictator. The constitutional authorities of Cohahuila and Texas assembled at Monclova, and earnestly protested against the usurpation. They were driven from office by military force under Gen. Cos, and the Government was dissolved. The Governor and members of the Local Legislature were imprisoned, and the central authority was established as supreme, contrary to the will of the people. At this juncture, Santa Anna, becoming alarmed at the demonstrations of determined opposition in Texas, released Austin, and sent him back to that country as a mediator. He had been absent over two years.

7. In a speech at a public meeting, soon after his return to Texas, he gave his opinions very fully on the state of affairs, and recommended such measures as he thought advisable to be adopted. Among other things in that memorable speech, he said:

"Under the Spanish Government, Texas was a separate and distinct Province; as such it had a separate and distinct local organization. It was one of the unities which composed the general mass of the nation, and as such participated in the War of the Revolution; and was represented in the Constituent Congress of Mexico, that formed the Constitution of 1824. The Constituent Congress confirmed this unity by the law of May 7th, 1824, which united Texas with Cohahuila provisionally, under the express guarantee of being made a State of the Mexican Confederation as soon as it possessed the necessary elements."

He further said, in speaking of the Revolution then progressing, that its object was-

"To change the form of Government; destroy the Federal Constitution of 1824, and establish a Central or Consolidated Government. The States are to become converted into Provinces. It is my duty," said he, "to state, as Gen. Santa Anna verbally and expressly author-

---

6. What is said of some of the Departments of Mexico styled "States"? What of Cohahuila and Texas? What did Gen. Cos do? What did Santa Anna do?

7. Give an account of Austin's speech on his return. What advice did Austin give?

ized me to say to the people of Texas, that he was their friend; that he wished for their prosperity, and would do all he could to promote it; and that in the new Constitution he would use his influence to give the people of Texas a special organization suited to their education, habits, and situation." He also said: "Whether the people of Texas ought or ought not to agree to this change, and relinquish all or a part of their constitutional and vested rights under the Constitution of 1824, is a question of the most vital importance, and one that calls for the deliberate consideration of the people, and can only be decided by them, fairly convened for the purpose."

8. These extracts from Austin's speech on the occasion referred to, are sufficient to show the positions of Mexico and Texas and the nature of the advice given by him at the time. In conformity with his views, Committees of Safety and Vigilance were raised, and resolutions passed to insist on their rights under the Federal Constitution of 1824. Troops were organized, and every preparation was made to resist the forces which they believed would be sent against them. They were not disappointed. Gen. Cos soon after arrived at Copano, from which place he marched to Bexar. The first engagement took place at Gonzales on the 2d of October, 1835. The Mexicans attacked the town, but were repulsed with considerable loss, both in killed and wounded. Shortly after, the Texans gained a more important victory at Goliad, on the 9th of October. The town was captured, and a large quantity of military stores were taken, besides three hundred stand of arms and two brass cannon. Austin was now Commander-in-chief of the Texan army.

9. On the 12th of November, 1835, a Convention of the people of Texas assembled at San Philipe de Austin, and a regular State Government was organized. In this body Gen. Sam. Houston made his appearance as a member, and exercised considerable influence in their proceedings. Soon

---

8. What did the people do in pursuance of his advice? What is said of Gen. Cos's movements? When and where was the first battle between the Texans and Mexicans fought? What was the result? When and where was the second fought, and with what results? Who was Commander-in-chief of the Texan army?
9. What occurred on the 12th of November, 1835? What is said of Gen. Houston? What is said of the movement on Bexar? What was the result? Who was elected Governor of Texas under the State organization? What became of Gen. Austin?

after, Gen. Austin resigned his position in the army, and the chief command was assigned to Gen. Houston. A movement without delay was made by the Texans against the town of Bexar, which was garrisoned by Mexican troops, under Gen. Cos. The place was taken after six days' siege. Gen. Cos surrendered on the 14th of December: he, with his troops, numbering over a thousand, were allowed to return to Mexico under their parole of honor that they would never in any way oppose the re-establishment of the Constitution of 1824. The country was thus freed for the present from Mexican military rule. Henry Smith was elected Governor under the State Government so organized, and Gen. Austin sent as an Agent or Commissioner to the United States.

10. Santa Anna, on receiving intelligence of the state of things in Texas, determined upon active measures for the reduction of the people to submission. He set out with an army of 7,500 men. He reached the Alamo late in February. This strong fort was garrisoned by 140 Texans, under Col. Travis. It was bombarded for eleven days, and finally carried by storm; but at a Mexican loss of 1,600. On the 6th of March the whole garrison was put to the sword. It was here that the brave, eccentric, and famous David Crockett, of Tenn., was killed. The Alamo is the Texan Thermopylæ.

On the 17th of March the Convention adopted a Constitution for an Independent Republic, and elected David G. Burnett President. Ten days after, Santa Anna attacked the Texan forces at Goliad, commanded by Col. Fannin. After a hard day's fighting, and the Mexicans having received reinforcements during the night, Col. Fannin deter-

---

10. What did Santa Anna do ? What occurred at the Alamo ? When did the Convention of the people of Texas resolve upon independence ? Who was the first President of the Republic thus declared ? What is said of the occurrences at Goliad, and when did they occur ? What effect did Santa Anna's advance, and his conduct at the Alamo and Goliad produce ? What is said of Houston's retreat ? When and where did the two armies meet ? What was the result ? What is further said of Gen. Houston ? Who succeeded him as President? Who succeeded Lamar ? What is said of the growth of Texas ?

mined to surrender, provided he could obtain honorable terms. His proposition was accepted by Santa Anna, who commanded the Mexicans in person, and the terms of the surrender were signed and formally interchanged. By the terms, Fannin, who was a Georgian, and his troops, were to give up their arms, and be allowed to retire to the United States. So soon as the surrender was complete, and the arms were delivered up, the whole force, consisting of about 300 men, were immediately massacred by order of Santa Anna. Few instances of such barbarous treachery and cruelty are to be found in the annals of the world. This advance of Santa Anna with so strong an army, and his conduct at the Alamo and Goliad, produced a temporary panic among the Texans. This was increased by the continued retreat of Gen. Houston—first to the Colorado, next to the Brazos, and finally to the San Jacinto. The seat of Government of the new Republic was moved temporarily to Galveston. Santa Anna pursued Houston to the San Jacinto, where he had taken position on the east side of that river. Here the two armies met on the 21st of April, and the Texans achieved a most brilliant victory. The Mexicans were greatly superior in numbers; but the Texans rushed to the fight with the shouts of "Remember the Alamo!" "Remember Goliad!" More than half of the Mexican forces engaged were among the killed, wounded, and captured, while the Texans engaged in the fight were not much over a third of their foe. Santa Anna, the Mexican President and Commander-in-Chief, was himself taken prisoner. Houston immediately entered into negotiations with him for the withdrawal of all Mexican forces from the territory of Texas. Orders were issued accordingly. The war was virtually at an end, and the independence of Texas achieved. On the 22d of October, after being duly elected, Gen. Houston was inaugurated as the 2d President of the Republic. Gen. Mirabeau B. Lamar was the 3d President. He came into office in 1838, and was succeeded by Anson Jones, the 4th President, in 1844. The young Republic, embracing some of the loveliest and richest regions of soil on the North American continent, during its short career was prosperous and rapid in growth. The population at this time was about 200,000.

11. On the 3d of March, 1837, the independence of this new power among the nations of the earth was recognized by the United States, in regular form. Two years afterwards it was likewise recognized by France and England, and very soon by most of the European powers. Not having fought for power, but for the right of local self-government, the thoughts of her people naturally turned towards the United States, and looked to a union with them. As early as the 4th of August, 1837, Texas proposed to unite herself with the United States. The proposition was at that time declined to be entertained by Mr. Van Buren, who was then President. It was not until Mr. Tyler's Administration, as we have seen, that the subject was renewed by either party. The results of the renewal then made thus far we have seen. The House proposition, or Mr. Milton Brown's Resolutions, setting forth the terms of a union which President Tyler submitted to President Jones, were adopted by the people of Texas in Sovereign Convention on the 4th of July, 1845, and a new Constitution formed preparatory for her admission as a State into the Federal Union.

---

11. When was her independence recognized by the United States? What is said of its recognition by other powers? What of the House proposition for her admission into the Union?

CHAPTER XVIII.

ADMINISTRATION OF POLK.
4th March, 1845—4th March, 1849.

THE WAR WITH MEXICO.

1. JAMES K. POLK, 11th President of the United States, was inaugurated on the 4th of March, 1845, in the 50th year of his age. The oath of office was administered by Chief-Justice Taney, in the presence of a very large assemblage of citizens, but greatly inferior in numbers to that which attended the inauguration of Harrison. In his Inaugural the new President spoke favorably of the late action of Congress in relation to Texas, and asserted that the title of the United States to the whole of Oregon was clear and indisputable, and intimated his intention to maintain it by force if necessary.

PRESIDENT POLK.

2. The new Cabinet consisted of James Buchanan, of Penn., Secretary of State; Robert J. Walker, of Miss., Secretary of the Treasury; William L. Marcy, of N. Y., Secretary of War; George Bancroft, of Mass., Secretary of the Navy; Cave Johnson, of Tenn., Postmaster-General, and John Y. Mason, of Va., Attorney-General.

3. General Almonte, the Mexican Minister Resident at Washington, after remonstrating against the course of the

---

CHAPTER XVIII.—**1.** Who was the 11th President, and what is said of his inauguration, and of his Inaugural Address?
2. Who constituted his Cabinet?
3. What is said of the position of Mexico at this time? When did Gen. Jackson die?

United States towards Texas, demanded his passports soon after Mr. Polk came into office. Mexico, never having recognized the independence of Texas, still claimed that Territory as belonging to her dominions. All friendly intercourse between the United States and Mexico now ceased. Immediately after the adoption by Texas, on the 4th of July of this year, as stated, of the proposition of the United States submitted by Mr. Tyler, Mr. Polk, apprehending difficulty with Mexico, immediately sent Colonel Zachary Taylor, now raised to the rank of Brigadier-General, with about five thousand troops, to repel any invasion that might be attempted. Early in August he took position at Corpus Christi, near the mouth of the Nueces River, which was the western boundary of the civil jurisdiction of Texas at that time; though she claimed the Rio del Norte as her rightful boundary.

In the mean time the country was filled with mourning at the intelligence of the death of General Jackson, who died at the Hermitage on the 8th of June, 1845, in the 79th year of his age.

4. The 29th Congress commenced its first session on the 1st of December, 1845, and continued to the 10th of August, 1846. It was largely Democratic. Among the first of its acts was the recognition, on the 29th of December, 1845, of Texas as a State of the Federal Union, on the terms proposed and agreed to. Other leading measures of a civil character adopted at this session were the repeal of the Whig Tariff of 1842, and the enactment of another, based upon the principles of Free Trade; the re-enactment of the Sub-Treasury or Independent Treasury system; the establishment of the Smithsonian Institute out of the funds received for this purpose in 1837; and a Resolution for terminating the joint occupation of Oregon

---

4. What was the political character of the 29th Congress? When did it meet. What was one of its first acts? What other leading measures of a civil character were adopted at this session? What Bills were vetoed?

under the then existing treaty with Great Britain. Internal Improvement Bills, and a Bill to pay citizens of the United States for French spoliations on their commerce, were vetoed by the President.

5. In the mean time, military acts of great importance were occurring. On the 13th of January, 1846, General Taylor was ordered to advance to the Rio Grande. On the 28th of March he reached the east bank of that river, and erected a fortress, called Fort Brown, directly opposite and within cannon-shot of the Mexican city of Matamoras. On the 26th of April, General Ampudia, the Mexican commander, gave notice to General Taylor that he considered hostilities commenced. On the same day sixty-three men, commanded by Capt. Thornton, were attacked on the east side of the Rio Grande above Matamoras, and all were either killed or captured. This was the first blood shed in the Mexican War.

6. As the movements of the Mexicans indicated the purpose of cutting off the supplies of Gen. Taylor by an attack upon Point Isabel, about twenty miles in his rear, he marched to the relief of that place with his principal force, leaving a small garrison at Fort Brown. Having garrisoned Point Isabel, which was a provision *dépôt*, on the 7th of May he set out on his return to Fort Brown. About noon on the next day he found the Mexican army, consisting of about six thousand men, drawn up in battle array across the prairie near Palo Alto, to oppose his progress. A battle immediately ensued, in which Gen. Taylor was victorious. The Mexican loss was one hundred killed. Taylor's loss was four killed and forty wounded. Among the mortally wounded was the lamented Major Ringgold. This was the battle of Palo Alto.

On the afternoon of the next day Gen. Taylor again advanced, and about 4 o'clock came in sight of the Mexicans.

---

5. What is said of the military acts in the mean time ?
6. What is said of the battles of Palo Alto and Resaca-de-la-Palma ?

occupying a strong position near Resaca-de-la-Palma, about three miles from Fort Brown. The battle was begun by the artillery on both sides. The Mexican guns were served much better than on the former occasion, and it was determined to capture them. Accordingly, Capt. May, with a squadron of dragoons, was ordered to charge them. In a few minutes the guns were in his possession, and Gen. La Vega, who commanded the artillery, was a prisoner. The charge was supported by the infantry, and the whole Mexican army was soon in complete rout. This was the battle of Resaca-de-la-Palma. By night not a Mexican soldier could be found east of the Rio Grande. On the next day Gen. Taylor resumed his position at Fort Brown. In a few days he crossed the river and took possession of Matamoras.

7. On the 11th of May, 1846, Mr. Polk, in a Message to Congress, declared that Mexico "had invaded our territory, and shed the blood of our fellow-citizens on our own soil;" and Congress, declaring that war existed "by the act of Mexico," authorized the President to accept the services of fifty thousand volunteers, and placed ten millions of dollars at his disposal. The President's call for volunteers was answered by the tender of the services of more than three hundred thousand men. Gen. Taylor's force was soon increased by a large number of volunteers from Texas and the adjoining States.

8. The plan of military operations now adopted by the Administration at Washington was, to strike Mexico on three different lines: one was from Matamoras to the interior, under the lead of Gen. Taylor; another through New Mexico to California, under the lead of Gen. Kearney, while a third column was to seize the Northern States, or Departments, of Mexico, under the lead of Gen. Wool.

9. In the latter part of August, Gen. Taylor began a for-

---

7. What of the President's Message of the 11th of May, and the action of Congress? What ensued?
8. What plan of military operations was adopted?
9. What is said of Taylor's movements?

ward movement, and on the 19th of September appeared before Monterey, the capital of the Department of New Leon, garrisoned by about 10,000 troops. Gen. Taylor's force was only sixty-five hundred men. He began the attack on the 21st of September, and on the 24th the Mexican General submitted propositions which resulted in the surrender and evacuation of Monterey. An armistice of eight weeks was agreed upon between the two Generals, or until instructions to renew hostilities could be received from their respective Governments. The truce was disapproved of by Mr. Polk, and on the 13th of October Gen. Taylor was ordered to renew offensive operations. About the middle of November the division of Gen. Worth occupied Saltillo, the capital of Coahuila. In December, Gen. Patterson took possession of Victoria, the capital of Tamaulipas, and the port of Tampico was captured by Commodore Perry.

10. Meantime Gen. Kearney made himself master of Santa Fé and all New Mexico without opposition. Having established a new government in New Mexico, he set out, on the 25th of November, with four hundred dragoons for California, on the Pacific Ocean. He learned on the way that California was already in possession of the United States by other forces which had been sent around by water in anticipation of a war with Mexico. So sending back three hundred of his men, he proceeded across the continent with only one hundred. In the early part of December, Col. Doniphan, who had been left in command at Santa Fé, with only nine hundred men, set out from Santa Fé southward, expecting to join Gen. Wool at Chihuahua. But he did not find him there. Wool, being impeded in his march by lofty and unbroken ranges of mountains, had turned southward and united his forces with those of Gen. Worth at Saltillo. Col. Doniphan was ignorant of this fact when he set out; but he successfully accomplished his march of a thousand miles through the enemy's country, from Santa Fé to Saltillo. He fought two battles on the way against superior forces, in both of which he was victorious, and captured Chihuahua, a city of great wealth, containing a population of forty thousand inhabitants.

11. During the preceeding Summer, California had been taken possession of by the United States forces under Col. Frémont, Commodore Sloat, and Commodore Stockton; and by the 22d of August, 1846, the whole vast region of California was in military possession of the United States. In December, soon after the arrival of Gen. Kearney, the Mexican inhabitants of California endeavored to regain possession, but the attempt was soon suppressed.

On the 22d and 23d of February, 1847, Gen. Taylor, with an army of only about five thousand men, met and defeated at Buena Vista, a few miles from Saltillo, an army of twenty thousand Mexicans, commanded by Santa Anna, the Dictator and Commander-in-chief. This important victory completely broke up the army of Santa Anna, and enabled the United States to turn their whole attention to the great design of the capture of Vera Cruz and the City of Mexico.

12. On the 9th of March, 1847, Gen. Scott, to whom this line of operations was committed, landed twelve thousand men, without opposition, a short distance south of Vera Cruz. He immediately invested the city. On the night of the 27th, articles of surrender were signed, and on the 29th the flag of the United States floated over the walls. On the 8th of April, Gen. Twiggs was sent forward towards the City of Mexico. On the 18th was fought the battle of Cerro Gordo, in which the armies of the United States were completely victorious. On the 15th of May, the advance under

---

11. What is said of the situation in California? What of the battle of Buena Vista?

12. To whom was assigned the command for the capture of the City of Mexico? What is said of the movements on this line? What was the effect of the capture of the Mexican capital? What were some of the features of the treaty of peace? By what name is this treaty known? What were the immediate results of the war as to losses and gains to the United States?

Gen. Worth occupied the city of Puebla. At Puebla, Gen. Scott waited for reinforcements. On the 7th of August, with about eleven thousand men, he began his march for the Capital of the Republic. In a few days they came in sight of the city. On the 20th occurred the battles of Contreras and Churubusco, in which the United States forces were again victorious, defeating an army of thirty thousand Mexicans. On the morning of the 8th of September, the Molino del Rey and the Casa de Moto, the outer defences of the castle of Chapultepec, were stormed and taken by Gen. Worth; but his loss was very great. All day long on the 12th the battle raged near and at the gate of the city; and when night put an end to the conflict, one division of Scott's army rested in the suburbs of Mexico, and another was actually within the gates. During the night the Mexican army and all the officers of the Government fled from the city, and at seven o'clock the next morning the flag of the United States floated in triumph from the walls of the national palace.

The conquest of the capital put an end to the war. A treaty of peace was not long after concluded between the two countries. The treaty was ratified by the United States Senate on the 10th of March, and by the Mexican Congress on the 30th of May. Mexico ceded to the United States all New Mexico and Upper California, and yielded also some important privileges. The United States paid Mexico fifteen millions of dollars, and assumed the payment of all debts due to citizens of the United States from the Mexican Government. This is known as the treaty of Guadaloupe Hidalgo.

The immediate results of this war were the loss to the United States of about twenty-five thousand men, and one hundred and sixty millions of dollars, with the acquisition of 632,157 square miles of territory, and a very great augmentation of military renown.

13. We will now return to civil affairs again. The most

notable remaining events of the civil administration of Mr. Polk will be briefly stated:

On the 8th of August, 1846, he sent a Message to Congress, asking an appropriation of three millions of dollars to enable him to negotiate a treaty of peace with Mexico, based upon the policy of obtaining a cession of territory outside of the then limits of Texas. It was on a Bill to grant this appropriation, that Mr. David Wilmot, of Penn., moved his celebrated "Proviso,"* or a restriction of Slavery in any newly-acquired territory, without any regard to the "Missouri Compromise" line, so called. The reading of the Amendment again sounded "like a fire-bell at night." It produced great sensation in the House and the country. The Bill with the Amendment passed the House; but was lost in the Senate.

14. The 2d session of the 29th Congress commenced on the 7th of December, 1846, and continued to the 3d of March, 1847, when it expired by the limitation of its term. During this period the question of Slavery was the chief topic of discussion and agitation; the controversy with England on the Oregon question having been amicably adjusted on a compromise line of the 49th degree or parallel of north latitude.

15. On the 15th of January, 1847, when the Bill for organizing Territorial Government in Oregon was pending in the House, with the Wilmot Proviso incorporated in it, it was moved by Mr. Burt, of S. C., to insert, just before the

---

13. What is said of Mr. Polk's Message of the 8th of August, 1846?
14. What is said of the 2d session of the 29th Congress? How had the Oregon question been settled?
15. What occurred in January, 1847, in the House, on a Bill organizing a Territorial Government for Oregon? Would the Restrictionists recognize the Missouri line? What is said of Mr. Calhoun and his resolutions at this time? What became of the Oregon Bill in the Senate?

---

* "*Provided*, That there shall be neither slavery nor involuntary servitude in any territory which shall hereafter be acquired, or be annexed to the United States, otherwise than in the punishment of crimes, whereof the party shall have been duly convicted. *Provided always*, That any person escaping into the same from whom labor or service is lawfully claimed in any one of the United States, such fugitive may be lawfully reclaimed and conveyed out of said territory, to the person claiming his or her labor or service."

restrictive clause, these words: "Inasmuch as the whole of said territory lies north of 36° 30' north latitude." This Amendment was rejected; showing that the Restrictionists did not intend to abide by that line, on the principle of a division of the public domain between the two great sections of the Union, upon which it was based. This Bill passed the House without any qualification of the Slavery restriction so incorporated in it. In the mean time, Mr. Calhoun, who had returned to the Senate, introduced in that body a series of resolutions which embodied the views of the Strict Constructionists. These resolutions gave rise to animated debates,* but never came to a vote. The bill to organize a Territorial Government for Oregon also failed in the Senate at this session.

16. The 1st session of the 30th Congress commenced on the 6th of December, 1847, and continued to the 14th of August, 1848. A majority of the House were against the Administration. The war with Mexico had not terminated when it met. The Slavery Question, however, was the most agitating of all others. The principles governing the discussions were those set forth in Mr. Calhoun's resolutions on the one side, and those embodied in the Wilmot Proviso on the other. In the midst of this excitement ex-President John Quincy Adams was stricken with paralysis

---

16. What is said of the 1st session of the 30th Congress? What of the agitation of the Slavery Question? What of the principles governing the discussions? What of the death of ex-President John Quincy Adams?

---

* "*Resolved*, That the Territories of the United States belong to the several States composing this Union, and are held by them as their joint and common property.

"*Resolved*, That Congress, as the joint agent and representative of the States of this Union, has no right to make any law, or do any act whatever, that shall directly, or by its effects, make any discrimination between the States of this Union, by which any of them shall be deprived of its full and equal right in any territory of the United States, acquired or to be acquired.

"*Resolved*, That the enactment of any law which should directly, or by its effects, deprive the citizens of any of the States of this Union from emigrating with their property into any of the Territories of the United States, will make such discrimination, and would, therefore, be a violation of the Constitution, and the rights of the States from which such citizens emigrated, and in derogation of their perfect equality which belongs to them as members of this Union, and would tend directly to subvert the Union itself.

"*Resolved*, That it is a fundamental principle in our political creed, that a people, in forming a Constitution, have the unconditional right to form and adopt the Government which they may think best calculated to secure their liberty, prosperity, and happiness, and that, in conformity thereto, no other condition is imposed by the Federal Constitution on a State, in order to be admitted into this Union, except that its Constitution shall be republican; and that the imposition of any other by Congress would not only be in violation of the Constitution, but in direct conflict with the principle on which our political system rests."

at his seat in the House, on the 21st of February, 1848. He was borne to the Speaker's room, where he remained two days, and there expired on the 23d, in the 81st year of his age.

17. While these agitations were going on, the people of Wisconsin, on the 29th of May, 1848, were admitted as a separate State into the Union.

18. After the Treaty of Peace with Mexico, various efforts were made to settle the Slavery Question between the States, in organizing Territorial Governments for Oregon, California, New Mexico, and Utah. Mr. Douglas, in the Senate, made an urgent appeal to adhere to the principle of a division of the public domain on the line of 36° 30′, known as "the Missouri Compromise" line. This was utterly repudiated by a controlling majority from the Northern States, both in the House and Senate. A Territorial Government was finally organized for Oregon, with an unqualified restriction on Slavery in it. All attempts to settle the question as to the other Territories utterly failed. In this state of things Congress adjourned on the 14th of August, 1848.

COAT OF ARMS OF WISCONSIN.

19. During the Fall of this year another Presidential election came off. The combined elements of opposition to the Administration, in the main, continued to bear the name of Whigs, though the anti-Slavery element now formed a distinct organization known as "Free-Soilers."

The Democratic party held their General Convention at Baltimore on the 22d of May, and put in nomination for the Presidency Gen. Lewis Cass, of Mich., and for the Vice-

---

17. When were the people of Wisconsin admitted as a State into the Union?
18. What is said of the attempts to settle the Slavery Question at this Congress, after the treaty of peace with Mexico?
19. What is said of the Presidential election in the Fall of 1848? Who were the candidates of the respective parties? What was the result of the election by the Colleges, and what by States?

Presidency Gen. William O. Butler, of Ky. The Whigs held their Convention at Philadelphia on the 1st of June, and put in nomination for the Presidency Gen. Zachary Taylor, of La., and for the Vice-Presidency Millard Fillmore, of N. Y. The Free-Soilers held their Convention at Buffalo, N. Y., on the 8th of August, and put in nomination for the Presidency Martin Van Buren, of N. Y., and for the Vice-Presidency Charles Francis Adams, of Mass. The result of the election was: 163 Electoral votes for the Whig ticket, and 127 for the Democratic. The Free-Soil ticket received no Electoral vote; but local returns showed that out of a popular vote of nearly three millions, there were polled for it nearly three hundred thousand individual votes. The vote for Taylor and Fillmore, by States, stood 15; and for Cass and Butler 15 also. The 15 States that voted for Taylor and Fillmore were: Massachusetts, Rhode Island, Connecticut, Vermont, New York, New Jersey, Pennsylvania, Delaware, Maryland, North Carolina, Georgia, Kentucky, Tennessee, Louisiana, and Florida; the 15 that voted for Cass and Butler were: Maine, New Hampshire, Virginia, South Carolina, Ohio, Mississippi, Indiana, Illinois, Alabama, Missouri, Arkansas, Michigan, Texas, Iowa, and Wisconsin. Taylor and Fillmore, therefore, having received a majority of the Electoral votes, were declared duly elected to the offices of President and Vice-President, after the 4th of March ensuing.

20. During the 2d session of the 30th Congress, which convened on the 4th of December, 1848, and expired on the 4th of March, 1849, no Act of importance was passed. Several efforts were made to settle the Question of Slavery in the Territories. Soon after the acquisition of California, gold mines were discovered in that country, which proved to be perhaps the richest in the world. These attracted a rapid and an immense immigration. The population soon

---

20. What is said of the 2d session of the 30th Congress? What of the gold mines in California? What of the population there? What of organizing governments in California, New Mexico, and Utah?

swelled to over 100,000. An organized government was greatly needed; but owing to the discordant elements of the political parties at Washington, the subject of a government for them, as well as for the people of Utah and New Mexico, was left to the councils of the incoming Administration and the patriotism of another Congress.

CHAPTER XIX.

ADMINISTRATIONS OF TAYLOR AND FILLMORE.

4th of March, 1849—4th of March, 1853.

1. The 4th of March, 1849, coming on Sunday, Zachary Taylor was duly inaugurated as the 12th President of the United States on the next day, Monday, the 5th of that month, in the 65th year of his age. The oath of office was administered by Chief-Justice Taney, in the presence of an immense concourse of people, in front of the East portico of the Capitol. He had received a majority of the Electoral votes of both sections of the Union, and intense interest was felt as to the line of policy he would pursue in regard to the exciting questions which then aroused so much bitterness of sectional strife. His Inaugural was conciliatory and satisfactory to "the friends of the Union under the Constitution." Having spent most of his life in the army, he had never taken any active part in politics, though his sympathies were well known to have been in early life with those of the Jeffersonian school.

PRESIDENT TAYLOR.

CHAPTER XIX.—1. What is said of Gen. Taylor's Inauguration, and his Address

2. The new Cabinet consisted of John M. Clayton, of Del., Sec'y of State; William M. Meredith, of Penn., Sec'y of the Treasury; George W. Crawford, of Ga., Sec'y of War; William B. Preston, of Va., Sec'y of the Navy; Thomas Ewing, of Ohio, Sec'y of the Interior (the new Executive Department just created); Jacob Collamer, of Vt., Postmaster-General, and Reverdy Johnson, of Md., Attorney-General.

3. Among the first subjects which occupied the attention of the new Administration was the state of things in California. Thomas Butler King, of Ga., was despatched as a Special Agent, with instructions to advise the people, in co-operation with Gen. Riley, then in command there, to adopt a Constitution for their own local self-government, preparatory to their admission into the Union as a State. In pursuance of this policy, a Convention was called, and a State Government instituted.

4. On the 15th of June, ex-President James K. Polk died in Nashville, Tenn., in the 54th year of his age.

5. The 1st session of the 31st Congress commenced on the 5th of December, 1849, and continued to the 30th of September, 1850. This was the longest and stormiest session of Congress ever before assembled. It is known as "the Congress of 1850." Among other things, it is noted for the return of Mr. Clay to the Senate, and the figuring in that arena again of "the Great Trio." Mr. Webster had returned soon after his retirement from Mr. Tyler's Cabinet; Mr. Calhoun had also returned soon after he retired from the same Cabinet. Mr. Clay now joined them in a most critical period of the country's history. On all the questions then most intensely agitating the public mind, the eyes of all true friends of the Union under the Constitution were hopefully turned to him as the great Pacificator.

---

2. Who formed his Cabinet?
3. What policy was adopted in regard to California?
4. When did ex-President Polk die?
5. When did the 1st session of the 31st Congress meet? What is said of it? What is it noted for? What is said specially of Mr. Clay?

CHAP. XIX.]   TAYLOR AND FILLMORE.   397

6. The subjects of public excitement at the time were: 1. The admission of California as a State under the Constitution she had during the previous Summer informally made and presented; 2. The organization of Territorial Governments for Utah and New Mexico; 3. The settlement of the boundary between New Mexico and Texas; 4. Slavery in the District of Columbia; 5. The non-rendition of fugitives from service. These were what Mr. Clay designated as "the five bleeding wounds."

7. In the House no party was in the majority. The Whigs and the Democrats, as they were called at the time, embodied the major portions; but these were divided among themselves upon what were deemed, by many, the vital principles of the crisis. A portion of the Strict-Construction Southern Whigs thought the time had come for a reorganization of parties upon the essential principles of the Federal Union. They endeavored to effect this reorganization on the election of Speaker; in this, however, they were not joined by other Strict-Constructionist Whigs nor Democrats from either of the two great sections of the Union. No Speaker was elected until the 22d of December, when Mr. Howell Cobb, of Ga., a Strict-Construction Democrat, was chosen under a resolution of the House, that whoever should receive the highest vote on a designated ballot, should be the Speaker, whether the vote so received should be a majority of the House or not.

8. On the 29th of January, 1850, Mr. Clay, in the Senate, presented a series of Resolutions, known as his "Compromise" of that year, embracing the five disturbing subjects

---

6. What five subjects of public excitement are stated? How did Mr. Clay designate them?
7. What is said of the House, and the state of parties therein? What of a portion of the Strict-Construction Southern Whigs? Did they fail in their object, and why? Who was elected Speaker? When and how?
8. What is said of Mr. Clay, and his Committee of Thirteen? What of "the Omnibus Bill" as a whole? What is said of that part of it relating to governments for Utah and New Mexico? What were the entire delegations from the South willing to do? When the principle of division on the Missouri line was repudiated by the Restrictionists, what did the Southern delegations then insist upon? What had all the Southern States done? What is said of that part of the Bill relating to the rendition of fugitive slaves?

referred to. These were referred to a Committee of Thirteen, of which he was chosen Chairman. This Committee reported what was known as "the Omnibus Bill"—that is, a Bill providing for all the separate subjects in one Act. This Bill, as a whole, was not satisfactory to many of any party. That part which provided for the admission of California under her then Constitution was strongly opposed by a majority of Southern Senators and members, though not by the Strict-Construction Whigs referred to. That part of the Bill providing Territorial Governments for Utah and New Mexico was unsatisfactory to the Strict-Construction Southern Whigs, because, notwithstanding it omitted a Congressional Territorial restriction on Slavery, yet it did not recognize and guarantee to the people of the Territories embraced the right to form and mould their institutions as they pleased, and to be admitted into the Union as States either with or without Slavery, as they might at the time determine for themselves; while it was denounced by the Restrictionists because it did not contain the Wilmot Proviso. The class of Whigs referred to, as well as the entire delegations from the South in the Senate and House, were willing to settle upon the principle of a division of the public domain between the two sections. Offers to abide by the line of 36° 30', known as "the Missouri Compromise" line, were repeatedly made; and as often as they were made they were rejected by the delegations of the Northern States. It was then, after the principle of a division of the public domain was abandoned by the North, that they insisted that the original Strict-Construction principle of Non-Interference by Congress with Slavery in the Territories, as well as on the admission of States into the Union, should be established as the future Federal policy on these questions. All the Southern States had declared that they would abide by the Missouri line of division; but would not submit to a total exclusion from participation in all the public domain, to the acquisition of which they had equally contributed in blood and treasure.

That part of the Bill which provided for an efficient mode for the reclamation and rendition of fugitive slaves from one State to another was violently assailed by the Abolition agitators.

Mr. Calhoun's views upon the whole subject were presented in a written speech on the 4th of March. This was read by Mr. Mason, a Senator from Virginia, as Mr. Calhoun, though present, was unable to deliver it. Mr. Webster followed three days afterwards in what was known as his "great Union speech of the 7th of March." In this he took position against territorial restriction; and declared that he would vote against the Wilmot Proviso. Few speeches ever produced greater sensation in the country than this did.

9. In this state of things Mr. Calhoun died, on the 31st of March, 1850, aged 68 years and 13 days. Due honors were paid to his memory, and appropriate tributes to his ability, integrity, and patriotism, by his compeers, including Mr. Clay and Mr. Webster.

10. The discussions on the exciting topics continued in the House and Senate until the 17th of June, when an Amendment to Mr. Clay's Bill, in that part relating to a Territorial Government for Utah, was adopted, which rendered it entirely satisfactory to the Southern Strict-Construction Whigs. It was that which provided that "when the said Territory, or any portion of the same, shall be admitted as a State, it shall be received into the Union, with or without slavery, as their Constitution may prescribe at the time of her admission." This was based upon the new principle now insisted upon. It was voted for by Mr. Webster, and was the turning-point in the settlement of 1850. By this, thereafter there was to be no Congressional restric-

---

9. What is said of the death of Mr. Calhoun?
10. What is said of the action of the Senate on the 17th of June?

tion on slavery in the public domain, either north or south of 36° 30'. The vote by States on this Amendment in the Senate stood, 20 for it; 6 against it; 2 divided, and 2 not voting.

11. In the midst of these agitations, the country was shocked and filled with mourning upon the announcement of the death of President Taylor. He died at the Executive mansion, after a few days of illness, on the 9th of July, 1850. The office of President, now for the second time in our history, devolved upon the Vice-President. Mr. Fillmore, who was in a cordial sympathy with Mr. Clay in his efforts at an adjustment of all these exciting questions, immediately assumed the duties of the Executive Chair, and became the 13th President. Gen. Taylor's Cabinet having all resigned on his death, Mr. Fillmore filled their places by appointing Mr. Webster Secretary of State; Thomas Corwin, of Ohio, Secretary of the Treasury; Charles M. Conrad, of La., Secretary of War; William A. Graham, of N. C., Secretary of the Navy; Alexander H. H. Stuart, of Va., Secretary of the Interior; Nathan K. Hall, of N. Y., Postmaster-General, and John J. Crittenden, of Ky., Attorney-General.

PRESIDENT FILLMORE.

12. In the mean time, Mr. Clay's Bill continued a subject matter of angry discussion in the Senate until the 31st of July, when it was so amended by striking out first one part and then another, that nothing of it was left but the portion providing a Government for the Territory of Utah,

---

11. What great event occurred on the 9th of July? Who acceded to the Presidency on the death of Gen. Taylor? Who composed the new Cabinet?
12. What became of Mr. Clay's "Omnibus Bill"? What is said of the new principle established in 1850 to govern the Territorial policy? When was California admitted into the Union?

with the Amendment of the 17th of June incorporated in it, as stated. This part of "The Omnibus Bill," as it was called, passed the Senate on the 1st of August. The other parts were taken up, and separately passed afterwards. All of them were severally taken up in the House, where they also passed, with the Senate Amendment of the 17th of June to the Utah Bill incorporated into Mr. Clay's original provision for a Territorial Government in New Mexico. In this way all these questions were disposed of, adjusted, and settled by the Congress of 1850. These Territorial Bills for governments in Utah and New Mexico, embraced in each portions of the Louisiana purchase, to which the Missouri line of 36° 30' was intended to apply. This line was no longer recognized after its repeated repudiation by the Restrictionists, to whom it was at first offered as a compromise upon the principle of a fair division of the public domain. When they refused to stand upon this principle, the other principle of non-intervention, in lieu of it, was established in 1850. Notwithstanding the discordant elements in Congress at the time, it received the sanction of a majority of the States in the Senate and House.

Under this adjustment the people of California were admitted as a separate State into the Union on the 9th of September, 1850.

13. The amicable settlement of these questions, thus effected, received public approval everywhere, and gave great gratification to an overwhelming majority of the people throughout the Union.

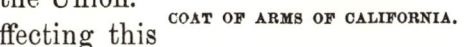

COAT OF ARMS OF CALIFORNIA.

Mr. Clay's acts in effecting this adjustment constituted the crowning glory of his life. The party animosities of former years were forgotten. He now had the confidence, friendship, and admiration of

---

13. What is said of the settlement of 1850? What of Mr. Clay?

Free-Traders and Protectionists, of Bank Whigs and Jackson Democrats. He never more took an active part in public affairs; but, continuing to hold his seat, he returned to Washington in the Winter of 1851, where he remained, gradually failing in health with the infirmities of age, until the 29th of June, 1852, when, after having passed the 75th anniversary of his birth, he gradually and quietly sank to his last rest, leaving the country at peace with the world and at peace with itself. The midday of the life of but few public men was ever more stormy than his had been, while that of none ever closed with a more tranquil and glorious sunset.

14. During the Fall of this year (1852) another Presidential election took place. The two great parties, Whig and Democratic, still held their nominal organizations, and both held their nominating Conventions at Baltimore this year. The Democratic Convention met on the 1st of June, and put in nomination for the Presidency General Franklin Pierce, of N. H., a Strict Constructionist of the "straitest sect" of the Jeffersonian school; and for the Vice-Presidency William R. King, of Ala., of the same class of statesmen. The Whigs met on the 16th of June, and put in nomination for the Presidency General Winfield Scott, the Commander-in-chief of the Army; and for the Vice-Presidency William A. Graham, of N. C.

The settlement of the Slavery Question by the adjustment, or "Compromise Measures," as they were called, of 1850, was so popular in the country that both these parties, in their platforms of principles, pledged themselves to stand by and maintain them. In accepting the nomination tendered him, Gen. Pierce gave the Democratic platform his cordial approval. In accepting the nomination

---

14. When did the next Presidential election come off? What is said of the parties, and their nominations for this election? What positions did the Democratic and Whig parties take upon the Compromise measures of 1850? What was the difference between Gen. Pierce and Gen. Scott upon these measures? What is said of the Free-Soil Party's nominations?

tendered him by the Whigs, Gen. Scott cautiously avoided endorsing that portion of the Whig platform which pledged the party to an "acceptance of, and an acquiescence in, the measures of 1850, the Act known as the Fugitive Slave Law included, as a settlement in principle and substance of the dangerous and exciting questions which they embraced."

The Anti-Slavery Agitators also held a Convention at Pittsburg, Penn., on the 11th of August, at which they put in nomination for the Presidency John P. Hale, of N. H., and for the Vice-Presidency George W. Julian, of Ind.

15. The result of the election by the Colleges was: 254 Electoral votes for Pierce and King, and 42 for Scott and Graham; by States, 27 for Pierce and King, and 4 for Scott and Graham. The States which voted for Pierce were: Maine, New Hampshire, Rhode Island, Connecticut, New York, New Jersey, Pennsylvania, Delaware, Maryland, Virginia, North Carolina, South Carolina, Georgia, Ohio, Louisiana, Mississippi, Indiana, Illinois, Alabama, Missouri, Arkansas, Michigan, Florida, Texas, Iowa, Wisconsin, California. Those that voted for Scott were: Massachusetts, Vermont, Kentucky, and Tennessee. The Free-Soil ticket received no Electoral vote, but out of the popular vote of nearly three millions and a half, it polled 155,825 individual votes, being little over half of what it polled at the previous election.

16. During the canvass preceding this election the whole country was again thrown into mourning by the announcement of the death of Mr. Webster, the last survivor of the great Senatorial "Trio." He expired at his residence at Marshfield, Mass., on the 23d of October, 1852, in the 71st year of his age. He was decidedly the favorite of a large portion of the people of the United States for the Presi-

---

15. What was the result of the election by the Colleges, and by the States?
16. What is said of the death of Mr. Webster? What of Mr. Fillmore, and his Administration?

dency in the election of 1852, and many thousands at the polls voted a ticket headed by his name, even after he was dead.

Mr. Calhoun, Mr. Clay, and Mr. Webster, were regarded as the three greatest statesmen of the country in their day. They were all men of very great ability, of very different characters of mind, as well as of styles of oratory. They differed also widely on many questions of public policy. But they were all true patriots in the highest sense of that term, and were all thoroughly devoted to the Union under the Federal Constitution. After the 4th of March, 1853, Mr. Fillmore retired to his residence, in Buffalo, N. Y. His Administration was distinguished for what was known as the "Compromise Measures of 1850," which restored peace and harmony to all sections of the Union for the time.

CHAPTER XX.

ADMINISTRATION OF PIERCE.

4th of March, 1853—4th of March, 1857.

1. On the 4th of March, 1853, Franklin Pierce, of N. H., the 14th President of the United States, was duly inaugurated, in the 49th year of his age. The oath of office was administered by Chief-Justice Taney, before a very large audience in front of the east portico of the Capitol, the usual place for ceremonies of this character. Gen. Pierce was the most accomplished orator of all his predecessors, and his Inaugural was delivered in his happiest style. It was responded to by shouts from the surrounding multitudes.

2. The new Cabinet consisted of William L. Marcy, of N. Y., Sec'y of State; James Guthrie, of Ky., Sec'y of the

---

CHAPTER XX.—**1.** What is said of Gen. Pierce's inauguration, and his Address?
2. What of his Cabinet?

Treasury; Jefferson Davis, of Miss., Sec'y of War; James C. Dobbin, of N. C., Sec'y of the Navy; Robert McClelland, of Mich., Sec'y of the Interior; James Campbell, of Penn., Postmaster-General, and Caleb Cushing, of Mass., Attorney-General.

3. Among the first things that occupied the new Administration, was the dispute that had arisen with Mexico on a question of boundary. This was settled by negotiation; and resulted in the acquisition by the United States of the region now known as Arizona.

PRESIDENT PIERCE.

This brought to the Union about 30,000 square miles of additional territory, known at the time as "Gadsden's Purchase," at the cost of ten millions of dollars. In the Summer of 1853, under the direction of the War Department, various expeditions were organized and sent out to explore routes for a railroad from the Valley of the Mississippi to the Pacific Ocean.

4. After the settlement of the Slavery Question by the Measures of 1850, which had quieted the excitement for a time, as we have stated, the Agitators changed the arena of their operations. They abandoned the halls of Congress for a season, and in their organizations directed their unceasing efforts to accomplish their objects by controlling local elections. The "Fugitive Slave Law," as it was called, of 1850, was now the main point of their assaults. The execution of this in various places was openly resisted

---

3. What was among the first things that occupied his attention? How was the matter settled?

4. How was the agitation of Slavery renewed? What were the Legislatures of several of the Northern States induced to do? What was the effect of the decision of the Federal Judiciary on the question involved? How were all denounced by the agitators who stood by the obligations of the Constitution?

by mobs and riots, gotten up at their instance. The Legislatures of several of the Northern States were induced by them to nullify the Federal law by the passage of State Acts, known as "Personal Liberty Bills." By these the Act of Congress on the subject was rendered inoperative for all practical purposes within the limits of these States, through the instrumentality of their respective Judiciary Systems. A decision by the Federal Judiciary, that the Act of Congress was constitutional and necessary to carry out one of the obligations of the common compact between the States had no effect upon the Agitators, except to cause them to denounce the court that rendered the decision, and any Union founded upon any such Compact. While little was said in Congress upon the subject, this was the exciting topic in the local elections in most of the Northern States, and unprecedented gains were thereby made to the Anti-Slavery Party. Every one who stood by the obligations of the Constitution was denounced by these Agitators as a "Pro-Slavery" advocate.

5. This was the state of things in December, 1853, when the 1st session of the 33d Congress met, and when it became necessary to organize a Territorial Government in a portion of the Louisiana cession not already embraced in the Utah and New Mexico Bills of 1850. For this purpose Mr. Douglas, Chairman of the Committee on Territories, on the 4th of January, 1854, reported a Bill in the Senate for the organization of a Government in the Territory of Nebraska. In this Bill, upon the subject of slavery, he used the same language as that set forth in the Utah and New Mexico Bills of 1850. He was careful to adhere faithfully to the territorial principle and policy then established, and which both of the two great parties were pledged to maintain. Then it was that the Restrictionists and Agitators again raised great excitement in the halls of Congress.

---

5. What is said of the agitation in Congress of 1854? Who began it, and how? What did the Restrictionists now say of the old Missouri line ?

Mr. Sumner, of Mass., on the 17th of January, introduced into the Senate a memorial against slavery, and gave notice of his intention, when the Nebraska Bill came up, to offer an amendment reaffirming the old slavery restriction of 1820 over this portion of the Louisiana cession. This opened *de novo* the whole territorial question that had been settled in 1850. The sectional controversy was thus again opened in the Federal Councils, with all its fierceness and bitterness. The Restrictionists and Agitators now spoke of the old Missouri line of division as "a sacred pledge" and "solemn compact" between the two great sections of the Union, which "the slavery propagandists" were about "most ruthlessly and wickedly to violate."

6. When the Nebraska Bill came up for action, it was amended in the Senate by the organization of two governments instead of one—a government for the Territory of Kansas as well as that of Nebraska. Upon the subject of slavery the same words were used in the organization of both governments. After a slight amendment, to make the object and policy of Congress more clearly to appear to be in strict conformity with the principle of Non-Intervention established in 1850, this Bill passed the Senate on the 3d of March, 1854, by a majority of nearly two to one; the yeas were 27, and the nays 14. By States, in that body, the vote stood: for it 21, and against it only 7; three States were divided. The same Bill, with one or two slight amendments, not changing the substance on any of the main points, passed the House on the 20th of May, by a vote of 113 in favor of it, and 100 against it. By States, in the House, the vote on this bill stood: 18 for it, and 13 against it. It received the prompt approval of the President, and is known as the Kansas and Nebraska Act. This is the legislation of 1854, about which so much has been said and written, and which constitutes the distinguishing feature of Gen. Pierce's Administration.

---

6. What amendment was made to the Nebraska Bill? What language was used in this and the Kansas Bill upon the subject of slavery?

7. Its object was to carry out in good faith the adjustment policy of 1850; but it was used by the Agitators in connection with the Fugitive Slave Act, another measure of that adjustment, in arousing the Anti-Slavery element everywhere to its intensest fury. A remnant of the Whig party, without regard to their solemn pledge to maintain the adjustment of 1850, "in principle and in substance," being now in opposition to the Administration, rather favored than opposed the agitation which ensued. Indeed, some of the leading men of this remnant took the lead in the agitation.

8. Under the Territorial policy of 1850, the public domain was to remain open and free alike for settlement and colonization by citizens of all the States with their " bondsmen," and property of every kind, without any discrimination for or against any class of persons; and the settlers were to regulate their own domestic institutions in their own way, with the perfect right of local self-government, without any limitations except such as are prescribed in the Constitution of the United States. The plan of operations adopted by the Agitators immediately after the passage of the Kansas and Nebraska Act, was to create trouble and dissensions among the settlers in these Territories. For this purpose Emigrant Aid Societies were formed by them in the Northern States; moneys were collected; arms were purchased and put into the hands of their mercenary emigrants, whose object was not colonization so much as agitation. Civil strife soon ensued, and what was known as the "Kansas War" followed. In this the celebrated John Brown obtained his first notoriety. The Administration, however, succeeded in preserving the general peace by strict and faithful maintenance of the laws.

---

7. What was the object of the Kansas-Nebraska Bill? How was it used by the agitators? What is said of a remnant of the Whig party?

8 What is said of the Territorial policy of 1850? What is said of the plan adopted by the agitators after the passage of the Kansas Bill? What followed? Who figured in it?

9. About this time a new political party sprung up, which soon extended throughout the Union. It was organized upon principles of secrecy. Its distinctive features were opposition to the election of Roman Catholics, and persons of foreign birth, to any office. The name assumed was the American Party; though it was most generally at the time designated by the appellation of "Know-Nothing."

In this state of things the elections of 1854 resulted adversely to the Administration. Those of 1855 were more favorable; but the combined opposition returned a large Anti-Administration majority to the House in the 34th Congress, which met in December, 1855.

10. Owing to the discordant elements of which this House was composed, no organization took place until the 1st of February, 1856, when Nathaniel P. Banks, of Mass., was declared Speaker, under a resolution similar to that adopted for the organization of the 31st Congress. In politics he was an Anti-Slavery American, or "Know-Nothing," as the party was commonly called, though he was not the regular nominee of that party. The Kansas difficulties were the chief subjects of discussion at this session. The seat of John W. Whitfield, a Democrat, who had been returned as a Delegate to the House from Kansas, was contested by the Agitators, upon the ground of fraud and violence resorted to by his supporters at the election. A committee was raised and sent to Kansas to make an investigation and report. Every means was resorted to to increase the excitement. The report consisted of over eleven hundred pages. The result was, that Whitfield was ultimately by vote of the House declared to be entitled to his seat. In this state of things the Presidential election of the Fall of 1856 took place. The Democratic party in the House

---

9. What is said of the new party that sprung up about this time? What is said of the elections in 1854-5?
10. What is said of the organization of the House on the meeting of the 34th Congress? What were the chief subjects of discussion at this session? What is said of the election of John W. Whitfield as a Delegate to the House? On what issue did the Democratic party then organize in the House?

organized themselves upon the principle of adhering to the Territorial policy of 1850, as carried out in the legislation of 1854.

11. The General Nominating Convention of this party met at Cincinnati on the 2d day of June, and presented the name of James Buchanan, of Penn., as their candidate for the Presidency, and that of John C. Breckinridge, of Ky., as their candidate for the Vice-Presidency.

After repeating their pledge to adhere to the adjustment of the questions of Slavery as made in 1850, they declared their distinct approval of the legislation of Congress of 1854, in carrying out the Territorial policy thereby established.

12. All the elements of the Anti-Slavery party met in Convention at Philadelphia, on the 17th of June, and organized for the first time under the popular name of "Republicans." They put in nomination for the Presidency, John C. Frémont, of Cal.; and for the Vice-Presidency, William L. Dayton, of N. J.

In their platform they proclaimed it to be "both the right and the duty of Congress to prohibit in the Territories, those twin relics of barbarism—Polygamy and Slavery."

13. The "American Party," so called, had previously held their Convention at Philadelphia, and nominated for the Presidency, Mr. Fillmore; and for the Vice-Presidency, Andrew J. Donelson, of Tenn.

The chief feature in their platform was opposition to what was called "Alien Suffrage." They affirmed the principles of the Compromise Measures of 1850.

Thus were presented the prominent issues in the canvass.

14. The result was the election of Mr. Buchanan and Mr. Breckinridge. The vote by the Colleges was: 174

---

11. What is said of the General Nominating Convention of the Democratic party?
12. What of the Convention of the elements of the Anti-Slavery party?
13. What of the American party, and the issues presented?
14. What was the result of the election by the Colleges? What by the States?

Electoral votes for Buchanan and Breckinridge; 114 for Frémont and Dayton, and 8 for Fillmore and Donelson. The vote by States was: 19 for the Democratic ticket; 11 for the Republican, and one for the American. The 19 States that voted for Mr. Buchanan were: New Jersey, Pennsylvania, Delaware, Virginia, North Carolina, South Carolina, Georgia, Kentucky, Tennessee, Louisiana, Mississippi, Indiana, Illinois, Alabama, Missouri, Arkansas, Florida, Texas, and California; the 11 that voted for Frémont were: Maine, New Hampshire, Massachusetts, Rhode Island, Connecticut, Vermont, New York, Ohio, Michigan, Iowa, and Wisconsin; the one that voted for Mr. Fillmore was Maryland.

This was not only a very emphatic popular re-endorsement of the Territorial policy established in 1850, but a like popular approval of the legislation of 1854, carrying it out.

15. The last session of the 34th Congress, which met the 1st of December, 1856, was distinguished for two measures. One was a further reduction of the Tariff, on the principle of free trade, which was approved on the 3d of March, 1857, and is known as the "Tariff of 1857." The other was the passage of an Act of Congress authorizing the people of Kansas to organize a State Constitution, preparatory to admission into the Union. This Act was exceedingly well guarded in its provisions for a full and fair expression of the popular will. After the expiration of his term of office, on the 4th of March, 1857, Gen. Pierce retired to his home in Concord, N. H., with the confidence and esteem of a large majority of the true friends of the Union under the Constitution in all sections of the country.

---

15. What two important Acts of Congress are referred to? What is said of President Pierce?

CHAPTER XXI.

ADMINISTRATION OF BUCHANAN.

4th of March, 1857—4th of March, 1861.

1. JAMES BUCHANAN, of Penn., the 15th President, was inaugurated on the 4th of March, 1857, in the 66th year of his age.

PRESIDENT BUCHANAN.

The oath of office was administered by Chief-Justice Taney. His Inaugural was conciliatory, and approbatory of the principles of the Kansas and Nebraska Bill, upon which he had been elected. These were, in his opinion, as declared in his letter accepting his nomination, "founded upon principles as ancient as free government itself."

2. The new Cabinet consisted of Lewis Cass, of Mich., Sec'y of State; Howell Cobb, of Ga., Sec'y of the Treasury; John B. Floyd, of Va., Sec'y of War; Isaac Toucey, of Conn., Sec'y of the Navy; Jacob Thompson, of Miss., Sec'y of Interior; Aaron V. Brown, of Tenn., Postmaster-General, and Jeremiah S. Black, of Penn., Attorney-General.

3. The two principal subjects which immediately engaged the attention of the new Administration were, the state of affairs in Utah and Kansas.

The trouble in Utah was with the Mormons. This sect of religionists, which tolerates a plurality of wives, had emigrated from Illinois, where they were not allowed to remain, to the Valley of the Great Salt Lake, some years

---

CHAPTER XXI.—**1.** What is said of the Inauguration of Mr. Buchanan?
2. What of his Cabinet?
3. What two subjects engaged his immediate attention? What of Utah?

before the acquisition of that territory by the United States. On the organization of a government for the Territory of Utah, which embraced this settlement, and the only settlement of white people in that wilderness region, Mr. Fillmore had appointed Brigham Young, the leader and chief apostle of this sect, Governor of the Territory. About the time of Mr. Buchanan's accession to office, intelligence was received of serious differences between Gov. Young and other subordinate officers of the Government. His whole religious organization were supposed to be preparing to resist the execution of the laws of the United States. Col. Albert Sidney Johnston, of the army, was therefore despatched with a sufficient military force to maintain law and order. The expedition set out early in the Summer of 1857.

4. A few days after the inauguration of Mr. Buchanan, the Supreme Court of the United States had, in a case before it, given a judicial decision upon the constitutionality of "the old Missouri Restriction," which embraced the Territory of Kansas. This court held, that Congress had no power to prohibit slavery in any of the territories of the Union; and that the restriction incorporated in the Missouri Act of 1820, whether as a compromise or not, was utterly inoperative and void from the beginning. This judgment was rendered in the famous "Dred Scott" case. The decision of the highest judicial tribunal of the country, thus pronounced upon the long-vexed question, so far from quieting the Agitators, only tended to arouse and inflame them. The strongest terms of abuse and vituperation were by them hurled against the court, and especially against the accomplished and venerable Chief Justice, by whom the judgment had been delivered. Every effort was now made by them to bring on a conflict of arms in Kan-

---

4. What of Kansas? What of the decision of the Supreme Court? How was this decision received by the Agitators? What plan was adopted by them in Kansas? What did the Administration do? What effect had it? What was the result? How was the question finally disposed of?

sas; while the Legislatures of Northern States were goaded to further acts of nullification of the Fugitive Slave Law. The plan of operations in Kansas adopted by them was to take no part in the organization of a State Government under the late Act of Congress; but to form a separate "Free State Constitution," as they called it. The policy of the Administration in this state of things in that quarter was harmony; and Mr. Robert J. Walker, a statesman of great eminence, who was in sentiment opposed to slavery, was sent as a special agent to persuade and induce the Abolitionists in Kansas to desist from their factious course, and to unite with all parties in the formation of a State constitution under the Act of Congress; assuring them that the constitution so formed should be ratified by a majority of the popular vote of the territory before it would be submitted to Congress. This also, so far from conciliating, only rendered the Agitators more desperate. They took no part in the formation of a constitution under the Act of Congress, nor any part in the vote on its ratification, when it was submitted to all the legal voters of the territory for adoption or rejection. The result was, the formation and ratification, by a popular vote, of a constitution tolerating slavery. Under this constitution, so made, the people of Kansas applied for admission into the Union at the 1st session of the 35th Congress, which assembled on the 7th day of December, 1857. On this application, the scenes in the Halls of Congress were more exciting, perhaps, than they had ever been before. A Bill to admit the State under the constitution so formed, known as the "Lecompton Constitution," passed the Senate, by a majority of 8, on the 23d of March, 1858. In the House a substitute was adopted in lieu of the Senate Bill, on the 30th day of April, by a majority of 9. Both Houses adhering to their previous votes, a Committee of Conference was finally raised. They reported a new Bill for the admission of Kansas under conditional terms as to boundary and public domain, first to be approved by them. The report of the Conference Committee was agreed to by both Houses; and thus the Kansas controversy was ended at that time. No serious difficulty arose in the territory afterwards.

5. It was on the admission of Kansas under the Lecompton Constitution, that a disastrous split took place in the Democratic party. Notwithstanding the intense Anti-Slavery agitation at the preceding elections, this party had a large majority, both in the House and Senate, at this time. The cause and reasons of the division which now occurred cannot be given in this brief sketch. It must suffice to say, that it was founded upon no practically essential principle, and might easily have been healed if considerations of public interests had prevailed over those of a personal character.

6. On the 11th of May, 1858, the people of Minnesota were admitted as a separate State into the Union.

7. Soon after this, the "Mormon War," as it was called, was brought to a close, under the auspices of Col. Johnston, and peace and order again prevailed in Utah.

MINNESOTA COAT OF ARMS.

8. The 16th day of August, 1858, is notable for an important event in the annals of the world. This was the successful accomplishment of the submarine Electro-telegraphic enterprise, bringing the people of the Eastern and Western hemispheres into instant communication with each other. It was on this day salutations between Queen Victoria and President Buchanan were sent among the first messages over the wires. This month also is notable for the appear-

---

5. What is said of the Democratic party?
6. When was Minnesota admitted into the Union?
7. What became of the "Mormon War," so called?
8. What is the 16th of August notable for? What is this whole month notable for?

ance of one of the largest and most magnificent comets of which we have any account. When its nucleus was near the horizon, its brilliant train stretched to the mid-heavens.

9. The 2d session of the 35th Congress was as distinguished for its quiet as the 1st had been for its excitement. Various efforts were made to effect a personal reconciliation between prominent leaders of the Democratic party, and to repair the breach that had been made, as before stated. These, however, failed.

The most important measure of this session was the admission of the people of Oregon as a separate State into the Union. It was consummated on the 14th of February, 1859.

OREGON COAT OF ARMS.

10. The quiet of the Slavery agitation, which followed the disposition of the Kansas troubles as stated, was of short duration. The celebrated John Brown, before referred to, who had figured in the Kansas War of 1856, and to whom the appellation had been given of "Osawatomie Brown," from the place of one of his murderous exploits in that Territory, made "a raid," as it was called, in Virginia, on the 17th of October, 1859. Instigated by the Agitators, and with moneys furnished by them, he raised arms and men, and concealing his movements under cover of night, succeeded in seizing the U. S. arsenal at Harper's Ferry. His design was, with this stronghold in his possession, to stir up and carry on a general servile war from Virginia South. Though he succeeded in getting possession of the arsenal and armory, yet his daring efforts utterly failed. None of the negroes of the vicinity joined him. His forces were soon routed. He was arrested, prose-

---

9. What is said of the 2d session of the 35th Congress? When was Oregon admitted?
10. What is said of the Slavery agitation at this time? What of "Osawatomie Brown"? What was the effect of his raid upon the Southern mind?

cuted for his crime, and hung under the laws of Virginia. This act greatly inflamed the Southern mind, especially as it was lauded by the official authorities of those Northern States which had refused to comply with their obligations under the Constitution in the matter of the rendition of fugitives from service.

11. It was in this state of things that the 1st session of the 36th Congress convened on the 5th of December, 1859. The discussions between the Agitators and the advocates of the maintenance of the Federal Union under the Constitution, with all its obligations and guarantees, were fierce and bitter. Very little attention was given to any other subject of importance, either domestic or foreign. Southern Senators and members openly proclaimed, that the nullification acts of the Northern States referred to, were a palpable breach of the Constitution; and, in the language of Mr. Webster in 1851, upon this identical point, that "a bargain cannot be broken on one side, and still bind the other," they asserted the reserved sovereign rights of the States, and declared that if those States North which had proven themselves faithless to the Federal Compact should persist in their course, the States South would withdraw from the Union. At this session all considerations nearly were merged in the questions of Slavery, the relations of the States of the Union towards each other under the Federal Compact, and the approaching Presidential election, which was to come off in the ensuing Fall. On the last of these subjects, most unfortunately for the country, the friends of the Union under the Constitution were never before so divided among themselves as they were at this time. They ran three tickets instead of one. One wing of the Democratic party put in nomination Stephen A. Douglas, of Illinois, for the Presidency, and

---

11. What is said of the 1st Session of the 36th Congress? What position did Southern Senators and members take? What is said of the friends of the Union under the Constitution in relation to the Presidential election of that Fall? What was the result of the election, and how might the result have been different?

Herschel V. Johnson, of Georgia, for the Vice-Presidency. Another wing of the same party put in nomination John C. Breckinridge, of Kentucky, for the Presidency, and Gen. Joseph Lane, of Oregon, for the Vice-Presidency. That portion of Conservatives known as the American party put in nomination for the Presidency John Bell, of Tenn., and for the Vice-Presidency Edward Everett, of Mass.; while the Agitators in the main rallied in mass and enthusiasm under the banner of the "Republicans," so-called, who had put in nomination for the Presidency Abraham Lincoln, of Illinois, and for the Vice-Presidency Hannibal Hamlin, of Maine.

The result was the election of the Republican ticket. The Electoral vote by the colleges stood: 180 for Lincoln and Hamlin; 72 for Breckinridge and Lane; 39 for Bell and Everett; and 12 for Douglas and Johnson. By a plurality count of the popular vote, Mr. Lincoln carried 18 States; Mr. Breckinridge, 11; Mr. Bell, 3; and Mr. Douglas but one. The 18 States thus carried by Mr. Lincoln were all north of what was known as "Mason and Dixon's Line;" the election, therefore, was entirely sectional. The popular vote cast for him in the aggregate amounted to 1,857,610; while the like aggregate vote cast against him (divided between the three other candidates) amounted to 2,804,560. This shows how differently the result might have been if the opponents of the schemes of the Agitators had united upon one ticket. As it was, Mr. Douglas carried but one State on the plurality count, though of the aggregate popular vote he carried 1,365,976. The 18 States that voted for Mr. Lincoln, under the plurality count of the popular vote, were: Maine, New Hampshire, Massachusetts, Rhode Island, Connecticut, Vermont, New York, New Jersey, Pennsylvania, Ohio, Indiana, Illinois, Michigan, Iowa, Wisconsin, California, Minnesota, and Oregon; the 11 that so voted for Mr. Breckinridge were: Delaware, Maryland, North Carolina, South Carolina, Georgia,

Louisiana, Mississippi, Alabama, Arkansas, Florida, and Texas; the 3 that so voted for Mr. Bell were: Virginia, Kentucky, and Tennessee; and the one that so voted for Mr. Douglas was Missouri. Mr. Lincoln did not receive the majority of the popular vote in but 16 of the 33 States then constituting the Union; so he had been elected without having received a majority of the popular vote of the States or of the people.

12. Most of the public men in the Southern States looked upon this election as an expression of a declared purpose on the part of the States North referred to, under the control of the Agitators, to continue their breach of faith in the matter of the rendition of fugitives from service, and as indicating such a tendency to a general centralization of the Government, as rendered a longer continuance in the Federal Union perilous to their rights, security, and safety. A Sovereign Convention of the people of South Carolina was immediately called, and by them an Ordinance of Secession was unanimously passed on the 20th day of December, 1860. It was styled—

"An Ordinance to dissolve the Union between the State of South Carolina and other States united with her under the compact entitled 'The Constitution of the United States of America;' and declared: 'that the Ordinance adopted by us in Convention, on the 23d day of May, in the year of our Lord one thousand seven hundred and eighty-eight, whereby the Constitution of the United States of America was ratified, and also all Acts and parts of Acts of the General Assembly of this State, ratifying Amendments of the said Constitution, are hereby repealed; and that the Union now subsisting between South Carolina and other States, under the name of the United States of America, is hereby dissolved."

13. The Ordinance was based expressly upon the grounds that "the States of Maine, New Hampshire, Vermont, Massachusetts, Connecticut, Rhode Island, New York, Pennsylvania, Illinois, Indiana, Michigan, Wisconsin, and Iowa" [all of which had voted for Mr. Lincoln], had enacted laws which either nullified the acts of Congress for

---

12. How was this election regarded by most of the public men in the Southern States? What was done by South Carolina?
13. What was her Ordinance of Secession based expressly upon?

the rendition of fugitives from service, or rendered useless any attempt to execute them, and that Iowa and Ohio had refused to surrender fugitives from justice charged with murder, and with inciting servile insurrection in the John Brown raid, as well as the danger to be apprehended from the centralizing doctrines and principles of the party soon to come into power in the Executive Department of the Federal Government.

14. Six other Southern States followed South Carolina in passing similar Ordinances. Mississippi, on the 9th of January, 1861; Florida, on the 10th; Alabama, on the 11th; Georgia, on the 19th; Louisiana, on the 26th; and Texas, on the 1st of February. These States met by delegations at Montgomery, in Ala., on the 4th of February, 1861, and immediately organized a new Union between themselves, and formed a new Constitution, under the name of "The Confederate States of America." Their Constitution was based upon all the essential principles of the Federal Compact of 1787, with its subsequent Amendments. A Provisional Government for one year was at first instituted, and Jefferson Davis, of Miss., and Alexander H. Stephens, of Ga., were elected President and Vice-President for that period. The Constitution for the permanent Government was to take effect on the 22d of February, 1862. Mr. Davis was inaugurated as President of the Provisional Government on the 18th day of February, 1861,

PRESIDENT DAVIS.

---

14. What is said of other Southern States? What did they do? Upon what were their Constitutions, provisional and permanent, based? Who were elected President and Vice-President, and for how long? When was the Constitution for a permanent Government to go into effect? What is said of the inauguration of Mr. Davis, and his Cabinet?

and selected for his Cabinet: Robert Toombs, of Ga., Secretary of State; Charles G. Memminger, of S. C., Secretary of the Treasury; Leroy P. Walker, of Ala., Secretary of War; Stephen R. Mallory, of Fla., Secretary of the Navy; and John H. Reagan, of Texas, Postmaster-General. The Attorney-Generalship was designated as the Department of Justice, and to this office Judah P. Benjamin, of La., was appointed. The new Government so organized went into immediate operation.

15. On the 29th of January, 1861, the people of Kansas were admitted as a separate State into the Federal Union, by Act of Congress, passed without any excitement.

16. In the mean time great efforts were made at reconciliation. At the instance of Virginia, an informal Peace Congress of all the States was called, to meet in Washington. This body met in February. Twenty States were represented in it— thirteen Northern and seven Southern. Ex-President Tyler presided over its deliberations. The Agitators were ably represented in it; and by them the Southern members were emphatically told that the Northern States never would fulfil their obligations under the Federal Constitution in the matter of the rendition of fugitives from service. This effort, therefore, to close the breach between the States tended only to widen it.

COAT OF ARMS OF KANSAS.

17. The Government at Montgomery despatched three Commissioners, John Forsyth, of Ala., Martin J. Crawford, of Ga., and Andrew B. Roman, of La., to Washington, to treat with the Federal authorities for a peaceful and amicable adjustment, upon the principles of equity and justice, of all

---

15. When was Kansas admitted into the Union as a State?
16. What is said of the "Peace Congress"?
17. What did the Confederate authorities at Montgomery do? How were the Commissioners received? What is said of Mr. Buchanan's position, and his retirement?

matters pertaining to the common property and public debt. Mr. Buchanan refused to receive them in their official capacity. The seceded States had before this taken possession of all the Federal forts and arsenals within their limits respectively, except Fort Sumter in Charleston harbor, Fort Pickens of Pensacola, and the fortifications in the Keys of the Southern coast of Florida, and had transferred the same jurisdiction over them to the Confederate States which had by their consent been exercised before by the United States. Mr. Buchanan made no attempt to retake these forts. While he maintained that a State could not rightfully secede, he also held that he could not, nor could Congress, rightfully and constitutionally resort to coercive measures against the regularly constituted authorities of a State to prevent it. In this condition of affairs Mr. Buchanan's term of office ended on the 4th of March, 1861, and he retired to his residence at Wheatland, near Lancaster, Pennsylvania.

CHAPTER XXII.

ADMINISTRATION OF LINCOLN.

4th of March, 1861—4th of March, 1865.

THE WAR BETWEEN THE STATES: FIRST YEAR.

1. ABRAHAM LINCOLN, of Illinois, 16th President of the United States, was duly inaugurated at the usual place on the 4th of March, 1861, aged 52 years and 20 days. Borne in an open carriage, he was escorted and guarded from Willard's Hotel to the Capitol by an armed military force, under the direction of Gen. Scott, the Commander-in-chief of the Army of the United States. The oath of office was administered by Chief-Justice Taney, in the presence

---

CHAPTER XXII.—1. What is said of the inauguration of President Lincoln? What of his Inaugural?

of an audience estimated at 10,000. His Inaugural Address was read from a manuscript. It indicated no decisive policy, except the maintenance of the "Union," which he claimed to be "older than the States," and his purpose to collect the public revenues at the ports of the seceded States, as well as to "hold, occupy, and possess" all the forts, arsenals, and other public property before held by the Federal authorities.

PRESIDENT LINCOLN.

2. The new Cabinet consisted of William H. Seward, of N. Y., Sec'y of State; Salmon P. Chase, of Ohio, Sec'y of the Treasury; Simon Cameron, of Penn., Sec'y of War; Gideon Welles, of Conn., Sec'y of the Navy; Caleb B. Smith, of Ind., Sec'y of the Interior; Montgomery Blair, of Md., Postmaster-General, and Edward Bates, of Mo., Attorney-General.

3. On the 12th of March the Confederate States Commissioners addressed a note to Mr. Seward, Secretary of State, setting forth the character and object of their mission. In it they said:

"The undersigned are instructed to make to the Government of the United States overtures for the opening of negotiations, assuring the Government of the United States that the President, Congress, and people of the Confederate States earnestly desire a peaceful solution of these great questions; that it is neither their interest nor their wish to make any demand which is not founded in strictest justice, nor do any act to injure their late Confederates."

---

2. Who composed the new Cabinet?
3. What is said of the Confederate Commissioners, and their overtures? What of the reply of Mr. Seward? What effect had this reply, made as it was, upon the Commissioners? What occurred in the mean time? What effect did the news of the sailing of the fleet from New York and Norfolk have upon the Commissioners? What did they do? What did Judge Campbell do? What answer did Mr. Seward give? When did the Commissioners first learn the actual state of things? What did they now say in a note to Mr. Seward?

This was replied to verbally and informally, through Mr. Justice John A. Campbell, of the Supreme Court of the United States. He was a citizen of Alabama, on terms of personal friendship with the Commissioners, and exceedingly anxious to effect a reconciliation, if possible. Mr. Seward selected him as a proper intermediary. In this way the Commissioners were given to understand by the most positive assurances, that Mr. Seward was "in favor of peace," and that an immediate official answer to the note of the Commissioners would "be productive of evil, not of good;" that "Fort Sumter, in Charleston harbor, would be evacuated in less than ten days, even before a letter could go from Washington to Montgomery;" and "as regarded Fort Pickens, in Florida, notice would be given of any design to alter the status there." Forts Sumter and Pickens were the only ones at this time held by the Federal authorities within the limits of the Confederate States, that they felt anxious about. Relying implicitly on these assurances, the Commissioners forebore to press an immediate reply to their note. In the mean time, however, it became known that the most active war preparations were going on in the Navy-Yard at New York. A squadron of 7 ships, carrying 285 guns and 2,400 men, was fitted out and put to sea, under sealed orders, from that port and Norfolk, early in April. When this became known also, as it did in a few days, apprehensions were immediately entertained by the Commissioners and others that it was intended for the reinforcement of Fort Sumter. The Commissioners waited upon Judge Campbell to know if he could get any information upon this point. On the 7th of April he addressed a letter to Mr. Seward, asking if the assurances which he had given were well or ill founded. Mr. Seward's reply was: "Faith as to Sumter fully kept; wait and see." This was when the fleet was near the harbor of Charleston for the purpose of reinforcing and provisioning Fort Sumter, "peaceably, if permitted; but forcibly, if necessary." The actual state of things was not known to the Commissioners until the 8th of April. On the next day, the 9th, they addressed Mr. Seward another note, in which they said, that the sending of the fleet to reinforce Fort Sumter, under the circumstances, was viewed by them, and could only be received by the world, as "a declaration of war against the Confederate States."

4. From subsequent disclosures, it appears that it was the intention of Mr. Lincoln to withdraw the Federal forces from Fort Sumter at an early day, when the assurance to that effect was given; but when this intention became known in his party circles, the Governors of seven of the Northern States, which were under the control of the Agitators, assembled in Washington, and prevailed on him to change his policy. It was after this that the war preparations mentioned were secretly commenced and carried on; and "faith as to Sumter" was only so far "kept" as to give notice, on the 8th of April, not to the Confederate Commissioners, but to Gov. Pickens, of S. C., of a change of the policy of the Administration in regard to the assurance given, and that a fleet was then on its way to reinforce the fort, as stated. Judge Campbell complained of the treatment he had received of Mr. Seward, but could get no reply or explanation. Believing in the rightfulness of the Southern cause, he soon after resigned his seat on the Supreme Court Bench. Fort Sumter at the time was commanded by Maj. Robert Anderson, of the U. S. Army, with a force less than a hundred, and with a very short supply of provisions.

5. Gen. Gustave T. Beauregard was in command of about

4. What is said of the assurance given by Mr. Seward, and the change of policy which caused it to be disregarded? What is said of Fort Sumter at this time? Who was in command there, and with what force?
5. What Confederate officer was in command at Charleston? What is said of his forces, and for what purpose were they collected? What is said of Gov. Pickens and Gen. Beauregard? What of the Secretary of War at Montgomery? What ensued? What was the Secretary's response to Maj. Anderson's verbal remarks to Beauregard's messenger? When and why did Beauregard open fire upon Sumter? How long did the bombardment last? What is said of the fleet? What of the capitulation? What is said of the firing on both sides during the bombardment?

6,000 Confederate volunteer troops in Charleston at the time, collected for the purpose of defending the place. Gov. Pickens informed him of the notice he had received. This was telegraphed by Beauregard to the authorities at Montgomery. The Secretary of War there replied, by ordering Beauregard, " if he had no doubt of the authenticity of the notice of the intention of the Washington Government to supply Fort Sumter by force, to demand at once its evacuation ; and if this should be refused, to proceed to reduce it." On the 11th of April the demand for its evacuation was made. Maj. Anderson, in writing, stated that the demand would not be complied with ; but added verbally to the messenger, " I will await the first shot, and if you do not batter us to pieces, we will be starved out in a few days." This written reply, as well as the verbal remarks accompanying it, was forthwith sent by Gen. Beauregard to the Secretary of War at Montgomery, who returned the following response: " Do not desire needlessly to bombard Fort Sumter. If Maj. Anderson will state the time at which, as indicated by himself, he will evacuate, and agree that, in the mean time, he will not use his guns against us, unless ours should be employed against Fort Sumter, you are authorized thus to avoid the effusion of blood. If this or its equivalent be refused, reduce the fort, as your judgment decides most practicable." This was communicated to Major Anderson. He refused to accede to the terms. The fleet was approaching; some of Beauregard's batteries and forces were between it and Fort Sumter. Should it arrive, while Anderson still held the

GEN. GUSTAVE T. BEAUREGARD.

fort, they would be exposed to attack in the rear as well as in the front. He therefore gave Maj. Anderson notice that he would at an early specified hour proceed to compel him to withdraw from the fort. He accordingly opened fire upon it, at 4.30 on the morning of the 12th of April. This was returned by the guns of the fort. The fleet came near, but took no part in the action. The bombardment lasted for 32 hours. Maj. Anderson then agreed to capitulate. Most liberal and honorable terms were granted; the entire garrison, 80 in all, officers and men, were permitted to be marched out with their colors and music; all private as well as company property was allowed to be taken by those to whom it belonged. As Providence ordered it, not a life was lost in this memorable and most frightful combat. The firing on both sides, at some times, particularly at night, was represented by those who witnessed it as "most grand and terrific." It was but the precursor, however, of many scenes of like character, not less grand and terrific, but infinitely more frightful and memorable from the loss of life and effusion of blood attending them.

6. This was the beginning of a war between the States of the Federal Union, which has been truly characterized as "one of the most tremendous conflicts on record." The din of its clangor reached the remotest parts of the earth, and the people of all nations looked on, for four years and upwards, in wonder and amazement, as its gigantic proportions loomed forth, and its hideous engines of destruction of human life and everything of human structure were terribly displayed in its sanguinary progress and grievous duration.

About this war—its origin, causes, conduct, guilt, crimes, consequences, and results, as well as its sufferings, sacrifices, and heroic exploits—many volumes have already been published, and many more will doubtless be published; but in reference to the whole, it may with reverence be

---

6. What was this the beginning of? What is said of this war?

said, that if *everything* done in it, and "every one" attending it deserving notice, should be duly recorded, "even the world itself could not contain the books that should be written." In this brief compendium its most prominent events only can be but barely chronicled, with very limited comments in elucidation or explanation.

7. The telegraphic announcement of the fall of Sumter enabled the Agitators to inflame the minds of the people of the Northern States under their influence to a higher pitch than ever, and to add to their ranks large accessions from the ranks of the Democratic and American parties. A cry was now raised by them for the maintenance of that Union which they had before denounced as "a covenant with death, and an agreement with hell." Upon the Confederates was charged the guilt of a desecration of the national flag, and with it the crime of treason. The beginning of the war with all its responsibilities was laid at their door. Mr. Lincoln, on the 15th of April, issued a Proclamation calling for 75,000 troops, and convening Congress to meet in Extra Session on the 4th of July. Thus stood the case on one side.

On the other, the Confederates maintained that the silencing by them of the guns of Sumter was only an act of defence in anticipation of an approaching attack from a hostile fleet, as announced by the notification to Gov. Pickens of the intention of the Federal authorities to "reinforce Fort Sumter, peaceably, if permitted; but forcibly, if necessary." This they regarded as a declaration of war, already initiated by the Federals. They held that the war was in fact begun when this fleet put to sea for the purpose stated, and that it was formally declared by the notification given. They stood upon the well-established principle of public law, that "the aggressor in a war" (that is, he who begins it) "is not the first who uses force, but the first who

---

7. What is said of the effect of the fall of Sumter at the North? What did President Lincoln do? How was the matter viewed in the Seceded States? How was Mr. Lincoln's Proclamation met by them?

renders force necessary." They held, that under the Constitution of 1787, by which the previously existing Federal Union between the States had been strengthened and made "more perfect," the sovereignty of the several States was still reserved by the parties respectively, and with it the right of eminent domain was retained by each within its limits—that the Federal authorities had no rightful military jurisdiction over the soil upon which Fort Sumter was erected, except by the consent of the State of South Carolina. This was expressly stipulated in the Constitutional Compact, and when South Carolina had re-assumed her sovereign jurisdiction over her entire territory, the possession of this fort (erected by her consent, for the special protection of her own chief city, as well as the common defence of the other States) justly belonged to her. They maintained further that she and her new Confederates had the right legally and morally to claim and take possession of it; and that any attempt by force to resist the exercise of this right by any other Power, was an act of war upon her and them. Mr. Lincoln's call for troops, therefore, was met by the Government at Montgomery by a similar call for volunteers to repel aggressions. So matters stood on both sides.

8. Mr. Lincoln's call for troops without authority of law, excited no less alarm than indignation in the Border States of Maryland, Virginia, North Carolina, Tennessee, Kentucky, Arkansas, and Missouri. Denunciatory replies were made to this call by the Governors of most of them. Four of these, to wit, Virginia (on the 17th of April), Arkansas (on the 6th of May), North Carolina (on the 20th of May—the 86th anniversary of her celebrated Mecklenburg Declaration of Independence), and Tennessee (on the 8th of June), by Sovereign Conventions of their people with-

---

8. What was the effect of the Proclamation in the Border States? What was its effect in the Northern States? What is said of the seven Governors? What of the riot in Baltimore?

drew from the Federal Union, and subsequently became separate members of the new Confederation.

Very different was the effect of the Federal Executive's call for troops elsewhere. It was promptly responded to by "the seven Governors" of the Northern States before mentioned. Within a few days their organized, equipped, and trained bands were on their way to the seat of war with all the speed that steam could afford. As some of them passed through Baltimore, a bloody riot occurred between them and citizens of that place on the 19th of April, in which several lives were lost on both sides.

9. On the same day of the riot in Baltimore, Mr. Lincoln issued another Proclamation ordering a blockade of all the ports of the Seceded States. This was succeeded on the 3d of May by a third Proclamation, ordering an increase to the Regular Federal Army of 64,748 men, and an increase to the navy of 18,000 seamen. This was followed by a fourth Proclamation on the 10th of May, authorizing the suspension of the privilege of the writ of *Habeas Corpus* in certain localities. Similar authority was soon after given to most of the Federal generals commanding in their respective districts. Under these Executive Orders, great numbers of citizens were arrested and put in close confinement without any charge or accusation. Application for redress was made to the venerable Taney, Chief-Justice of the United States, in the case of John Merryman. This high judicial officer held the Executive Edict to be unconstitutional, and ordered the discharge of the prisoner. The decision was set at defiance. Members of the Cabinet issued "*Lettres de Cachet*" at will. It was about this time Mr. Seward is reported to have said to Lord Lyons, the British Minister at Washington: "I can touch a bell at my right hand, and order the arrest of a citizen of

---

9. What other Proclamation did Mr. Lincoln issue, and when? What is said of the suspension of the writ of *Habeas Corpus?* What of the decision of Chief-Justice Taney upon it? What did members of the Cabinet now do at will? What is Mr. Seward reported to have said to Lord Lyons?

CHAP. XXII.] ADMINISTRATION OF LINCOLN. 431

Ohio; I can touch the bell again, and order the arrest of a citizen of New York. Can Queen Victoria do as much?" Some time after, the Legislature of Maryland was prevented from meeting by the arrest and imprisonment of its most prominent members, by order of the Secretary of War. No criminal charge was then or afterwards brought against them.

10. On the 21st of May, after the accession of Virginia, the seat of Government of the Confederate States was transferred to Richmond, the capital of that State. The Federal Congress assembled in Washington on the 4th of July. Attempts were made to pass resolutions legalizing President Lincoln's Proclamations. These failed. But his acts were excused on the grounds of the "necessities of war." This Congress, however, promptly passed Acts authorizing the raising of and putting in the field 525,000 men, and appropriating over $500,000,000 for equipping and provisioning this immense force; as well as fitting out a most formidable navy, for the prosecution of the war. They also passed a resolution in which they declared "that this war is not prosecuted on our part in any spirit of oppression, nor for any purpose of conquest or subjugation, nor for the purpose of overthrowing or interfering with the rights or established institutions of those [the Southern] States; but to defend and maintain the supremacy of the Constitution and all laws made in pursuance thereof, and to preserve the Union, with all the dignity, equality, and rights of the several States unimpaired; that as soon as these objects are accomplished the war ought to cease."

11. Meantime large armies were marshalling on both sides. Virginia was to be the theatre of active operations. The first movement for an invasion was made on the 24th

---

10. What occurred on the 21st of May? What is said of the Federal Congress which assembled on the 4th of July, and their Acts? What of a resolution passed by them?
11. What was going on in the meantime? When was the first invasive movement commenced by the Federals? What was the point of attack? What is said of Col. Ellsworth and his slayer? What is said of the battles which followed this movement?

of May. This was by Col. Elmer E. Ellsworth, in command of a regiment of N. Y. Fire Zouaves. On that day he took possession of Alexandria. He was killed by J. W. Jackson, the proprietor of the "Marshall House," who was quickly killed in turn. This movement of Federal troops was soon followed by the engagements at Grafton, the 29th of May; at Philippi, the 3d of June; at Big Bethel, the 10th of June; at Rich Mountain, the 11th of July; at Laurel Hill, or Carrick's Ford, the 14th; at Scary Creek, the 17th, and the great battle of Manassas, on the 21st of July. In this, the Confederates, under Gens. Beauregard and Joseph E. Johnston, with a force of about 30,000, met and routed the Federal army, under Gen. Irwin McDowell, of about 60,000, killing, wounding, and capturing "between four and five thousand" men, and taking 28 pieces of artillery, about 5,000 muskets, besides a great amount of army stores.

12. The Confederate Congress met in its first session in Richmond on the 20th of July, 1861, the day before the great battle at Manassas. Mr. Toombs resigned his position as Secretary of State on the 21st, and took commission as Brigadier-General in the Provisional Army. Mr. Robert M. T. Hunter, of Va., succeeded him in the State Department. The most energetic measures were adopted by Congress to raise men and munitions of war to repel the formidable invasion, now threatened.

13. Within a few days after the battle of Manassas, Gen. Scott, Commander-in-chief of the Federal army, at his own request, on account of age and infirmities, was relieved from all further active duty. His place was filled by Gen. Geo. B. McClellan. On the 29th of August, the Federals captured the forts on Hatteras Inlet on the coast of North Carolina, with 65 guns and 615 prisoners.

---

12. When did the Confederate Congress meet in Richmond? What is said of Mr. Toombs and Mr. Hunter? What of the action of the Confederate Congress at this session?

13. What is said of Gen. Scott, of the Federal army? What of the military operations that soon followed?

On the 2d of October was fought the battle of Leesburg, in Virginia, where the Confederates achieved another signal victory under Gen. Nathan G. Evans. On the next day, the 3d, the Federal forces under Gen. Reynolds met with a disastrous repulse at Cheat Mountain Pass, by the Confederates under Gen. Henry R. Jackson. On the 7th of November, the Federals took possession of the forts at Port Royal, S. C.

14. While these things were going on in the East, operations in the West were not less active or portent, politically and militarily. Gov. Jackson and the State authorities of Missouri had attempted, at first, to maintain a neutral position between the parties at war; but Capt. Lyon, the Federal officer in command at St. Louis, believing that they would ultimately join the Confederates, seized the State arsenal and arms on the 25th of April, and routed the State militia at Camp Jackson on the 10th of May. On the 20th of June, raised to the rank of Brigadier-General, he took possession of Booneville, then held by Col. Marmaduke of the State troops. Civil war commenced in Missouri. Gov. Jackson and those acting with him saw that the position of "armed neutrality" could not be maintained. They were compelled to take sides with the Confederates or Federals. They cast their fortunes with the Confederates. Gen. Sterling Price, in command of Missourians, and Gen. McCulloch, in command of a Confederate force from Texas and Arkansas, met the Federals at Carthage on the 5th of July, where they achieved a victory. On the 10th of August, their success was much more signal at Oak Hill. It was in this battle that Gen. Lyon was killed. On the 20th of September, Price took Lexington, with upwards of 3,000 prisoners. On the 7th of November, the day on which the

---

14. What was going on in the West in the meantime? What was the position of Gov. Jackson and the State authorities of Missouri at first? What did Capt. Lyon, of the Federal army, do? When did he take the State arms? When Camp Jackson? When Booneville? What was now the state of things in Missouri? What did Gov. Jackson and those acting with him now see and do? What is said of the battles of Carthage, Oak Hill, Lexington, and Belmont?

19

Federals took Port Royal, S. C., was fought the battle of Belmont, in Missouri; in which the Confederates carried the day.

15. On the 6th of November, an election was held in the Confederate States for President and Vice-President, for a term of six years, to begin on the 22d of February, 1862, under their Constitution for permanent Government. Mr. Davis and Mr. Stephens received the unanimous vote of the Electoral Colleges for these offices respectively. As soon as the fall of the fortresses at Port Royal was known in Richmond, Gen. Robert E. Lee was despatched to take command on the sea-coast of South Carolina and Georgia.

About this time occurred an event at sea which came near involving the Federal Government in a war with Great Britain. It was the seizure by Capt. Wilkes, commanding the U. S. steam-frigate *San Jacinto*, of the Confederate Ambassadors Slidell and Mason, on board the British steam packet *Trent*. The matter was ultimately disposed of by a disavowal of the act of Wilkes on the part of the Federal Administration, and the restoration of the Ambassadors to a British deck.

16. The Governor and State authorities in Kentucky, as those of Missouri, had at first attempted to hold the position of "armed neutrality" between the States at war; but this attempt failed in this instance as it had in the other. A provisional Government was organized by a portion of the people of Kentucky, headed by John C. Breckinridge, William C. Preston, Humphrey Marshall, and other distinguished statesmen, which during the Fall allied itself with the Southern cause. In this way, before the close of the year, the States of Missouri and Kentucky were both, under their Provisional Governments, recognized as equal members of the Confederate States.

15. What occurred on the 6th of November, 1861 ? Who was put in Confederate command on the coast of South Carolina and Georgia after the taking of Port Royal by the Federals? What is said of the *Trent* affair ?

16. What is said of the state of things in Kentucky ? What s said of Missouri and Kentucky ?

CHAP. XXII.] ADMINISTRATION OF LINCOLN. 435

17. The Confederate naval operations during this period deserve special notice, though it must be brief. The Federals at the beginning of the war having possession of the entire common navy, the Confederates at first had no resort in this particular but the enlistment of armed ships under letters of marque. Very soon quite a number of small vessels were thus put in commission, and reached the high seas by running the blockade. Among these were the *Calhoun,* the *Petrel,* the *Spray,* the *Ivy,* the *Webb,* the *Dixie,* the *Jeff Davis,* the *Bonita,* the *Gordon,* the *Coffee,* the *York,* the *McRae,* the *Savannah,* the *Nina,* the *Jackson,* the *Tuscarora,* besides others. In less than a month, more than twenty prizes were taken and run into Southern ports. The steamers *Sumter* and *Nashville* were fitted out by the Government, and went to sea as soon as possible, under the command of regular officers, who had resigned their positions in the Federal navy. The *Sumter* ran the blockade at the mouth of the Mississippi, on the 30th of June, in charge of Commander Raphael Semmes. It soon made many captures of merchant-vessels. The *Nashville* was put in command of Capt. Robert B. Pegram, who at a later day got his ship out of the port of Charleston. By this little navy, so put afloat, several millions' worth of merchandise was captured, which produced a great sensation throughout the Northern States. Their foreign trade was not only crippled, but nearly driven from the ocean.

18. The foregoing presents a brief sketch of the rapid progress of great events, and the general state of affairs at the end of December, 1861. The contest upon the whole thus far was greatly to the advantage of the Confederates,

---

17. What is said of the Confederate naval operations? Name some of the privateers put in commission. What is said of the *Sumter* and the *Nashville?* Who commanded the *Sumter,* and who the *Nashville?* What amount of property was captured by the Confederate navy? What was the effect of this in the Northern States and on their foreign trade?

18. How stood affairs upon the whole at the end of December, 1861? Which side had the greater number of prisoners? What is said of an exchange, and Mr Davis's position in regard to it?

in view of the number of victories achieved and prisoners captured. Of the latter the excess was largely on their side. No cartel of exchange had yet been agreed upon, though Mr. Davis had made repeated and earnest efforts to bring about a conformity in this particular with the usages of civilized nations. Every proposition of this sort made by him had been refused even an entertainment of, by the Administration at Washington. This brings us to the close of a period which, for the better understanding of dates and classification of events, we shall in this Compendium designate as the First Year of the War.

CHAPTER XXIII.

ADMINISTRATION OF LINCOLN—CONTINUED.

SECOND YEAR OF THE WAR.

1. IN January, 1862, at the opening of the second year of the war, the Confederates had in the field, distributed at various points, including all branches of service, in round numbers, about 300,000 men; while the Federals, in like manner, and in like round numbers, had not less than 800,000. About this time Edwin M. Stanton was put at the head of the War Department at Washington, in place of Cameron. The programme of the ensuing campaign, on the part of the Federals, was another movement on Richmond from the Potomac, and a general invasion southward, from the junction of the Ohio and Mississippi rivers. For this purpose two large armies had been organized— one at Washington, under the immediate direction of Gen. McClellan; and the one in the West under Gen. Halleck. To meet these, the Confederates had collected what forces they could in Virginia, under command of Gen. Joseph E.

CHAPTER XXIII.—1. What is said of the numbers of the respective armies in the beginning of 1862 ? What of Mr. Stanton ? What of the programme for the ensuing campaign ? What is said of the battles of Fishing Creek, Forts Henry and Donelson, and Sidney Johnston's movements ?

Johnston, still at Manassas; and in like manner had collected what forces they could in the West, under the command of Gen. Albert Sidney Johnston, whose headquarters were at Bowling Green, Ky. Their other forces were kept mainly in defence of the extensive sea-coast, besides a small trans-Mississippi army. The general campaign opened by operations in Halleck's department. On the 19th of January, the battle of Fishing Creek, in Ky., was fought, in which the Federals, under the immediate command of Gen. G. H. Thomas, were successful. In this battle the Confederates, early in the action, lost their commander, Gen. Felix K. Zollicoffer. This was soon succeeded by two other Federal successes of much greater importance: these were the capture of Fort Henry, on the Tennessee River, the 6th, and Fort Donelson, on the Cumberland River, in Tennessee, the 16th of February. At these places the Confederate losses, in killed, wounded, and captured, amounted to about 9,000 men; and by these reverses, Gen. Albert Sidney Johnston was compelled to fall back from Kentucky, and to take a position south of the Tennessee River. It was in the gloom of these disasters that Mr. Davis, on the 22d of February, was duly inaugurated President of the Confederate States, for six years, under their Constitution for permanent government.

2. The Federals, encouraged by their successes in the West, pushed their movements southward in that quarter. They took Nashville without opposition, on the 23d of February, and there captured millions' worth of commissary stores. Their forces were soon pushed forward and concentrated at Pittsburg Landing, on the Tennessee River. The Confederate forces, under Sidney Johnston and Beauregard (who had been transferred to the West), were likewise concentrated as fast as possible at Corinth, a few miles south of the Landing. Their forces west of the

---

2. What is said of the Federal movements after their successes? What of the Confederates? What of the battle of Elkhorn?

Mississippi could not be brought over, as they were pressed by a large body of Federals in that quarter, and were forced to a bloody engagement on the 7th of March. This is known as the battle of Elkhorn, or Pea Ridge. In it the Confederates, under Price and McCulloch, with a force of 20,000, held their ground against a force of 25,000 under the lead of Gen. Curtis. Maj. Gen. Earl Van Dorn was now the chief in command of the Confederates in that quarter. It was in this conflict the gallant McCulloch fell

3. On the 6th and 7th of April, the two armies concentrated at Pittsburg Landing and at Corinth, met in two memorable combats, known as the battles of Shiloh. In the first day's engagement the Confederates lost their great leader, Gen. Albert Sidney Johnston; but gained a brilliant victory under Beauregard, who succeeded him. The Federals, under Gen. Grant, were completely routed; and nothing saved them from entire capture or utter destruction, but the shelter they found on the banks of the river under the protection of the heavy metal of their gun-boats. With large reinforcements, under Gen. Buell, the battle was renewed on the next day, the 7th, and desperately fought on both sides, without any decisive results either way. The Federals regained the ground from which they were driven on the 6th, while the Confederates continued to hold their original position. These two battles were the bloodiest of the war up to that time. The slaughter was great on both sides. The losses of the Confederates, in killed, wounded, and missing, were 10,699, while the losses of the Federals, according to their own accounts, were over 15,000. The whole number of the Confederates engaged in these battles, according to official returns, amounted to 40,355; while the number of the Federals, under Grant and Buell united, was, according to the most reliable accounts, not less than 78,000—nearly double.

On the 29th of May, Gen. Beauregard withdrew his forces

---

3. What is said of the battles at Shiloh ? What of Beauregard and Bragg ?

from Corinth, and fell back to Tupelo, Miss. Soon after this (on the 4th of June), Fort Pillow, on the Mississippi, was abandoned by the Confederates; and on the 6th, the city of Memphis was occupied by the Federals. Beauregard's health failing, he was succeeded by Gen. Braxton Bragg, in command of what was known as the Army of the Tennessee.

4. While these events were occurring in the West, others of vast importance were transpiring in the East, which now require notice. Under the programme stated, McClellan had organized in Washington, during the winter, a new army, known as the Army of the Potomac, thoroughly drilled, disciplined, and equipped, numbering at least 120,000 men. Its object was the capture of Richmond, and for this purpose it was put in motion on the 8th of March. It was first directed against Joseph E. Johnston, at Manassas, with a force of not over 30,000, all told. Johnston by great adroitness withdrew his small army towards Richmond, and thus eluded the threatened crushing blow. This caused McClellan to change the line of his operations. The plan then adopted by him was to make his approaches upon Richmond by the Chesapeake Bay, up the Peninsula, using the York River as a base for supplies. For this purpose, his forces were conveyed by transports to Fortress Monroe. The Peninsula at that time was defended by Gen. John B. Magruder, with a small

GEN. GEORGE B. M'CLELLAN.

---

4. What is said of McClellan and his army? What of Gen. Joseph E. Johnston? What of Magruder? What of the battle of Williamsburg? What of the battle of Seven Pines? When did Gen. Lee take command of the Confederate army in Virginia?

Confederate force, not exceeding 11,000. To support these, and to check McClellan's movements when they were known, Johnston, by rapid movements, concentrated, as soon as possible, all the available forces that he could command at Yorktown, or its vicinity. By these manœuvres considerable delay was caused in McClellan's advance, and it was not until early in May that he reached as far as Yorktown. Several encounters took place on his advance before and after he reached that place, as Johnston, with consummate strategy, retired before his overwhelming numbers. The most important of these engagements was the battle of Williamsburg, on the 5th of May, between detachments of the two armies. This resulted very much to the advantage of the Confederates. McClellan, with his superior forces, however, continued to advance until he reached the Chickahominy, in the latter part of the month. On the 31st of May, portions of the two armies met in battle on the right side of that stream. This is known as the battle of the Seven Pines, or Fair Oaks. The losses on both sides were great. In the action, Gen. Johnston received a severe wound in his shoulder, by which he was disabled to continue in the field. The chief command of his forces was then assigned to Gen. Robert E. Lee, who had been recalled from the Southern sea-coast. But while Johnston, with his great skill and tactics, had been thus holding McClellan in check, or retarding his advance on the Confederate capital, very important military operations were going on in another part of Virginia.

GEN. ROBERT E. LEE.

CHAP. XXIII.] ADMINISTRATION OF LINCOLN. 441

5. The wonderful Valley Campaign of the celebrated "Stonewall" Jackson,* as he was called, commenced on the 23d of March, with the bloody conflict between his forces and those of Gen. Shields, at Kernstown. This was followed by his notable victory over Milroy, at McDowell, on the 8th of May; over Banks, at Winchester, on the 25th of May; over Frémont, at Cross Keys, on the 8th of June, and over Shields, at Port Republic, on the 9th of June. This most extraordinary chieftain, in

GEN. (STONEWALL) JACKSON.

this campaign, 'within forty days, marched his little army of not much above 15,000, during this period, over 400 miles; sent 3,500 prisoners to the rear; left as many more of the enemy killed or disabled on the field, and defeated four separate armies, amounting in the aggregate to at least three times his numbers." This is the man the thunder of whose guns, seventeen days after his victory at Port Republic, on the evening of the 26th of June, on the rear right flank of McClellan's army (which now stood astraddle the Chickahominy, within a few miles of Richmond), was the opening signal of the ever-memorable Six Days' terrible fighting around the Confederate capital. The whole of these grand military exploits were now, on the Confederate side, under the immediate and entire direction of Gen. Lee. The result of these repeated conflicts—at Mechanicsville and Beaver Dam Creek, the 26th; Gaines's Mill, the 27th; Savage Station, the 29th; Frayser's Farm and

---

5. What is said of "Stonewall" Jackson, and his Valley Campaign in 1862?

* This appellation, which became famous, owed its origin to a remark of Gen. Bee, just before he fell in the battle of Manassas, on the 21st of July, 1861. While rallying his men, he said: "*There is Jackson, standing like a stone wall.*"

White Oak Swamp, the 30th; and Malvern Hill, the 1st of July—was a series of successful victories, which, when the numbers and equipments on the respective sides are considered, have few parallels in history. The loss in killed and wounded was about 20,000 on each side; but the Confederates, with a force greatly less in the aggregate than their adversary, captured over 10,000 prisoners, 52 pieces of artillery, with 30,000 stand of small-arms, and an immense amount of army stores. McClellan's army sought and obtained refuge under the protection of his gun-boats at Harrison's Landing, on James River. So ended the Peninsular Campaign, as it was called. Mr. Lincoln immediately called for 300,000 more men.

6. After McClellan's signal repulse in his movement against Richmond, a new Federal army was organized and styled the Army of Virginia. Its chief command was assigned to Maj. Gen. John Pope. The remnant of McClellan's forces was ordered to Acquia Creek, and put under the direction of the new chieftain, whose plan was to attack Richmond on a different line. Lee despatched Jackson to watch the new Federal commander's movements. His advance under Gen. Banks was met by Jackson, on the 9th of August. The battle of Cedar Run ensued. In this Jackson was victorious. When Lee learned the state of affairs, and the number of forces concentrated under Pope, with his intention to move on Richmond overland from that direction, he moved all his forces from about Richmond, with which he set out to meet and repel the threatened advance. The two armies met on the 30th of August, on the rolling grounds of Manassas, where the first great battle of the war had been fought, the year before. In this another great victory was achieved by Lee: Pope was completely routed, and driven to his fortifications near Washington. The Federal loss was not less than 30,000

---

6. Who succeeded McClellan in command of the Federal forces? What is said of the battles of Cedar Run and the second battle of Manassas?

men. Eight generals were killed; 9,000 prisoners taken, with 30 pieces of artillery, and 30,000 stand of small-arms. McClellan was again put in command of all the Federal forces in and around Washington.

7. While these things were going on in the East, equally stirring events were occurring in the West. The Army of Tennessee having been recruited to the number of about 50,000, Bragg set out upon a campaign for the recovery of Tennessee and Kentucky. This terminated with the two battles of Richmond and Perryville in the latter State. The one at Richmond was fought near the last of the month, by Gen. E. Kirby Smith on the Confederate side, and Gens. Manson and Nelson on the Federal. It closed with a complete Confederate victory; the Federals were utterly routed. The battle of Perryville was fought on the 7th of October, under the auspices of Gen. Bragg himself. The end of this was his retirement, with all his forces, from Kentucky, and his taking position at or near Murfreesboro', Tenn. The fruits of this campaign were not very satisfactory to the authorities on either side. Gen. Buell, who was chief in command of the Federal forces against Bragg, was superseded on the 30th of October by Gen. Rosecrans. This new commander commenced active operations to drive Bragg from Murfreesboro'. Meantime Bragg was making active preparations for renewed aggressive movements himself. These two armies being about equally matched in numbers—40,000 on each side—met on the 31st of December. The result was the bloody conflict known as the battle of Murfreesboro'. It

GENERAL ROSECRANS.

---

7. What is said of Bragg's Western Campaign? What of the battles of Richmond, Ky., Perryville, Ky., and Murfreesboro, Tenn. ?

lasted two days. The fighting on both sides was heroic and desperate. A Federal writer, in giving an account of it, gives the loss of killed and wounded on both sides at "near 25,000 men, of which appalling aggregate the sum of above 10,000 was from the Confederate, and of about 14,000 from the Union army." Neither side acknowledged defeat.

8. We turn again to the East, and note the operations in the meantime of the Army of Virginia under Lee. Soon after his great victory at the second battle of Manassas, this renowned chieftain made a movement over the Potomac into Maryland. On the 14th of September the battle of Boonesboro', or South Mountain, was fought between detachments of the two armies, in which the Confederates sustained a loss. On the 15th, Harper's Ferry, occupied by the Federals, was taken by Gen. Stonewall Jackson. The Confederates here captured 11,000 prisoners, besides 73 pieces of artillery and 13,000 stand of small-arms. Two days afterwards, on the 17th, was fought the great drawn battle between Lee and McClellan, at Sharpsburg. The relative forces were about 60,000 men under Lee, and 120,000 under McClellan. The combat raged all day. The losses on both sides were great—not less in the aggregate than 25,000. Both armies held their ground. But upon McClellan's receiving large reinforcements, Lee returned to Virginia.

9. On the 22d of September the "Seven Governors," before mentioned, joined by five others of like character and intent (after having waited upon Mr. Lincoln by deputation), met in secret junto at Altoona, Penn. What was said by them to Mr. Lincoln, or done by them during their session at Altoona, was not made known. It was understood, however, that their business was to demand of the

---

8. What is said of Lee's campaign into Maryland, and the battles of Harper's Ferry, Boonesboro', and Sharpsburg?
9. What is said of the Seven Governors, and Mr. Lincoln's Proclamation of Emancipation? What of McClellan and Burnside?

Administration the abolition of slavery, and not "the maintenance of the Union under the Constitution," as the object for which the war should be prosecuted, and "to place in the hands of persons of strict Anti-Slavery views the execution of military affairs." It was on this day that Mr. Lincoln issued his celebrated Emancipation Proclamation; and shortly afterwards, on the 5th of November, McClellan was again removed from the command of the Army of the Potomac, and Gen. Ambrose E. Burnside, supposed to be in sympathy with the Agitators, was assigned to the position.

10. This new chief immediately commenced active operations for another movement against Richmond. His chosen line of attack was by way of Fredericksburg. He found himself confronted by Lee, and here, on the 13th of December, the two armies again tried their strength. The Federals still greatly exceeded the Confederates in numbers. The result, however, was the achievement by Lee of another most brilliant victory. The aggregate loss of the Confederates was 4,361; while that of the Federals was 12,321. By this shock Burnside's movement was completely arrested. Both armies thus quietly remained, confronting each other, on the opposite banks of the Rappahannock, during the remainder of the year.

11. While all these operations by the land forces on both sides were going on in the East and the West, the doings of the respective navies in the meantime deserve notice. On the 8th of February of this year, Gen. Burnside, by the aid of the Federal fleets, captured Roanoke Island on the coast of North Carolina. On the 8th of March the *Virginia*, a Confederate iron-clad war-vessel, which had been constructed at Norfolk, a sort of sea-monster, attacked the Federal fleet near the mouth of James River. It soon de-

---

10. What is said of Burnside's movement on Richmond, and of the battle of Fredericksburg?
11. What is said of the naval movements during the year? What of the *Virginia?* What of the fall of Newbern? What of the fall of Island No. 10? What of Fort Pulaski? What of Forts Jackson and St. Philip? What of Fort Macon? What of the attack on **Drury's Bluff?** What of the doings of the Confederate war-ships *Florida* and *Alabama?*

stroyed the Federal sloop-of-war *Cumberland* and the frigate *Congress*, and promised to clear the port in a few days; but her career was soon checked. During the night of the 8th, the *Monitor*, a new and curiously constructed iron-clad war-ship, arrived from New York. She attacked the *Virginia* on the 9th, and so damaged her that she was compelled to return to her moorings. On the 14th of March, Newbern, N. C., was taken by aid of a Federal fleet. On the 7th of April, Island No. 10, on which the Confederates had erected their strongest fortifications in the Mississippi River, was taken by the Federals, with their iron-clad boats, after a frightful bombardment of twenty-four days. The Confederate loss here was 17 killed and 600 prisoners, with 70 rifled cannon, varying from 32 to 100-pounders. Fort Pulaski, near Savannah, Ga., was bombarded by a Federal fleet and taken on the 12th of April. On the 24th, Forts Jackson and St. Philip, which guarded the mouth of the Mississippi, were, after several days' unsuccessful bombardment, adroitly run past by a Federal fleet under the command of Admiral Farragut, which resulted in the loss of these forts, and the capture of New Orleans. On the 25th, Fort Macon, in North Carolina, was taken by aid of a Federal fleet. On the 15th of May, a Federal fleet of their most powerful water-crafts, in iron panoply, led by the monitors *Galena* and *Aroostook*, made a most formidable bombardment of the Confederate works at Drewry's Bluff, which defended Richmond against approach by the waters of James River. This frightful display of power was unsuccessful in its objects. The fleet retired somewhat disabled, without accomplishing anything. During the Summer and Fall of this year the Confederate navy, particularly two new war-ships that had been got out from England, the *Florida* and *Alabama*, did immense injury to the commerce of the Federals. Such was the general situation of affairs on both sides, on land and sea, when the curtain of time dropped upon the scenes at the close of the Second Year of the War.

CHAPTER XXIV.

ADMINISTRATION OF LINCOLN—CONTINUED.

THIRD YEAR OF THE WAR.

1. THE plan of the campaign adopted by the Federals for 1863, the third year of the war, looked to two objects— the capture of Richmond in the East, and the opening of the Mississippi River in the West. The Confederates still held Port Hudson and Vicksburg, which commanded the navigation of that river. The first and most desired of these objects was the capture of Richmond. This, in the latter part of January, was committed to Gen. Joseph Hooker, who superseded Gen. Burnside, at Fredericksburg. The other was committed to Gen. Ulysses S. Grant, who had won great distinction and *éclat* for his victories at Forts Henry and Donelson, the year before.

2. Hooker commenced his movements against Richmond on the 27th of April. He had massed opposite Fredericksburg at least 132,000 men, thoroughly drilled and instructed in every branch of the service: for efficiency in every respect it was regarded superior by far to any military organization which had ever before taken the field in America. He himself pronounced it "the finest army on the planet." To meet this most formidable array, Gen. Lee had an effective force not exceeding 50,000 men. Hooker seemed to take it for granted that Lee would instantly retire before these frightful odds, or that he was inevitably doomed to speedy capture with his entire command. Lee, however, did not retire. He gave battle for four days, beginning on the 29th—meeting Hooker's divisions at every point of assault, and by skilful manœuvres made several successful assaults himself. The result of the four

---

CHAPTER XXIV.—**1.** What is said of the Federal plan of campaign for 1863? To whom was the command of their two great armies given? **2.** What is said of Hooker's army, and when did he move? What is said of Lee and his army? What is said of the fighting which ensued? What of the respective losses? What of "Stonewall" Jackson? What is said of both armies after these conflicts?

days' terrible conflict was his driving back the entire body of the invading host. Hooker's whole plan was well conceived, and all his operations for an advance were faultlessly arranged: they failed in execution from nothing but the transcendent skill with which they were met, checked, and thwarted at and around Chancellorsville. The military genius displayed by Lee, in his various movements in repelling this advance of Hooker, will ever place him high in the rank of the first class of commanders who have figured in the world's history. His aggregate losses were 10,281. Hooker's like aggregate losses were not officially reported; on the most reliable estimates, however, they could not have been much if any under 25,000. It was in one of the actions during these four days' fighting that the great Confederate chieftain "Stonewall" Jackson lost his life. The

THE NIGHT ATTACK IN WHICH STONEWALL JACKSON FELL.

fatal shot that ended his days came by mistake from his own lines. Hooker's grand army was so shattered and demoralized by this signal repulse that no further attempts to advance were made by him. Neither was Lee able to do anything for some time but to hold his position and recruit his forces as best he could. By the last of May his numbers were increased to about 68,000. Hooker was still confronting him with between 70,000 and 80,000.

3. We turn now to the operations going on meantime in

---

3. What is said of Grant and his movements in the West? What plan of taking Vicksburg did he finally adopt? When did his transports pass the Vicksburg forts? What is said of his subsequent movements? What is said of the siege of Vicksburg, and the respective forces of Grant and Pemberton?

the West. Grant commenced his movements first against Vicksburg. This was early in the year. During February and March he tried unsuccessfully several lines of approach to the coveted stronghold: first by way of Holly Springs; then by Chickasaw Bayou; then by Williams's Canal; then by Lake Providence; then by Yazoo Pass; then by Steele's Bayou; then by Milliken's Bend, and New Carthage Cut-off; and finally adopted the plan of sending his army down the west side of the Mississippi to Grand Gulf, some distance below, and boldly running his transports past the Vicksburg batteries down to the same point, where his army would cross the river, and, coming up from below, attack Vicksburg in the rear. In this enterprise he succeeded. His transports passed the batteries on the night of the 22d of April. From Grand Gulf he moved up towards Vicksburg, and after several engagements—at Port Gibson, Raymond, Jackson, Edwards's Dépôt, and at the Big Black—and after being joined by Sherman with his forces from Haines's Bluff, he laid a regular siege to Vicksburg, held by the Confederates under Gen. Pemberton with a force of about 30,000. Grant's whole army now, on water and land, amounted to not less than 150,000. The siege lasted for months.

4. Meantime, while these events were occurring in the West, we turn again to what was going on in the East. First it is proper to note, that the people in forty-eight counties of Western and Northern Virginia, who sided with the Federals, and had formed a Provisional Government for that portion of the State, were admitted into the Federal Union as a separate State, on the 20th of April. This was consummated by a Proclamation, issued on

COAT OF ARMS OF WEST VIRGINIA.

---

4. What is said of Western Virginia? When was she admitted into the Union?

that day by Mr. Lincoln. But the business we have in hand at present relates mainly to events of a military character. With these we proceed.

5. About the middle of June, Lee, feeling strong enough, with his army increased to near 80,000, to undertake a Confederate aggressive movement, set out on an invasion of Pennsylvania. *En route* he recovered Winchester from Milroy, and Martinsburg, occupied by the Federals. At these places he captured 34 large guns, many small-arms, and upwards of 5,000 prisoners. He crossed the Potomac at Shepherdstown and Williamsburg. Hooker followed him. Several cavalry engagements ensued without any important results. Lee himself crossed the Potomac on the 25th of June. Hooker was superseded on the 27th of June, and succeeded by Gen. George G. Meade as the commander of the Federal army. The object of Lee's movement seems to have been, first to obtain subsistence for his troops, and secondly to relieve Pemberton in Vicksburg, by drawing off large numbers of the besieging forces to arrest his progress. Advanced detachments of his army reached and took York and Carlisle, in Pennsylvania. Meade hastened with an immense army now collected by the Federals, not less than 100,000, to repel the invasion. The two armies encountered each other on the 1st of July, 1863, near Gettysburg. Here were fought the great battles which take the name of that place. The Federals held an exceedingly strong posi-

GEN. GEORGE G. MEADE.

---

5. What is said of Lee's movements in June? Who succeeded Hooker in command of the Federal army? What is said of the battle of Gettysburg? Where did Lee after this take position? What is said of Meade's and Lee's armies during the Fall?

tion, well selected for defence. This the Confederates attacked with great valor and fury on the 2d, but were repulsed with heavy loss. They renewed the attack with equal spirit and energy on the 3d; but were again compelled to retire, after immense slaughter. Meade held the field and won the day. The Federal loss was about 25,000; that of the Confederates was, in killed, wounded, and missing, not less than 30,000—a loss which they were ill able to repair. Lee returned to Virginia, and took position on the south side of the Rapidan. Meade followed him. Several encounters took place between detachments of the two armies—one at Centreville, one at Bristow Station, one at Mine Run, at different times during the Fall; but no general engagement between these two armies occurred again in this year.

6. We turn once more to the progress of events in the West. On the 4th of July, 1863, the same day that Lee commenced his retreat from Gettysburg, Vicksburg was surrendered to Grant by capitulation, with over 200 guns, and near 30,000 prisoners, who by the capitulation were paroled. This was another loss the Confederates were ill able to repair. After the surrender of Vicksburg, efforts were no longer made to hold Port Hudson. This place was surrendered to the Federals on the 9th of July. The Mississippi was now opened, and the Confederate States cut in twain by this high-road, thus secured to the Federals.

7. We left the armies of Rosecrans and Bragg at the close of the last year sullenly facing each other, after their direful conflict at Murfreesboro'. Bragg fell back to Tullahoma, where he remained for some time. Rosecrans made no active movements until June, 1863. On his advance then made, Bragg continued to retire and fall back

---

6. What is said of the surrender of Vicksburg? Of Port Hudson? What was the result?
7. What is said of the armies under Bragg and Rosecrans? When and where did they again meet in regular battle? What was the result? What is said of the battle of Missionary Ridge?

from place to place until he reached Georgia. There was no renewal of regular conflict between these two armies until September. Rosecrans had been largely reinforced; and after Lee had taken his position on the Rapidan, in Virginia, as stated, he ventured to weaken his force there to the extent of about 5,000 men, which he sent to aid Bragg in repelling Rosecrans's further advance. Soon after the arrival of this reinforcement to Bragg the great battles of the Chickamauga were fought. These were on the 19th and 20th of September. The result of both was a brilliant victory by the Confederates. The Federal forces amounted to not less than 55,000, while the Confederates numbered not more than 40,000. The Confederate loss was heavy—not less than 10,000; while the Federal loss was fully 20,000 men (8,000 of whom were prisoners), besides 49 pieces of artillery, and 15,000 small-arms. Rosecrans fell back to Chattanooga, and sought refuge in his fortifications. There Bragg on Missionary Ridge confronted him for some time. Grant was soon put at the head of the Southwestern Federal forces. About this time a portion of Bragg's forces were sent against Knoxville, where an unsuccessful assault upon the Federal strong works was made on the 17th of November. While Bragg was thus weakened, Grant planned and executed those movements of his forces which resulted in the signal victory achieved by the Federals in the battle of Missionary Ridge. This was fought on the 25th of November. Bragg's army was completely routed. He was soon, at his own request, relieved of its command. He was succeeded by Gen. Joseph E. Johnston. Grant was soon after appointed Lieutenant-General of all the Federal forces. His headquarters after this were transferred to the Army of the Potomac. So stood military affairs on land on both sides in December, 1863.

8. Naval operations in the meantime on the Federal side,

---

8. What is said of naval operations during the year 1863?

though of a stupendous character, practically amounted to nothing, except in the continued blockade of Southern ports. Their other naval efforts were directed chiefly against Fort Sumter and Charleston, and resulted in battering Sumter to pieces; but the Confederates still held and occupied the ruins. The Confederate fleet was still actively at work in the destruction of Federal commerce, but having no port into which they could carry their prizes, it resulted in no available material benefit to their cause. So closed the scenes on both sides at the end of the Third Year of the War.

CHAPTER XXV.

ADMINISTRATION OF LINCOLN—CONTINUED.

FOURTH YEAR AND END OF THE WAR.

1. In 1864, the fourth year of the war, active military operations began in February. They were commenced by the Federals by an invasion of Florida, from Jacksonville, with an army under Gen. Seymour. On the 20th of this month was fought the battle of Olustee, or Ocean Pond. Here the Confederates gained a brilliant victory under Colquitt and Finnegan. Twenty-five hundred prisoners were taken, with three Napoleon guns, two 10-pounder Parrotts, and three thousand stand of arms. Florida was saved by the action. On the 22d of February, the Confederate cavalry, under Forrest, achieved a great victory at Okolona, Miss. By this Sherman's expedition from Vicksburg to Mobile, with 50,000 men, was checked and stopped at Meridian, Miss. He returned to Vicksburg. This was succeeded by other triumphs of considerable importance west of the Mississippi. In the early part of March, Gen. Banks had set out from New Orleans for Texas, by way of Shreveport,

---

CHAPTER XXV.—1. What is said of operations in the beginning of 1864? What of the battle of Olustee, or Ocean Pond? What of the battle of Okolona? What of Banks's movement towards Texas, and the result?

with forces in his command numbering in all not less than 40,000. Detachments of these were successfully attacked by the Confederates at Mansfield and Pleasant Hill, and the invasion arrested. Banks was compelled to return, after having lost in the expedition 14,000 men, besides 35 pieces of artillery, 20,000 small-arms, one gun-boat, and 3 transports. The Confederate forces, operating against Banks, in all did not exceed 25,000 men. Their losses were small.

2. While these events were occurring in the South and West, others of a stirring character were taking place in the East, which deserve special notice. These were the celebrated raids of Kilpatrick and Dahlgren in Virginia. These officers set out from the Federal lines in the latter part of February, on a cavalry expedition against Richmond. The object was to enter the city, release the Federal prisoners, and leave them to burn the city and kill the Confederate President and Cabinet. They both reached the vicinity of Richmond on the 1st of March. Their forces had divided and taken different routes. Kilpatrick came up first, and being met by a force that he did not venture to encounter, retired, and made his escape down the Peninsula. Dahlgren, during the night of the same day, coming up and meeting with a similar repulse, attempted to make his escape in a similar manner, but was killed by citizens of the country in his retreat. We now proceed with operations on a grander scale.

3. Not long after the return of Sherman and his army from Meridian to Vicksburg, he was transferred to the chief command of the Federal forces at Chattanooga. Two grand campaigns were now clearly developed by the Federals for the Summer of 1864, as in 1863—one against Richmond, to be under Grant himself; the other against Atlanta, in Georgia, under Sherman. To Grant's movements, Lee was

---

2. What is said of the raids of Kilpatrick and Dahlgren? What were their object and result?
3. What was the Federal plan of general operations for 1864? Who opposed Grant, and who opposed Sherman?

opposed in Virginia; and to Sherman's, Johnston, in Georgia. To the movements of these two great Federal armies the chief attention and energies on both sides were henceforth directed.

4. We will look first to Virginia. Grant had under his immediate control an army of not less than 200,000 men. Early in May he put about 6,000 of these in motion, under Gen. Crook, up the Kanawha; about 10,000 under Sigel, from Winchester, with a view of taking Staunton and Lynchburg, and operating on Lee's rear. At the same time he sent Gen. Butler up James River with 30,000, to take Petersburg, and approach Richmond on the south; while he himself, with about 100,000, set out simultaneously on an overland march to attack the Confederate Capital on the north, leaving the rest in the rear to be drawn on as reinforcements might be required. The powerful army, under his immediate command, reached and crossed the Rapidan on the 4th of May. Lee, with about 60,000 men, set himself to work to check, thwart, and stay the advancing host in its movement on the Confederate Capital. This he did in a series of battles, beginning on the 6th of May and ending on the 12th of June, as Grant, with his overwhelming numbers, continued to pass his right—first in the Wilderness, then at Spottsylvania C. H., then at North Anna, and lastly at Cold Harbor—which will ever stand among the most memorable of history. Grant, being unable to dislodge him from his fortifications in and around Richmond, which he had thus reached, was compelled finally to seek a new base for further operations on James River, as McClellan had done before. He established his headquarters at City Point about the middle of June. His losses by the time he reached his new headquarters were

---

4. What was the number of Grant's forces? When did he begin operations, and how did he dispose of his forces? When did he with his main body cross the Rapidan? What force had Lee to meet him with? What is said of Lee's conduct in checking Grant's advance? What battles are mentioned? What was Grant compelled finally to do? What is said of his losses from the time he left the Rapidan until he reached City Point?

not much, if any, under 60,000—a number equal to Lee's entire army.

5. In the meantime his co-operative movements so set on foot, had been equally checked and thwarted. First, the movement under Butler was arrested by Beauregard; who, as soon as it was known, hastened up from Charleston with all the available force at his command, and reached Petersburg about the time Butler effected his landing at Bermuda Hundreds, on the west side of James River, between Petersburg and Richmond. This was on the 6th of May, the day on which the fighting between Lee and Grant commenced in the Wilderness. By this quick movement of Beauregard, Petersburg was saved from the grasp of Butler. During the whole of Grant's progress from the Rapidan to City Point, Butler, with his army of 30,000, was "bottled up" at Bermuda Hundreds, as he expressed it, by the superior skill and strategy of Beauregard, with a force of less than half the number of his adversary. The only engagement of importance that took place between them was on the 16th of July, in which Beauregard achieved a great success. Butler's loss was about 5,000 men in killed, wounded, and captured, while Beauregard's was comparatively small.

Secondly, the conjoint movement of Crook and Sigel was arrested by Breckinridge, who met Sigel at New Market, on the 15th of May, and with a greatly inferior force completely routed his command. Sigel was superseded by Hunter. He, with the rallied forces of Sigel, Crook, and Averill, was, on the 18th of June, met at Lynchburg by Early, whom Lee had despatched to that point. Hunter was here routed, as Sigel had been.

6. Grant, being thus baffled in his entire plan, ceased all active operations except laying close siege to Petersburg.

---

5. How was the co-operative movement under Butler met and checked? How was the co-operative movement under Crook and Sigel arrested?
6. What occurred after Grant ceased all active operations, except laying siege to Petersburg? What is said of Early's campaign? What of Sheridan?

In this state of things, Lee sent Early with his small command on an expedition into Maryland, northward of Washington. This was intended to threaten, and, if possible, perhaps seize the Federal Capital, supposed at the time to be bare of forces; or, at least, to compel the withdrawal of a portion of Grant's army around Petersburg and the vicinity of Richmond. Early was met at Monocacy by a Federal force, which he routed; but on approaching the works around Washington, he found them too strong to be successfully assailed by him. He returned after securing a large supply of provisions. Grant sent Sheridan after Early. Two battles ensued between the forces under these generals; one at Winchester, on the 19th of September, in which Early was defeated; the other was at Cedar Creek, on the 19th of October. Here Early attacked Sheridan's forces, he being absent at the time, and completely routed them. Sheridan arrived late in the day, rallied his men, and routed the Confederates in turn. He then proceeded to lay waste and devastate the rich and fertile Valley of the Shenandoah—destroying everything within his reach upon which man or domestic animals could subsist.

7. In the meantime Grant was incessant in his operations against Petersburg. Many gallant exploits were performed on both sides, in making and in repelling attacks upon the works. The most notable of all the events attending the siege this year was the horrible powder-mine explosion under one of the Confederate forts. This was resorted to by the Federals as means to break the Confederate lines. It was fired on the 30th of July, and resulted much more disastrously to the Federals than to the Confederate side. About 5,000 Federals, who rushed into the breach, in hopes of thus entering within the lines of their adversary, were hurled and driven by that adversary into the frightful crater, and there put to slaughter.

---

7. What is said of the siege of Petersburg, and the mine explosion?

8. We again turn our attention to what was going on in Georgia while these events were occurring in Virginia. Sherman, with a force in front and rear about equal to that of Grant, commenced his movements on Atlanta about the same time that Grant commenced his on Richmond. In front of him Johnston stood at Dalton, on the 7th of May, with an army of about 45,000. With this, by his unsurpassed, masterly skill and strategy, he succeeded in checking and thwarting Sherman's designs for months; as Lee had baffled those of Grant. Sherman, instead of offering him battle, flanked him to the right; Johnston took position at Resaca, where a severe conflict ensued, on the 14th of May. Sherman again turning his left by his overwhelming numbers, Johnston again met him in the vicinity of New Hope Church, near Dallas, where conflicts again occurred, on the 25th, 26th, and 27th of May. Sherman again flanking the Confederates, Johnston met his advancing column at Kenesaw Mountain. Here Sherman made two desperate assaults, on the 27th of June, which were both repulsed with great slaughter. He then again swung his hosts around the Confederate forces; but Johnston succeeded in safely reaching, without loss, his fortifications at Atlanta, on the 9th of July.

About this time he was reinforced with the reserved

GENERAL SHERMAN.

---

8. What is said of the movements of the two armies in Georgia in the mean time? What of their relative size? What of Johnston's movements and battles? When did he reach his fortifications at Atlanta? What is said of the Georgia militia? What of Gens. Smith and Toombs? What of Johnston's losses from Dalton to Atlanta? When was Johnston removed? What is said of Hood and the battles of the 20th and 22d of July? When did Sherman enter Atlanta?

Georgia militia, numbering about 5,000 strong, under the command of Gustavus W. Smith, a distinguished officer, who had resigned his position in the regular Confederate service, the year before, on account of some disagreement with the War Department at Richmond. Gen. Toombs, who had, in like manner, resigned his position in the Provisional Confederate army, was now in command of a portion of the militia under Gen. Smith. Johnston's position at Atlanta was quite as strong as that of Lee at Petersburg

GEN. JOSEPH E. JOHNSTON.

and Richmond. His losses, from Dalton to the Chattahoochee, were not over 5,000; while those of Sherman, between the same points, were not less than Grant's from the Rapidan to Cold Harbor. In this condition of things, however, Johnston was removed on the 17th of July, and Gen. John B. Hood put in his place. He has been well characterized as "a successor brave, indeed, but rash." Instead of remaining behind his works to repel assaults upon them, he rushed out to attack the Federals in front. Within a few days, on the 20th and 22d of July, were thus fought the great battles of Atlanta. Hood, with unequal forces, assailed the Federals outside of his works, and lost in all about 8,000 men, without inflicting any serious injury upon his adversary. On the 31st of August he gave up the city, and retired towards Newnan. Sherman took possession of his prize on the 2d of September.

9. Hood soon after projected his famous Tennessee campaign. This was commenced on the 28th of September.

---

9. What is said of Hood's Tennessee campaign? What of Sherman's movements after Hood left Georgia?

His army at this time, after all the recruits that could be brought to its ranks, amounted to only about 35,000. The result of this Tennessee movement was the battles of Franklin and Nashville. The battle of Franklin was fought on the 30th of November. In this Hood gained a signal victory, though at considerable loss. The battle of Nashville was fought on the 15th and 16th of December. It lasted two days. The Confederates here were finally utterly defeated, and almost routed, by Thomas, whom Sherman had left in his rear, with forces amply sufficient to meet this meditated blow of Hood, of which he was fully apprised. In the mean time, Sherman, after destroying and burning Atlanta, had set out anew from that point (on the 15th of November), on his grand march to the sea, with an army of 65,000. As there was no sufficient Confederate force to oppose him, he passed through the State almost unmolested, laying waste the country in a belt of nearly thirty miles in breadth, and reached Savannah on the 22d of December, 1864. So stood the military operations on land on both sides at this time.

10. We will now note the naval operations during the same period. The Confederate war-cruiser *Alabama*, commanded by Admiral Semmes, was encountered this year, on the 19th of June, by the U. S. steamer *Kearsarge*, near Cherbourg, on the coast of France, and was sunk by her. The Confederate iron-clad *Albemarle*, lying at Plymouth, N. C., was blown up by a Federal torpedo, during the month of July. The *Florida* was also captured, on the 7th of October, by the *Wachusett*, a Federal war-ship, in the neutral port of San Salvador, Brazil. The Federals during the year had kept an immense fleet afloat, engaged in keeping up the blockade of Confederate ports. Besides this, they sent a squadron of 28 ships, under Admiral Far-

---

10. What is said of naval operations during 1864? What of the forts commanding Mobile Harbor? What was the only remaining port to the Confederates at which the blockade could be run? What fort defended the entrance to Wilmington? What is said of the attempt to reduce it? What other war-ships did the Confederates get to sea this year?

ragut, to reduce the forts which defended Mobile Bay. This was early in August. The Confederate ram *Tennessee* made a desperate resistance, but was taken on the 5th of August. Fort Powell was evacuated and blown up by its garrison the same day. On the 7th of August, Fort Gaines capitulated. On the 23d, Fort Morgan surrendered. So this harbor was finally and effectually closed. Wilmington, N. C., was now the only remaining port through which the Confederates had any communication with the outside world by sea; and this only by running the gauntlet of the blockade. Fort Fisher still stood in defence of the entrance to its harbor. Against this last Confederate sea-coast stronghold, a powerful fleet was fitted out during the Fall. It consisted of fifty war-ships, including seven iron-clads, and put under command of Admiral Porter, with a large land force under Gen. Butler. A terrific bombardment was commenced on the 24th, which lasted for two days, without accomplishing anything. The horrible explosion of the Butler ship-torpedo, loaded with 250 tons of gunpowder, was equally ineffectual. The enterprise was finally abandoned.

During the Fall of this year the Confederates got to sea, from a British port, another formidable war-ship, the *Shenandoah,* which did immense damage, estimated at $6,000,000, to the Federal whaling-ships in the Pacific Ocean.

11. Two other events of the same year deserve notice. One was the admission of the people of Nevada into the Federal Union as a separate State. This was consummated by a proclamation of Mr. Lincoln, on the 31st of October, 1864. The other was the Federal election of the 8th of November, for President and Vice-President, for another term, after the ensuing 4th of March. Mr. Lincoln had been previously nominated by his party for re-election; and

---

11. What two other events of this year deserve notice? When was Nevada admitted as a State? What is said of the Federal election for President and Vice-President?

with him had been nominated, for the Vice-Presidency, Andrew Johnson, of Tennessee. The latter was a U. S. Senator when his State allied itself to the Confederacy. He, however, continued to hold his seat, and was the only Senator, from any of the States, who did so after the withdrawal of their States from the Federal Union. In this election the Democratic party nominated for the Presidency, Gen. George B. McClellan, of the Federal army; and for the Vice-Presidency, George H. Pendleton, of Ohio. The result was, Messrs. Lincoln and Johnson carried the Electoral votes of every State except three, to wit: New Jersey, Delaware, and Kentucky; though of the popular vote the Democratic ticket received 1,802,237, against 2,213,665 cast for Lincoln and Johnson. So matters stood on both sides at the close of the fourth year of the war.

NEVADA COAT OF ARMS.

12. The year of 1865 opened gloomily upon the Confederates. The greater part of their territory was occupied by the Federals, who had over a million of men now in the field; while they could muster under arms but little, if any, over 150,000. Their supply of subsistence was also nearly exhausted.

13. Early in January of this year was initiated, by Francis P. Blair, Sr., the celebrated Hampton Roads Conference, between Mr. Lincoln and Confederate Commissioners. This, however, did not take place until the 3d of February, and was attended with no practical results. In the mean time, between the initiation and holding of this conference, another tremendous Federal fleet, under Ad-

---

12. What is said of the opening of 1865?
13. What is said of the Hampton Roads Conference? What of the fall of Fort Fisher? What of the movements of Sherman? Who was again put at the head of the Confederate forces to meet him? What was the number of the Confederates now under Johnston? What encounters took place?

CHAP. XXV.]   ADMINISTRATION OF LINCOLN.   463

miral Porter, with a large land force, under Gen. Terry, had been sent on another expedition against Fort Fisher; and, by their conjoint operations, this Malakoff of the Confederates had fallen on the 15th of January. The end was now rapidly approaching. Sherman commenced, about the 1st of February, his advance from Savannah through South Carolina, laying everything waste before him, as he had done in Georgia. Columbia was burnt by the Federals under him on the 17th of February. On the same day the small Confederate force which had continued to hold Charleston and Fort Sumter was withdrawn from that place. This, with the fragments of other shattered armies, amounting in all to about 35,000 men, constituted the entire force that could be brought to face Sherman's legions in their progress to join Grant in Virginia. At the head of this, Gen. Jos. E. Johnston was again, in the last extremity, placed in command. Two bloody encounters took place between his reduced columns and Sherman's increased army: one at Averasboro', on the 16th, the other at Bentonville, on the 19th, of March. On the 23d, Sherman reached Goldsboro', N. C., where he was joined by large additional reinforcements, under Schofield and Terry, and Johnston withdrew to Raleigh. So matters stood here for some time.

14. While Sherman was thus proceeding through the Carolinas, Sheridan, with a large cavalry force, was in motion in Virginia. He came down from the Shenandoah Valley, laying waste the country, and joined Grant near Petersburg, on the 26th of March. Lee, with less than 45,000 muskets, was now pressed in his trenches, extending thirty-five miles in length, in defence of the Confederate capital, by forces numbering over 200,000. On the 1st of April his right was turned, and the battle of Five Oaks

---

14. What is said of the movements in Virginia in the mean time? When were Lee's lines broken? When and where did Lee's forces surrender? To what number were they reduced? What is said of Mr. Davis and his Cabinet? What of the " Sherman-Johnston Convention?"

was fought. On the 2d, Grant, by a concentration of forces, succeeded in making a breach in the Confederate general line of defence, near Petersburg. Lee was now compelled to retire, and give up Richmond at last. Several sanguinary and heroic struggles ensued. The remaining thinned but resolute and undaunted columns of the Confederate chief, like the Spartan band at Thermopylæ, were soon brought to their last death-grapple with the monster army of the Potomac. The tragic *finale* was at hand. On the 9th of April, at Appomattox C. H., the sword of Lee was surrendered, under liberal terms of capitulation. Not much else pertaining to the "annihilated" army of Virginia was left to be passed under the formula of the general surrender then made. On this occasion Grant exhibited the greatest magnanimity. He declined to receive the sword of Lee, and in his capitulation paroled him and the less than 8,000 Confederates who then and there grounded their arms. Mr. Davis and his Cabinet, with the other officials, had left Richmond on the night of the 2d, after Lee's lines were broken, and thus made their escape. At Greensboro', N. C., the Confederate President, in consultation with Generals Johnston and Beauregard, and his Cabinet, authorized Johnston to make such terms as he might be able to do with Sherman, for a termination of the war, and general pacification. The result of this was what was known as the "Sherman-Johnston Convention," which was formally agreed to, and signed by them, on the 18th of April.*

---

* MEMORANDUM, OR BASIS OF AGREEMENT, MADE THIS 18TH DAY OF APRIL, A.D. 1865, NEAR DURHAM'S STATION, AND IN THE STATE OF NORTH CAROLINA, BY AND BETWEEN GEN. JOSEPH E. JOHNSTON, COMMANDING THE CONFEDERATE ARMY, AND MAJOR-GEN. W. T. SHERMAN, COMMANDING THE ARMY OF THE UNITED STATES IN NORTH CAROLINA, BOTH PRESENT.

I.—The contending armies now in the field to maintain their *status quo* until notice is given by the Commanding General of either one to its opponent, and reasonable time, say forty-eight hours, allowed.

II.—The Confederate armies now in existence to be disbanded and conducted to the several State Capitals, there to deposit their arms and public property in the State Arsenal; and each officer and man to execute and file an agreement to cease from acts of war, and abide the action of both State and Federal authorities. The number of arms and munitions of war to be reported to the Chief of Ordnance at Washington City, subject to the future action of the Congress of the United States, and in the mean time to be used solely to maintain peace and order within the borders of the States respectively.

III.—The recognition, by the Executive of the United States, of the several State Governments on their officers and Legislatures taking the oath prescribed by the Constitution of the

15. While negotiations were going on between these Generals, and four days before the Convention was signed, on the night of the 14th of April, Mr. Lincoln was assassinated, at Ford's Theatre, in Washington City, by John Wilkes Booth, an actor of note, and son of Junius Brutus Booth, the famous English tragedian. By the death of Mr. Lincoln the Presidency of the United States again devolved upon the Vice-President. Mr. Andrew Johnson, holding this position at the time, therefore immediately succeeded to the Federal Executive Chair. From the great excitement created by the horrible act by which Mr. Lincoln had been taken off, or from some other cause, the Sherman-Johnston Convention was disapproved by the newly-installed President. Upon being notified of this fact by Gen. Sherman, Gen. Johnston then, on the 26th of April, entered into a capitulation with him, by which he surrendered all the Confederate forces under his command, upon similar terms agreed upon between Lee and Grant. The course of Johnston was promptly followed by all the other Confederate commanders everywhere. The last surrender was that by E. Kirby Smith, in Texas, on the 26th of May. Three days after this, the 29th, President Johnson announced the facts by proclamation, with offer of amnesty,

---

15. What is said of Mr. Lincoln's assassination? Who succeeded him as President? What course did President Johnson adopt in reference to the Sherman-Johnston Convention? What ensued? When, where, and by whom was the last Confederate surrender made? What Proclamation did President Johnson issue on the 29th of May? What number of Confederates under arms were surrendered? What was the number of Federals mustered out of service?

United States; and where conflicting State Governments have resulted from the war, the legitimacy of all shall be submitted to the Supreme Court of the United States.
IV.—The re-establishment of all Federal Courts in the several States, with powers as defined by the Constitution and the laws of Congress.
V.—The people and inhabitants of all States to be guaranteed, so far as the Executive can, their political rights and franchises, as well as their rights of person and property, as defined by the Constitution of the United States and of the States respectively.
VI.—The Executive authority of the Government of the United States not to disturb any of the people, by reason of the late war, so long as they live in peace and quiet, abstain from acts of armed hostility, and obey laws in existence at the place of their residence.
VII.—In general terms, it is announced that the war is to cease; a general amnesty, so far as the Executive power of the United States can command, on condition of the disbandment of the Confederate armies, the distribution of arms, and resumption of peaceful pursuits by officers and men hitherto composing the said armies. Not being fully empowered by our respective principals to fulfil these terms, we individually and officially pledge ourselves to promptly obtain necessary authority, and to carry out the above programme.

W. T. SHERMAN, *Major-General,*
Commanding the Army of the United States in North Carolina.
J. E. JOHNSTON, *General,*
Commanding Confederate States Army in North Carolina.

upon certain conditions, to all who had participated in the conflict on the Confederate side, except fourteen designated classes. The whole number of Confederates thus surrendered, including Lee's and all, amounted to about 150,000 under arms. The whole number of Federals then in the field, and afterwards mustered out of service, as the records show, amounted, in round numbers, to 1,050,000.

16. Thus ended the war between the States. It was waged by the Federals with the sole object, as they declared, of "maintaining the Union under the Constitution;" while by the Confederates it was waged with the great object of maintaining the inestimable sovereign right of local self-government on the part of the Peoples of the several States. It was the most lamentable as well as the greatest of modern wars, if not the greatest in some respects "known in the history of the human race." It lasted four years and a little over, as we have seen, with numerous sanguinary conflicts, and heroic exploits on both sides not chronicled in this Compendium; but many of which will live in memory, and be perpetuated as legends, and thus be treasured up as themes for story and song for ages to come.

17. In conclusion, a few comments only will be added. One of the most striking features of the war was the great disparity between the numbers on the opposite sides. From its beginning to its end, near, if not quite, two millions more of Federals were brought into the field than the entire forces of the Confederates. The Federal records show that they had from first to last two million six hundred thousand men in the service; while the Confederates, all told, in like manner, had but little over six hundred thousand. The aggregate Federal population at its commencement was above twenty-two millions; that of the Confeder-

---

16. What is said of the war thus brought to a close?
17. What was one of the most striking features of the war? What is said of the relative population of the respective sides? What was the number of prisoners taken, and the mortality of those held by each side respectively? What of the aggregate loss of life, etc., on both sides? On what did both sides rely for means to support the war? What was the result? What was the aggregate loss in money expended on both sides, including the loss of property?

ates, was less than ten, near four millions of these being Negro slaves, and constituting no part of the arms-bearing portion of their population. Of Federal prisoners during the war, the Confederates took in round numbers 270,000; while the whole number of Confederates captured and held in prisons by the Federals was in like round numbers 220,000. In reference to the treatment of prisoners on the respective sides, about which much was said at the time, two facts are worthy of note: one is, that the Confederates were ever anxious for a speedy exchange, which the Federals would not agree to; the other is, that of the 270,000 Federal prisoners taken, 22,576 died in Confederate hands; and of the 220,000 Confederates taken by the Federals, 26,436 died in their hands: the mortuary tables thus exhibiting a large per cent. in favor of Confederate humanity. The entire loss on both sides, including those who were permanently disabled, as well as those killed in battle, and who died from wounds received and diseases contracted in the service, amounted upon a reasonable estimate "to the stupendous aggregate of one million of men." Both sides during the struggle relied for means to support it upon the issue of paper-money, and upon loans secured by bonds. An enormous public debt was thus created by each, and the aggregate of money thus expended on both sides, including the loss and sacrifice of property, could not have been less than eight thousand millions of dollars—a sum fully equal to three-fourths of the assessed value of the taxable property of all the States together when it commenced.

CHAPTER XXVI.

ADMINISTRATION OF JOHNSON.

15th of April, 1865—4th of March, 1869.

ACCESSION OF GRANT, 4TH OF MARCH, 1869.

1. ANDREW JOHNSON, of Tennessee, 17th President of the United States, succeeded to the Chief Magistracy thereof, on the 15th of April, 1865, in the 57th year of his age. He was Vice-President, as we have seen, at the time of the death of Mr. Lincoln, and thereby became President. Before the war he had been attached to the Strict Construction school of statesmen; but favored the war for "the maintenance of the Union under the Constitution." He was the author of the resolution of the Federal Congress declaring the objects for which the war should be waged, and which has been noted in its proper place. Great anxiety, therefore, was felt everywhere as to the course he would now adopt.

PRESIDENT JOHNSON.

2. The first indication of his course given by the new President was the retention of all Mr. Lincoln's Cabinet then in office. Some changes in this had been made by Mr. Lincoln. On the death of Chief-Justice Taney, the 12th of October, 1864, in the 88th year of his age (who had presided on the Bench of the Supreme Court with eminent ability for over 28 years), Mr. Chase had been promoted to

---

CHAPTER XXVI.—1. What is said of President Johnson, and his political antecedents?
2. What of his Cabinet? What is said of Chief-Justice Taney?

this high position; and Mr. Hugh McCulloch, of Ind., at the time of Mr. Johnson's accession, was Secretary of the Treasury, in place of Mr. Chase; James Harlan, of Iowa, was also Secretary of the Interior, in place of Caleb B. Smith; William Dennison, of Ohio, was Postmaster-General, in place of Mr. Blair; and James J. Speed, of Ky., was Attorney-General, in place of Mr. Bates.

3. The next important act of President Johnson was his disapproval of the "Sherman-Johnston Convention," for a general pacification and a restoration of all the States to their position in the Federal Union, as we have seen. After this came his Proclamation of Peace, on the 29th of May, as stated. This was after the surrender of all the Confederate forces under arms, and after the arrest and imprisonment of Mr. Davis and all the civil officers of the Confederate States Government and State Executives that could be found. He still continued, however, to hold all the Seceded States under military rule.

4. On the same day of his Proclamation of Peace, 29th of May, he issued another Proclamation as Commander-in-chief of the armies of the United States, appointing a Provisional Governor of the State of North Carolina, and providing for the assemblage of a Convention in that State, to form a new Constitution under which the State would be recognized by him as a member of the Federal Union. This Convention was to be chosen by certain classes of electors under the Constitution of North Carolina as it existed when the war commenced, to the exclusion of others. No new element of constituency was introduced. A similar course was pursued by him towards the States of Virginia, South Carolina, Georgia, Florida, Alabama, Mississippi, Arkansas, Louisiana, and Texas. The people of North Carolina, and of the other nine States named, complied with the terms required of them—annulled their Ordi-

---

3. What is said of the next important acts of President Johnson?
4. What is said of the other Proclamation of the 29th of May? What was the result?

nances of Secession; renewed their obligations to the Federal Union; made new Constitutions for their own government; and also accepted and adopted the Thirteenth Amendment to the Constitution of the United States as a result of the war, which provided for the prohibition of slavery forever in all the States. This had been proposed to the States by the Federal Congress at its last session. They moreover elected Senators and Members to the Federal Congress in pursuance of what was known as the "President's Policy."

5. On the assembling of the 39th Congress of the United States, in December, 1865, the policy thus inaugurated by Mr. Johnson was bitterly assailed by the Agitators, who, about this time, came to be known by the party name of "Radicals." They had a majority in both Houses of the Federal Congress as then constituted, and denied to the ten States referred to, representation in either. They insisted that the Federal Union should not be restored as it was before, but be "reconstructed" upon a new basis of constituency in these ten States. They proposed what is known as the Fourteenth Amendment to the Federal Constitution; but in proposing it, refused ten States of the Union any voice or hearing. This led to an open and violent rupture between the President and a majority of both branches of Congress. Their proposed Fourteenth Amendment was refused adoption by every one of the ten States which was denied a voice in its proposal, and by several of the Northern States. In this state of things the Agitators at the next session resorted to the revolutionary course of declaring the ten Southern States named, to be in a state of rebellion, and dividing them into five military districts, over each of which a military commander was placed. The State officials, Executive, Legislative, and Judicial, in each of these ten States, were all removed; the

---

5. What is said of the Agitators on the assembling of Congress in 1865? What of their policy of "Reconstruction"? What was done in time of profound peace? What is said of the new war thus inaugurated by the Agitators? What of Mr. Johnson's vetoes? What of Mr. Stanton? What of Mr. Johnson's impeachment?

writ of *Habeas Corpus* was suspended in time of profound peace, and near nine millions of people put under absolute military sway. This was all done to compel the people of these States to comply with the exactions made on their line of " Reconstruction." Their line was, to disfranchise hundreds of thousands of the white people of the States to be " reconstructed," with the general enfranchisement of the males of the Negro race of 21 years of age and above, in the same States. It also looked to the fixing of what was called political " disabilities," or " disqualifications" to hold office, on every man in these States who had ever before the war held any office of honor or trust, State or Federal, from the highest to the lowest.

Thus was inaugurated by the Agitators a new war, not only upon these States, but upon the Constitution itself, and upon all the fundamental and essential principles on which the entire fabric of American free institutions was based.

Mr. Johnson vetoed the reconstructive measures thus passed; but his veto was overruled by a two-thirds vote in both Houses. He vetoed other measures of like character, with the same result. A quarrel ensued between him and Mr. Stanton, Secretary of War, who continued to hold his office in defiance of the Executive order dismissing him therefrom. This led to the impeachment of the President by the House on the 22d of February, 1868. The Senate, sitting as a high court of impeachment, Chief-Justice Chase presiding, came to a decision on the 26th of May following, when a conviction failed by a majority of one vote only.

6. Under the military domination of the Radical Revolutionary Reconstructive measures, new Conventions were called in the ten Southern States. The old constitutional constituencies of these States were ignored in the formation of these Conventions. Many thousands of the white race in each of them were disfranchised, while unlimited suffrage

---

6. What is said of the result of the "Reconstructive" measures of Congress?

was extended to the black race, as stated. By these bodies, so constituted, and under bayonet dictation, the exacted Fourteenth Amendment was declared adopted by the requisite number of States to make it part of the Federal Constitution.

7. All the Confederate officials except Mr. Davis, and all other "State prisoners," as they were called, caused to be arrested by Mr. Johnson after the surrender of their armed forces, in May, 1865, as stated, were discharged within twelve months, on parole to answer any prosecution that might thereafter be brought against them by the Federal authorities. Mr. Davis was continued in close confinement, in irons part of the time, at Fortress Monroe. Against him a prosecution for treason was instituted in the Federal Court embracing that part of Virginia. He, however, was never put on trial, though he constantly urged it. Bail was allowed him on the 13th of May, 1867, and the indictment was finally quashed by the Government the year afterwards.

8. During the Fall of 1868, another Federal election took place for President and Vice-President. The Radicals, still bearing the name of "Republicans," met in Convention at Chicago on the 19th of May, and put in nomination for the Presidency, Gen. Grant, of Illinois; and for the Vice-Presidency, Schuyler Colfax, of Indiana. The Democrats held their General Convention in the city of New York, on the 4th of July, and nominated Horatio Seymour, of New York, for the Presidency, and Gen. Francis P. Blair, of Missouri, for the Vice-Presidency. General Blair had taken a most active and prominent part in the war for "the maintenance of the Union under the Constitution;" but was bitterly opposed to the new Radical war upon the Constitution itself. This he held to be revolutionary, and founded upon most glaring usurpations of

---

7. What is said of the Confederate officials and other "State prisoners"? What of Mr. Davis?
8. What is said of the Presidential election in the Fall of 1868?

CHAP. XXVI.] ADMINISTRATION OF JOHNSON. 473

power. The result of the election was the choice of Grant and Colfax by the Electoral Colleges; they received 217 of the Electoral votes, while Seymour and Blair received but 77. Of the popular vote cast, Grant and Colfax received 2,985,031, and Seymour and Blair received 2,648,830. The States of Mississippi, Texas, and Virginia were not allowed to vote, because they had not complied with the "Reconstruction" exactions. Had they and the disfranchised in other States been allowed to vote, the popular majority would most probably have been against the Radical ticket; as it was, it was only 336,201.

9. Some other events of Mr. Johnson's Administration deserve special notice. One of these is, the admission of the people of Nebraska as a separate State in the Union. This took place on the 1st of March, 1867; the whole number of the States now constituting the Union being thereby swelled to the number of thirty-seven, and all, according to the Constitution, and according to the terms of their admission, being "upon an equal footing with the original thirteen."

COAT OF ARMS OF NEBRASKA.

During the Summer of the same year, the Territory of Alaska, containing 500,000 square miles, was acquired by purchase from Russia, at the price of $7,200,000 in coin. The islands of St. Thomas and St. John were also acquired during Mr. Johnson's Administration, by purchase from Denmark, at the price of $7,500,000. It may be further noted that it was during his Administration that ex-President Buchanan died, at Wheatland, on the 1st of June, 1868, in the 78th year of his age.

At the expiration of his term of office, President John-

---

9. When was Nebraska admitted as a State into the Union? What was the number of States after her admission? What acquisitions of territory were made during Mr. Johnson's Administration? How were the acquisitions made? When did ex-President Buchanan die, and at what age?

son retired to his home, in Greenville, Tenn., where he still resides.

10. On the 4th of March, 1869, Gen. Ulysses S. Grant, of Illinois, the 18th President of the United States, was duly inaugurated for a term extending from that day to the 4th of March, 1873. He was at the time in the 47th year of his age. His Cabinet at first consisted of Hamilton Fish, of N. Y., Sec'y of State; George S. Boutwell, of Mass., Sec'y of the Treasury; John A. Rawlins, of Ill., Sec'y of War; Adolph E. Borie, of Penn., Sec'y of the Navy; Jacob D. Cox, of Ohio, Sec'y of the Interior; John A. J. Cresswell, of Md., Postmaster-General, and Ebenezer R. Hoar, of Mass., Attorney-General. Several changes in it have been made since; but none deserve special note.

PRESIDENT GRANT.

11. Gen. Lee, after his surrender in 1865, took the Presidency of Washington College, Lexington, Va., where he continued to reside, and discharge the duties of his new position with great fidelity and ability, until the 12th of October, 1870, when he died, in the 64th year of his age.

The news of the death of this renowned Chieftain produced a profound sensation everywhere. Appropriate honors were paid to his memory in all parts of the country, North as well as South.

12. On the 9th of October, 1871, occurred the greatest conflagration ever witnessed in any of the States. It was the burning of the city of Chicago, in Illinois. The loss was estimated at over one hundred millions of dollars.

13. The administration of Gen. Grant thus far has been

10. What is said of the 18th President of the United States and his Cabinet?
11. What is said of Gen. Lee? When did he die?
12. What is said of the fire in Chicago?
13. What is said of Gen. Grant's Administration thus far?

thoroughly on the line of Radical policy, and strongly marked by measures of very great importance—all tending directly to the centralization of power in the Federal head, and the destruction of the reserved rights of local self-government by the several States of the Union. Of this character may be named, among others of these measures, the Fifteenth Amendment to the Constitution of the United States; which was carried and declared to be part of the Constitution under his auspices; and in like manner as the Fourteenth. His attempt to acquire St. Domingo without authority of law may also be specially mentioned. But the most notable of all these measures is the "Enforcement Act," so called, known as the "Ku-Klux Act of 1871." This goes far beyond anything in the Sedition Act of 1798, under the elder Adams, in its direct attacks upon public liberty. But without further specification, it may be stated, that all the leading features of the present Administration and its general policy point directly, and, if not arrested by the Peoples of the several States at the ballot-box, will lead ultimately, to the entire overthrow of the Federal system, and the subversion of all the free institutions thereby attempted to be secured on the American Continent, and the history of which we have traced.

14. It has not been within the range of the object of this work to treat of the general economic statistics—social, moral, and intellectual—either of the Colonies separate, or of the States united, which mark the progress of Commonwealths, or Nations, in the scale of civilization.

In relation to this exceedingly important view of the subject, it must suffice here to state a few facts only, from which the grandeur of their development in these respects may be seen, by a glance at the general outlines.

15. The whole area of country then, let it be noted, embraced within the limits of the States and their Territo-

---

14. What is said of statistics?
15. What is said of the area of the country?

ries, at the beginning, was less than one million of square miles: it is now near four millions.

16. There were, as we have seen, but thirteen States at first united in a Federal Union: now there are thirty-seven.

17. The aggregate population of the original thirteen Colonies, when they assumed the powers of separate, sovereign, self-governing States, was under three millions, about one half-million of which were slaves, of the black race: the like aggregate population is at present near forty millions, of which over four millions and a half are of the same black, or negro race, now rendered free, as one of the accepted results of the war between the States.

18. The regular and rapid increase of this aggregate population appears from the official decennial census returns. The number in 1790 had reached 3,929,214. This number continued to increase during each subsequent decade as follows: In the year 1800, the entire population of the old as well as the new States that had then been admitted was 5,308,483. In the year 1810 it was 7,239,884. In 1820 it was 9,633,822. In 1830 it was 12,866,020. In 1840 it was 17,069,453. In 1850 it was 23,191,876. In 1860 it was 31,443,321; and in 1870 it was 38,558,371. The figures thus given show an increase of population unequalled in the history of any country; but the advance during the same period in everything else which indicates progress in prosperity and happiness, is no less apparent and striking from the following facts:

19. The tonnage of the United States engaged in foreign trade, in 1789, was only a little over half a million. In 1860, just before the war, it was above six millions.

20. In 1789 the exports were in value a little over nine millions of dollars, and the imports a little over twenty-nine millions. In 1860, the exports amounted in value to

---

16. What is said of the number of the States?
17. What of the population?
18. What of the increase of the population by decades?
19. What is said of the tonnage?
20. What is said of the exports?

over four hundred millions of dollars, and the imports not much under that sum.

21. In 1790, the culture of cotton was just beginning to be introduced. In 1860, the production of this great staple, which has revolutionized the commerce of the world, had reached to upwards of four millions of bales, and constituted the chief article of the enormous exports at that period. Even since the war, in 1870, the exports of cotton amounted in value to over two hundred millions of dollars, and constituted in value more than half the entire exports of that period.

22. In 1800, there were but about two hundred newspapers published in the United States. In 1860, there were, including political, religious, scientific, literary, and miscellaneous, not much under four thousand, circulating in the aggregate not much, if any, under ten millions of copies.

23. In 1790, there were very few Colleges in the United States; not many, if any, over a dozen. In 1860, there were, including male and female, not much under two hundred and fifty, with about thirty thousand students. There were at the same time not much under four millions of pupils at schools of a lower grade.

24. Progress in religious culture and teaching, up to the same period, was not less marked than that in the barely intellectual training. In 1860, there were not less than fifty thousand churches and forty thousand clergymen in the various denominations, with not less than ten millions of worshippers, according to their modes of faith.

25. The value of real and personal property had, in the aggregate, during the same period, swelled to the amount of over sixteen thousand millions of dollars.

26. Railroads, operated by steam-engines, were unknown

---

21. What is said of cotton?
22. What is said of newspapers?
23. What is said of colleges and other schools?
24. What of progress in religious culture?
25. What of the aggregate value of property?
26. What of railroads?

in the world in 1825. It was in 1830 that the first locomotive of this sort ever constructed on this continent, called the "Best Friend," was put upon the South Carolina Road from Charleston to Hamburg. There are now so in operation in the United States, not less than fifty thousand miles of railroads, extending in all directions, from the Atlantic to the Pacific oceans, at a cost that would have seemed fabulous to the fathers of the last generation.

27. The magnetic telegraph was unknown in the world until 1843. It now stretches, with its network of wires, not only over the entire extent of this vast country, from ocean to ocean, but across the Atlantic; and brings all parts of the earth under the influence of a power, which acts upon the whole as if it were pervaded by a common living sensorium. To the genius of Samuel Finley Breese Morse, a citizen of Massachusetts, mankind is indebted for this greatest of all discoveries yet made, in rendering the abstruse laws of nature subservient to the cause of human progress and the highest attainments in civilization.

28. These facts must suffice for the purpose stated. To go into anything like a detail of the instrumentalities by which such results have been reached—of the numerous inventions and discoveries which have been made—of the advances in the various arts and sciences—of the achievements in agriculture and mechanical industries—of the products of spindles, looms, and factories—of furnaces and forges—of the wonders of steam in the shops, and on water, as well as on rail—of the innumerable other instruments of creative power, which contributed so much to the grand whole of public and private prosperity, which are apparent from the glance thus taken,—would require many volumes much larger than the present condensed view of the forms and nature of the Governments of the

---

27. What of the magnetic telegraph? To whom is mankind indebted for it?
28. What further is said upon the subject of progress?

States, and their political relations towards each other, in Federal union, from which these most stupendous results have sprung.

29. In bringing the subject to a close, it may be stated with confidence, that for nearly ninety years, from the very date of their thus entering into union, and up to the breaking out of the late most lamentable war between them, no People in the annals of history made a more brilliant career in all that secures liberty, prosperity, and happiness, and adds dignity, power, and renown to Nations, than did the Peoples of the United States. Rome, in the acme and splendor of her glory, after five centuries of growth and development, from the expulsion of her Kings, did not surpass the point of national greatness to which these States had attained in less than one, from the time they freed themselves from the British Crown. Rome, the most renowned of ancient Republics, it is said fell at last by the weight of Empire. This under her system was inevitable. She was a single Republic. In her growth she did not recognize the Federative principle. In extending her jurisdiction over neighboring States, by not adopting this principle and securing the sovereign right of local self-government to all Peoples thus falling within her limits, but by assuming absolute dominion over them, she necessarily became a Centralized Empire, with ultimate despotism as a necessary consequence. The United States, on the contrary, are founded on the directly opposite principle. They do not constitute a single Republic, but a Federal Republic. Under their system of Federative Union, no apprehension need arise for the safety and security of liberty from any extent of either their boundaries or their numbers.

Now, therefore, that the chief cause which led to the late war between them is forever removed, if they shall adhere to the principle of the sovereign right of local self-

---

29. What is said of the future?

government, on the part of the States respectively, which lies at the foundation of the whole fabric, then there is no perceived reason why they should not go on in a still higher career in all that constitutes true greatness in human development and achievement. But if this principle shall be abandoned—as the present indications threaten—then all that is so glorious in the past and so hopeful in the future will, sooner or later; be lost in the same inevitable despotism of a Consolidated Centralized Empire, which eventuated in the overthrow and destruction of the liberties of Rome.

APPENDIX.

A.

In Congress, July 4th, 1776.

THE UNANIMOUS DECLARATION OF THE THIRTEEN UNITED STATES OF AMERICA.

When, in the course of human events, it becomes necessary for one people to dissolve the political bands which have connected them with another, and to assume, among the powers of the earth, the separate and equal station to which the laws of nature and of nature's God entitle them, a decent respect to the opinions of mankind requires that they should declare the causes which impel them to the separation.

We hold these truths to be self-evident, that all men are created equal; that they are endowed by their Creator with certain unalienable rights; that among these, are life, liberty, and the pursuit of happiness. That, to secure these rights, governments are instituted among men, deriving their just powers from the consent of the governed; that, whenever any form of government becomes destructive of these ends, it is the right of the people to alter or to abolish it, and to institute a new government, laying its foundation on such principles, and organizing its powers in such form, as to them shall seem most likely to effect their safety and happiness. Prudence, indeed, will dictate, that governments long established should not be changed for light and transient causes; and, accordingly, all experience hath shown, that mankind are more disposed to suffer, while evils are sufferable, than to right themselves by abolishing the forms to which they are accustomed. But when a long train of abuses and usurpations, pursuing invariably the same object, evinces a design to reduce them under absolute despotism, it is their right, it is their duty, to throw off such government, and to provide new guards for their future security. Such has been the patient sufferance of these colonies, and such is now the necessity which constrains them to alter their former systems of government. The history of the present King of Great Britain is a history of repeated injuries and usurpations, all having, in direct object, the establishment of an absolute tyranny over these States. To prove this, let facts be submitted to a candid world:

He has refused his assent to laws the most wholesome and necessary for the public good.

He has forbidden his Governors to pass laws of immediate and pressing importance, unless suspended in their operation till his assent should be obtained: and, when so suspended, he has utterly neglected to attend to them.

He has refused to pass other laws for the accommodation of large districts of people, unless those people would relinquish the right of representation in the legislature; a right inestimable to them, and formidable to tyrants only.

He has called together legislative bodies at places unusual, uncomfortable, and distant from the depository of their public records, for the sole purpose of fatiguing them into compliance with his measures.

He has dissolved representative houses repeatedly, for opposing, with manly firmness, his invasions on the rights of the people.

He has refused, for a long time after such dissolutions, to cause others to be elected; whereby the legislative powers, incapable of annihilation, have returned to the people at large for their exercise; the State remaining, in the mean time, exposed to all the danger of invasion from without, and convulsions within.

He has endeavored to prevent the population of these States; for that purpose, obstructing the laws for naturalization of foreigners; refusing to pass others to encourage their migration hither, and raising the conditions of new appropriations of lands.

He has obstructed the administration of justice, by refusing his assent to laws for establishing judiciary powers.

He has made judges dependent on his will alone for the tenure of their offices, and the amount and payment of their salaries.

He has erected a multitude of new offices, and sent hither swarms of officers to harass our people, and eat out their substance.

He has kept among us, in times of peace, standing armies, without the consent of our legislature.

He has affected to render the military independent of, and superior to, the civil power.

He has combined, with others, to subject us to a jurisdiction foreign to our constitution, and unacknowledged by our laws; giving his assent to their acts of pretended legislation:

For quartering large bodies of armed troops among us:

For protecting them, by a mock trial, from punishment, for any murders which they should commit on the inhabitants of these States:

For cutting off our trade with all parts of the world:

For imposing taxes on us without our consent:

For depriving us, in many cases, of the benefits of trial by jury:

For transporting us beyond seas to be tried for pretended offences:

For abolishing the free system of English laws in a neighboring province, establishing therein an arbitrary government, and enlarging its boundaries, so as to render it at once an example and fit instrument for introducing the same absolute rule into these colonies:

For taking away our charters, abolishing our most valuable laws, and altering, fundamentally, the powers of our governments:

For suspending our own legislatures, and declaring themselves invested with power to legislate for us in all cases whatsoever.

He has abdicated government here, by declaring us out of his protection, and waging war against us.

He has plundered our seas, ravaged our coasts, burnt our towns, and destroyed the lives of our people.

He is, at this time, transporting large armies of foreign mercenaries to complete the works of death, desolation, and tyranny, already begun, with circumstances of cruelty and perfidy scarcely paralleled in the most barbarous ages, and totally unworthy the head of a civilized nation.

He has constrained our fellow-citizens, taken captive on the high seas, to bear arms against their country, to become the executioners of their friends and brethren, or to fall themselves by their hands.

He has excited domestic insurrections amongst us, and has endeav-

APPENDIX. 483

ored to bring on the inhabitants of our frontiers, the merciless Indian savages, whose known rule of warfare is an undistinguished destruction of all ages, sexes, and conditions.

In every stage of these oppressions we have petitioned for redress in the most humble terms; our repeated petitions have been answered only by repeated injury. A prince, whose character is thus marked by every act which may define a tyrant, is unfit to be the ruler of a free people.

Nor have we been wanting in attention to our British brethren. We have warned them, from time to time, of attempts made by their legislature to extend an unwarrantable jurisdiction over us. We have reminded them of the circumstances of our emigration and settlement here. We have appealed to their native justice and magnanimity, and we have conjured them, by the ties of our common kindred, to disavow these usurpations, which would inevitably interrupt our connections and correspondence. They, too, have been deaf to the voice of justice and consanguinity. We must, therefore, acquiesce in the necessity which denounces our separation, and hold them, as we hold the rest of mankind, enemies in war, in peace, friends.

We, therefore, the representatives of the UNITED STATES OF AMERICA, in GENERAL CONGRESS assembled, appealing to the Supreme Judge of the World for the rectitude of our intentions, do, in the name, and by the authority of the good people of these colonies, solemnly publish and declare, that these United Colonies are, and, of right, ought to be, **Free and Independent States**; that they are absolved from all allegiance to the British crown, and that all political connexion between them and the state of Great Britain is, and ought to be, totally dissolved; and that, as *FREE AND INDEPENDENT STATES*, they have full power to levy war, conclude peace, contract alliances, establish commerce, and to do all other acts and things which INDEPENDENT STATES may of right do. And, for the support of this declaration, with a firm reliance on the protection of **Divine Providence**, we mutually pledge to each other our lives, our fortunes, and our sacred honor.

The foregoing declaration was, by order of Congress, engrossed and signed by the following members:

JOHN HANCOCK.

New Hampshire.
Josiah Bartlett,
William Whipple,
Matthew Thornton.

Massachusetts Bay.
Samuel Adams,
John Adams,
Robert Treat Paine,
Elbridge Gerry.

Rhode Island.
Stephen Hopkins,
William Ellery.

Connecticut.
Roger Sherman,
Samuel Huntington,
William Williams,
Oliver Wolcott.

New York.
William Floyd,
Philip Livingston,
Francis Lewis,
Lewis Morris.

New Jersey.
Richard Stockton,
John Witherspoon,
Francis Hopkinson,
John Hart,
Abraham Clark.

Pennsylvania.
Robert Morris,
Benjamin Rush,
Benjamin Franklin,
John Morton,
George Clymer,
James Smith,

George Taylor,
James Wilson,
George Ross.

Delaware.

Cæsar Rodney,
George Read,
Thomas M'Kean.

Maryland.

Samuel Chase,
William Paca,
Thomas Stone,
Charles Carroll, of Carrollton.

Virginia.

George Wythe,
Richard Henry Lee,
Thomas Jefferson,
Benjamin Harrison,

Thomas Nelson, jun.,
Francis Lightfoot Lee,
Carter Braxton.

North Carolina.

William Hooper,
Joseph Hewes,
John Penn.

South Carolina.

Edward Rutledge,
Thomas Heyward, jun.,
Thomas Lynch, jun.,
Arthur Middleton.

Georgia.

Button Gwinnett,
Lyman Hall,
George Walton.

Resolved, That copies of the Declaration be sent to the several assemblies, conventions, and committees, or councils of safety, and to the several commanding officers of the continental troops; that it be proclaimed in each of the United States, and at the head of the army.

B.

ARTICLES OF CONFEDERATION AND PERPETUAL UNION BETWEEN THE STATES.

To all to whom these presents shall come, we, the undersigned Delegates of the States affixed to our names, send greeting.—Whereas the Delegates of the United States of America, in Congress assembled, did, on the 15th day of November, in the Year of our Lord 1777, and in the Second Year of the Independence of America, agree to certain articles of Confederation and Perpetual Union between the States of New Hampshire, Massachusetts Bay, Rhode Island and Providence Plantations, Connecticut, New York, New Jersey, Pennsylvania, Delaware, Maryland, Virginia, North Carolina, South Carolina, and Georgia, in the words following, viz.:

" Articles of Confederation and Perpetual Union between the States of New Hampshire, Massachusetts Bay, Rhode Island and Providence Plantations, Connecticut, New York, New Jersey, Pennsylvania, Delaware, Maryland, Virginia, North Carolina, South Carolina, and Georgia.

ARTICLE I. The Stile of this confederacy shall be " The United States of America."

ARTICLE II. Each state retains its sovereignty, freedom, and independence, and every Power, Jurisdiction, and right, which is not by this confederation expressly delegated to the United States, in Congress assembled.

ARTICLE III. The said states hereby severally enter into a firm league of friendship with each other, for their common defence, the security of their liberties, and their mutual and general welfare, binding themselves to assist each other, against all force offered to, or attacks made upon them, or any of them, on account of religion, sovereignty, trade, or any other pretence whatever.

ARTICLE IV. The better to secure and perpetuate mutual friendship and intercourse among the people of the different states in this Union, the free inhabitants of each of these states, paupers, vagabonds, and fugitives from justice excepted, shall be entitled to all privileges and immunities of free citizens in the several states; and the people of each state shall have free ingress and regress to and from any other state, and shall enjoy therein all the privileges of trade and commerce, subject to the same duties, impositions, and restrictions as the inhabitants thereof respectively, provided that such restriction shall not extend so far as to prevent the removal of property imported into any state, to any other state of which the owner is an inhabitant; provided, also, that no imposition, duties, or restriction shall be laid by any state on the property of the United States, or either of them.

If any person guilty of, or charged with treason, felony, or other high misdemeanor in any state, shall flee from justice, and be found in any of the United States, he shall, upon demand of the governor or executive power of the state from which he fled, be delivered up and removed to the state having jurisdiction of his offence.

Full faith and credit shall be given in each of these states to the records, acts, and judicial proceedings of the courts and magistrates of every other state.

ARTICLE V. For the more convenient management of the general interest of the United States, delegates shall be annually appointed in such manner as the legislature of each state shall direct, to meet in Congress on the first Monday in November, in every year, with a power reserved to each state to recall its delegates, or any of them, at any time within the year, and to send others in their stead, for the remainder of the year.

No state shall be represented in Congress by less than two, nor by more than seven members; and no person shall be capable of being a delegate for more than three years in any term of six years; nor shall any person, being a delegate, be capable of holding any office under the United States, for which he, or another for his benefit, receives any salary, fees, or emolument of any kind.

Each state shall maintain its own delegates in any meeting of the states, and while they act as members of the committee of the states.

In determining questions in the United States, in Congress assembled, each state shall have one vote.

Freedom of speech and debate in Congress shall not be impeached or questioned in any court, or place out of Congress, and the members of Congress shall be protected in their persons from arrests and imprisonments, during the time of their going to and from, and attendance on Congress, except for treason, felony, or breach of the peace.

ARTICLE VI. No state, without the consent of the United States in Congress assembled, shall send any embassy to, or receive any embassy from, or enter into any conference, agreement, alliance, or treaty with any king, prince, or state; nor shall any person holding any office of profit or trust under the United States, or any of them, accept of any present, emolument, office, or title of any kind whatever from any king, prince, or foreign state; nor shall the United States, in Congress assembled, or any of them, grant any title of nobility.

No two or more states shall enter into any treaty, confederation or alliance whatever between them, without the consent of the United

States, in Congress assembled, specifying accurately the purposes for which the same is to be entered into, and how long it shall continue.

No state shall lay any imposts or duties, which may interfere with any stipulations in treaties, entered into by the United States in Congress assembled, with any king, prince, or state, in pursuance of any treaties already proposed by Congress, to the courts of France and Spain.

No vessels of war shall be kept up in time of peace by any state, except such number only as shall be deemed necessary by the United States, in Congress assembled, for the defence of such state, or its trade; nor shall any body of forces be kept up by any state, in time of peace, except such number only, as in the judgment of the United States, in Congress assembled, shall be deemed requisite to garrison the forts necessary for the defence of such state; but every state shall always keep up a well regulated and disciplined militia, sufficiently armed and accoutred, and shall provide, and have constantly ready for use, in public stores, a due number of field pieces and tents, and a proper quantity of arms, ammunition, and camp equipage.

No state shall engage in any war without the consent of the United States, in Congress assembled, unless such state be actually invaded by enemies, or shall have received certain advice of a resolution being formed by some nation of Indians to invade such state, and the danger is so imminent as not to admit of a delay till the United States, in Congress assembled, can be consulted; nor shall any state grant commissions to any ships or vessels of war, nor letters of marque or reprisal, except it be after a declaration of war by the United States, in Congress assembled, and then only against the kingdom or state, and the subjects thereof, against which war has been so declared, and under such regulations as shall be established by the United States, in Congress assembled, unless such state be infested by pirates, in which case vessels of war may be fitted out for that occasion, and kept so long as the danger shall continue, or until the United States, in Congress assembled, shall determine otherwise.

ARTICLE VII. When land forces are raised by any state for the common defence, all officers of or under the rank of colonel shall be appointed by the legislature of each state respectively by whom such forces shall be raised, or in such manner as such state shall direct, and all vacancies shall be filled up by the state which first made the appointment.

ARTICLE VIII. All charges of war, and all other expenses that shall be incurred for the common defence or general welfare, and allowed by the United States, in Congress assembled, shall be defrayed out of a common treasury, which shall be supplied by the several states, in proportion to the value of all land within each state, granted to or surveyed for any person, as such land and the buildings and improvements thereon shall be estimated according to such mode as the United States, in Congress assembled, shall from time to time direct and appoint. The taxes for paying that proportion shall be laid and levied by the authority and direction of the legislatures of the several states within the time agreed upon by the United States, in Congress assembled.

ARTICLE IX. The United States, in Congress assembled, shall have the sole and exclusive right and power of determining on peace and war, except in the cases mentioned in the 6th article—of sending and receiving ambassadors—entering into treaties and alliances; provided that no treaty of commerce shall be made whereby the legislative power of the respective states shall be restrained from imposing such imposts and duties on foreigners, as their own people are subjected to, or from prohibiting the exportation or importation of any species of goods or commodities whatsoever—of establishing rules for deciding in all cases, what captures on land or water shall be legal, and in what manner prizes taken by land or naval forces in the service of the United States shall be divided or appropriated—of granting letters of marque and reprisal in times of peace—appointing courts for the trial of piracies and felonies committed on the high seas, and establishing courts for receiving and determining finally appeals in all cases of captures, provided that no member of Congress shall be appointed a judge of any of the said courts.

The United States, in Congress assembled, shall also be the last resort on appeal in all disputes and differences now subsisting, or that hereafter may arise, between two or more states concerning boundary, jurisdiction, or any other cause whatever; which authority shall always be exercised in the manner following. Whenever the legislative or executive authority or lawful agent of any state in controversy with another shall present a petition to Congress, stating the matter in question and praying for a hearing, notice thereof shall be given by order of Congress to the legislative or executive authority of the other state in controversy, and a day assigned for the appearance of the parties by their lawful agents, who shall then be directed to appoint, by joint consent, commissioners, or judges, to constitute a court for hearing and determining the matter in question; but if they cannot agree, Congress shall name three persons out of each of the United States, and from the list of such persons each party shall alternately strike out one, the petitioners beginning, until the number shall be reduced to thirteen; and from that number not less than seven, nor more than nine names, as Congress shall direct, shall, in the presence of Congress, be drawn out by lot, and the persons whose names shall be so drawn, or any five of them, shall be commissioners or judges, to hear and finally determine the controversy, so always as a major part of the judges who shall hear the cause shall agree in the determination: and if either party shall neglect to attend at the day appointed, without showing reasons which Congress shall judge sufficient, or, being present, shall refuse to strike, the Congress shall proceed to nominate three persons out of each state, and the secretary of Congress shall strike in behalf of such party absent or refusing; and the judgment and sentence of the court to be appointed, in the manner before prescribed, shall be final and conclusive; and if any of the parties shall refuse to submit to the authority of such court, or to appear or defend their claim or cause, the court shall nevertheless proceed to pronounce sentence, or judgment, which shall, in like manner, be final and decisive. the judgment or sentence and other proceedings being in either case transmitted to Congress, and lodged among the acts of Congress for the security of the parties concerned: provided that every commissioner, before he sits in judgment, shall take an oath to be administered by one of the judges of the supreme or superior court of the state where the cause shall be tried, " well and truly to hear and determine the matter in question, according to the best of his judgment, without favor, affection, or hope of reward:" provided, also, that no state shall be deprived of territory for the benefit of the United States.

All controversies concerning the private right of soil claimed under different grants of two or more states, whose jurisdictions as they may respect such lands, and the states which passed such grants, are adjusted, the said grants or either of them being at the same time claimed to have originated antecedent to such settlement of jurisdiction, shall, on the petition of either party to the Congress of the United States, be finally determined, as near as may be, in the same manner as is before prescribed for deciding disputes respecting territorial jurisdiction between different states.

The United States, in Congress assembled, shall also have the sole and exclusive right and power of regulating the alloy and value of coin struck by their own authority, or by that of the respective states —fixing the standard of weights and measures throughout the United States—regulating the trade and managing all affairs with the Indians, not members of any of the states, provided that the legislative right of any state within its own limits be not infringed or violated—establishing or regulating post-offices from one state to another, throughout all the United States, and exacting such postage on the papers passing through the same, as may be requisite to defray the expenses of the said office—appointing all officers of the land forces in the service of the United States, excepting regimental officers—appointing all the officers of the naval forces, and commissioning all officers whatever in the service of the United States—making rules for the government and regulation of the said land and naval forces, and directing their operations.

The United States, in Congress assembled, shall have authority to appoint a committee, to sit in the recess of Congress, to be denominated "A Committee of the States," and to consist of one delegate from each state; and to appoint such other committees and civil officers as may be necessary for managing the general affairs of the United States under their direction—to appoint one of their number to preside, provided that no person be allowed to serve in the office of president more than one year in any term of three years; to ascertain the necessary sums of money to be raised for the service of the United States, and to appropriate and apply the same for defraying the public expenses; to borrow money, or emit bills on the credit of the United States, transmitting every half year to the respective states an account of the sums of money so borrowed or emitted; to build and equip a navy; to agree upon the number of land forces, and to make requisitions from each state for its quota, in proportion to the number of white inhabitants in such state, which requisition shall be binding; and thereupon the legislature of each state shall appoint the regimental officers, raise the men, and clothe, arm, and equip them, in a soldier-like manner, at the expense of the United States; and the officers and men so clothed, armed, and equipped, shall march to the place appointed, and within the time agreed on by the United States, in Congress assembled; but if the United States, in Congress assembled, shall, on consideration of circumstances, judge proper that any state should not raise men, or should raise a smaller number than its quota, and that any other state should raise a greater number of men than the quota thereof, such extra number shall be raised, officered, clothed, armed, and equipped in the same manner as the quota of such state, unless the legislature of such state shall judge that such extra number cannot be safely spared out of the same, in which case they shall raise, officer, clothe, arm, and equip as many of such extra number as they judge can be safely spared. And the officers and men so clothed, armed, and equipped, shall march to the place appointed, and within the time agreed on by the United States, in Congress assembled.

The United States, in Congress assembled, shall never engage in a war, nor grant letters of marque and reprisal in time of peace, nor enter into any treaties or alliances, nor coin money, nor regulate the value thereof, nor ascertain the sums and expenses necessary for the defence and welfare of the United States, or any of them, nor emit bills, nor borrow money on the credit of the United States, nor appropriate money, nor agree upon the number of vessels of war to be built or purchased, or the number of land or sea forces to be raised, nor appoint a commander-in-chief of the army or navy, unless nine states assent to the same: nor shall a question on any other point, except for adjourning from day to day, be determined, unless by the votes of a majority of the United States, in Congress assembled.

The Congress of the United States shall have power to adjourn to any time within the year, and to any place within the United States, so that no period of adjournment be for a longer duration than the space of six months, and shall publish the journal of their proceedings monthly, except such parts thereof relating to treaties, alliances, or military operations, as in their judgment require secrecy, and the yeas and nays of the delegates of each state on any question shall be entered on the journal when it is desired by any delegate, and the delegates of a state, or any of them, at his or their request, shall be furnished with a transcript of the said journal, except such parts as are above excepted, to lay before the legislatures of the several states.

ARTICLE X. The committee of the states, or any nine of them, shall be authorized to execute, in the recess of Congress, such of the powers of Congress, as the United States, in Congress assembled, by the consent of nine states, shall from time to time think expedient to vest them with; provided that no power be delegated to the said committee for the exercise of which, by the articles of confederation, the voice of nine states in the Congress of the United States assembled is requisite.

ARTICLE XI. Canada, acceding to this confederation, and joining in the measures of the United States, shall be admitted into, and entitled to all the advantages of this union; but no other colony shall be admitted into the same, unless such admission be agreed to by nine states.

ARTICLE XII. All bills of credit emitted, moneys borrowed, and debts contracted by, or under the authority of Congress, before the assembling of the United States, in pursuance of the present confederation, shall be deemed and considered as a charge against the United States, for payment and satisfaction whereof the said United States and the public faith are hereby solemnly pledged.

ARTICLE XIII. Every state shall abide by the determinations of the United States, in Congress assembled, on all questions which, by this confederation, is submitted to them. And the articles of this confederation shall be inviolably observed by every state, and the union shall be perpetual; nor shall any alteration, at any time hereafter, be made in any of them, unless such alteration be agreed to in a Congress of the United States, and be afterwards confirmed by the legislatures of every state.

And Whereas it hath pleased the great Governor of the world to incline the hearts of the legislatures we respectively represent in Congress, to approve of, and to authorize us to ratify, the said articles of confederation and perpetual union. Know ye that we, the undersigned delegates, by virtue of the power and authority to us given for that purpose, do, by these presents, in the name and in behalf of our respective constituents, fully and entirely ratify and confirm each and every of the said articles of confederation and perpetual union, and all and singular the matters and things therein contained: and we do further solemnly plight and engage the faith of our respective constituents, that they shall abide by the determinations of the United States, in Congress assembled, on all questions which, by the said confederation, are submitted to them. And that the articles thereof shall be inviolably observed by the states we respectively represent, and that the union shall be perpetual. In witness whereof, we have hereunto set our hands in Congress. Done at Philadelphia, in the state of

Pennsylvania, the 9th day of July, in the year of our Lord 1778, and in the 3d year of the Independence of America.

Josiah Bartlett,	John Wentworth, jun., August 8th, 1778,	On the part and behalf of the state of New Hampshire.
John Hancock, Samuel Adams, Elbridge Gerry,	Francis Dana, James Lovell, Samuel Holten,	On the part and behalf of the state of Massachusetts-Bay.
William Ellery, Henry Marchant,	John Collins,	On the part and behalf of the state of Rhode-Island and Providence Plantations.
Roger Sherman, Samuel Huntington, Oliver Wolcott,	Titus Hosmer, Andrew Adam,	On the part and behalf of the state of Connecticut.
Jas Duane, Fras Lewis,	William Duer, Gouv^r Morris,	On the part and behalf of the state of New York.
Jno Witherspoon,	Nathl Scudder,	On the part and behalf of the state of New Jersey, November 26th, 1778.
Robt Morris, Daniel Roberdeau, Jon^a Bayard Smith,	William Clingan, Joseph Reed, 22d July, 1778,	On the part and behalf of the state of Pennsylvania.
Tho. M'Kean, Feb. 12th, 1779, John Dickinson, May 5th, 1779,	Nicholas Van Dyke,	On the part and behalf of the state of Delaware.
John Hanson, March 1st, 1781,	Daniel Carroll, March 1st, 1781,	On the part and behalf of the state of Maryland.
Richard Henry Lee, John Banister, Thomas Adams,	Jno Harvie, Francis Lightfoot Lee,	On the part and behalf of the state of Virginia.
John Penn, July 21st, 1778,	Corns Harnett, Jno Williams,	On the part and behalf of the state of North Carolina.
Henry Laurens, William Henry Drayton,	Jno Matthews, Richd Hutson, Thos. Heyward, jun.,	On the part and behalf of the state of South Carolina.
Jno Walton, 24th July, 1778,	Edwd Telfair, Edwd Langworthy,	On the part and behalf of the state of Georgia.

C.

CONSTITUTION OF THE UNITED STATES OF AMERICA.

We the People of the United States, in order to form a more perfect Union, establish Justice, insure domestic Tranquillity, provide for the common defence, promote the general Welfare, and secure the Blessings of Liberty to ourselves and our Posterity, do ordain and establish this Constitution for the United States of America.

ARTICLE I.

Section 1. All legislative Powers herein granted shall be vested in a Congress of the United States, which shall consist of a Senate and House of Representatives.

Section 2. [1]The House of Representatives shall be composed of Members chosen every second Year by the People of the several States, and the Electors in each State shall have the Qualifications requisite for Electors of the most numerous Branch of the State Legislature.

[2]No Person shall be a Representative who shall not have attained to the Age of twenty-five years, and been seven Years a Citizen of the United States, and who shall not, when elected, be an Inhabitant of that State in which he shall be chosen.

[3]Representatives and direct Taxes shall be apportioned among the several States which may be included within this Union, according to their respective Numbers, which shall be determined by adding to the whole Number of free Persons, including those bound to Service for a Term of Years, and excluding Indians not taxed, three fifths of all other Persons. The actual Enumeration shall be made within three Years after the first Meeting of the Congress of the United States, and within every subsequent Term of ten Years, in such Manner as they shall by Law direct. The Number of Representatives shall not exceed one for every thirty Thousand, but each State shall have at Least one Representative; and until such enumeration shall be made, the State of New Hampshire shall be entitled to chuse three, Massachusetts eight, Rhode Island and Providence Plantations one, Connecticut five, New York six, New Jersey four, Pennsylvania eight, Delaware one, Maryland six, Virginia ten, North Carolina five, South Carolina five, and Georgia three.

[4]When vacancies happen in the Representation from any State, the Executive Authority thereof shall issue Writs of Election to fill such Vacancies.

[5]The House of Representatives shall chuse their Speaker and other Officers; and shall have the sole Power of Impeachment.

Section 3. [1]The Senate of the United States shall be composed of two Senators from each State, chosen by the Legislature thereof, for six Years; and each Senator shall have one Vote.

[2]Immediately after they shall be assembled in Consequence of the first Election, they shall be divided as equally as may be into three Classes. The Seats of the Senators of the first Class shall be vacated at the Expiration of the second Year, of the second Class at the Expiration of the fourth Year, and of the third Class at the Expiration of the sixth Year, so that one-third may be chosen every second Year; and if Vacancies happen by Resignation, or otherwise, during the Recess of the Legislature of any State, the Executive thereof may make temporary Appointments until the next Meeting of the Legislature, which shall then fill such Vacancies.

[3]No Person shall be a Senator who shall not have attained to the

Age of thirty Years, and been nine Years a Citizen of the United States, and who shall not, when elected, be an Inhabitant of that State for which he shall be chosen.

[4]The Vice President of the United States shall be President of the Senate, but shall have no Vote, unless they be equally divided.

[5]The Senate shall chuse their other Officers, and also a President pro tempore, in the Absence of the Vice President, or when he shall exercise the Office of President of the United States.

[6]The Senate shall have the sole Power to try all Impeachments. When sitting for that Purpose, they shall be on Oath or Affirmation. When the President of the United States is tried, the Chief Justice shall preside: And no Person shall be convicted without the Concurrence of two-thirds of the Members present.

[7]Judgment in Cases of Impeachment shall not extend further than to removal from Office, and Disqualification to hold and enjoy any Office of Honour, Trust or Profit under the United States: but the Party convicted shall nevertheless be liable and subject to Indictment, Trial, Judgment and Punishment, according to Law.

SECTION 4. [1]The Times, Places and Manner of holding Elections for Senators and Representatives, shall be prescribed in each State by the Legislature thereof; but the Congress may at any time by Law make or alter such Regulations, except as to the places of chusing Senators.

[2]The Congress shall assemble at least once in every Year, and such Meeting shall be on the first Monday in December, unless they shall by Law appoint a different Day.

SECTION 5. [1]Each House shall be the Judge of the Elections, Returns and Qualifications of its own Members, and a Majority of each shall constitute a Quorum to do Business; but a smaller Number may adjourn from day to day, and may be authorized to compel the Attendance of absent Members, in such Manner, and under such Penalties as each House may provide.

[2]Each House may determine the Rules of its Proceedings, punish its Members for disorderly Behaviour, and, with the Concurrence of two-thirds, expel a Member.

[3]Each House shall keep a Journal of its Proceedings, and from time to time publish the same, excepting such Parts as may in their Judgment require Secrecy; and the Yeas and Nays of the Members of either House on any question shall, at the Desire of one-fifth of those Present, be entered on the Journal.

[4]Neither House, during the Session of Congress, shall, without the Consent of the other, adjourn for more than three days, nor to any other Place than that in which the two Houses shall be sitting.

SECTION 6. [1]The Senators and Representatives shall receive a Compensation for their Services, to be ascertained by Law, and paid out of the Treasury of the United States. They shall in all Cases, except Treason, Felony and Breach of the Peace, be privileged from Arrest during their Attendance at the Session of their respective Houses, and in going to and returning from the same; and for any Speech or Debate in either House, they shall not be questioned in any other Place.

[2]No Senator or Representative shall, during the Time for which he was elected, be appointed to any civil Office under the Authority of the United States, which shall have been created, or the Emoluments whereof shall have been encreased during such time; and no Person holding any Office under the United States, shall be a Member of either House during his Continuance in Office.

SECTION 7. [1]All Bills for raising Revenue shall originate in the House of Representatives; but the Senate may propose or concur with Amendments as on other Bills.

²Every Bill which shall have passed the House of Representatives and the Senate, shall, before it become a Law, be presented to the President of the United States; If he approve he shall sign it, but if not he shall return it, with his Objections, to that House in which it shall have originated, who shall enter the Objections at large on their Journal, and proceed to reconsider it. If after such Reconsideration two thirds of that House shall agree to pass the Bill, it shall be sent, together with the Objections, to the other House, by which it shall likewise be reconsidered, and if approved by two thirds of that House, it shall become a Law. But in all such Cases the Votes of both Houses shall be determined by Yeas and Nays, and the Names of the Persons voting for and against the Bill shall be entered on the Journal of each House respectively. If any Bill shall not be returned by the President within ten Days (Sundays excepted) after it shall have been presented to him, the Same shall be a law, in like Manner as if he had signed it, unless the Congress by their Adjournment prevent its Return, in which Case it shall not be a Law.

³Every Order, Resolution, or Vote to which the Concurrence of the Senate and House of Representatives may be necessary (except on a question of Adjournment) shall be presented to the President of the United States; and before the Same shall take Effect, shall be approved by him, or being disapproved by him, shall be repassed by two thirds of the Senate and House of Representatives, according to the Rules and Limitations prescribed in the Case of a Bill.

SECTION 8. The Congress shall have Power

¹To lay and collect Taxes, Duties, Imposts, and Excises, to pay the Debts and provide for the common Defence and general Welfare of the United States; but all Duties, Imposts, and Excises shall be uniform throughout the United States;

²To borrow Money on the credit of the United States;

³To regulate Commerce with foreign Nations, and among the several States, and with the Indian Tribes;

⁴To establish an uniform Rule of Naturalization, and uniform Laws on the subject of Bankruptcies throughout the United States;

⁵To coin Money, regulate the Value thereof, and of foreign Coin, and fix the Standard of Weights and Measures;

⁶To provide for the Punishment of counterfeiting the Securities and current Coin of the United States;

⁷To establish Post Offices and post Roads;

⁸To promote the progress of Science and useful Arts, by securing for limited Times to Authors and Inventors the exclusive Right to their respective Writings and Discoveries;

⁹To constitute Tribunals inferior to the supreme Court;

¹⁰To define and punish Piracies and Felonies committed on the high Seas, and Offences against the Law of Nations;

¹¹To declare War, grant Letters of Marque and Reprisal, and make Rules concerning Captures on Land and Water;

¹²To raise and support Armies, but no Appropriation of Money to that Use shall be for a longer Term than two Years;

¹³To provide and maintain a Navy;

¹⁴To make Rules for the Government and Regulation of the land and naval Forces;

¹⁵To provide for calling forth the Militia to execute the Laws of the Union, suppress Insurrections and repel Invasions;

¹⁶To provide for organizing, arming, and disciplining, the Militia, and for governing such Part of them as may be employed in the Service of the United States, reserving to the States respectively, the Appointment of the Officers, and the Authority of training the Militia according to the Discipline prescribed by Congress;

[17]To exercise exclusive Legislation in all Cases whatsoever, over such District (not exceeding ten Miles square) as may, by Cession of particular States, and the Acceptance of Congress, become the Seat of the Government of the United States, and to exercise like Authority over all Places purchased by the Consent of the Legislature of the State in which the same shall be, for the Erection of Forts, Magazines, Arsenals, Dock-Yards, and other needful Buildings;—And

[18]To make all Laws which shall be necessary and proper for carrying into Execution the foregoing Powers, and all other Powers vested by this Constitution in the Government of the United States, or in any Department or Officer thereof.

SECTION 9. [1]The Migration or Importation of such Persons as any of the States now existing shall think proper to admit, shall not be prohibited by the Congress prior to the Year one thousand eight hundred and eight, but a Tax or Duty may be imposed on such Importation, not exceeding ten dollars for each Person.

[2]The Privilege of the Writ of Habeas Corpus shall not be suspended, unless when in Cases of Rebellion or Invasion the public Safety may require it.

[3]No Bill of Attainder or ex post facto Law shall be passed.

[4]No Capitation, or other direct, Tax shall be laid, unless in Proportion to the Census or Enumeration herein before directed to be taken.

[5]No Tax or Duty shall be laid on Articles exported from any State.

[6]No Preference shall be given by any Regulation of Commerce or Revenue to the Ports of one State over those of another: nor shall Vessels bound to, or from, one State, be obliged to enter, clear, or pay Duties in another.

[7]No Money shall be drawn from the Treasury, but in Consequence of Appropriations made by Law; and a regular Statement and Account of the Receipts and Expenditures of all public Money shall be published from time to time.

[8]No Title of Nobility shall be granted by the United States: And no Person holding any Office of Profit or Trust under them, shall, without the Consent of the Congress, accept of any present, Emolument, Office, or Title, of any kind whatever, from any King, Prince, or foreign State.

SECTION 10. [1]No State shall enter into any Treaty, Alliance, or Confederation; grant Letters of Marque and Reprisal; coin Money; emit Bills of Credit; make any Thing but gold and silver Coin a Tender in Payment of Debts; pass any Bill of Attainder, ex post facto Law, or Law impairing the Obligation of Contracts, or grant any Title of Nobility.

[2]No State shall, without the consent of the Congress, lay any Imposts or Duties on Imports or Exports, except what may be absolutely necessary for executing it's inspection Laws: and the net Produce of all Duties and Imposts, laid by any State on Imports or Exports, shall be for the use of the Treasury of the United States; and all such Laws shall be subject to the Revision and Controul of the Congress.

[3]No State shall, without the Consent of Congress, lay any Duty of Tonnage, keep Troops, or Ships of War in time of Peace, enter into any Agreement or Compact with another State, or with a foreign Power, or engage in War, unless actually invaded, or in such imminent Danger as will not admit of Delay.

ARTICLE II.

SECTION 1. [1]The executive Power shall be vested in a President of the United States of America. He shall hold his Office during the

APPENDIX. 495

Term of four Years, and, together with the Vice President, chosen for the same Term, be elected, as follows

²Each State shall appoint, in such Manner as the Legislature thereof may direct, a Number of Electors, equal to the whole number òf Senators and Representatives to which the State may be entitled in the Congress: but no Senator or Representative, or Person holding an Office of Trust or Profit under the United States, shall be appointed an Elector.

[* The Electors shall meet in their respective States, and vote by Ballot for two Persons, of whom one at least shall not be an Inhabitant of the same State with themselves. And they shall make a List of all the Persons voted for, and of the Number of Votes for each; which List they shall sign and certify, and transmit sealed to the Seat of the Government of the United States, directed to the President of the Senate. The President of the Senate shall, in the Presence of the Senate and House of Representatives, open all the Certificates, and the Votes shall then be counted. The Person having the greatest Number of Votes shall be the President, if such Number be a Majority of the whole Number of Electors appointed; and if there be more than one who have such Majority, and have an equal Number of Votes, then the House of Representatives shall immediately chuse by Ballot one of them for President; and if no Person have a Majority, then from the five highest on the List the said House shall in like Manner chuse the President. But in chusing the President the Votes shall be taken by States, the Representation from each State having one Vote; A Quorum for this Purpose shall consist of a Member or Members from two thirds of the States, and a Majority of all the States shall be necessary to a Choice. In every Case, after the Choice of the President, the Person having the greatest Number of Votes of the Electors shall be the Vice President. But if there should remain two or more who have equal Votes, the Senate shall chuse from them by Ballot the Vice President.]

³The Congress may determine the time of chusing the Electors, and the Day on which they shall give their Votes; which Day shall be the same throughout the United States.

⁴No Person except a natural born Citizen, or a Citizen of the United States, at the time of the Adoption of this Constitution, shall be eligible to the Office of President: neither shall any Person be eligible to that Office who shall not have attained to the Age of thirty five Years, and been fourteen Years a Resident within the United States.

⁵In Case of the Removal of the President from Office, or of his Death, Resignation, or Inability to discharge the Powers and Duties of the said Office, the same shall devolve on the Vice President, and the Congress may by Law provide for the Case of Removal, Death, Resignation, or Inability, both of the President and Vice President, declaring what Officer shall then act as President, and such Officer shall act accordingly, until the Disability be removed, or a President shall be elected.

⁶The President shall, at stated Times, receive for his Services, a Compensation, which shall neither be encreased nor diminished during the Period for which he shall have been elected, and he shall not receive within that Period any other Emolument from the United States, or any of them.

⁷Before he enter on the Execution of his Office, he shall take the following Oath or Affirmation:—

"I do solemnly swear (or affirm) that I will faithfully execute the "Office of President of the United States, and will to the best of my "Ability, preserve, protect and defend the Constitution of the United "States.

SECTION 2. ¹The President shall be Commander in Chief of the Army and Navy of the United States, and of the Militia of the several States, when called into the actual Service of the United States; he may require the Opinion, in writing, of the principal Officer in each of the executive Departments, upon any Subject relating to the Duties of their respective Offices, and he shall have Power to grant Reprieves

---

* This clause within brackets has been superseded and annulled by the 12th amendment, on page 500.

and Pardons for Offences against the United States, except in Cases of Impeachment.

²He shall have Power, by and with the Advice and Consent of the Senate, to make Treaties, provided two thirds of the Senators present concur; and he shall nominate, and by and with the Advice and Consent of the Senate, shall appoint Ambassadors, other public Ministers and Consuls, Judges of the supreme Court, and all other Officers of the United States, whose Appointments are not herein otherwise provided for, and which shall be established by Law: but the Congress may by Law vest the Appointment of such inferior Officers, as they think proper, in the President alone, in the Courts of Law, or in the Heads of Departments.

³The President shall have Power to fill up all Vacancies that may happen during the Recess of the Senate, by granting Commissions which shall expire at the End of their next Session.

SECTION 3. He shall from time to time give to the Congress Information of the State of the Union, and recommend to their Consideration such Measures as he shall judge necessary and expedient; he may, on extraordinary Occasions, convene both Houses, or either of them, and in Case of Disagreement between them, with Respect to the Time of Adjournment, he may adjourn them to such Time as he shall think proper; he shall receive Ambassadors and other public Ministers; he shall take Care that the Laws be faithfully executed, and shall Commission all the officers of the United States.

SECTION 4. The President, Vice President and all civil Officers of the United States, shall be removed from Office on Impeachment for, and Conviction of, Treason, Bribery, or other high Crimes and Misdemeanors.

ARTICLE III.

SECTION 1. The judicial Power of the United States, shall be vested in one supreme Court, and in such inferior Courts as the Congress may from time to time ordain and establish. The Judges, both of the supreme and inferior Courts, shall hold their Offices during good Behavior, and shall, at stated Times, receive for their Services, a Compensation, which shall not be diminished during their Continuance in Office.

SECTION 2. ¹The judicial Power shall extend to all Cases, in Law and Equity, arising under this Constitution, the Laws of the United States, and Treaties made, or which shall be made, under their Authority;—to all Cases affecting Ambassadors, other public Ministers, and Consuls;—to all Cases of admiralty and maritime Jurisdiction;—to Controversies to which the United States shall be a Party;—to Controversies between two or more States;—between a State and Citizens of another State;—between Citizens of different States,—between Citizens of the same State claiming Lands under Grants of different States, and between a State, or the Citizens thereof, and foreign States, Citizens or Subjects.

²In all Cases affecting Ambassadors, other public Ministers and Consuls, and those in which a State shall be Party, the supreme Court shall have original Jurisdiction. In all the other Cases before mentioned, the supreme Court shall have appellate Jurisdiction, both as to Law and Fact, with such Exceptions, and under such Regulations as the Congress shall make.

³The Trial of all Crimes, except in Cases of Impeachment, shall be by Jury; and such Trial shall be held in the State where the said Crimes shall have been committed; but when not committed within

any State, the Trial shall be at such Place or Places as the Congress may by Law have directed.

SECTION 3. [1]Treason against the United States, shall consist only in levying War against them, or in adhering to their Enemies, giving them Aid and Comfort. No Person shall be convicted of Treason unless on the Testimony of two Witnesses to the same overt Act, or on Confession in open Court.

[2]The Congress shall have Power to declare the Punishment of Treason, but no Attainder of Treason shall work Corruption of Blood, or Forfeiture except during the Life of the Person attainted.

ARTICLE IV.

SECTION 1. Full Faith and Credit shall be given in each State to the public Acts, Records, and judicial Proceedings of every other State. And the Congress may by general Laws prescribe the Manner in which such Acts, Records and Proceedings shall be proved, and the Effect thereof.

SECTION 2. [1]The Citizens of each State shall be entitled to all Privileges and Immunities of Citizens in the several States.

[2]A Person charged in any State with Treason, Felony, or other Crime, who shall flee from Justice, and be found in another State, shall on Demand of the executive Authority of the State from which he fled, be delivered up, to be removed to the State having Jurisdiction of the Crime.

[3]No Person held to Service or Labour in one State, under the Laws thereof, escaping into another, shall, in Consequence of any Law or Regulation therein, be discharged from such Service or Labour, but shall be delivered up on Claim of the Party to whom such Service or Labour may be due.

SECTION 3. [1]New States may be admitted by the Congress into this Union; but no new State shall be formed or erected within the Jurisdiction of any other State; nor any State be formed by the Junction of two or more States, or Parts of States, without the Consent of the Legislatures of the States concerned as well as of the Congress.

[2]The Congress shall have Power to dispose of and make all needful Rules and Regulations respecting the Territory or other Property belonging to the United States; and nothing in this Constitution shall be so construed as to Prejudice any Claims of the United States, or of any particular State.

SECTION 4. The United States shall guarantee to every State in this Union a Republican Form of Government, and shall protect each of them against Invasion, and on Application of the Legislature, or of the Executive (when the Legislature cannot be convened) against domestic Violence.

ARTICLE V.

The Congress, whenever two thirds of both Houses shall deem it necessary, shall propose Amendments to this Constitution, or, on the Application of the Legislatures of two thirds of the several States, shall call a Convention for proposing Amendments, which, in either Case, shall be valid to all Intents and Purposes, as Part of this Constitution, when ratified by the Legislatures of three fourths of the several States, or by Conventions in three fourths thereof, as the one or the other Mode of Ratification may be proposed by the Congress; Provided that no Amendment which may be made prior to the Year one thousand eight hundred and eight shall in any Manner affect the first and fourth Clauses in the Ninth Section of the first Article; and that no State, without its Consent, shall be deprived of its equal Suffrage in the Senate.

ARTICLE VI.

[1] All Debts contracted and Engagements entered into, before the Adoption of this Constitution, shall be as valid against the United States under this Constitution, as under the Confederation.

[2] This Constitution, and the Laws of the United States which shall be made in Pursuance thereof; and all Treaties made, or which shall be made, under the authority of the United States, shall be the supreme Law of the Land; and the Judges in every State shall be bound thereby, any Thing in the Constitution or Laws of any State to the Contrary notwithstanding.

[3] The Senators and Representatives before mentioned, and the Members of the several State Legislatures, and all executive and judicial Officers, both of the United States and of the several States, shall be bound by Oath or Affirmation, to support this Constitution; but no religious Test shall ever be required as a Qualification to any Office or public Trust under the United States.

ARTICLE VII.

The Ratification of the Conventions of nine States, shall be sufficient for the Establishment of this Constitution between the States so ratifying the Same.

DONE in Convention by the Unanimous Consent of the States present the Seventeenth Day of September in the Year of our Lord one thousand seven hundred and Eighty seven and of the Independance of the United States of America the Twelfth **In Witness** whereof We have hereunto subscribed our Names,

GEO WASHINGTON—
Presidt and deputy from Virginia.

New Hampshire.

JOHN LANGDON, NICHOLAS GILMAN.

Massachusetts.

NATHANIEL GORHAM, RUFUS KING.

Connecticut.

WM. SAML. JOHNSON, ROGER SHERMAN.

New York.

ALEXANDER HAMILTON.

New Jersey.

WIL: LIVINGSTON, DAVID BREARLEY,
WM. PATERSON, JONA. DAYTON.

Pennsylvania.

B. FRANKLIN, THOMAS MIFFLIN,
ROBT. MORRIS, GEO: CLYMER,
THO: FITZSIMONS, JARED INGERSOLL,
JAMES WILSON, GOUV: MORRIS.

Delaware.

GEO: READ, GUNNING BEDFORD, **Jun'r**,
JOHN DICKINSON, RICHARD BASSETT.
JACO: BROOM,

APPENDIX.

Maryland.

James M'Henry,
Danl. Carroll.
Dan: of St. Thos. Jenifer,

Virginia.

John Blair,
James Madison, Jr.

North Carolina.

Wm. Blount,
Hu. Williamson.
Rich'd Dobbs Spaight,

South Carolina.

J. Rutledge,
Charles Pinckney,
Charles Cotesworth Pinckney,
Pierce Butler.

Georgia.

William Few,
Abr. Baldwin.

Attest: **WILLIAM JACKSON**, *Secretary.*

The following is prefixed to the first ten Amendments:

"CONGRESS OF THE UNITED STATES,

" Begun and held at the City of New York, on Wednesday, the fourth of March, one thousand seven hundred and eighty-nine.

" The Conventions of a number of the States, having at the time of their adopting the Constitution, expressed a desire, in order to prevent misconstruction or abuse of its powers, that further declaratory and restrictive clauses should be added: And as extending the ground of public confidence in the Government, will best insure the beneficent ends of its institution;

" *Resolved by the Senate and House of Representatives of the United States of America, in Congress assembled,* two thirds of both Houses concurring, That the following Articles be proposed to the Legislatures of the several States, as amendments to the Constitution of the United States, all, or any of which articles, when ratified by three fourths of the said Legislatures, to be valid to all intents and purposes, as part of the said Constitution; viz.

" Articles in addition to, and Amendment of the Constitution of the United States of America, proposed by Congress, and ratified by the Legislatures of the several States pursuant to the fifth article of the original Constitution."

ARTICLES *in addition to, and amendment of, the Constitution of the United States of America, proposed by Congress, and ratified by the Legislatures of the several States, pursuant to the fifth article of the original Constitution.*

Article I. Congress shall make no law respecting an establishment of religion, or prohibiting the free exercise thereof; or abridging the freedom of speech, or of the press; or the right of the people peaceably to assemble, and to petition the Government for a redress of grievances.

Article II. A well regulated Militia, being necessary to the security of a free State, the right of the people to keep and bear Arms, shall not be infringed.

Article III. No soldier shall, in time of peace be quartered in any house, without the consent of the Owner, nor in time of war, but in a manner to be prescribed by law.

ARTICLE IV. The right of the people to be secure in their persons, houses, papers, and effects, against unreasonable searches and seizures, shall not be violated, and no Warrants shall issue, but upon probable cause, supported by Oath or affirmation, and particularly describing the place to be searched, and the persons or things to be seized.

ARTICLE V. No person shall be held to answer for a capital, or otherwise infamous crime, unless on a presentment or indictment of a Grand Jury, except in cases arising in the land or naval forces, or in the Militia, when in actual service in time of War or public danger; nor shall any person be subject for the same offence to be twice put in jeopardy of life or limb; nor shall be compelled in any Criminal Case to be a witness against himself, nor be deprived of life, liberty, or property, without due process of law; nor shall private property be taken for public use, without just compensation.

ARTICLE VI. In all criminal prosecutions, the accused shall enjoy the right to a speedy and public trial, by an impartial jury of the State and district wherein the crime shall have been committed, which district shall have been previously ascertained by law, and to be informed of the nature and cause of the accusation; to be confronted with the witnesses against him; to have compulsory process for obtaining Witnesses in his favour, and to have the assistance of Counsel for his defence.

ARTICLE VII. In Suits at common law, where the value in controversy shall exceed twenty dollars, the right of trial by jury shall be preserved, and no fact tried by a jury shall be otherwise re-examined in any Court of the United States, than according to the rules of the common law.

ARTICLE VIII. Excessive bail shall not be required, nor excessive fines imposed, nor cruel and unusual punishments inflicted.

ARTICLE IX. The enumeration in the Constitution, of certain rights, shall not be construed to deny or disparage others retained by the people.

ARTICLE X. The powers not delegated to the United States by the Constitution, nor prohibited by it to the States, are reserved to the States respectively, or to the people.

ARTICLE XI. [*Proposed in* 1794, *and ratified in* 1797.] The Judicial power of the United States shall not be construed to extend to any suit in law or equity, commenced or prosecuted against one of the United States by Citizens of another State, or by Citizens or Subjects of any Foreign State.

ARTICLE XII. [*Proposed in* 1803, *and ratified in* 1804.] The Electors shall meet in their respective states, and vote by ballot for President and Vice-President, one of whom, at least, shall not be an inhabitant of the same state with themselves; they shall name in their ballots the person voted for as President, and in distinct ballots the person voted for as Vice-President, and they shall make distinct lists of all persons voted for as President, and of all persons voted for as Vice-President, and of the number of votes for each, which lists they shall sign and certify, and transmit sealed to the seat of the government of the United States, directed to the President of the Senate;—The President of the Senate shall, in presence of the Senate and House of Representatives, open all the certificates and the votes shall then be counted;—The person having the greatest number of votes for President, shall be the President, if such number be a majority of the whole number of Electors appointed; and if no person have such majority, then from the persons having the highest numbers not exceeding three on the list of those voted for as President, the House of Representatives shall choose immediately, by ballot, the President. But in choosing the President, the votes shall be taken by states, the representation from each state having one vote; a quorum for this purpose shall consist of a member or members from two-thirds of the states, and a majority of all the states shall be necessary to a choice. And if the House of Representatives shall not choose a President whenever the right of choice shall devolve upon them, before the fourth day of March next following, then the Vice-President shall act as President, as in the case of the death or other constitutional disability of the President. The person having the greatest number of votes as Vice-President, shall be the Vice-President, if such number be a majority of the whole number of Electors appointed, and if no person have a majority, then from the two highest numbers on the list, the Senate shall choose the Vice-President; a quorum for the purpose shall consist of two-thirds of the whole number of Senators, and a majority of the whole number shall be necessary to a choice. But no person constitutionally ineligible to the office of President shall be eligible to that of Vice-President of the United States.

THE following are the three recent Amendments referred to in the Compendium:

ARTICLE XIII.

SECTION 1. Neither slavery nor involuntary servitude, except as a punishment for crime, whereof the party shall have been duly convicted, shall exist within the United States, or any place subject to their jurisdiction.

SECTION 2. Congress shall have power to enforce this article by appropriate legislation.

ARTICLE XIV.

SECTION 1. All persons born or naturalized in the United States, and subject to the jurisdiction thereof, are citizens of the United States, and of the States wherein they reside. No State shall make or enforce any law which shall abridge the privileges or immunities of citizens of the United States; nor shall any State deprive any person of life, liberty, or property, without due process of law, nor deny to any person within its jurisdiction the equal protection of the laws.

SECTION 2. Representatives shall be apportioned among the several States according to their respective numbers, counting the whole number of persons in each State, excluding Indians not taxed; but when the right to vote at any election, for the choice of Electors for President and Vice-President of the United States, Representatives in Congress, the executive and judicial officers of a State or the members of the Legislature thereof, is denied to any of the male inhabitants of such State (being twenty-one years of age, and citizens of the United States), or in any way abridged except for participation in rebellion or other crime, the basis of representation therein shall be reduced in the proportion which the number of such male citizens shall bear to the whole number of male citizens twenty-one years of age, in said State.

SECTION 3. No person shall be a Senator or Representative in Congress, or Elector of President and Vice-President, or hold any office, civil or military, under the United States, or under any State, who, having previously taken an oath as a member of Congress, or as an officer of the United States, or as a member of any State Legislature, or as an executive or judicial officer of any State, to support the Constitution of the United States, shall have engaged in insurrection or rebellion against the same, or given aid or comfort to the enemies thereof; but Congress may, by a vote of two-thirds of each House, remove such disability.

SECTION 4. The validity of the public debt of the United States authorized by law, including debts incurred for payment of pensions and bounties for services in suppressing insurrection or rebellion, shall not be questioned; but neither the United States nor any State shall assume or pay any debt or obligation incurred in aid of insurrection or rebellion against the United States, or any claim for the loss or emancipation of any slave; but all such debts, obligations and claims shall be held illegal and void.

SECTION 5. The Congress shall have power to enforce, by appropriate legislation, the provisions of this article.

ARTICLE XV.

SECTION 1. The right of citizens of the United States to vote shall not be denied or abridged by the United States, or by any State, on account of race, color, or previous condition of servitude.

SECTION 2. The Congress shall have power to enforce this article by appropriate legislation.

D.

THE FIRST TWO OF MR. JEFFERSON'S DRAFT OF THE KENTUCKY RESOLUTIONS OF 1798.

1. *Resolved*, That the several States composing the United States of America, are not united on the principle of unlimited submission to their General Government; but that, by a compact under the style and title of a Constitution for the United States, and of Amendments thereto, they constituted a General Government for special purposes, —delegated to that Government certain definite powers, reserving, each State to itself, the residuary mass of right to their own self-government; and that whensoever the General Government assumes undelegated powers, its acts are unauthoritative, void, and of no force: that to this compact each State acceded as a State, and is an integral party, its co-States forming, as to itself, the other party: that the Government created by this compact, was not made the exclusive or final judge of the extent of the powers delegated to itself; since that would have made its discretion, and not the Constitution, the measure of its powers; but that, as in all other cases of compact among powers having no common judge, each party has an equal right to judge for itself, as well of infractions as of the mode and measure of redress.

2. *Resolved*, That the Constitution of the United States, having delegated to Congress a power to punish treason, counterfeiting the securities and current coin of the United States, piracies, and felonies committed on the high seas, and offences against the law of nations, and no other crimes whatsoever; and it being true, as a general principle, and one of the amendments to the Constitution having also declared, that " the powers not delegated to the United States by the Constitution, nor prohibited by it to the States, are reserved to the States respectively, or to the people," therefore the act of Congress,

passed on the 14th day of July, 1798, and intituled, "An Act in Addition to the act intituled An Act for the punishment of certain crimes against the United States," as also the act passed by them on the ―― day of June, 1798, intituled "An Act to punish frauds committed on the bank of the United States," (and all their other acts which assume to create, define, or punish crimes, other than those so enumerated in the Constitution,) are altogether void, and of no force; and that the power to create, define, and punish such other crimes is reserved, and, of right, appertains solely and exclusively to the respective States, each within its own territory.

E.

VIRGINIA RESOLUTIONS, 1798–1799.

Resolved, That the General Assembly of Virginia, doth unequivocally express a firm resolution to maintain and defend the Constitution of the United States, and the Constitution of this State, against every aggression either foreign or domestic; and that they will support the Government of the United States in all measures warranted by the former.

That this Assembly most solemnly declares a warm attachment to the Union of the States, to maintain which it pledges its powers; and, that for this end, it is their duty to watch over and *oppose every infraction of those principles which constitute the only basis of that Union*, because a faithful observance of them, can alone secure its existence and the public happiness.

That this Assembly doth explicitly and peremptorily declare, that it views the powers of the Federal Government, as resulting from the compact to which the States are parties, as limited by the plain sense and intention of the instrument constituting that compact, as no further valid than they are authorized by the grants enumerated in that compact; and that, in case of a deliberate, palpable, and dangerous exercise of other powers, not granted by the said compact, the States, who are parties thereto, have the right, and are in duty bound, to interpose, for arresting the progress of the evil, and for maintaining, within their respective limits, the authorities, rights, and liberties, appertaining to them.

That the General Assembly doth also express its deep regret, that a spirit has, in sundry instances, been manifested by the Federal Government, to enlarge its powers by forced constructions of the constitutional charter which defines them; and that indications have appeared of a design to expound certain general phrases (which, having been copied from the very limited grant of powers in the former Articles of Confederation, were the less liable to be misconstrued) so as to destroy the meaning and effect of the particular enumeration which necessarily explains and limits the general phrases, and so as to consolidate the States, by degrees, into one Sovereignty, the obvious tendency and inevitable result of which would be, to transform the present Republican system of the United States into an absolute, or, at best, a mixed monarchy.

That the General Assembly doth particularly protest against the palpable and alarming infractions of the Constitution, in the two late cases of the "Alien and Sedition Acts," passed at the last session of

Congress; the first of which, exercises a power nowhere delegated to the Federal Government, and which by uniting Legislative and Judicial powers to those of Executive, subverts the general principles of free government, as well as the particular organization and positive provisions of the Federal Constitution; and the other of which acts, exercises in like manner, a power not delegated by the Constitution, but on the contrary, expressly and positively forbidden by one of the amendments thereto; a power, which more than any other, ought to produce universal alarm, because it is levelled against the right of freely examining public characters and measures, and of free communication among the people thereon, which has ever been justly deemed, the only effectual guardian of every other right.

That this State having by its Convention, which ratified the Federal Constitution, expressly declared, that among other essential rights, "the liberty of conscience and the press cannot be cancelled, abridged, restrained, or modified by any authority of the United States," and from its extreme anxiety to guard these rights from every possible attack of sophistry and ambition, having with other States, recommended an amendment for that purpose, which amendment was, in due time, annexed to the Constitution, it would mark a reproachful inconsistency, and criminal degeneracy, if an indifference were now shown, to the most palpable violation of one of the rights, thus declared and secured; and to the establishment of a precedent which may be fatal to the other.

That the good people of this Commonwealth, having ever felt, and continuing to feel the most sincere affection for their brethren of the other States; the truest anxiety for establishing and perpetuating the union of all; and the most scrupulous fidelity to that Constitution, which is the pledge of mutual friendship, and the instrument of mutual happiness; the General Assembly doth solemnly appeal to the like dispositions in the other States, in confidence, that they will concur with this Commonwealth, in declaring, as it does hereby declare, that the acts aforesaid, are unconstitutional; and, that the necessary and proper measures will be taken *by each* for co-operating with this State, in maintaining unimpaired the authorities, rights, and liberties, reserved to the States respectively, or to the people.

That the Governor be desired to transmit a copy of the foregoing resolutions to the Executive authority of each of the other States, with a request, that the same may be communicated to the Legislature thereof; and that a copy be furnished to each of the Senators and Representatives representing this State in the Congress of the United States.

GENERAL INDEX.

ABORIGINES, 10.
ADAMS, JOHN, elected Vice-President in 1788, 258; in 1792, 261; elected President in 1796, 265; death of, 338.
ADAMS, JOHN QUINCY, Minister to Russia, 309; Secretary of State, 323; elected President, 333; member of the House, 344; course in the House, 359; death of, 392.
ADAMS, SAMUEL, 173; what he said of the new Constitution, 251.
ADÉT, M., speech of Washington to, 265; further accounts of, 266-269.
ADMINISTRATIONS:—Washington's, 253; John Adams', 269; Jefferson's, 281; Madison's, 292; Monroe's, 323; John Quincy Adams', 334; Jackson's, 340; Van Buren's, 355; Harrison's, 365; Tyler's, 367; Polk's, 384; Taylor's, 395; Fillmore's, 400; Pierce's, 404; Buchanan's, 412; Lincoln's, 422; Johnson's, 468; Grant's, 474.
ALABAMA, admitted into the Union as a State, 325; secession of, 420.
ALLEN, ETHAN, 176.
ALIEN AND SEDITION ACTS, 272; prosecution under, 278; Jefferson's opinion of, 283.
AMBRISTER AND ARBUTHNOT, executed by Jackson, 324.
AMENDMENTS OF THE CONSTITUTION, first ten ratified, 255; eleventh do., 262; twelfth do., 286; thirteenth do., 470; fourteenth and fifteenth, 472 and 474.
AMERICA, discovery of, 5; South, 12, 14; North, 12; Central, 14.
AMERICUS VESPUCIUS, for whom the continent was named, 13.
ANDRÉ, MAJOR, British spy, 220.
ANDROS, SIR EDMUND, the tyrant, 56, 71, 102; outrages by, in New England Colonies, 117.
ARCHDALE, JOHN, Governor of North Carolina, 85, 92.
AURORA BOREALIS, first observed in this country, 121.
ARKANSAS, admitted into the Union as a State, 353; secession of, 429.
ARNOLD, BENEDICT, GEN., 176, 199; treason of, 220; invades Virginia, 222.
ATHERTON, CHARLES G., resolutions by, in the House, and votes thereon, on the subject of negro slavery in the States, 362.
AUSTIN, STEPHEN F., founder of the Mexican Colony of Texas, 376 et seq.
AZTECS, 11, 12.

BACON, NATHANIEL, proclaimed rebel and traitor in Virginia, 97.
BALTIMORE, LORD, founder of the Colony of Maryland, 66.
BANK OF THE UNITED STATES, first, 257; second, chartered, 321; re-charter vetoed, 344; public deposits removed from, 350.
BARRÉ, COL., speech in defence of Colonies, 160.
BARRINGTON, GOVERNOR, of North Carolina, 87.
BATTLES ON LAND DURING THE COLONIAL CONDITION:—Mystic River, 58; Fort Casimir, 76; Roanoke, 83; Tuscarora, 94; Indian in New York, 103; Schenectady, 105; Quebec, 106; Montreal, 107; battles with King Philip, 115; Salmon Falls, Port Royal, and Haverhill, 120; first at Louisbourg, 124; Combahee, 127; Fort Necessity, 148; Braddock's with the Indians, 150; Fort Edward, 150; Alleghany River, 152; Fort William Henry, 153; second at Louisbourg, 154; Fort Frontenac, 154; Plains of Abraham, 156; Etchoe, 157; Fort Loudon, 158; Concord, Lexington, Ticonderoga and Crown Point, 170; Bunker Hill, 174; Fort Moultrie, 180.
BATTLES ON LAND AFTER THE INDEPENDENCE OF THE STATES DECLARED:—Fort Washington, 194; Trenton, 195; Princeton, 195; Bennington, 200; Saratoga, 201; Brandywine and Germantown, 202; Monmouth, 205; Kettle Creek, 209; Savannah, 212; Camden, 217; King's Mountain, 218; Cow Pens, 224; Guilford, 225; Eutaw Springs, 227; Yorktown, 229.
BATTLES ON LAND BY THE STATES IN THE BRITISH AND INDIAN WAR OF 1812:—Indian in Northwest, 259, 263; Tippecanoe, 298; York, in Canada, 310; Fort Meigs, 311; Sackett's Harbor, Fort George, and the Thames, 311; Callebee, Autossee, Tallushatchee, Talladega, Emuckfau, Horse Shoe, 312; Chippewa, Lundy's Lane, Fort Erie, and Plattsburg, 315; Bladensburg and North Point, 316; New Orleans, 319; Okeechobee, 358.
BATTLES IN REPUBLIC OF TEXAS:—Gonzales, Bexar, Alamo, Goliad, and San Jacinto, 380-82.
BATTLES ON LAND BY THE UNITED STATES IN MEXICAN WAR:—Palo Alto and Resaca de la Palma, 386-87; Monterey and

506 GENERAL INDEX.

Buena Vista, 388–89; Cerro Gordo, Contreras, Churubusco, Molino del Rey, and Chapultepec, 389–90.

BATTLES ON LAND IN WAR BETWEEN THE STATES:—Grafton, Philippi, Big Bethel, Rich Mountain, Laurel Hill, Carrick's Ford, Scary Creek, and first Manassas, 432; Leesburg, Cheat Mountain, Booneville, Carthage, Oak Hill, and Lexington, 433; Belmont, 434; Fishing Creek, Fort Henry, Fort Donelson, 437; Elk Horn, or Pea Ridge, Corinth, or Shiloh, 438; Williamsburg and Seven Pines, 440; Kernstown, McDowell's, Cross Keys, Port Republic, Mechanicsville, Beaver Dam Creek, Gaines's Mill, Savage Station, Fraser's Farm, White Oak Swamp, and Malvern Hill, 441 ; Cedar Run and Second Manassas, 442; Richmond (in Ky.), Perryville and Murfreesboro, 443; South Mountain, Harper's Ferry, and Sharpsburg, 444; Fredericksburg, 445; Chancellorsville, 448; Port Gibson, Raymond, Jackson, Edwards' Depot, and Big Black, 449; Gettysburg, 450; Chickamauga and Missionary Ridge, 452; Olustee and Okolona, 453; Mansfield and Pleasant Hill, 454; Wilderness, Spottsylvania Court House, North Anna, and Cold Harbor, 455; Bermuda Hundreds, New Market, and Lynchburg, 456; Monocacy, Winchester, and Cedar Creek, 457; Resaca, New Hope Church, and Kenesaw Mountain, 458; Atlanta, 459; Franklin and Nashville, 460; Five Oaks, Petersburg, Appomattox Court House, 464; Averasboro and Bentonville, 463.

BATTLES ON WATER, OR SEA FIGHTS BY UNITED STATES NAVY:—Paul Jones, 213. *In war against Tripoli:* Commodores Preble and Barron, 287. *In British war of 1812:* Fight between the *President* and *Little Belt* (Com. Rogers), 296; the *Constitution* (Capt. Hull), and *Guerriere*, 307; the *Essex* (Capt. Porter) and *Alert*, the *Wasp* (Capt. Jones) and the *Frolic*, the *United States* (Capt. Decatur) and *Macedonian*, the *Constitution* (Com. Bainbridge) and *Java*, 308; the *Hornet* (Capt. Lawrence) and the *Peacock*, the *Chesapeake* (Capt. Lawrence) and the *Shannon*, the *Argus* (Capt. Allen) and the *Pelican*, the *Enterprise* and the *Boxer*, 313; Commodore Perry's fleet on Lake Erie, 311; Commodore McDonough's flotilla at Plattsburg, 315. *In war against Algiers:* Decatur's fleet and operations in the Mediterranean, 320.

BATTLES ON WATER, or naval operations in the War between the States, 434, 435, 445, 446, 449, 460, 461.

BERKELEY, SIR WM., Governor of Virginia, 43, 44, 83, 97.

BEDFORD, DUNNING, in Federal Convention, 247.

BEAUREGARD, GUSTAVE T., General, at

Fort Sumter, 425 ; at First Manassas, 432 ; at Shiloh, 438; at Petersburg, 456.

BELL, JOHN, 418.

BELLAMONT, LORD, Governor of New York, 109.

BENTON, THOMAS H., defender of Jackson's Administration, 350 ; do. Van Buren's, 359.

BOSTON, settlement of, 37 ; massacre in, 165 ; Port Bill of, 166; "The cause of, cause of all," 167.

BRADDOCK, General, defeat in the French war, 149.

BRAGG, BRAXTON, General, in command of the Army of the Tennessee, 439; in Kentucky, 443; at Chickamauga and Missionary Ridge, resigns command, 452.

BRECKINRIDGE, JOHN C., 410, 418, 434; victory by, at New Market, 456.

BROUGHAM, LORD HENRY, on the new Constitution, 252.

BROWN JOHN, or "Ossawatomie," 408,416.

BROWN, MILTON, Resolutions by, for the admission of Texas, 373 (note).

BUCHANAN, JAMES, Secretary of State, 384; elected President, 410; retires from office, March 4, 1861, 422; death of, 473.

BURGOYNE, JOHN, British General, 173, 199 ; defeat of, at Saratoga, 201.

BURNETT, DAVID G., first President of the Republic of Texas, 381.

BURNSIDE, AMBROSE E., supersedes McClellan, and defeated at Fredericksburg, 445 ; superseded by Hooker, 447.

BURGESSES, House of, in Virginia, 39, 42, 44.

BURR, AARON, 266 ; elected Vice-President, 280 ; tried for treason, 287, 288.

CABINETS:—Washington's, 256; John Adams', 269; Jefferson's, 283; Madison's, 292; Monroe's, 323; John Quincy Adams', 335; Jackson's, 341; Van Buren's, 356 ; Harrison's, 367 ; Tyler's, 368; Polk's, 384; Taylor's 396 ; Fillmore's, 400 ; Pierce's, 404 ; Buchanan's, 412; Lincoln's, 423; Johnson's, 468 ; Grant's, 474.

CABOT, JOHN and SEBASTIAN, 15.

CALHOUN, JOHN C., 297, 300 ; Secretary of War, 323; and Vice-President, 332; do. 340; rupture with Jackson, 343; in the Senate, 344; accepts Clay's Tariff Compromise of 1833, 348; debate with Webster 349; separates from the Whigs, 358; Resolutions on the nature of the Government, 359; vote upon them, 360; Secretary of State, 371; Resolutions of, in Senate, in 1847, on slavery restrictions in the Territories, 392, (note); last speech in Senate, death of, 399.

CALIFORNIA, admitted into the Union as a State, 401.

CALVERT, SIR GEORGE, Lord Baltimore, 65; CECIL, 67.

CALVERT, LEONARD, 67, 69; PHILIP, 69.

GENERAL INDEX. 507

CAMDEN, LORD, on taxation and representation, 160.
CAMPBELL, JOHN A., Justice of Supreme Court of United States, resigns, 424, 425.
CAMPBELL, DUNCAN G., 335.
CANONICUS, Indian Chief, 52, 61.
CARY, THOMAS, Governor of North Carolina, 85.
CARTERET, SIR GEORGE, 70.
CASS, LEWIS, at Hull's surrender, 305; Secretary of War, 344; defeated for Presidency, 394.
CASSACUS, Indian chief, 57.
CHARLES I., King of England, 42, 66.
CHARLES II., King of England, 44, 45, 56, 63, 70, 78, 84, 113.
CHARLESTON, city of, South Carolina, 178, 214, 215, 425, 463.
CHATHAM, Earl of, 153, 164, 168-9.
CHASE, SALMON P., Secretary of Treasury, 423; fifth Chief Justice, 468.
CHICAGO, city of, great fire in, 474.
CHOLERA, ASIATIC, first appearance of, in United States, 345.
CHRISTIANA, Queen of Sweden, 75.
CHURCH OF ENGLAND, established in Virginia, 43, 101.
CLAY, HENRY, 297; at Ghent, 314; on Missouri Compromise, 329 (note), 331; Secretary of State, 335; in Senate, 344; defeat of, for Presidency, 345; Tariff Compromise of, 348; opposition to Jackson, 350; do. Van Buren, 359; supports Calhoun's Resolutions, 361; "rather be right than President," 364; retires from Senate, 370; second defeat for Presidency, 372; returns to the Senate, Compromise of 1850, 397; death of, 402.
CLAYBORNE, WILLIAM, 65, 67, 68.
CLARKE, ELIJAH, Colonel, 209, 216.
CLINCH, DUNCAN L., General, 353.
CLINTON, DE WITT, 301.
CLINTON, GEORGE, 287, 291; death of, 300.
CLINTON, GEORGE, Governor of New York, 112.
CLINTON, SIR HENRY, British General, 173, 178, 179, 191, 204, 208, 214, 222.
COBB, HOWELL, Sec'y of Treasury, 412.
COCHRANE, SIR ALEXANDER, British Admiral, 316.
COCKBURN, SIR GEORGE, British Admiral, 313, 316.
COLLETON, JAMES, Governor of South Carolina, 89, 90.
COLFAX, SCHUYLER, 472.
COLONIES, BRITISH, 3, 15; Virginia, 14; New York, 26; Massachusetts, 28; New Hampshire, 45; Connecticut, 48; Rhode Island, 50; Maryland, 65; New Jersey, 70; Delaware, 74; Pennsylvania, 7;, North Carolina, 82; South Carolina, 87; Georgia, 130; causes that led to the independence of, 159 et sequens; new governments instituted in, 175; their independence declared, 181 et sequens; confederation between, 183; articles of union between, as States, 186.
COLUMBUS, CHRISTOPHER, 5, 6, 7, 8.
COMPROMISE, Missouri, 326 (note); line of division on which it was based repudiated, 393; new compromise on the subject in 1850, 397; principles of this compromise, 406-8.
CONFEDERATION of the thirteen Colonies in 1776 as States, 186.
CONFEDERATION, the New England, 56, 61, 113; King Philip's war with, 114, 115; end of, by abrogation of charters, 117.
CONGRESS of all the Colonies called by Virginia, 167; met in Philadelphia, 1774, 167; organization and action of, 168; second session of, 171; action of, 172; receives Washington's resignation, 237; a Convention to amend Constitution, 241; first Congress under new Constitution, first movement in, to abolish negro slavery, 257.
CONNECTICUT, Colony of, 48; settlement of, 49; first government of, 50; new charter to, under Charles II., 63; government overthrown by Andros, 117; charter preserved in old oak, 117; old officers restored on the expulsion of Andros, 119.
CONSTITUTION, first, of the United States, 186; propositions to amend, 238; "three-fifths clause," 239; Madison's proposition, 240; Resolutions of Congress for a Convention of the States to this end, 241; Convention meets in Philadelphia in 1787, 242; new Constitution agreed upon and referred to Congress, and by Congress submitted to the States, 242-50; changes in new Constitution, under it the United States still a Confederated Republic, 248, 249, 251; full copies of first and second Constitutions with Amendments, 479 et sequens.
CORNWALLIS, CHARLES, British Lord and General, 194, 216, 223; moves into Virginia, to Yorktown, 228; surrender of, 229.
CRAVEN, CHARLES, Governor of South Carolina, 94.
CRAWFORD, MARTIN J., Confederate Commissioner, 421, 423.
CRAWFORD, WILLIAM H., Minister to France, 300, 313; Secretary of War, 320; Secretary of Treasury, 323; defeated for Presidency, 332.
CROSBY, WILLIAM, Governor of New York, 111.
CUTTS, JOHN, Governor of New Hampshire, 116.
DALE, SIR THOMAS, Governor of Virginia, 23.
DALLAS, GEORGE M., 372.
DARK DAYS, 215.
DAVIS, JEFFERSON, Secretary of War, 405; President of Confederate States, 420-434; leaves Richmond, 464; arrested and discharged, 472.

GENERAL INDEX.

DAYTON, WILLIAM, 410.
DEANE, SILAS, 196, 204.
DEARBORN, HENRY, General, 304, 310.
DELAWARE, LORD, 23.
DELAWARE, Colony, settlement of, 74.
DE KALB, BARON, General, killed, 217.
DE SOTO, FERNANDO, 140 et sequens.
D'ESTAING, COUNT, French Admiral, 204, 206, 212.
DE TOCQUEVILLE on the new Constitution, 252.
DISTRICT OF COLUMBIA, founded, 259; movement to abolish slavery in, 358.
DONELSON, ANDREW J., 410.
DOUGLAS, STEPHEN A., on Missouri Compromise, 393; on Compromise of 1850, 406; on Kansas and Nebraska Act, 407; defeat of, for Presidency, 418.
DRAKE, SIR FRANCIS, 83.
DRUMMOND, WILLIAM, Governor of Albemarle settlement in North Carolina, 83.
DUDLEY, JOSEPH, Governor of New England Colonies on abrogation of their charters, 117.
EARTHQUAKES, 64, 122; great one of 1812, 300.
EARLY, JUBAL A., General, defeats Hunter at Lynchburg, 456; moves into Maryland, 457.
ELIZABETH, QUEEN, 15, 29.
ELLSWORTH, OLIVER, motion by, to strike out "National" in the Federal Constitution, 246; second Chief Justice, 269.
EMBARGO ACT, 290, 291, 295.
ENGLAND, or GREAT BRITAIN, acknowledgment of the Independence of the States by, 230; Jay's treaty with, 264; orders in council by, 288, 295; right of search; affair of the *Leopard* and *Chesapeake*, 289; war of 1812 with, 301; treaty of peace with, at Ghent, 320.
E PLURIBUS UNUM, 190, 198.
EVERETT, EDWARD, 418.
EVERHARD, SIR RICHARD, Governor of North Carolina, 87.
FAUCHET, M., 262.
FEDERAL UNION, established in 1776, 186; Jefferson's new idea of the proper structure of, 244; second Constitution of, 242-250.
FILLMORE, MILLARD, 394 President, 400—410.
FLAG OF THE UNITED STATES, 198, 259.
FLETCHER, BENJAMIN, Governor of Pennsylvania, 81.
FLORIDA, 140; admitted into the Union, 374; secession of, 420.
FLOYD, JOHN, General, 311.
FLOYD, JOHN B., Secretary of War, 412.
FORSYTH, JOHN, Senior, defender of Jackson's Administration, 350; Secretary of State, 356.
FORSYTH, JOHN, Junior, Confederate Commissioner, 421, 423.
FRANCE, war between, and England, 104, 109, 120, 146; treaty of the United States with, 204; *quasi* war with, 273; Berlin and Milan decrees by, 288, 289.

FREMONT, JOHN C., 389, 410, 441.
FRENCHTOWN, slaughter of United States prisoners at, 310.
GAGE, THOMAS, British General, last Royal Governor of Massachusetts, 168 et sequens.
GALLATIN, ALBERT, 283, 309.
GATES, HORATIO, General, 201, 203, 216; defeat at Camden, 217, 235.
GATES, SIR THOMAS, Governor of Virginia, 23.
GENET, M., 261.
GEORGIA, settlement of Colony of, 130 et sequens; cession of Western Territory by, to United States, 286, 335; controversy with the United States about, 336; secession of, 420.
GERRY, ELBRIDGE, 270, 301; death of, 317.
GIBBES, ROBERT, Governor of South Carolina, 94.
GILBERT, SIR HUMPHREY, first grant of land in America to, by Queen Elizabeth, 15.
GORGES, SIR FERNANDO, 45, 116.
GREENE, NATHANIEL, General, 207, 223.
GRAHAM, WM. A., 402.
GUSTAVUS ADOLPHUS, 74.
GRANT, ULYSSES S., at Shiloh, 438; at Vicksburg, 451; at Missionary Ridge, 452; as Lieutenant General, moves against Richmond, 455; lays siege to Petersburg, 456; captures Richmond, 464; elected President, 472.
HALE, JOHN P., 403.
HALE, NATHAN, 193.
HAMILTON, ALEXANDER, in Federal Convention, 243, 250; Secretary of Treasury, 256; head of Federal Party, 258; retired from office, 264; death of, 288.
HAMLIN, HANNIBAL, 418.
HANCOCK, JOHN, 168, 171.
HARMAR, JOSIAH, General, 259.
HARRISON, WM. HENRY, General, 298; succeeds Hull, 306, 310; voted for for President, 353; elected President, 364; his inaugural and cabinet, 366; death of, 367.
HARTFORD, Convention at, 317.
HARVEY, SIR JOHN, Governor of Virginia, 42, 67.
HARVARD, University of, 60.
HAYNE, ISAAC, sad fate of, 227.
HAYNE, ROBERT Y., debate with Webster, 342.
HEATH, SIR ROBERT, 83.
HENRY, JOHN, British secret agent, 299.
HENRY, PATRICK, 162, 242, 251.
HOOD, JOHN B., General, supersedes Johnston at Atlanta, 459.
HOOKER, JOSEPH, General, 447; superseded by Meade, 450.
HOUSTON, SAMUEL, General, in Texas, 381; second President of Texas, 382.
HOWE, SIR WM., British commander at Boston, 175, 190, 202.
HOWE, British Admiral and Earl, 191, 204.

GENERAL INDEX.

HOWE, ROBERT, United States General, 203.
HUGUENOTS, 90, 92.
HULL, WM., General, 304; surrender of Detroit by, 305.
HULL, ISAAC, Captain in the Navy, 307.
HUTCHINSON, MRS. ANN, 59.
HYDE, EDWARD, Governor of North Carolina, 85.
INDEPENDENCE, causes that led to it, 159 et sequens; declaration of, 181 et sequens; Confederation to maintain, 186; acknowledgment of, by Great Britain, 231; full copy of the Declaration, 481.
INDIANA, admitted as a State, 321.
ILLINOIS, admitted as a State, 325.
INTERNAL IMPROVEMENTS, 330, 343.
IOWA, admitted as a State, 374.
JACKSON, ANDREW, Major-General, 311; victory at New Orleans, 319; in Seminole war of 1818, 324 ; 333; elected President, 340; rupture with Calhoun, 343; explanation of proclamation, 347; protest against Senate censure, 350; farewell address, 354; death of, 385.
JACKSON, THOMAS J., "Stonewall;" Valley Campaign of, 441; in the battles at Richmond, 442; at Harper's Ferry, 444; death of, 448.
JAMESTOWN, settlement of, 17.
JASPER, SERGEANT, 179; mortally wounded, 212.
JAY, JOHN, 230, 250; first Chief-Justice of the United States, 256.
JEFFERSON, THOMAS, author of the Declaration of Independence, 183; 230, 242; new idea of, on the structure of a Federal Union, 244; 256, 258, 262; elected Vice-President, 267; elected President, 280; inaugural and views of the nature of the Government, 283; acquisition of Louisiana, 285; re-elected President, 287; retirement from public life, 292; death of, 338.
JOHNSON, ANDREW, elected Vice-President, 462; becomes President, 465; Cabinet and Administration of, 468 et sequens; impeachment and acquittal, 471; retirement from office, 473.
JOHNSON, HERSCHEL V., 418.
JOHNSON, NATHANIEL, Governor of South Carolina, 93.
JOHNSON, RICHARD M., 354.
JONES, ANSON, fourth President of the Republic of Texas, 383.
JONES, JACOB, Commodore, 308.
JONES, PAUL, 213.
JOHNSTON, ALBERT SIDNEY, Colonel and General, 413, 415, 437, fall of, at Shiloh, 438.
JOHNSTON, JOSEPH E., General at First Manassas, 432, 436; wounded at Seven Pines, 440; succeeds Bragg in command at Dalton, 452; opposes Sherman's advance, 458; superseded by Hood at Atlanta, 459; replaced at the head of Southern Army, 463; Convention of, with Sherman, 464; surrender of, 465.

JULIAN, GEORGE W., 403.
KANSAS, Territorial Bills relating to, 406, 408, 411, 414; admitted as a State, 421.
KEARNEY, STEPHEN W., General in Mexican war, 389.
KENTUCKY, admitted as a State into the Union, 260; attempts neutrality in the war between the States, 434.
KEY, FRANCIS, "Star-Spangled Banner," 316.
KIDD, CAPTAIN, the Pirate, 108.
KING PHILIP, Indian chief, his war with the New England Confederation, 114.
KING, THOMAS BUTLER, special agent to California, 396.
KING, RUFUS, in Federal Convention, 243; voted for for Vice-President and President, 287, 291, 321.
KING, WILLIAM R., elected Vice-President, 403.
KYRLE, RICHARD, Governor of South Carolina, 89.
LA FAYETTE, MARQUIS, 196; General, 197, 202, 205, 223, 228; revisit to the United States, 331.
LAMAR, MIRABEAU, third President of the Republic of Texas, 382.
LANE, JOSEPH, 418.
LANE, RALPH, Governor of North Carolina, 83.
LANSING, JOHN, in Federal Convention, 247.
LA SALLE, 143.
LAURENS, HENRY, 230.
LAWRENCE, JAMES, Captain in the Navy, 312.
LEE, ARTHUR, 196, 204.
LEE, CHARLES, General, 179, 194, 205.
LEE, HENRY, Major, "Light-Horse Harry," 211.
LEE, RICHARD HENRY, 183.
LEE, ROBERT E., General, in command of Southern sea-coast, 434; takes command at Richmond, 440; at second Manassas and Sharpsburg, 442, 444; at Fredericksburg, 445; at Chancellorsville, 448; at Gettysburg, 451; in the Wilderness, and at Cold Harbor, 455; final surrender of, to Grant, 464; death of, 474.
LENOX, DUKE OF, head of "Grand Council of Plymouth" Company, 36.
LINCOLN, ABRAHAM, elected President, 418; inaugural, Cabinet, and Administration of, 422 et sequens; assassination of, 465.
LINCOLN, BENJAMIN, General, 199, 210, 212, 214.
LIVINGSTON, ROBERT R., 184, 255.
LONDON COMPANY, organized, 17; dissolved, 41.
LOUDON, EARL OF, 151.
LOUISIANA, named by La Salle, 144; acquired by Jefferson, 285; admitted as a State into the Union, 300; secession of, 420.
LOWNDES, WILLIAM, 297.
LYON, MATTHEW, M. C., imprisoned under the Sedition Act, 277.

LYON, GENERAL, killed in Missouri, 433.
LUDWELL, PHILIP, Governor of North Carolina, 85.
MACOMB, ALEXANDER, General, 315.
MADISON, JAMES, movement of, to amend Constitution, 240; in Federal Convention, 243, 250, 278; Secretary of State, 283; elected President, 291; Cabinet, *status* in politics, and Administration of, 292 et sequens; re-elected President, 301; retirement to private life, 322; death of, 353.
MAINE, settlement of, 28, 116; admitted as a State, 326.
MANGUM, WILLIE P., 353.
MARION, FRANCIS, General, 157, 218, 219.
MARTIN, LUTHER, in Federal Convention, 247.
MARSHALL, JOHN, 270; third Chief-Justice, 283; death of, 352.
MARYLAND, settlement of, Colony of, 65; name of, 66; charter of, to Lord Baltimore, 66.
MASON, JOHN, Captain, grant to, by Plymouth Company, 47.
MASON AND DIXON'S LINE, 160.
MATHER, COTTON, 118.
MAY FLOWER, 32.
MASSACHUSETTS, settlement of, 28, 37; first Government of, 38; dispute with New Hampshire, 47; cited to answer Royal Commissioners, 114; purchase by, of Maine, 116; dispute with New Hampshire settled, 116; charter of, abrogated, 116; expulsion of Andros, and union with Plymouth under new charter, 119; opposition by, to stamp duties, 161; Boston Port Bill, 166; organized Provisional Government, 168; declared to be in a state of rebellion, 169.
MASSACRES, Indian, in Virginia, 40; in North Carolina, 86; Wyoming, in Pennsylvania, 207.
MASSASOIT, Indian chief, 34, 51, 114, 115.
McCLELLAN, GEORGE B., General, Commander-in-Chief of Federal Army, 432, 436; Peninsular Campaign, 439; defeat of, 442; battle of Sharpsburg, 444; superseded by Burnside, 445; voted for for President, 462.
McCREA, MISS JANE, 199.
McDONOUGH, COMMODORE, 315.
McDOWELL, IRWIN, General, at First Manassas, 432.
McCULLOCH, BENJAMIN, General, 433, 438.
McDUFFIE, GEORGE, 337.
MEADE, GEORGE G., General, supersedes Hooker, 450; battle of Gettysburg, 451.
MECKLENBURG, Declaration of Independence, 182.
MERCER, HUGH, General, 152; killed, 195.
MINNESOTA, admitted as a State into the Union, 415.
MINUITS, PETER, 75.
MISSISSIPPI, admitted as a State into the Union, 324; secession of, 420

MISSOURI, admitted as a State into the Union, 328; attempts neutrality in the war between the States, 434.
MOHEGANS, 57, 61.
MONROE, JAMES, 285; elected President, 321; Cabinet and Administration of, 323 et sequens; Missouri Compromise, so called, 326 (note); Monroe Doctrine, so called, 331; death of, 344.
MONTGOMERY, RICHARD, General, 157, 175; captures Montreal, and is killed, 176, 177.
MONTGOMERY, city, Confederate States Government organized at, 420.
MOORE, JAMES, Governor of South Carolina, 93.
MORGAN, DANIEL, General, 199, 201, 223.
MORRIS, ROBERT, 222.
MORTON, JOSEPH, Governor of South Carolina, 89.
MOULTRIE, FORT, battle of, in 1776, 180.
MOULTRIE, WILLIAM, Colonel and General in South Carolina, 157, 179, 209.
MUTINY, in Pennsylvania line in 1781, 222; at Newburg, New York, in 1783, 232 et sequens; Washington's great speech in suppression of, 235, 236.
NEBRASKA, admitted into the Union as a State, 473.
NEVADA, admitted into the Union as a State, 462.
NEW AMSTERDAM, first name of New York city, 27.
NEW ENGLAND, name of, given to, 22; Confederation of, 56; Constitution of, 61, 113; end of Confederation, 117.
NEW HAMPSHIRE, settlement of, 45; name of, 47; first Government of, 47; new charter of, 116.
NEW HAVEN, settlement of, 49; first Government of, the "Blue Laws," 50.
NEW JERSEY, settlement of, by the Danes, and how it became a British Colony, 70.
NEW NETHERLANDS, first name of New York, 70, 76, 78, 88.
NEW ORLEANS, 145; battle of, 319.
NEW SWEDEN, first name of Delaware, 76, 77.
NEW YORK, Colony of, settlement of, as New Netherlands, 26; became a British Colony, 28; first Government of, as British Colony, 101, 102.
NEW YORK, city of, threatened by British in 1776; Washington arrives at, 181; evacuates, 193; great fire in 1835, 352.
NINETY-SIX, 209, 216, 223; siege of, 226.
NORTH CAROLINA, first settlement of the Colony of, 82; first Government of, 84; first Colony to declare independence, 182; accession of, to the Union under the new Constitution, 259; secession of, 429.
NORTH, LORD, head of Tory Administration in England, 165, 169.
NULLIFICATION, Ordinance of, by South Carolina, 346; repeal of, 348.
OGLETHORPE, JAMES EDWARD, General,

founder of the colony of Georgia, 130 et sequens.
OHIO, State of, admitted into the Union, 286.
"OLD DOMINION," why applied to Virginia, 44, 101.
OREGON, admitted as a State into the Union, 416.
PANAMA MISSION, 337.
PARKER, SIR PETER, British Admiral, 178, 179.
PARLIAMENT, British, 44, 95.
PARTIES, Old Federal, headed by Hamilton, 258; Old Republican or Democratic, headed by Jefferson, 258; first contest between, 276; second, 287; Old Federal extinct, 326; Democratic or strict construction against latitudinous construction, 258, 262, 330; National Republican, headed by Clay, 340; strict constructionists, by Jackson, 341; Anti-Masonic organized, 344; first General Convention of Democratic, 345; Whig organized, 350; Anti-Slavery organized, 372; Free-Soil organized, 394; American or Know-Nothing organized, 409; Anti-Slavery assumes name of Republican, 410.
PATTERSON, WILLIAM, in Federal Convention, 245.
PECK, JARED, prosecuted under Sedition Act, 278.
PENDLETON, GEORGE H., 462.
PENN, WILLIAM, 71, 72, 77, 78.
PENNSYLVANIA, settlement of the Colony of, 77; name, charter, and first Government of, 78, 80.
PEQUODS, war with, 57; made slaves of and tribe extinguished, 59.
PERRY, OLIVER H., Commodore, 311.
PERSONAL LIBERTY BILLS, 406.
PETERS, HUGH, 59.
PHENOMENA, extraordinary, 64, 121, 215, 351, 352, 416.
PHILADELPHIA, founded, 80; meeting of first Congress of Colonies at, 167; independence declared at, 185; seat of Government for ten years, 259.
PHIPPS, SIR WM., first Governor of the United Colonies of Plymouth and Massachusetts, 119.
PICKENS, ANDREW, Colonel, 209, 216.
PICKENS, FRANCIS W., Governor of South Carolina, 425.
PIERCE, FRANKLIN, elected President, 403; Cabinet and Administration of, 404 et sequens; Kansas and Nebraska Act, 407; retirement from office, 411.
PINCKNEY, CHARLES, in Federal Convention, 245.
PINCKNEY, CHARLES COTESWORTH, 270, 287, 291.
PINCKNEY, WILLIAM, 297.
PLYMOUTH, COMPANY of, organized for North Virginia, in England, 16; dissolved, 36; 45, 48.
PLYMOUTH, Colony of, 28, 33; first Governor of, John Carver, 33; Colonists called pilgrims, 35; first Government of, 38; old officers restored on expulsion of Andros, 119; union with Massachusetts under new charter, 119.
POCAHONTAS, 21, 24.
POLK, JAMES K., elected President, 372; Cabinet and Administration of, 384 et sequens; Mexican War, 386; death of, 396.
POPE, JOHN, General, 442.
PORTER, DAVID, Commodore, 308, 313.
POWHATAN, Indian chief, 24, 39.
PRESCOTT, British General, taken prisoner, 197.
PRESIDENTIAL ELECTIONS:—In 1788, 253; in 1792, 261; in 1796, 266; in 1800, 278; in 1804, 287; in 1808, 290; in 1812, 301; in 1816, 321; in 1820, 326; in 1824, 332; in 1828, 339; in 1832, 345; in 1836, 353; in 1840, 364; in 1844, 371; in 1848, 393; in 1852, 402; in 1856, 410; in 1860, 417; in 1864, 461; in 1868, 472.
PREVOST, British General, 209, 210.
PRICE, STERLING, General in Missouri, 433, 438.
PRINCETON, College of, founded, 73; battle of, 196.
PRINTING PRESS, first established in America, 60.
PRISONERS, exchange of, 436; number taken on both sides in the War between the States, and treatment of, 467.
PULASKI, COUNT, 202; mortally wounded, 212.
PURITANS, character of, 29, 43.
PUTNAM, ISRAEL, General, 192, 210.
QUAKERS, 71, 72, 78.
QUARRY, ROBERT, Governor of South Carolina, 89.
RALEIGH GILBERT, 28.
RALEIGH, SIR WALTER, 16, 82.
RANDOLPH, EDMUND, leader of "Nationals" in Federal Convention, 243, 250, 256, 293.
RANDOLPH, JOHN, of Roanoke, 302.
RANDOLPH, PEYTON, President of the Congress of 1774, 167.
RAWDON, LORD, British General, 217, 226.
REBELLIONS, Clayborn's in Maryland, 67, 68; Culpepper's in North Carolina, 85; Bacon's in Virginia, 97; Shay's in Massachusetts, 238.
REGICIDES, 63.
RESOLUTIONS, Madison's, in 1786, which led to a revision of the Constitution, 240; of the Annapolis Convention, do.; of the Congress, for the call of a Convention for that purpose, 241; of Congress, on the powers of the Federal Government on the subject of Negro Slavery in the States, 257; Calhoun's in the Senate, on the nature of the Government, and its powers, 359; Atherton's in the House, on the subject of Negro Slavery, 362; Milton Brown's, for the admission of Texas, 373 (note); Calhoun's, on Slavery re-

GENERAL INDEX.

striction in the Territories, 392 (note); first two of Jefferson's *Kentucky* Resolutions of 1798, 497; Virginia Resolutions of 1798–99, 498.
RESTORATION, Charles II., of, 113.
RHODE ISLAND, settlement of the Colony of, 50; accession to the Union under the new Constitution, 359.
RICHMOND, city of, theatre burned in, 299; capital of Confederate States, 431; captured, 464.
RIVES, WILLIAM C., defender of Tyler's Administration in the Senate, 369.
ROMAN, ANDREW B., Confederate Commissioner, 421, 423.
ROSS, British General, captured Washington City, 316.
RUSSELL, JONATHAN, Commissioner to Ghent, 314.
RUTLEDGE, EDWARD, Governor of South Carolina, 179.
SANDYS, SIR EDWIN, 32.
SANTA ANNA, ANTONIO LOPEZ, Dictator of Mexico, 379 et sequens; captured at San Jacinto, 382.
SAVANNAH, city of, settlement of, 130; taken by the British in 1778, 208.
SAVANNAH, STEAMER, first that crossed the Atlantic, 325.
SAYLE, WILLIAM, first Governor of South Carolina, 87.
SALZBURGERS, 130.
SCHUYLER, PETER, Governor of New York, 110.
SCHUYLER, PHILIP, General, 175, 199.
SCOTT, WINFIELD, General, wounded at Lundy's Lane, 315; captured Black Hawk, 345; in chief command against Mexico, 389-90; defeated for Presidency, 402; retired from chief command of Federal Army, 432.
SEAL, of United States, 190, 259.
SECESSION, causes of, 418, 419, 428.
SEMMES, RAPHAEL, Confederate Commodore, 435, 446, 453, 460.
SEVIER, COLONEL, 218.
SEWARD, WILLIAM H., Secretary of State, 423; remark to Lord Lyon, 430.
SEYMOUR, HORATIO, 472.
SHAY, DANIEL, rebellion of 238.
SHERMAN, ROGER, 184.
SHERMAN, WILLIAM T., General, march of, from Vicksburg, 453; in command at Chattanooga, 454; advance on Atlanta, 458; takes Atlanta, 459; march to the Sea, 460; advance through South Carolina, 463; convention and capitulation with Johnston, 464.
SHELBY, ISAAC, Colonel, 218.
SLAVERY, INDIAN, established in New England, 59; 115.
SLAVERY, NEGRO, introduced into Virginia, 26; into Massachusetts, 59; into South Carolina, 88; into Georgia and all the Colonies, 136; number of slaves at Independence, 189; first movement in Congress for abolition of, and result, 257; Missouri Compromise upon, 326 (note); Resolutions of Senate upon, in 1838, 359 (note); Resolutions of House upon, 362; Wilmot Proviso upon, 391 (note); Calhoun's Resolutions of 1848 upon, 392 (note); Clay's Compromise upon, in 1850, 397; principles of this Compromise, 406–8.
SMITH, GUSTAVUS, General, 459.
SMITH, JOHN, Captain, of Virginia, 18, 65.
SMITH, E. KIRBY, General, 443, 465.
SMITH, THOMAS, Governor of South Carolina, 92.
SMITHSON, JAMES, bequest by, to United States, 361; Institute founded, 385.
SMYTH, ALEXANDER, General, 307.
SOTHEL, SETH, Governor of North Carolina, 85, 90.
SOUTH CAROLINA, settlement of Colony of, 87; first Government of, 88; Yamassee War in, 126; nullification, 346; secession ordinance of, 419.
STANTON, EDWIN M., 436, 471.
STARK, JOHN, Colonel and General, 200.
ST. CLAIR, ARTHUR, General, 198, 199, 259.
STEPHENS, ALEXANDER H., 420, 434.
STIRLING, GENERAL, 192.
STRIKER, GENERAL, at North Point, 316.
STUYVESANT, PETER, Governor of New York, 76, 101.
SUMNER, CHARLES, 407.
SUMTER, FORT, taken by Confederates, 428; evacuated, 463.
SUMTER, WILLIAM, Colonel in South Carolina, 218, 219.
SUPREME COURT, of the United States organized, 256, 262; decision of, on the powers of the Federal Government over the subject of Negro Slavery, 413.
TALLEYRAND, 271.
TANEY, ROGER B., Attorney General, 344; Secretary of Treasury, 350; fourth Chief-Justice, 352; decision against suspension of Habeas Corpus, 430; death of, 468.
TARIFF, Protective, 330, 338; bill of, in 1828, 339; bill of, in 1832, 344; compromise of, in 1833, 348; violated, 370; protection again abandoned, 385, 411.
TARLETON, B., British Colonel, 218, 219; anecdote about, 224.
TAYLOR ZACHARY, Colonel and General, 358, 385, 386, 387; at Monterey, 388; at Buena Vista, 389; elected President, 394; Cabinet and Administration of, 395 et sequens; death of, 400.
TEA, tax on, how received in Boston, New York, Philadelphia, and Charleston, S. C., 166.
TECUMSEH, Indian warrior, 298; killed, 311.
TELEGRAPH, electro-magnetic, 375, 415, 478.
TENNESSEE, admitted into the Union as a State, 266; secession of, 429.
TEXAS, 44; Republic of, 376 et sequens; Resolutions for the admission of, into

GENERAL INDEX. 513

the Union, 373 (note); admission of, 385; secession of, 420.
"THE GREAT TRIO," 351, 396, 403.
"THE THREE-FIFTHS CLAUSE," 239.
THOMAS, JOHN, General, 177, 178.
TOMPKINS, DANIEL D., 321, 326.
TOBACCO, 24.
TOOMBS, ROBERT, 421, 432, 459.
TROUP, GEORGE M., Governor of Georgia, controversy with United States, 335.
TRYON, last of the Royal Governors of Connecticut, ravages of, 211.
TUSCARORAS, Indian, 86, 94.
TWIGGS, DAVID E., General, gallantry at Cerro Gordo, 389.
TYLER, JOHN, 354, 364; President by death of Harrison, Cabinet and Administration of, 368 et sequens; Treaty of Washington, 370; explosion on Princeton, 371; action on Texas question, 374; retirement of, 375; President of Peace Congress, 421.
UNCAS, Indian chief, 62.
UNITED STATES, history of, 3; union between Federal, 4; first Constitution of, 186, 479; second Constitution of, 242, 486; seal of, 190; flag of, 198.
VALLEY FORGE, Washington's winter quarters, 203.
VAN BUREN, MARTIN, 341, 346; elected President, 353; Cabinet and Administration of, 355 et sequens; defeat for re-election, 364-65; voted for by the Free-Soil Party, 394.
VANE, SIR HENRY, 59.
VAN RENSSELAER, STEPHEN, General, 304, 306.
VERMONT, admitted as a State into the Union, 260.
VICKSBURG, taken by Grant, 451.
VIRGINIA, settlement of the Colony of, under London Company, 18; birth of American free institutions in, 25, 39; why called "Old Dominion," 44; secession of, 429.
VIRGINIA, WEST, admitted as a State into the Union, 449.
WARREN, JOSEPH, General, 174.
WARS:—Indian in Virginia, 40; Pequod in New England, 57; Coree and Tuscorora in North Carolina, 86; Appalachee and Yamassee in South Carolina, 93, 94; Five Nations in New York, 103; French, 105, 121, 146; King Philip's, 114; Cherokee, 157; of the Revolution, 190 et sequens; with Tripoli, 286; British, of 1812, 301; with Algiers, 320; Seminole, 324; Black Hawk, 345; Seminole again, 352, 358; with Mexico, 387; between the States, 427.
WASHINGTON, GEORGE, Major, 147; General in command of the forces of the United Colonies, 171; at New York in 1776, 181; refuses General Howe's letter, 191; evacuates New York, 193; retreats through New Jersey, 194; victory by, at Trenton, 195; battle at Princeton, 196; defeat at Brandywine,

202; victory at Monmouth, 205; capture of Cornwallis at Yorktown, 229; speech at Newburg, 235-6; resigns his commission, 237; advises change in Federal Constitution, 240; President of Convention to propose changes, 242; elected President of the United States, 253; Administration of, 253 et sequens; speech of, to Adét, 265; veto of Apportionment Bill, 258; retirement, 268; death of, 275.
WASHINGTON, WILLIAM, Colonel, wounds Tarleton; anecdote about, 224.
WASHINGTON, City of, founded, 259; taken by the British, 316.
WAYNE, ANTHONY, General, 211, 263.
WEBSTER, DANIEL, debate with Hayne, 342; do. with Calhoun, 349; Secretary of State, 367; resigns, 370; 7th of March Speech, 399; again Secretary of State, 400; death of, 403.
WESLEY, REV. JOHN, 135.
WEST, JOSEPH, Governor of South Carolina, 88, 89.
WEST, FRANCIS, Governor of Virginia, 42.
WEST INDIES, 10.
WILKINSON, JAMES, General, succeeds Dearborn, 311, 315.
WILLIAMS, BENJAMIN, Colonel, 218.
WILLIAMS, ROGER, 50 et sequens.
WILLIAM and MARY, King and Queen of England, 73, 81, 100, 104, 118.
WILMOT, DAVID, celebrated "Proviso," of, 391 (note).
WILSON, JAMES, 243, 248, 356.
WINDER, General, at Bladensburg, 316.
WINTHROP, JOHN, first Governor of Massachusetts, 37, 49.
WIRT, WILLIAM, Attorney General, 323, 335; voted for for President, 344.
WISCONSIN, admitted as a State, 393.
WISE, HENRY A., defender of Tyler's Administration in the House, 369.
WITCHCRAFT, 122.
WHITE, HUGH L., 353.
WHITEFIELD, REV. GEORGE, 135.
WITHERFORD, Indian warrior, speech of, 312.
WOLF, JAMES, General, 154, 156.
WOOL, JOHN E., General in Mexican War, 388.
WORTH, WILLIAM J., General, gallantry of, at Monterey, Saltillo, Molino del Rey, and Casa de Moto, 389-90.
WRIGHT, SILAS, able defender of Van Buren's Administration, 359.
WYATT, SIR FRANCIS, Governor of Virginia, 39, 42.
WYOMING, Massacre at, 207.
YAMASSEES, 94, 126.
YATES, ROBERT, in Federal Convention, 247.
YEAMANS, SIR JOHN, Governor of South Carolina, 88.
YEARDLEY, GEORGE, Governor of Virginia, 24, 25, 39.
YORK, DUKE OF, 28, 70, 76, 80.
YORKTOWN, city of, Cornwallis captured at, 229.